Battlegrounds of Freedom

Ed,
Thank you very much for
all you do with the scouts.
They are the future of our nation.

Norman Desmarais

Battlegrounds Of Freedom

A Historical Guide to the Battlefields of the War of American Independence

Norman Desmarais

Edited by June Fritchman

Busca, Inc.
Ithaca, New York

Busca, Inc.
P.O. Box 854
Ithaca, NY 14851
Ph: 607-546-4247
Fax: 607-546-4248
E-mail: info@buscainc.com
www.buscainc.com

First Edition

Printed in the United States of America

ISBN: 0-9666196-7-6

Library of Congress Cataloging-in-Publication Data

Desmarais, Norman.
Battlegrounds of freedom : a historical guide to the battlefields of the War of American Independence / Norman Desmarais.— 1st ed.
     p. cm.
Includes bibliographical references and index.
   ISBN 0-9666196-7-6 (alk. paper)
   1. United States—History—Revolution, 1775–1783—Battlefields—Guidebooks. 2. United States—History—Revolution, 1775–1783—Campaigns. 3. Battlefields—United States—Guidebooks. I. Title.
E230.D47 2005
973.3'3—dc22

             2005011908

All maps Copyright © 2003 DeLorme (www.delorme.com) Street Atlas USA® Plus.
Reprinted with permission.

Cover design by Cayuga Digital Imaging and Helena Cooper, incorporating author's photo of 2nd Rhode Island Regiment charging with bayonets

Gallery photography: author

Image editing: Jack Dickard

Composition: P.S. We Type ◆ Set ◆ Edit

To our ancestors who sacrificed to win and to preserve our freedom.

To the members of the 2nd Rhode Island Regiment who nurtured an interest in living history

and

To the members of the Brigade of the American Revolution, Continental Line, and British Brigade who generously give of themselves to help re-create the era of the War for American Independence.

The publisher dedicates this book to the beloved memory of Harold G. Cooper (1927–2005).

CONTENTS

Maps and photographs follow page 108

LIST OF ILLUSTRATIONS

Following Page 108

Maps

Photos

FOREWORD

Who among us at one time or another has not traveled from historic site to historic site as part of a family vacation? This may sound like the lead-in to a comedy routine but it would not be so funny if it were not so true. Something about these places attracts us to them. Some of us travel to them like a pilgrimage while others are on a nostalgia trip. Perhaps we are looking for a way to make our own, personal commemoration. Maybe we feel some sense of civic duty. Perhaps it's just fun. Whether through the imagination of an excited child or the reverent study of adults, we are all drawn to these places.

The first battlefield commemoration ever held may have been a reunion of Revolutionary War veterans at Bunker Hill in the 1820s, and in 1824 the Marquis de Lafayette returned to the United States as the "nation's guest," laying cornerstones to monuments and receiving the honors of grateful Americans during his year long tour. Reflecting on the sentiments of his times, Benson J. Lossing, who in 1848 traveled the vast landscape of the American Revolution, prefaced his observations in his book *The Pictorial Field-Book of the Revolution* by saying:

For years a strong desire was felt to embalm those precious things of our cherished household, that they might be preserved for the admiration and reverence of remote posterity. I knew that the genius of our people was the reverse of antiquarian reverence for things of the past; that the glowing future, all sunlight and eminence, absorbed their thoughts and energies, and few looked back to the twilight and dim valleys of the past through which they had journeyed. I knew that the invisible fingers of decay, the plow of agriculture, and the behests of Mammon, unrestrained in their operations by the prevailing spirit of our people, would soon sweep away every tangible vestige of the Revolution, and that it was time the limner was abroad. I knew that, like stars at dawn which had beamed brightly through a long night, the men of old were fast fading away, and the relics associated with their trials and triumphs would soon be covered up forever.

During the nation's Centennial dozens of monuments were erected on hallowed grounds, seemingly rediscovered and to be preserved for future generations. In the succeeding years travelers came to view those sources of national identity, touching the past as their lives moved faster and faster with every step of progress.

Beginning again with the United States' Bicentennial there has been a flurry of activity to recognize and protect Revolutionary War historic sites. Legislation has been passed and agencies have been created at all levels of government to preserve, protect, and make accessible scores of previously little known historic places, and like during the Bicentennial and the Centennial before, this activity seems to have intensified in the midst of the 225th anniversary of our War for Independence as communities feel a sense of importance saying "history happened here."

It is timely that such a work as this is published now in light of these facts and hopefully future generations will continue that long-held tradition of traveling from historic site to historic site, using this guide to enlighten them in their journeys.

Paul Ackermann
Past Commander
Brigade of the American Revolution

PREFACE

The United States is the only country to have gained its independence from Great Britain by force of arms. The war that won that independence was also the longest one in American history, except for the Vietnam War. Yet, it is a forgotten war. It gets very brief coverage in history textbooks; and many people confuse it with the War of Rebellion (Civil War).

There have been no major historical guidebooks to Revolutionary War sites published since the nation's Bicentennial almost 30 years ago. Many of these books focused on 18th-century houses and structures, some of which had little or no connection with the War for American Independence other than dating from the same period. Others had cursory information about the sites.

This book intends to serve as a historical guide to the battlefields of the War for American Independence. It is intended for several audiences: readers interested in American history, re-enactors, tourists, and visitors. Each site begins with the name of the city, the dates of significant actions discussed in this text, and the name (and alternate names) of the battle or action. Historical background to understand what happened at a site follows. Specially formatted text also identifies the location of the site, indicates what the visitor can expect to see, and identifies any interpretive aids. In any case, this book is not meant to replace the guides produced for specific sites and available at the visitor centers. These guides usually provide more details about the features of that particular site.

This book takes a hybrid geographical/chronological approach to accommodate the various audiences. Going from north to south and east to west, the book begins with Maine, the most northeastern state (which was part of Massachusetts during the War for American Independence) and proceeds west to Vermont and New York before going south to Massachusetts, Rhode Island, Connecticut, etc. Some states with many actions—for instance, New York and South Carolina—are subdivided using this scheme. These divisions are reflected with references to their respective maps. Within each geographical subdivision, the text generally follows a chronological sequence so readers can follow the text as a historical sequence or "story" involving many of the same characters. Some locations or battles, for instance, Fort Ticonderoga or West Point, have chronological subdivisions covering that site's importance at different times of the war. Cross references have been added as necessary.

Travelers should take care to map the route for most efficient travel as many sites are not along main roads. Sometimes one must backtrack to visit a place thoroughly. Travelers should also be aware that some locations in a particular state may be further than other locations in a neighboring state. Consulting maps allows the visitor to proceed from one location to another with the least amount of backtracking. It also offers options for side trips as desired. See Appendix 3 of battle sites grouped and keyed to major cities/locations.

For those who desire such information, Appendix 2 provides a chronological list of battles, actions, and skirmishes. History books often present events in purely chronological order. However, that is not a good approach for a guidebook to follow, as events can occur simultaneously great distances apart. For example, the powder alarm in Williamsburg, Virginia occurred on the same day as the battles of Lexington and Concord in Massachusetts.

Appendix 1 is an alphabetical state-by-state list of battles, etc., the usual guidebook approach. Consider the TourBooks produced by the American Automobile Association (AAA). This approach requires the traveler to plan a trip carefully beforehand or to thumb through the book to determine whether a particular city or town has any points of interest.

Other books take a thematic approach, covering campaigns or specific themes like the war on the frontier. This technique, while more focused, often ignores information relevant to a site that properly belongs to another theme. This book does not take this approach, in any case.

Battlegrounds of Freedom includes other important features. Each state is keyed to a map or maps to facilitate orientation. These maps have pointers to battlefield locations, and have been reproduced on high quality paper.

There are over 100 photographs, also reproduced on high quality paper, with descriptive captions, and keyed to the text. These photos are important for identifying details of historic buildings, monuments, and battlefields. Many of the photos are of battle and event re-enactments. Although these photos are black and white reproductions, where relevant the caption indicates the color of the uniform (for instance, Tarleton's Legionnaires wore green, etc.) All photos, unless otherwise indicated, are by the author.

Another feature that modern readers and visitors will find useful are URLs for websites of various parks and tourist organizations, and which are correlated with various battle sites. Visitors may want to consult these websites ahead of time for important, updated information on special events, hours, fees, etc. These URLs were active and accurate at the time this book went to press.

Cognizant that one may begin a tour anywhere, the first occurrence of a person's name in a section identifies him or her as completely as possible with full name and dates.

Chapters 1 through 16 describe the important battles by state or colony and provide information about their location. Chapter 17 "(Re)Living History is about War of Independence re-enactors, their associations, and additional resources. Appendix 1 lists most of the battles and actions of the war (listing many more than are covered in this book), arranged alphabetically by colony and then chronologically. Some battles have several names and appear under more than one designation like the First Battle of Saratoga which is also known as the Battle of Freeman's Farm. Appendix 2 provides a purely chronological listing. Appendix 3 is for visitors, indicating sites near a city or within a general geographic area. The Glossary provides definitions for some 18th-century military and historical terms. There is also a Bibliography and an Index.

The author is currently working on a book that covers more of the battles, skirmishes, and actions not covered by *Battlegrounds of Freedom* and that are listed in the appendices.

Most of the sites described in this book are reconstructions or restorations. Many buildings were damaged during the War of Independence or fell into disrepair over the years. They were refurbished, for the most part, for the nation's Bicentennial in 1975–1976. Battlefield fortifications were sometimes destroyed after a battle so they could not be re-used by the enemy at a later time. For example, the hornworks and siege trenches at Yorktown, Virginia were destroyed after the surrender of General Charles Cornwallis (1738–1805) so the Crown forces could not re-use them for a subsequent assault. They were, however, rebuilt and used again during the War of Rebellion (Civil War).

There are many houses and structures still standing that demonstrate what life was like in the 18th century. Only those related to the battles are covered. There are also descriptions of a few locations, such as Valley Forge and Philadelphia, Pennsylvania and Morristown, New Jersey where there were no battles but that were significant for the outcome of the war.

Many of the sites have been obliterated by urban development and have nothing to see or visit. Houses and other construction have demolished them. One battlefield is covered by a shopping mall; another has been submerged under a man-made lake; others were destroyed by high-rise apartment or office buildings. Many are remembered only with a roadside marker. Some don't even have that.

Many sites have little importance to the outcome of the war which took on the nature of a civil war—particularly in the South. Here, neighbors apparently took advantage of opportunities to settle feuds with each other. Some actions were mere skirmishes or raids lasting only a few minutes. For example, some actions consisted of a single volley. After one of the forces fired, it fled. Yet, some important events, such as the capture of Fort Kaskaskia in Illinois by George Rogers Clark (1752–1818) and the capture of Fort Ticonderoga by Benedict Arnold (1741–1801), Ethan Allen (1738–1790), and the Green Mountain Boys were effected without firing a single shot. The battle at Black Mingo Creek, South Carolina lasted only 15 minutes. Other engagements, particularly those involving Lieutenant Colonel Francis Marion (1732–1795) known as the Swamp Fox, were fought in the swamps of South Carolina and are hard to find.

Some sites remain undeveloped and virtually ignored. This is not necessarily bad. While erosion, neglect, and plant or tree growth slowly undermine earthworks, they do significantly less damage than the rapid deterioration resulting from bikers and walkers.

One cannot easily cover all the sites of the War for American Independence. However, one can visit all the sites and events that affected the outcome of the war. One can also visit enough locally significant spots to get an understanding of what the war was like for the people of that region. This book tries to cover the extant battle sites and hopes to serve as a companion on the voyage of discovery.

Norman Desmarais
normd@providence.edu

ACKNOWLEDGMENTS

I would like to express my gratitude to Jack Montgomery for igniting the spark to write this book and to Michael Cooper for fanning the flame, nurturing the idea and bringing it to fruition. Much of the research was conducted in the collections of the libraries of Providence College and the other academic libraries in Rhode Island whose staffs aided in making the materials available. Francine Mancini, interlibrary loan librarian at Providence College, deserves special mention for obtaining the many items not owned by libraries in Rhode Island.

The members of the Brigade of the American Revolution, the Continental Line, and the British Brigade generously give of themselves to help re-create the era of the War for American Independence. Without their efforts, many of the pictures in this book would not be possible. Carl Becker and Paul Bazin provided additional photographs and DeLorme allowed us to use their maps. Ted McCrorie, Carl Becker, Kirk Hindman, and John Cook, my readers, provided valuable feedback and insights that guided the project through the various stages of revision to completion.

June Fritchman, my editor, corrected inconsistencies and revised the manuscript into a coherent whole. I wish to extend special thanks to my wife Barbara and daughters Jeanne and Denise for their patience and support during the long periods of research and writing. In addition, Jeanne provided valuable advice for bringing the book to market.

1

MAINE

See the Maine map.

Maine was part of Massachusetts at the time of the War for American Independence.

Castine (July 24 to August 11, 1779)

Fort George

Fort George State Historical Site is at the intersection of Battle Avenue and Wadsworth Street in Castine.

`http://coastlinememories.com/castine.points.interest.fort.george.html`

The British finished the construction of Fort George and held it until the end of the War of 1812. They used it as a base to attack New England coastal towns. Almost 4 months after the Treaty of Ghent, they blew up the works and left on April 25, 1815. The fort is partially restored and maintained as a memorial.

Castine, coveted by world powers for its strategic port, endured two centuries of disputes among Native Americans, French, British, Dutch, and Americans. The Americans used it as a base for hit-and-run missions against the King George's navy.

By 1779, the British economy was suffering from loss of trade with the American colonies. A particular concern was the inability to get tall masts for ships. The Royal Navy relied on Maine's white pine forests for the resource, and the 3-year supply that was stockpiled was now almost exhausted.

Colonel Francis McLean led 2 regiments (about 700 men) from Halifax, Nova Scotia to Penobscot Bay on the coast of Maine on June 17, 1779 to improve the source of supply. They sailed in 4 or 5 transports, accompanied by 3 sloops of war under the command of Captain Henry Mowatt. Colonel McLean also planned to establish an outpost for Nova Scotia, a haven for fleeing Loyalists, and a base for future raids into New England. The troops, along with some citizens of the village, began building Fort George on Bagaduce Peninsula (present-day Castine).

The Massachusetts General Court was in session when news of the British expedition to Penobscot Bay reached Boston. The delegates quickly resolved, on June 24, to force the British out of Massachusetts without consulting the Continental Congress or the Continental Army. They petitioned Congress for the use of 3 vessels of the Continental Navy then in Boston harbor. The rest of the navy of some 45 vessels (22 armed ships and 23 transports) consisted of ships from the Massachusetts State Navy and private vessels. The Commonwealth promised the owners that it would make good any losses incurred on the expedition. Commodore Dudley Saltonstall (1738–1796) was placed in command.

Massachusetts called up 800 marines and 1,200 militia to accompany the navy—the largest American amphibious force of the entire war. It located 6 small field guns and appointed Lieutenant Colonel Paul Revere (1735–1818) (see Photos MA-11 through MA-13) to command the artillery and Brigadier General Solomon Lovell (d. 1801) to command the "army." The expedition set sail on July 24, 1779, and arrived off Penobscot Bay the following day.

The American militia thought the fort, which jutted into the bay and commanded the principal passage into the inner harbor, looked imposing. In fact, it was a dirt fortification with walls no higher than 4 feet and completely open on the eastern side with no platforms for artillery. The British did not occupy it until July 26, 2 days after the Americans arrived.

Although the fort was weak and the Americans outnumbered the British, the different American contingents maintained their independence and Saltonstall could not organize them effectively. Nor could he and Lovell cooperate.

The Americans fought several small skirmishes near the fort for 47 days but failed to take it. They even began building a fortification of their own about half a mile away from the British works. Saltonstall called a council of war on July 31, but he and Lovell still could not agree on what to do. Saltonstall tried to convince Lovell for a week to attack the fort with his militia, but Lovell argued that the militia could not assault fortifications defended by British Regulars. Lovell tried to convince Saltonstall to attack the 3 small British warships in the harbor, but Saltonstall argued that it was foolish to risk his ships to the fire of shore fortifications. At their meeting on August 6, the two commanders agreed to send for reinforcements.

On August 11, Lovell and about 250 Americans tried to trick the British and lure them out of their defenses. They occupied a battery which the British had recently abandoned. Small parties approached Fort George to entice some of the British to come out. About 55 redcoats advanced toward the concealed Americans. When they approached the American battery, they fired a single volley. The whole American detachment fled to the safety of their main fort. Saltonstall called another council of war and decided to try a naval attack.

The delays resulting from Saltonstall's and Lovell's inability to come to agreement gave MacLean time to request reinforcements. The British sent 5 frigates from New York to Penobscot Bay. When the reinforcements arrived the next day, the larger American navy which included some 40 ships against a handful of British sloops of war, fled in panic up the Penobscot River. British guns destroyed some of the vessels and the Americans ran the remaining ships aground and burned them.

The Americans then fled into the woods and returned to Boston on foot, leaving 500 dead or missing behind. Saltonstall and Revere were court-martialed for treason, unsoldierly conduct, and cowardice—for destroying what amounted to the entire Massachusetts Navy at that time. Saltonstall was found guilty and summarily dismissed from the service. Paul Revere was convicted of negligence, but a second court-martial later cleared him.

2

VERMONT (AND NEW HAMPSHIRE)

See the Vermont map.

Vermont was not a colony at the time of the War for American Independence. Both New York and New Hampshire claimed it as their own.

New Hampshire saw no military action but it contributed 3,700 militia and 12,497 men to the Continental Army—a total of 16,197 men.

East Hubbardton (July 7, 1777)

The Hubbardton Battlefield State Historic Site is 7 miles north of U.S. 4 at East Hubbardton. This is the site of the only Revolutionary War battle fought on Vermont soil.
http://www.dhca.state.vt.us/HistoricSites/html/hubbardton.html

The Hubbardton Battle monument was erected in 1859 at about the midpoint of the semicircle formed by the Green Mountain Boys and the Massachusetts militia. It marks the spot where Colonel Ebeneezer Francis was supposedly buried. A 1-mile trail shows the difficult terrain the British were forced to traverse on their march through a mountain pass and the deadly climb up Monument Hill.

Major General John Burgoyne (1722–1792) marched his army south from Canada intending to split the colonies, to capture Albany, and to join the British forces in New York City. His expedition was proceeding swiftly and with better results than anticipated in early July, 1777.

After Burgoyne captured Fort Ticonderoga on his march to Albany, the majority of the American defenders fled across Lake Champlain into present-day Vermont. A secondary group escaped by boat with supplies and invalids down South Bay to Skenesboro (now Whitehall, New York). Burgoyne's troops chased the main body east through Skenesboro, New York and over hilly terrain to Hubbardton, Vermont. Here, American Major General Arthur St. Clair (1737–1818) ordered Colonel Seth Warner (1743–1784), the commander of the Green Mountain Boys, to form a rear guard of some 1,000 men to help cover his tired and tattered main army as they moved southwest to Castleton. Warner was supposed to follow St. Clair to Castleton, but he disobeyed orders and camped at Hubbardton along the Crown Point Military Road which connected the garrisons on Lake Champlain with sites on the Connecticut River. He failed to post adequate pickets, however.

Native American scouts reported the location of Warner's camp to Brigadier General Simon Fraser (1737–1777) who was camped about 3 miles west. Fraser and his German counterpart, Major General Baron Friedrich von Riedesel (1738–1800), plotted a dawn attack. At about 4:40 on the morning of Monday, July 7, Fraser's 750 men surprised the 2nd New Hampshire Regiment of the Continental Army under Colonel Nathan Hale (d. 1781) (not the executed spy) as they were having breakfast near Sucker Brook. The Continentals formed for battle with their left on the slopes of a 1,200-foot hill now called Mount Zion. Their first volley killed 21 redcoats, including an officer. (Major Balcarres who commanded the flank companies of Fraser's Advanced Corps was slightly wounded, but his clothes had 30 bullet holes.)

Fraser tried to turn Hale's left flank by attacking the slope on the other side of the road and through the woods. This action left his left flank vulnerable. A detachment of Seth Warner's Green Mountain Boys and a detail of Massachusetts militia under Colonel Ebenezer Francis (d. 1777), quickly assembled behind a stone wall at the top of Monument Hill. They formed a semicircle and offered resistance, inflicting a large number of casualties as the Crown forces advanced up the steep slope through brush and fallen trees. The battle seemed like a repetition of the Battle of Bunker Hill. American troops held their ground against an enemy attacking up a hill.

Colonel Francis's Massachusetts militia pushed the redcoats back until Major General von Riedesel arrived with reinforcements. The Hessian jaegers and grenadiers (see Photos VT-1 and VT-2) advanced singing to the music of their band. This encouraged his men, dramatized the arrival of reinforcements, and exaggerated their size. The Hessians broke through the Massachusetts line on the right, killing Francis. They also reinforced the British attack on the main American position in a bayonet charge that forced the front to collapse. Warner ordered his Vermont troops to retreat with the nonmilitary order: "Scatter and meet me in Manchester."

The Americans lost 40 dead and 300 men captured, including Colonel Hale and 70 of his men, in the 2-hour battle. They also lost 12 guns. The Crown forces lost about 35 dead and 150 wounded. Warner's failure to comply with orders cost the Americans a large number of needless casualties and prisoners. Although they were caught off guard, they managed to recover and offer a stiff defense and showed the Crown forces they were willing to fight.

Colonel Ebenezer Francis's bravery under fire was greatly admired at Hubbardton. When his body was found after the battle, Baron von Riedesel personally directed that the young colonel receive a proper military burial.

Bennington (August 16, 1777)

During the War for American Independence, part of Vermont was claimed by New York. The Battle of Bennington was actually fought in/near Hoosick Falls, NY.
     http://www.dhca.state.vt.us/HistoricSites/html/bennington.html

The Bennington Battle Monument is in Bennington, Vermont, 0.5 mile west of the junction of State Route VT 9 and U.S. 7, then north to the end of Monument Avenue to 15 Monument Circle. The Bennington Battle Monument was the tallest battle monument in the world when completed in 1891. At 306 feet, it is still the tallest structure in Vermont. It offers a good view of three states from the upper lookout chamber which is reached by elevator. A diorama and exhibit illustrate the battle and the monument.

In New York state, the Bennington Battlefield State Historic Site is located 3 miles east of Hoosick Falls, New York, on State Route NY 67. An interpretive sign explains the course of the battle and a hilltop picnic area overlooks the battlefield. (See North Hoosick, NY.)
`http://nysparks.state.ny.us/cgi-bin/cgiwrap/nysparks/historic.cgi?p+1`

Major General John Burgoyne (1722–1792) marched his army south from Canada in early July, 1777, intending to split the colonies, to capture Albany, and to join the British forces in New York City. His expedition was proceeding swiftly and with better results than anticipated by the end of July, but it soon bogged down.

Burgoyne's army passed through Fort Edward on July 30. The Americans abandoned and burned the fort before leaving for Stillwater, New York, about 30 miles north of Albany. It became apparent that the expected Loyalist support would be minimal and that the 185-mile supply route from Canada was too long. Burgoyne needed more baggage animals to continue his slow march, so he decided to take Major General Baron Friedrich von Riedesel's (1738–1800) advice and raid a magazine established by the New England militia at Bennington. They had reports that the magazine contained large supplies of food and ammunition and had at least 100 horses.

Burgoyne sent Lieutenant Colonel Friedrich Baum (d. 1777), commander of the Brunswick dragoons, to Bennington on August 11 with about 800 men. The force was composed of 374 dismounted Hessian dragoons, grenadiers, and light infantry; about 300 Canadians and American Loyalists; 80 Native Americans; and a company of about 50 of Brigadier General Simon Fraser's (1737–1777) marksmen. Burgoyne expected that Baum would find large supplies of food, forage, and horses guarded by only a few militia. He also thought Bennington was full of Loyalists who would help him, so he didn't send a larger detachment. Baum even insisted on taking a German band that destroyed any attempt at surprise.

A large portion of Baum's soldiers were dragoons who carried heavy packs (knapsacks and blankets) with their arms and accoutrements, 60 rounds of ammunition, haversacks of provisions, hatchets, a portion of the equipment for their tents, an enormous sword, a large canteen capable of holding about a gallon. They wore long skirted coats and heavy leather gauntlets reaching almost to their elbows. They also wore heavy leather boots and found the 40-mile trek slow going (see Photo VT-3).

The Native Americans ran ahead, plundering and burning any homesteads they could find along the way. They slaughtered cattle along the way to keep the cowbells rather than round them up for food for the army. News that the Native Americans were on the warpath caused the inhabitants to drive their horses and cattle away, making Colonel Baum's task more difficult.

Brigadier General John Stark (1728–1822), of New Hampshire, organized and equipped a brigade of 1,500 men by the first week of August. He marched them to Bennington to defend the frontier. Stark met Baum about 9:00 AM on August 14 at Sancoick's Mill about 5 miles from Bennington, but the two forces did not conduct battle then. Nor did they do battle on the 15th, even though both sides received reinforcements, because it rained. The Americans now numbered 2,000 militia and a few Native Americans.

Baum sent word to Burgoyne for reinforcements and entrenched on high ground between the Walloomsac River and Little White Creek.

On Saturday, August 16, the sun came out around noon, and both sides prepared for battle. Several men had scouted the enemy force, so the Americans knew their strength and dispositions. Baum had scattered his forces about the hillside. Therefore General Stark sent a column of 200 New Hampshire men to the north flank while another column of 300 Vermont rangers and Bennington militia marched around to the south. An additional 300 men attacked the nearest position east of the Walloomsac River. When the flanking columns began their attack about 3:00 PM, Stark would make the main assault toward the center with 1,200 men.

When Baum, who spoke no English, saw small groups of armed men approaching, he thought they were Loyalists from the area coming to help him or to seek safety. The American flanking columns took advantage of this error and disguised themselves as small groups of farmers to get into position. They said they were Loyalists and offered to join him and to swear the customary oath of allegiance. Brigadier Major Philip Skene (1725–1780) assured Baum that the men were sincere and that he could add them to his force. After having them sworn in, Baum gave them slips of white paper to wear in their hats to identify them as friendly forces so the Native Americans would not harm them.

A German officer wrote about the deception:

> How Colonel Baum became so completely duped as to place reliance on these men, I know not. But . . . he was somehow or other persuaded to believe [that they wished] to offer their services to the leader of the King's troops . . . I cannot pretend to describe the state of excitation and alarm into which our little band was now thrown. With the solitary exception of our leader, there was not a man among us who appeared otherwise than satisfied that those to whom he had listened were traitors . . . [But] he remained convinced of their fidelity.

When a large group of militia blocked the road, the "new allies" took up positions around Colonel Baum and in his rear. But when the firing started, they began shooting German officers in the back. The Native Americans were caught between two lines of fire and ran off into the forest, followed by the Canadians and the Loyalists after firing one volley. Colonel Baum had only his German and British troops and a few others left. They were running low on ammunition when a wagon containing their reserve supply caught fire and exploded. As the Americans moved in, the Hessians drew their great swords to defend themselves. The attackers had no bayonets to counter this move and were at a disadvantage until Baum received a mortal wound in the abdomen about 5:00 PM. The Hessians then surrendered.

Lieutenant Colonel Heinrich Christoph von Breymann (d. 1777), sent to support Baum, took 16 hours to march 24 miles through the forest in the pouring rain. When he and his company arrived at Sancoick's Mill about 4:30, they heard no firing and assumed Baum was still holding out. Flank patrols on the hill drove off the small militia bands that tried to impede their progress.

Breymann forced Stark back as Colonel Seth Warner (1743–1784) arrived with reinforcements that gave the Americans enough strength to repel the German attacks and assault the enemy on both flanks. Heavy firing continued until about sunset when Colonel Breymann, almost out of ammunition, ordered a retreat. The Hessians retreated with as many wounded as they could carry. The Americans immediately pursued them, changing the retreat into a rout. The German drums beat the signal for a parley, but the Americans did not understand it and kept firing until dark. Breymann, wounded in the leg and with 5 bullet holes in his clothes, commanded the rear guard action that permitted two-thirds of his command to escape after dark. Stark ordered his men not to pursue the enemy after dark when they might shoot at each other.

Colonel Baum died without ever knowing that there were never any horses in Bennington. He was buried on the road to Bennington.

Stark reported American casualties as 14 killed and 40 wounded. The Crown forces' casualties amounted to 207 men killed, an unknown number of wounded, and more than 600 captured. The Crown forces also lost 12 drums, 250 broadswords, 4 ammunition wagons, several hundred muskets, a few rifles, and 4 brass cannon captured by Wolfe at Quebec in 1759. This defeat at Bennington deprived Burgoyne of approximately 1,000 troops at the Battle of Saratoga.

3

NEW YORK

New York contributed a total of 21,647 men to the war effort—3,866 militia and 17,781 in the Continental Army.

This chapter has three sections: Upstate New York, Downstate New York/Hudson River Valley, and New York City.

UPSTATE

See the map of Upstate New York.

General William Howe (1732–1786) proposed to make the Hudson River his main campaign objective for 1776 by landing at New York. He also wanted to capture ports in South Carolina. He would secure a base of operations in New York and position his forces to push north to clear the riverway of Americans. The overwhelming dominance of the British navy on the waterways would assure him control of the river. General Howe wanted to concentrate the entire British force in America in New York, but the British government had diverted part of it to Canada in early 1776 to repel an American invasion. This diversion of forces laid the groundwork for the divided command structure that plagued British operations throughout the war.

On the American side, General George Washington's (1732–1799) problem was to guess accurately where the Crown forces would attack and to make preparations to meet them. He foresaw correctly that New York would be the focus of their assault. He deemed it necessary to build new fortifications along the Hudson River and to fortify New York City and Long Island.

Overall British strategy for 1776 planned for two attacks on the Hudson-St. Lawrence line in the northern colonies. Yet, the British also proposed to mount a separate attack in the South. The objective of this southern attack was to enlist the help of Loyalists, seize some of the major southern cities, and control the southern colonies. General Henry Clinton (1730–1795) left Boston en route to North Carolina on January 20, 1776, with a force of 1,500 troops to secure the South, while Howe remained in New York to begin the campaign for the Hudson Valley.

With their command of New York and of the sea, the British could move north up the Hudson to Lakes George and Champlain and to Canada, or south to the Delaware and Chesapeake Bays, to Virginia, and the Carolinas. They could also support the many Loyalists they believed lived in Albany and along the Mohawk valley. Moreover, they could encourage the people of the New Hampshire Grants in their dispute with the Continental Congress over boundary claims and administration. (The New Hampshire

Grants, now the state of Vermont, were so-called because most of the land had been settled by people from New England under grants of land made by the governor of New Hampshire. The residents were particularly uneasy because they were nearest the enemy.) Even though Ethan Allen (1738–1790) and his Green Mountain Boys came home heroes after capturing Fort Ticonderoga, Major General John Burgoyne (1722–1792) considered the area ripe for British recruitment as long as the disputes over land grants remained unresolved.

If the British controlled the water route along the Hudson River and Lakes George and Champlain, they would separate the rebels from both the Iroquois League of Six Nations—the Mohawk, the Oneida, the Onondaga, the Cayuga, the Seneca, and the Tuscarora—and the Native Americans of the Western Confederation. General Burgoyne did not yet have a command. He could only advise, so he suggested that the British might enlist some of the 160,000 Native Americans to carry arms to the black slaves of the south. Otherwise, the British could prevent them from joining the rebels.

In 1777, General Burgoyne concluded that the strategic key to military success was British control of the interior water route between New York and the St. Lawrence River. His "Thoughts for Conducting the War from the Side of Canada" called for his army, Lieutenant Colonel Barry St. Leger's (1737–1789) army, and Gen. William Howe's army to divide New England, the heart of the rebellion, from the colonies farther south. Burgoyne thought that this division of the rebellion would go a long way toward ending it. The plan, however, required close coordination between the three armies, and this, as it turned out, was its fatal flaw.

Burgoyne set out from Canada in June, 1777, expecting to reach Albany by fall. His force was divided into two parts: General Sir Guy Carleton (1724–1808) would remain in Canada to defend that province and provide logistic support to the 2 columns moving south. The first and largest part—7,200 British and Hessian Regulars, and 650 Loyalists, Canadians, and Native Americans, under his personal command—was to take the route down Lake Champlain to Ticonderoga and thence via Lake George to the Hudson. The second—700 Regulars and 1,000 Loyalists and Native American braves under Lieutenant Colonel Barry St. Leger—was to move via Lake Ontario to Oswego and thence down the Mohawk Valley to join Burgoyne at Albany.

General Sir Guy Carleton (1724–1808) gave Burgoyne the task, required by the government, of issuing a proclamation offering a pardon to any rebel who deserted and went home. Burgoyne's proclamation (June 23, 1777) called on the Loyalists to join him, offered protection to those who sided with the King, and threatened to turn the Native Americans loose on the rebels. He made this announcement using language that caused laughter and ridicule both in the colonies and in the House of Commons in London. A few days later, he told his Native American allies they must make war in a civilized manner. They were not to scalp or torture the wounded and prisoners, and they must not harm old men, women, and children.

In his preparations, Burgoyne evidently forgot the lesson the British had learned in the French and Indian War, that troops had to be prepared to travel light in the wilderness and fight like Native Americans. He carried 138 pieces of artillery and a heavy load of officers' personal baggage. Numerous ladies of high and low rank accompanied the expedition. When he started down the lakes, Burgoyne did not have enough horses and wagons to transport his artillery and baggage once he had to leave the water and move overland.

Fort Ticonderoga
(July 8, 1758; May 10, 1775; July 1–6, 1777)

Fort Ticonderoga is on Route NY 74, 1 mile northeast of the town of Ticonderoga.
http://www.fort-ticonderoga.org/

William Ferris Pell purchased the site of Fort Ticonderoga in 1820. The fort remained in his family until Stephen Pell decided to restore it in 1908—10 years before the creation of any national park and 20 years before the reconstruction of Williamsburg, Virginia. The reconstruction restored most of the stone walls and two interior barracks. The four-sided fort faces south on its long axis (see Photo NY-1). Each of its four corners has a bastion shaped like an arrowhead to protect the side walls. The north and west walls also have freestanding triangular bastions called demilunes in front of them for added protection, as they face land approaches where attackers could place heavy artillery to knock holes through the walls. The apex of the demilunes points outward, forming angled walls to deflect cannonballs and shells to the side. Wooden bridges connect the demilunes to the fort proper. If enemy forces capture the demilunes, the bridges could be raised. Some of the bastions house dungeons, storehouses, and other quarters. Ramps lead from the parade to the ramparts for impressive views of the surrounding area. Scores of cannon line the bastions of the fort (see Photo NY-2).

The South Barracks houses a museum which fills the three floors. Pell's private collection became the basis of the museum's collection. It includes Ethan Allen's blunderbuss, General Schuyler's personal flag made of wool with a ring of circular white linen stars, and a hollow silver bullet that concealed a secret message from the British General Clinton to Burgoyne telling him of the capture of the Hudson River forts. (The soldier who carried the message tried to swallow the bullet when he was captured and was hanged as a spy.) There are musket balls with the tooth marks of the men who chewed on them during surgery or punishment (hence the term "bite the bullet"), and a rum horn made by Paul Revere. Some of the rooms are set up to depict the original quarters, a soldier's canteen, and the officer of the day's quarters.

Mount Defiance (835 feet), where British general William Phillips placed four 12-pound cannon forcing the evacuation of Fort Ticonderoga, is off Route NY 22/74, 1 mile southeast of town. A paved road goes to the top.

Fort Mount Hope, 2 miles northwest of Fort Ticonderoga, is privately owned. Mount Independence is in Vermont, across Lake Champlain from the fort.

Crown Point is a large British fort 11 miles north of Ticonderoga off NY 9N. There is a museum.
http://nysparks.state.ny.us/cgi-bin/cgiwrap/nysparks/historic.cgi?p+5

The location of Fort Ticonderoga controls a 2-mile portage from Lake Champlain to Lake George and consequently the entire route between Canada and New York. The Native Americans called the place "between the waters." The French began building the first fort here in October, 1755, and called it Carillon because the builders thought the water from Lake George sounded like a "chime of bells" as it fell over the rocks into Lake Champlain.

The fort originally consisted of squared-off timbers laid horizontally and backed by embankments, but the wood eventually rotted and was replaced by stone (see Photos NY-1 and NY-2). As the fort's outer entrenchment was nearing completion, the British attacked it on July 8, 1758 with 15,000 men—the largest British Army yet fielded in North America. Louis Joseph Marquis de Montcalm de Saint-Véran, (1712–1759) did not wait for the attack. He ordered wooden fortifications built in the woods $\frac{3}{4}$ mile west of the fort. Unlike stone which shatters and acts like shrapnel when struck by artillery, wood was better able to withstand artillery fire and could be easily repaired. The British lost 2,000 men killed and wounded in an unsuccessful attempt to penetrate the defenses. The defenders lost only 300 out of 3,500.

General Jeffrey Amherst, Baron Amherst (1717–1797) returned the following summer to find the fort's garrison drastically reduced. After a 4-day siege, the French blew up their powder and evacuated the fort. Amherst had the damage repaired and renamed the fort Ticonderoga. The British occupied Fort Ticonderoga for the next 16 years, but it no longer had any military importance with the French removed from eastern North America, so it was only guarded by a few men and fell into disrepair.

1775–1776

Early in May, 1775, the Massachusetts Committee of Safety authorized Captain Benedict Arnold (1741–1801) to recruit a company of 400 men to capture Fort Ticonderoga. About the same time, the Connecticut assembly made a similar offer to Lieutenant Colonel Ethan Allen (1738–1790) and his Green Mountain Boys. When Arnold learned of this, he rode to Castleton, Vermont, to confront Allen, but the Green Mountain Boys refused to serve under anybody but Allen. So Arnold and Allen agreed to share the command.

Allen, Arnold, and 83 men boarded the only boats available, a couple of scows, at Hand's Cove on the east shore of Lake Champlain near Shoreham, Vermont. By the time they landed, it was too light for the boats to return for the remainder of the assault party which totaled two to three hundred men. With less than one-third of his total strength, Allen decided to attack the fort about 3:30 AM on May 10, 1775. They caught the redcoats by surprise and both the commanding officer and the second-in-command asleep in bed. Allen and Arnold climbed the wooden outside stairs leading to the top floor, with swords drawn and demanded the fort's surrender. Allen shouted something like "Come on out, you damn old rat!" He later embellished the statement in his memoirs published in 1779 where he recorded he called for the surrender "In the name of the Great Jehovah and the Continental Congress." The second-in-command described Benedict Arnold as requesting surrender in a "genteel manner." He described Ethan Allen as highly agitated, brandishing a sword, and demanding the keys of the fort.

The position was not as critical as the cannon and ammunition stored there (see Photos NY-1 and NY-2; also Photo MA-10). Allen, Arnold, and the raiding party captured 78 guns in good condition, 6 mortars, 3 howitzers, thousands of cannonballs,

30,000 flints, and other supplies at Ticonderoga and Crown Point (about 12 miles further north), which they seized the next day. The captives were marched to a prison in Hartford, Connecticut.

General George Washington (1732–1799) sent Colonel Henry Knox (1750–1806), later to be his chief of artillery, to Fort Ticonderoga to remove the artillery he needed so badly. Knox arrived on December 5 and began the task of loading 43 cannon and 16 mortars—119,000 pounds of artillery—for the journey to Boston. He also took 2,300 pounds of lead and a supply of flints. The train of 42 heavy sledges pulled by 80 yoke of oxen traveled 300 miles, despite the poor or nonexistent roads in icebound western New England. They arrived at Framingham (20 miles from Cambridge, Massachusetts) by January 25. The guns were eventually installed on Dorchester Heights, overlooking Boston, in March, 1776, and contributed greatly to convincing the redcoats to evacuate the city (see Photo MA-10).

1777

American defenses in the north were very weak in 1777. There were only about 2,500 Continentals at Ticonderoga, with 450 occupying old Fort Stanwix in the Mohawk Valley. Dissension was rife among the Americans. New Englanders refused to support Major General Philip Schuyler (1733–1804), the aristocratic New Yorker who commanded the Northern Army, and openly intrigued to replace him with their own favorite, Major General Horatio Gates (1728–1806).

The British returned in 1777 as Major General John Burgoyne (1722–1792) marched from Canada to Albany. His first task was to retake the old British position controlling Lake Champlain at Fort Ticonderoga. Burgoyne's army landed north of Fort Ticonderoga on both sides of the lake on July 1. The Germans landed on the east, the British on the west.

Major General Arthur St. Clair (1737–1818) was in command at Ticonderoga. His orders required that he defend the fort itself, Mount Independence across the lake, and Mount Hope 2 miles to the northwest of the fort. He neglected to occupy Sugar Loaf (Mount Defiance), a mile to the southwest. This was the highest point in the area and dominated both the fort and Mount Independence, but St. Clair considered it inaccessible and did not have enough men to defend the mountain. Major General William Phillips (1731–1781), Burgoyne's second in command and an artilleryman, directed his engineers and artillery to begin work on July 4. He reportedly told his men: "Where a goat can go, a man can go, and where a man can go, he can drag a gun." He then led his men up the mountain. He had four 12-pounders in position by noon of July 6. The cannon did not threaten the fort but could destroy the floating bridge and boats needed for evacuation. St. Clair recognized his danger and evacuated Ticonderoga on the night of July 5-6, leaving behind cannon and valuable supplies.

Burgoyne pursued the retreating Americans to Skenesboro, New York (now Whitehall), arriving on the afternoon of July 6 in time to capture 2 ships. The Americans burned the rest as they evacuated the area. Brigadier General Simon Fraser (1737–1777), and Major General Baron Friedrich von Riedesel (1738–1800) pursued the main body and surprised and defeated the rear guard near Hubbardton, Vermont the next day. General St. Clair managed to escape with the rest of his men and rejoined the army at Fort Edward, New York.

As the British pursued the Patriots after the fall of Fort Ticonderoga, they left their wounded in bark huts under the charge of Sergeant Roger Lamb who tore up his shirt to make bandages, as there were no supplies to dress their wounds. Burgoyne left several hundred men behind to garrison Fort Ticonderoga after capturing it. He hoped that General Sir Guy Carleton (1724–1808) would send reinforcements for this purpose, but Carleton told him his orders from London forbade him doing so.

Burgoyne could choose one of two routes to reach Fort Edward on the Hudson. He could continue overland via Fort Ann, a distance of 23 miles through a wilderness of tall trees and deep ravines with poor or nonexistent roads; or he could return to Fort Ticonderoga, go up Lake George and across country to a point on the Hudson north of Fort Edward. This route also had its difficulties because the falls and rapids between Lake Champlain and Lake George would require a portage of about 3 miles. The poor road between Lake George and the Hudson would reduce the distance to only 10 miles.

Burgoyne did not want to appear to be retreating by going back to Ticonderoga to take the second and easier route. He decided to continue overland through the forest to the Hudson, but he sent his boats, his artillery, and other heavy equipment by the first route. The overland line of advance was already a nightmare, running along wilderness trails, through marshes, and across wide ravines and creeks that had been swollen by abnormally heavy rains. Major General Philip Schuyler (1733–1804) (see Photo NY-5) adopted the tactic of making it even worse by destroying bridges, cutting trees in Burgoyne's path, and digging trenches to let the waters of swamps onto drier ground. The Americans encouraged local residents to drive off their horses and cattle and to burn their crops to prevent the British from getting them. The British averaged about a mile a day, arriving at Fort Edward on July 29, 3 weeks later. By that time, Burgoyne was desperately short of horses, wagons, and oxen. Yet Schuyler, with an unstable force of 4,500 men discouraged by continual retreats, was in no position to give battle.

General George Washington (1732–1799) did what he could to strengthen the Northern Army. He first dispatched Major General Benedict Arnold (1741–1801), his most aggressive field commander, and Major General Benjamin Lincoln (1733–1810), a Massachusetts man noted for his influence with the New England militia. On August 16, he detached Colonel Daniel Morgan (1736–1802) with 500 riflemen from the main army in Pennsylvania and ordered them along with 750 men from Colonel Rufus Putnam's (1738–1824) force in the New York highlands to join Schuyler. The riflemen were intended to furnish an antidote for Burgoyne's Native Americans who, despite his efforts to restrain them, were terrorizing the countryside. (See Photo VA-1, American rifleman.)

After Burgoyne surrendered at Saratoga, the Americans once again took control of Fort Ticonderoga which served as the rallying point for raiding parties through the end of the war. The fort was never garrisoned again after the war and fell into disrepair, serving as a quarry for building material.

Plattsburgh (October 11–13, 1776)

Valcour Island

Valcour Island is about 6 miles south of Plattsburgh, about 900 yards off the west shore of Lake Champlain.

The Clinton County Historical Museum has a diorama that depicts the engagement. When it moved to smaller quarters (Cumberland Avenue and Sailly Avenue, Plattsburgh) in the summer of 2004, it loaned the diorama to an exhibit in the old high school on Front Street in Keeseville, New York.

http://www.clintoncountyhistorical.org/museum.html

The Smithsonian Institution's National Museum of American History in Washington, D.C. houses the gunboat *Philadelphia* which was one of the 5 two-masted galleys and 8 gunboats constructed for Benedict Arnold's fleet for the Battle of Valcour Island. The *Philadelphia,* commanded by Captain Benjamin Rue, was outfitted with a 12-pound cannon, two 9-pounders, and swivel guns. It was sunk by a 24-pound shot through the bow. It lay at the bottom of Lake Champlain with the top of the white pine mast barely 10 feet below the surface of Valcour Bay until 1935 when it was dredged up and restored. The original timbers still show evidence of holes from the musket and cannon fire. The National Museum of American History also displays many items of iron, wood, and pewter from the *Philadelphia* along with reproductions of 18th century shipboard items.

During the autumn of 1776, while General William Howe (1732–1786) was routing General George Washington (1732–1799) around New York City, other British forces under Sir Guy Carleton (1724–1808) attempted to take advantage of a previous British achievement, the repulsion of an American attack on Canada the previous year. Carleton rather leisurely built a flotilla of boats to carry British forces from Canada down Lake Champlain and Lake George, intending to reduce the fort at Ticonderoga before winter set in. Brigadier General Benedict Arnold (1741–1801) countered by having 150 soldiers and craftsmen build a much weaker flotilla of 16 vessels in the summer of 1776.

The comparatively shallow water of the lake required specially designed ships, most of which consisted of small craft propelled by oars and by small sails on short, stumpy masts. The British fleet consisted of the *Inflexible,* a three-masted sloop; 2 schooners, the *Maria* and the *Carleton;* the *Loyal Convert;* a large gundalow (open boat about 53 feet long, 15 feet wide and almost 4 feet deep in the center), and about 20 gunboats, each with one gun. They also had 4 longboats armed with field cannon; 24 bateaux which carried provisions; and a 422-ton sailing scow, the *Thunderer.* The *Thunderer* was 92 feet long and more than 33 feet wide and carried 300 men, howitzers, and 24-pound and 6-pound guns. However, Arnold disposed his fleet in such a way as to make it impossible for the *Thunderer* to take part in the battle.

Arnold's fleet consisted of the schooners *Liberty* and *Royal Savage* and the sloop *Enterprise.* He also had another schooner built called the *Revenge,* as well as the *Lee,* a cutter; 4 galleys: the *Washington, Congress, Trumbull,* and *Gates,* (about 72 feet long, 20 feet wide and 6 feet deep); and 8 flat-bottomed gundalows. These ships which comprised the colonial navy carried from 45 to 80 men each and were armed with everything from 2-pounders and smaller swivel guns to 18-pounders (18th-century artillery is classified by the weight of the shot fired).

Arnold's boats waited behind Valcour Island between the island and the west shore of Lake Champlain. They were arranged in a line with their broadside guns facing south. Carleton sailed south with his flotilla on October 11, searching for Arnold's boats. Carleton came around the north of Valcour Island and bypassed Arnold by 2 miles without realizing it. When he realized his mistake, he had to turn around and sail into a strong north wind.

While Arnold's line position gave him maximum advantage against a superior enemy force, he made the mistake of sending the *Royal Savage* toward the enemy with orders to return to the line of battle when spotted. Four of the fastest boats, *Royal Savage, Congress, Trumbull,* and *Washington,* would inflict whatever damage they could. When he saw the size of the enemy fleet, Arnold signaled all his ships back to the line of battle, but most of the crew were amateur sailors at best. The *Royal Savage* ran aground in shallow water near the southwest tip of Valcour Island (a marker on Route NY 9 is directly opposite the spot). The *Carleton* approached the *Royal Savage* to fire on her, but she experienced the same trouble with the adverse wind. She dropped anchor and prepared to fire. Most of the British gunboats lined up with the *Carleton* across the channel and a general engagement followed at about 12:30. The *Carleton* was severely damaged and her skipper seriously wounded. Two smaller boats had to tow the *Carleton* out of the action.

The *Royal Savage* continued firing until the *Thunderer* sent a landing party of Native Americans and Regulars to drive off the gunners. Later, a crew from the *Maria* burned the *Royal Savage* which exploded when the flames reached the magazine. The battle continued until the *Inflexible* managed to bring her guns into effective range. She fired 5 broadsides and put most of Arnold's guns out of action. The engagement lasted until darkness set in.

Believing he had Arnold trapped, Sir Guy Carleton held his position and prepared to destroy the rebel fleet the next day. But Arnold took advantage of a fog cover and a good northeast wind at his back to sail his boats in single file between the British line and the shore to escape out into the lake. He left the burned-out hulk of the *Royal Savage* behind and the gundalow *Philadelphia* which sank about an hour after the battle ended.

The wind turned during the night and blew from the south. Arnold was only 8 miles from Carleton's ships by daybreak and both fleets had to row into the wind. The wind turned again on October 13, allowing the British to close the gap. They began raking Arnold's boats with broadsides about 11:00 AM, forcing the galley *Washington* to surrender and the cutter *Lee* to run aground. Arnold's flagship, the *Congress,* and 4 gundalows continued to resist, moving south as fast as they could.

Carleton recognized *Arnold* on board the *Congress* and concentrated his attention on him, but Arnold turned into the wind and rowed across the lake to the Vermont shore to escape. He beached the rest of his fleet in Buttonmold Bay (near Panton, Vermont) and marched 10 miles to Crown Point with 200 men. The *Trumbull, Enterprise, Revenge,* and *Liberty* arrived at Crown Point before him. Arnold burned the fort there and withdrew to Fort Ticonderoga.

Arnold lost the naval battle along with 11 of his boats and more than 100 men killed, wounded, and captured. But he delayed Carleton's advance down the Hudson

Valley by more than 6 months—long enough that the British commander reached Ticonderoga too late in the year to undertake a siege. Carleton returned his army to winter quarters at St. John's, Canada, leaving the British with no advance base from which to launch the following year's campaign. This limited victory did little to dispel the gloom that fell on the Patriots after General George Washington's (1732–1799) defeats in New York.

The British, aware that Continental enlistments expired at the end of the year, had high hopes that the rebel Army would simply fade away and the rebellion collapse. Howe halted General Charles Cornwallis's (1738–1805) pursuit of Washington and sent General Henry Clinton (1730–1795) with a detachment of troops under naval escort to seize Newport, Rhode Island. Clinton occupied Rhode Island without resistance, and used Newport as a base to harass American shipping. Howe then dispersed his troops in winter quarters, establishing a line of posts in New Jersey at Perth Amboy, New Brunswick, Princeton, Trenton, and Bordentown, and retired himself to New York. Howe had gained the object of the 1776 campaign, a strong foothold, and possibly, as he thought at the time, a great deal more.

Fort Edward (July 27, 1777)

Fort Edward is on the portage trail between the Hudson River and Lake Champlain on Route U.S. 4.
        `http://www.revolutionaryday.com/usroute4/ftedward/default.htm`

A small pyramid on the west side of Route U.S. 4 marks the site of the house Jane McCrea was visiting when she was captured. The house (modern street number 219) is opposite the high school. Jane McCrea was originally buried off U.S. 4, 2 miles south of Fort Edward, but her remains were later moved to the Union Cemetery on Broadway.

A marker on the west side (right) of Route U.S. 4 south marks the approximate location of the northeast bastion of Fort Edward. Following U.S. 4 and proceeding straight on Montgomery Street when U.S. 4 turns to the left, one comes to Old Fort Street. Turning right onto Old Fort Street, one can see a marker on the right (north) identifying the low ground as part of the old moat. A few hundred feet further down the road toward the river, a marker identifies the site of the barracks and other parts of the fort opposite Rogers Island.

The Rogers Island Visitors Center (11 Rogers Island Drive, Fort Edward, New York) includes historical displays, videos, and archaeological artifacts that detail Fort Edward's earliest known Native American inhabitants through the War for American Independence. The location was one of the largest British forts in the colonies during the Seven Years' War and the main base camp for Rogers Rangers, 1757–1759. It is strategically located on the military trail during the War for American Independence.
        `http://www.thenortherncampaign.org/rogislandsite.htm`

The Old Fort House Museum (29 Broadway, U.S. Route 4), located just to the west of U.S. 4 and 0.1 mile beyond its junction with Route NY 197, is a regional museum which has a scale model of old Fort Edward. Constructed in 1772 as a private residence for Patrick Smyth, the Old Fort House is one of the oldest frame structures in upstate New York. It served as headquarters for both British and American generals in the War for

American Independence. General George Washington and his party dined here on two different occasions in July, 1783. The museum includes five additional buildings.
`http://www.ftedward.com/History/OldFort/oldFort.htm`

Fort Ann is on U.S. 4 about midway between Fort Edward and Whitehall (formerly Skenesboro). A marker to the east of U.S. 4 and just south of the bridge identifies the "Oldest House" which was part of the site of the stockaded fort. A well that served the fort is diagonally across the highway and 100 feet west on Charles Street. A reconstructed blockhouse just north of the Oldest House is a replica of what is presumed to be the British fort of 1757.

Major General John Burgoyne (1722–1792), in a psychological ploy to terrorize the rebels, issued a proclamation on June 23, 1777, that called on the Loyalists to join him, offered protection to those who sided with the king, and threatened to turn the Native Americans loose on the rebels. A few days later, however, he told his Native American allies they must conduct the war in a civilized manner. They were not to scalp or torture the wounded and prisoners, nor were they to harm old men, women, or children. Burgoyne's announcement, though meant to be threatening, used stilted language that provoked only laughter and ridicule in the colonies and even in the House of Commons in London.

Moving south, Burgoyne's next logical objective after the capture of Fort Ticonderoga was Fort Edward on the Hudson River. Burgoyne could choose one of two routes to reach Fort Edward. He could travel overland via Fort Ann, a distance of 23 miles over poor or nonexistent roads through a wilderness of tall trees, deep ravines, marshes, and creeks swollen by abnormally heavy rains. Or he could travel up Lake George and cross the country to a point on the Hudson north of Fort Edward. This latter route had its own difficulties, for the falls and rapids between Lake Champlain and Lake George would require a portage (carrying gear overland) of about 3 miles. Yet taking the poor road between Lake George and the Hudson would reduce his total march to only 10 miles.

Burgoyne proceeded through the forest with his troops but sent his boats, artillery, and other heavy equipment by the easier roundabout route. Major General Philip Schuyler (1733–1804) made his trek even more difficult by destroying bridges, cutting trees across the path, and digging trenches to let the waters of swamps onto usually dry ground. To further hinder the British troops, the Americans encouraged local residents to drive off their horses and cattle and burn their crops. Such obstacles reduced the British advance to a snail's pace, an average of 1 mile a day. The British persisted, however, and arrived at Fort Edward on July 29, 1777. Burgoyne was desperately short of horses, wagons, and oxen, yet Schuyler, with an unstable force of only 4,500 men who had been discouraged by continual retreats, was in no position to give battle.

Burgoyne's army passed through Fort Edward on July 30. The Americans abandoned and burned the fort before leaving for Stillwater, about 30 miles north of Albany. Burgoyne needed more baggage animals to continue his slow march, so he decided to take Major General Baron Friedrich von Riedesel's (1738–1800) advice and raid a magazine established by the New England militia at Bennington. They had reports that the magazine contained large supplies of food and ammunition and had at least 100 horses.

General George Washington (1732–1799) did what he could to strengthen the Northern Army, sending Major General Benedict Arnold (1741–1801), his most aggressive field commander, and Major General Benjamin Lincoln (1733–1810), a Massachusetts man noted for his influence with the New England militia, to join the northern force. On August 16, Washington detached an additional unit under Colonel Daniel Morgan (1736–1802) with 500 riflemen and ordered them, along with 750 men from Colonel Rufus Putnam's force in the New York highlands, to join Schuyler. The riflemen were intended to furnish an antidote to Burgoyne's Native Americans who, despite his efforts to restrain them, were terrorizing the countryside.

The worst single incident for the British-Native American alliance happened away from the field of battle. A 23-year-old white woman named Jane "Jenny" McCrea (1754–1777), the daughter of a Presbyterian minister, was being escorted through the woods by a Native American war party to meet her fiancé, Lieutenant David Jones, a Loyalist officer serving with the British. Somewhere along the way, she was killed on July 27 by her "protectors" in a quarrel over their reward money. When the news spread across the New York frontier, it caused both terror and anger among the people. Wyandot Panther was accused of the crime but went unpunished because Burgoyne felt he could not afford to offend his Native American allies. The incident occurred at a time when the Native Americans raided the farms and settlements of eastern New York and western Vermont, stiffening the resolve of the Americans to resist Burgoyne and thus contributed to his defeat.

After the McCrea incident, British commanders encouraged the Native Americans to return to small-scale raids on frontier farms and settlements. The British hoped that this strategy would damage civilian morale, disrupt food production, and force the Americans to transfer troops from the major eastern battlefields to garrison duty in the West.

Rome (August, 1777)

Fort Stanwix

> Fort Stanwix National Monument is off Route NY 26 in downtown Rome, New York. (See Photo NY-3.)
>
>   `http://www.nps.gov/fost/`
>
> The fort was leveled by 1830. However, it was later reconstructed, before the nation's Bicentennial, to its 1777 appearance.

The British built Fort Stanwix in 1758 after the outbreak of the French and Indian War to replace 3 smaller forts that protected the Oneida Carry, a short stretch of level ground between the Mohawk River and the Wood Creek. This short portage was the only obstacle for canoe travelers to go from the Great Lakes to the Atlantic Ocean. The fort, named for its builder Brigadier General John Stanwix, never saw action in the French and Indian War, so the British neglected and abandoned it when they won Canada in 1763.

American rebels, under Colonel Elias Dayton (1737–1807), repaired and restored the fort in June, 1776 at the outbreak of the War for American Independence. For a while it was called Fort Schuyler in honor of Major General Philip Schuyler (1733–1804), a leading and powerful figure in this part of the state.

By July, 1777, the fort was garrisoned with 750 troops when Major General John Burgoyne (1722–1792) made it a prime objective in his New York campaign. He sent Lieutenant Colonel Barry St. Leger (1737–1789) with 700 Regulars and 1,000 Loyalists and Native Americans as a diversion to move via Lake Ontario to Oswego, and then march down the Mohawk Valley to join Burgoyne outside of Albany. Joseph Brant (1742–1807), Mohawk Chief Thayendanagea, led another 900 Native American allies to augment St. Leger's force. Most of the Native warriors came from the Mohawk tribe, the most powerful tribe in the Iroquois League, whose Six Nations included the Mohawks, Onondagas, Cayugas, Senecas, Oneidas, and Tuscaroras. They marched against Fort Stanwix on July 26 to clear the western approach to Albany and to serve as a diversion to draw troops away from Albany. They traveled about 10 miles a day through the wilderness with some light pieces of artillery. Meanwhile, Burgoyne led the main army of 7,200 British and Hessian Regulars along with 650 Loyalists, Canadians, and Native Americans down Lake Champlain to Fort Ticonderoga and then via Lake George to the Hudson.

St. Leger arrived at Fort Stanwix on August 3—the same day that Burgoyne learned General William Howe (1732–1786) was not headed north, but south to Philadelphia. The American garrison at Fort Stanwix consisted of only 750 men commanded by Colonel Peter Gansevoort (1749–1812). St. Leger demanded Gansevoort's surrender, threatening to massacre the defenders and the settlers along the Mohawk. Fearing massacre by the Native Americans, Gansevoort's men were determined to hold out to the bitter end. He "rejected with disdain" St. Leger's demand for surrender. St. Leger, lacking adequate artillery, decided against a frontal assault, so he and his 1,700 men surrounded the fort and settled into a siege (see Photo NY-3).

On August 4, the Patriot Tryon County militia under Brigadier General Nicholas Herkimer (1728–1777) set out to relieve the fort; however, they were ambushed in a wooded ravine near Oriskany about a mile or two from Fort Stanwix. The militia, under the direction of a mortally wounded Herkimer, scattered in the woods and fought a bloody afternoon's battle in a summer thunderstorm. Both sides suffered heavy losses, and though the militia were unable to relieve Fort Stanwix, the casualties they inflicted on St. Leger's Native Americans and Loyalists discouraged the Native Americans, who had already become restless during the static siege operation. Moreover, a sortie from the fort pillaged the camps. The departure of the Native Americans forced the British and Loyalists to abandon the siege.

When Schuyler learned of the plight of the Stanwix garrison, he detached Major General Benedict Arnold (1741–1801) with 950 Continentals to relieve them, despite his own weak position before Burgoyne. Arnold left from Fort Dayton (present day village of Herkimer), 30 miles to the south, and took advantage of the dissatisfaction of St. Leger's Native Americans. Employing a Dutchman, his clothes shot full of holes, and a friendly Oneida as his messengers, he spread the rumor that the Continentals were approaching "as numerous as the leaves on the trees." The Native Americans, who had special respect for any insane person, departed in haste, scalping many of their Loyalist allies as they went. With half his force gone, St. Leger was forced to abandon the siege and retreat to Oswego. The British never conquered Fort Stanwix; the American defenders in Albany never turned away from Burgoyne's army; and the British initiative to win the upper Hudson River was over. With St. Leger in retreat and Howe gone to Philadelphia, Burgoyne was strictly on his own.

Fort Stanwix was garrisoned until 1781 but never saw action again. American and Iroquois representatives met here in October, 1784, to negotiate the Treaty of Fort Stanwix which set peace terms with the Native Americans and forced the Iroquois Confederacy to cede large tracts of their ancestral lands to the United States.

Oriskany (August 6, 1777)

Oriskany Battlefield is 6 miles east of Oriskany, New York on State Route NY 69, and is marked by a large shaft on the highest point of ground.
`http://nysparks.state.ny.us/cgi-bin/cgiwrap/nysparks/historic.cgi?p+20`

This large 84-foot granite-limestone obelisk on the highest point of ground lists the names of the militia killed at Oriskany. This is where the Americans rallied after breaking out of the ambush. A small granite marker to the right of the battle monument and down the slope marks the spot where Herkimer is believed to have directed the defense.

Brigadier General Nicholas Herkimer (1728–1777) assembled a militia force of 800 men and boys—all males in the Mohawk Valley between 16 and 60 years of age—and set out from Fort Dayton, now the town of Herkimer, on the morning of August 4, 1777 to relieve Fort Stanwix and oppose Lieutenant Colonel Barry St. Leger (1737–1789). He followed a military supply road and camped about 10 miles from Stanwix on the night of August 5.

He sent a message to Colonel Peter Gansevoort (1749–1812), the fort's commander, to fire 3 cannon when he received the letter and to conduct a diversionary attack on the British siege line. Herkimer had still not heard any cannon 2 days later. He was inclined to halt his advance, but his regimental commanders pressed him to continue the assault, impugning his loyalty and bravery.

Unaware that his position had been revealed to St. Leger the night before by Molly Brant who was Joseph Brant (1742–1807) Mohawk Chief Thayendanagea's sister and Sir William Johnson's (1715–1774) (a British general and Superintendent of Indian Affairs) mistress and mother of several of his children, Herkimer's mile-long column descended into a gully 6 miles below the fort at Oriskany. Most of the advance force of 600 men were deep into the ravine when about 400 of Brant's Native Americans and some Loyalists opened fire on them from both sides of the road where it dipped down into the ravine and crossed a creek and marshy area. They killed or wounded more than a dozen officers, including Herkimer, in the initial volley. Herkimer's rear guard of 200 had fled down the road.

Herkimer, shot in the thigh, demanded to be propped against a beech tree to direct the operation. He ordered his men to form a circle against the snipers. They managed to keep the line intact for about $\frac{3}{4}$ hour when a heavy rainstorm broke, wetting everyone's priming pan and delaying the battle about an hour. The same storm delayed the start of Gansevoort's diversionary attack on the enemy camp.

Herkimer took advantage of this relief to order his men to fight in pairs. The Native Americans would wait for a militiaman to fire, then rush in to tomahawk him before he could reload. By fighting in pairs, one man loaded his musket while the other protected him from a tomahawk charge.

When the storm subsided, some of the militia broke away and managed to reach higher ground and formed a new line of defense. Brant received reinforcements from the siege lines at Fort Stanwix. They turned their coats inside out in an attempt to trick the militia into thinking they were friends (hence the term "turncoat"), but one of the men recognized his Loyalist neighbor. The stiff resistance began to dispirit the Native Americans who were now engaged in protracted hand-to-hand combat. They began to desert, forcing the Loyalists to withdraw.

Although the exact number of casualties at Oriskany has never been determined with certainty, both sides suffered heavy losses in the 6-hour battle. It was one of the bloodiest engagements of the war, with one of the highest ratios of casualties suffered to the number of men involved. The militia lost more than 160 killed and 50 wounded; several men were taken prisoner and the rest returned to Fort Dayton. Nicholas Herkimer died 11 days later after an amputation.

The militia never managed to relieve Fort Stanwix, but they inflicted such heavy casualties on St. Leger's Native Americans and Loyalists that the Native Americans, who had already become restless during the static siege operation, became discouraged and left. A sortie from the fort pillaged the camps and gave the Native Americans further reason to leave. The departure of the Native Americans forced the British and Loyalists to abandon the siege.

North Hoosick (August 16, 1777)
Battle of Bennington

During the War for American Independence, part of Vermont was claimed by New York. The Battle of Bennington was actually fought in/near Hoosick Falls, New York where the Bennington Battlefield State Historic Site is located. It is 3 miles east of Hoosick Falls, New York, on State Route NY 67.

`http://nysparks.state.ny.us/cgi-bin/cgiwrap/nysparks/historic.cgi?p+1`

An interpretive sign explains the course of the battle. A hilltop picnic area overlooks the battlefield.

See Bennington, Vermont, for a discussion of this battle.

Stillwater/Schuylerville
(September 19 and October 7–17, 1777)
(Battle of) Saratoga

Saratoga National Historical Park in Stillwater, New York, is 8 miles south of Schuylerville (then called Saratoga) on U.S. 4. It covers 2,800 acres and embraces partially wooded country along the west side of the Hudson River. (The traveler should realize that the battle of Saratoga site is no longer in the town of Saratoga.)
http://www.nps.gov/sara/index.htm

A visitor center on Fraser Hill, the highest point in the park, affords a view of the battlefield and surrounding area. A 9.5-mile scenic driving tour has 10 stops in the park, including the key British redoubts and scenes of action. A unique monument depicts a granite boot, epaulets, and an inscription documenting Arnold's heroics but does not mention his name.

Eight miles from the battlefield stands the Saratoga Battle Monument (see Surrender, Schuylerville, below) commemorating Burgoyne's surrender.

Major General John Burgoyne (1722–1792) submitted a plan to the British ministry called "Thoughts for Conducting the War from the Side of Canada" on February 28, 1777. This plan which became the basis for British military strategy in 1777 aimed to cut the American states along the Hudson River by moving on Albany. However, Burgoyne suffered defeats at Bennington and Fort Stanwix on the way to Albany. He lost a large percentage of his troops; most of his Native Americans became disheartened and left. He dared not send another detachment in search of supplies fearing it would meet a similar fate as at Bennington. So he had to get everything he needed from Canada which meant a month's delay. Every day that he waited in position, the American forces grew stronger.

Congress deferred to New England sentiment on August 19 and replaced Major General Philip Schuyler (1733–1804) with Major General Horatio Gates (1728–1806). Gates was more the beneficiary than the cause of the improved situation, but his appointment helped morale and encouraged the New England militia. General George Washington's (1732–1799) emissary, Major General Benjamin Lincoln (1733–1810), also did his part.

In the first week of September, Major General Benedict Arnold (1741–1801) returned from a successful expedition against General Barry St. Leger (1737–1789) at Fort Stanwix. Colonel Daniel Morgan (1736–1802) arrived with riflemen from Washington's army. General Gates understood Burgoyne's plight perfectly and adapted his tactics to take full advantage of it. He advanced his forces 4 miles northward on September 12, the day after the Battle of the Brandywine, and took up a position, surveyed and prepared by the Polish engineer, Colonel Thaddeus Kosciusko (1746–1817), on Bemis Heights, a few miles south of Saratoga. Gates placed 3 brigades—about 3,000 men—and most of his artillery on the right. He placed his center brigade under Brigadier General Ebenezer Learned (1728–1801) a little to the west near Mr. Nielson's farmhouse.

Freeman's Farm

By early September, 1777, Burgoyne knew he could expect help from neither General William Howe (1732–1786) nor Lieutenant Colonel Barry St. Leger (1737–1789). Disillusioned about the Loyalists, he wrote Colonial Secretary Sir George Germain (1716–1785):

> The great bulk of the country is undoubtedly with Congress in principle and zeal, and their measures are executed with a secrecy and dispatch that are not to be equalled. Wherever the King's forces point, militia in the amount of three or four thousand assemble in twenty-four hours; they bring with them their subsistence, etc., and the alarm over, they return to their farms.

Nevertheless, gambler that he was, General Burgoyne began crossing to the west bank of the Hudson at Saratoga (now Schuylerville) on his southward march. He crossed on a bridge of boats during September 13 and 14, signaling his intention to get to Albany or lose his army. While his supply problem daily became worse, his Native Americans, with a natural instinct for sensing approaching disaster, drifted off into the forests, leaving him with little means of gaining intelligence of the American dispositions.

On the morning of September 19, 1777, General Burgoyne engaged the Americans in the Battle of Freeman's Farm. He advanced toward the American position about 10:00 AM with an army reduced to 6,000 men (he had left Canada with 10,000). He planned to use 4,200 to attack and 1,800 to act as a reserve and guard his boats and supplies. He divided the 4,200 men into 3 columns. Brigadier General Simon Fraser (1737–1777) commanded the strongest column of about 2,000 men on the right or the west end of the line. His objective was to take the unfortified high ground overlooking the American defenses from the west. Brigadier General James Hamilton (ca. 1710–1783) commanded the center column of 1,100 men. Major General Baron Friedrich von Riedesel (1738–1800) led the left column of about 1,100 men near the Hudson River.

General Gates waited for the Crown forces to attack. His scouts could see the enemy moving through the trees and kept reporting to Gates for 3 hours, from 10:00 AM until 1:00 PM. General Fraser's troops had to march a considerable distance to get into position, so the other 2 columns waited in place until about 1:00 PM when Fraser would fire 3 guns as a signal for the army to advance. The battle swayed back and forth over the farm for more than 3 hours.

Arnold persuaded Gates to let him move forward to counter the attack of the Crown forces and to send Colonel Morgan's riflemen into a wooded ravine south of Freeman's Farm. Morgan used a turkey call to rally his men. Together, they took a heavy toll of officers and men. When the British advanced against Arnold, they soon found themselves in serious trouble. They charged, and Arnold moved forward. Arnold asked Gates for some reinforcements, saying he could defeat the enemy easily. Gates refused and ordered Arnold back to the lines. Arnold ignored the orders. Baron von Riedesel arrived, driving off Arnold's forces.

The Crown forces held the field at the end of the day, but they lost about 600 men—twice as many as the American casualties—many of them officers. One regiment lost over three-quarters of its men. The morale of the men was broken, and they knew that Major General Horatio Gates still blocked their intended route.

After the Battle of Freeman's Farm, Burgoyne planned to resume the attack the next day but changed his mind when he heard that General Henry Clinton (1730–1795) left New York to relieve him. Clinton, in fact, stormed Forts Clinton and Montgomery on the Hudson on October 6, but, exercising that innate cautious characteristic of all his actions, he refused to gamble for high stakes. He simply sent an advance guard on to Kingston while he returned to New York, leaving Burgoyne to his fate.

The lines in Saratoga remained stable for 3 weeks. Burgoyne built an extensive system of field fortifications extending over 2 miles. His ranks, however, were being depleted by desertion and disease. There was not enough food for both horses and soldiers.

Bemis Heights

Burgoyne's situation was critical by now. He had no hope of assistance and his supplies were dwindling daily. Food was running out; the meadows were grazed bare by the animals; and every day more men slipped into the forest, deserting the lost cause. He strengthened his position by constructing redoubts, digging trenches, and chopping down trees to provide a field of fire in front of his position. Burgoyne had to decide whether to advance or retreat. Gates strengthened his entrenchments and awaited the attack he was sure Burgoyne would have to make. He occupied and fortified the high ground which was Burgoyne's objective since September 19. Military reinforcements increased his forces to around 10,000 by October 7.

With little intelligence of American strength or dispositions, Burgoyne sent out a "reconnaissance in force" with 1,500 men and 8 cannon on October 7 to attack the American left flank and feel out their positions. On learning that the British were approaching Gates sent out a contingent including Morgan's riflemen to meet them, and a second battle developed, usually known as Bemis Heights.

Burgoyne's troops marched about $\frac{3}{4}$ mile southwesterly and deployed in a clearing on the Barber farm. Most of the Crown forces' front faced an open field, but both flanks rested in woods, exposed to surprise attack.

The Americans attacked in 3 columns under Colonel Morgan, General Ebenezer Learned, and Brigadier General Enoch Poor (1736–1780) at about 3:00 PM. General Poor attacked the east flank first, as he had a shorter distance to go. Colonel Morgan engaged the west flank, breaking the line repeatedly. The Crown forces rallied but were driven back. Both flanks came under tremendous pressure from all sides and could not rally, so they retreated into the fortifications on the Freeman farm.

General Benedict Arnold, who had been relieved of command after a quarrel with Gates, rode onto the field and led Learned's brigade against the German troops holding the British center. Under tremendous pressure from all sides, the Germans joined a general withdrawal into the fortifications on the Freeman farm.

When Arnold saw General Fraser riding back and forth on his horse encouraging his men, he recognized this officer's importance to the Crown forces. He asked Morgan to have his riflemen shoot him. Morgan selected Tim Murphy, who mortally wounded Fraser on the third shot.

Believing victory close at hand, Arnold led 1 column in a series of attacks on the Balcarres redoubt (see Photo NY-4). After failing repeatedly to take this position, Arnold wheeled his horse and dashed through the crossfire of both armies toward the Breymann redoubt. He arrived just as the American troops began to assault the fortification, so he joined in the attack, overwhelming the German soldiers defending the work. He was shot in the left leg after entering the redoubt and suffered a fractured thigh on the same leg wounded at Quebec. Had the shot been fatal, he would have died one of America's greatest heroes. Lieutenant Colonel Heinrich Christoph von Breymann (d. 1777) was also mortally wounded defending the Breymann redoubt which the Germans lost and could not regain.

Burgoyne suffered about 600 casualties to the Americans' 150. With his position open to attack from the right rear, he had only one choice: to retreat that night if he could, leaving the sick and wounded behind. He withdrew to a position in the vicinity of Saratoga. Militia soon worked around to his rear and cut his supply lines. His position hopeless, Burgoyne finally capitulated on October 17 at Saratoga. The total prisoner count was nearly 6,000, and great quantities of military stores fell into American hands.

The victory at Saratoga brought the Americans out well ahead in the campaign of 1777 despite the loss of Philadelphia. What had been at stake soon became obvious. American morale improved considerably at a time when General George Washington's (1732–1799) army was being pushed around New York, and it convinced the King of France to support the American cause.

Surrender, Schuylerville

Schuylerville, known as Saratoga in 1777, was originally a Native American camping ground. French refugees settled here by 1688 and named it Saratoga. It was renamed Schuylerville in 1831 to honor Major General Philip Schuyler (1733–1804).

The Battle Monument in Schuylerville on Burgoyne Street (Route NY 338) west of Route U.S. 4 commemorates Major General John Burgoyne's (1722–1792) surrender. The monument was started during the Battle of Saratoga Centennial in 1877 and finished 6 years later. Its 184 iron stairs lead to the top of the 154-foot, 6-inch monument which overlooks the battlefield sites. Niches around the monument contain life-size bronze statues of Philip Schuyler facing his home to the east (See Photo NY-5.); Daniel Morgan, commander of his celebrated riflemen, facing west; Horatio Gates looking to the north. The fourth niche remains empty, commemorating the leadership of Benedict Arnold who later turned traitor.

The Field of Grounded Arms is on Ferry Street (Route NY 29), 1 block east of Route U.S. 4. The site is noted only by a small marker.

`http://www.victoryatsaratoga.com/visitors.htm`

Philip Schuyler's country home in Schuylerville was the center of his farming and milling operations. His main home was in Albany. The British burned the original house and its outbuildings in Schuylerville. The present house was erected later in 1777, shortly after Burgoyne's surrender. It is administered as part of the Saratoga National Historical Park.

Ten days after the Battle of Bemis Heights, with his army of 5,700 surrounded by an army that grew to 20,000 men, Major General John Burgoyne (1722–1792) finally capitulated on October 17, 1777, at Saratoga. Instead of a surrender, he suggested a "convention" in which the Americans would let the British return to England if they promised not to fight again in the war. Major General Horatio Gates (1728–1806) accepted, but Congress later cancelled this agreement and sent Burgoyne's soldiers to prison camps in Virginia until the end of the war. These prisoners are sometimes referred to as the "convention army."

The surrender of an entire British army with all its equipment had a tremendous psychological impact on the American cause. What had been at stake soon became obvious, however. On February 6, 1778 France signed a treaty pledging full military support to the American states, tantamount to a declaration of war against England.

When news of Burgoyne's surrender at Saratoga reached London, Lord Chatham addressed the House of Lords:

> No man thinks more highly than I of the virtue and valour of British troops; I know they can achieve anything except impossibilities; and the conquest of English America is an impossibility. You cannot, I venture to say it, *you cannot conquer America . . .* What is your present situation there? We do not know the worst, but we know that in three campaigns we have done nothing, and suffered much . . . Conquest is impossible: you may swell every expense and every effort still more extravagantly; pile and accumulate every assistance you can buy or borrow; traffic and barter with every little pitiful German prince that sells his subjects to the shambles of a foreign power; your efforts are forever vain and impotent; doubly so from this mercenary aid on which you rely; for it irritates to an incurable resentment the minds of your enemies. To overrun them with the mercenary sons of rapine and plunder; devoting them and their possessions to the rapacity of hireling cruelty! If I were an American, as I am an Englishman, while a foreign troop was landed in my country, I never would lay down my arms, never—never—never!

Cherry Valley (November 11, 1778)

Settled in 1740, Cherry Valley was an important stagecoach stop on the Cherry Valley Turnpike, now U.S. 20.

A large stone monument in the village cemetery commemorates the victims of the Massacre of 1778. The Cherry Valley Museum on 49 Main Street maintains the local history and the stone memorial in the village cemetery.
                    http://www.cherryvalleymuseum.org/

Walter Butler (ca. 1752–1781) and Joseph Brant (1742–1807) Mohawk Chief Thayendanagea joined forces against the strategic but poorly defended settlement of Cherry Valley on November 11, 1778. Snow had already fallen and weather conditions seemed too severe for campaigning, so the residents were not prepared for an attack by 700 Native Americans and Loyalist rangers.

The raiders had already completed a march of 150 miles when they arrived in the vicinity of Cherry Valley. They attacked the village on the morning of November 11, a foggy, rainy Wednesday, killing or capturing most of the officers. They ransacked the village and settlement of 40 homes spread out in an imperfect semicircle over about 6 miles. They killed 15 militia and about 30 of the 300 residents in a 4-hour period. They captured the rest of the residents but released them the next day, except for 2 women and 7 children who they kept as hostages to trade for the release of the relatives of Loyalist officers being held prisoner in Albany. The only buildings still standing when the raiders left were the fort, the church, and one or two homes.

Port Jervis (July 19–22, 1779)
Minisink

> Minisink is now called Port Jervis. The battlefield is located in the vicinity of the junction of NY 97 and County Road 168. Minisink Ford is on the Delaware River northwest of Port Jervis and opposite Lackawaxen, Pennsylvania.
>
> The place of the massacre came to be known as Hospital Rock. It is reached by a short path 100 yards west of the battle monument erected in 1830 that lists the names of some 45 casualties. Sentinel Rock, a large boulder about 100 yards to the southwest, is where Brant stormed through the militia defenses. There are many historical markers along NY 97 commemorating the events. Port Jervis was called Minisink in the 18th century, and there were three Native American villages using the name Minisink in the area, including Minisink Ford on the Delaware River.

Joseph Brant (1742–1807) Mohawk Chief Thayendanagea and a party of 60 Native Americans and 27 Loyalists burned and looted Minisink on the night of July 19, 1779. They were more intent on looting and destruction, taking only 3 prisoners and 4 scalps. Lieutenant Colonel (Dr.) Benjamin Tusten (d. 1779) and about 150 local militia pursued Brant for 17 miles the following day before camping for the night.

The militia was about a mile away from Brant at about 9:00 AM on July 22 and tried to catch him crossing a ford in the Delaware River. When the woods and high ground hid the 2 forces from each other, Brant circled around to the American rear and set up an ambush along the retreat route.

The militia were surprised and disappointed not to find the enemy around the ford. They began to return home when they ran into the ambush. Brant cut off a third of the militia while the rest took a position on the high ground and held it for several hours. As dusk fell and the defenders ran low on ammunition, Brant identified a weak point in the defense and attacked.

Organized resistance collapsed and the defenders were massacred. The casualties included Lieutenant Colonel Benjamin Tusten, a physician, and the 17 wounded he was tending. Several men were also shot trying to swim across the Delaware. There were only 30 survivors from the initial party.

Elmira (August 29, 1779)
Battle of Newtown
Battle of Chemung

Newtown Battlefield is on Route U.S. 17, 3 miles east of Elmira. The Battle of Newtown is also known as the Battle of Chemung.

http://www.mizar5.com/cvlh/camp.htm

Newtown Battlefield Reservation memorializes Sullivan's victory with a 60-foot-tall stone obelisk that was erected in 1912. The 300-acre park atop 600-foot high Sullivan Hill lies 1,000 feet east of the Chemung River and offers a marvelous view of the Chemung Valley, but it has little relationship to the battle which was fought along the ridge below it and near the river. The battle area is largely undeveloped and is privately owned. Some historical markers along U.S. 17 and on the Wellsburg turnoff identify sites and actions associated with the fight.

http://www.mizar5.com/cvlh/home.htm

General Henry Clinton's (1730–1795) inaction allowed General George Washington (1732–1799) to attempt to deal with British-inspired Native American attacks in 1779. Although Major General John Burgoyne's (1722–1792) defeat ended the threat of invasion from Canada, the British continued to incite the Native Americans all along the frontier to bloody raids on American settlements. From Fort Niagara and Detroit they sent out their bands, usually led by Loyalists, to pillage, scalp, and burn in the Mohawk Valley of New York, the Wyoming Valley of Pennsylvania, and the new American settlements in Kentucky.

Washington detached Major General John Sullivan (1740–1795) with a force of 4,000 seasoned Continentals to deal with the Iroquois in Pennsylvania and New York. Washington wanted a punitive expedition that would end the problems with the Native Americans. He ordered "the total destruction and devastation of their settlements" and the taking of prisoners, including women and children who would be kept as hostages to insure future cooperation from the Iroquois.

Sullivan organized his troops in Easton, Pennsylvania, on May 7 but waited 6 weeks before setting out for western New York on June 18. He made no effort to hide his movements, so his prey soon learned of his advance. The force of some 800 Iroquois, under Joseph Brant (1742–1807) Mohawk Chief Thayendanagea, 250 Loyalists, and 15 men of the British 8th Regiment, were determined to destroy Sullivan's army before it gained momentum. They decided on a surprise attack over the objections of Walter Butler (ca. 1752–1781), a despised Mohawk Valley Loyalist. They fortified the mountain pass along the Chemung River, just south of Elmira, with a camouflaged log breastwork and waited as Sullivan approached early on August 29.

The advancing column included 3 companies of Colonel Daniel Morgan's (1736–1802) Virginia riflemen in the lead. They spotted the trap and Sullivan directed Brigadier General Enoch Poor (1736–1780) to lead the main assault on the hill on the enemy's left. As Poor advanced, the artillery fired on the breastwork.

Nathan Davis recorded this account of the battle of Newtown:

When our front had advanced within a short distance of them, they commenced a fire from behind every tree, and at the same time gave a war whoop. Not all the infernals of the Prince of Darkness, could they have been let loose from the bottomless pit, would have borne any comparison to these demons of the forest.

We were expressly ordered not to fire, until we had obtained permission from our officers, but to form a line of battle as soon as possible and march forward. This we did in good order, and at the same time the Indians kept up an incessant fire upon us from behind trees; firing and retreating back to another tree, loading and firing again, still keeping up the war whoop. They continued this mode of warfare till we had driven them halfway up the hill, when we were ordered to charge bayonets and rush on. No sooner said than done. We then, in our turn, gave our war whoop, in the American style, which completely silenced the unearthly voice of their stentorian throats. We drove them, at once, to the opposite side of the hill, when we were ordered to halt, as the Indians were out of sight and hearing.

How many we killed I never could exactly ascertain, but some were killed, and one scalped to my knowledge, and much blood was seen on their track. We also took two prisoners, one Negro and one white man, said to be a Tory. The white man was found painted black, lying on his face, and pretending to be dead. As no blood was seen near him, after a proper discipline he was soon brought to his feelings. He was then stripped and washed, and found to be white. A rope was then tied round his neck, and he was led in front of the troops, whilst every one gave him his sentence, "You shall be hung tomorrow." This, however, was not put into execution.

The defenders retreated under Sullivan's artillery. Other Americans had taken the enemy's right. The Native Americans, outnumbered 5 to 1 and facing encirclement, began to flee. Most retreated over the mountains with much difficulty. Those who remained fought bravely. Sullivan lost 3 men killed and 39 wounded. The Native Americans lost approximately 12 men killed.

Sullivan did not pursue but kept marching for the next 6 weeks without encountering much resistance. He destroyed 40 Native American settlements and many fields and orchards, returning to Easton on October 15 with a few prisoners. His men had been as brutal as their foes, scalping the wounded and mutilating the dead. Sullivan failed to crush the Six Nations, and their warriors renewed their raids in 1780 and 1781 with unprecedented ferocity. (See also Wyoming Valley, Pennsylvania.)

Schoharie (October 17, 1780)

The Old Stone Fort in the village of Schoharie, near the intersection of NY 30 and NY 443, was originally built as a church in 1772. It was enclosed by a stockade in 1778 and called Lower Fort. Blockhouses at the southwest and northeast corners of the stockade mounted small cannon. Sharpshooters manned the church's square tower which once was topped by a belfry and spire (removed in 1830). The roof cornice at the rear of the church has a hole supposedly made by a small cannonball fired by the attackers in 1780.

The Old Stone Fort Museum Complex contains exhibits of the Schoharie County Historical Society that include electrified maps. An audio-visual program interprets Revolutionary War activities of the region. Other buildings comprise a 1740 Palatine house, an 18th-century Dutch barn, an 1850 law office, an 1860 schoolhouse, and a historical and

genealogy library. David Williams, one of the three men who captured Major John André (1751–1780) at Tarrytown, is buried in front of the church. A tall pillar marks the grave.
http://www.schohariehistory.net/OSF.htm

A highway marker on NY 30 at Watsonville about 4 miles southwest of Middleburgh identifies the site of the house where Timothy Murphy lived for several years and where he died in 1818 at the age of 67. A marker for the Upper Fort appears on the left side of NY 30 about a 0.25 mile south of the marker for Murphy's house.

The long, flat, fertile Schoharie Valley was a major source of provisions (mainly grain) for the Patriots. Each harvest produced about 80,000 bushels of wheat for General George Washington's (1732–1799) army. This made the valley an attractive objective for Loyalist and Native American raiders.

The inhabitants of the valley formed a committee of safety in 1775, organized 5 companies of minutemen, and eventually built 3 forts to protect the valley. Sir John Johnson and Joseph Brant (1742–1807), Mohawk Chief Thayendanagea, joined forces at Unadilla late in September, 1780, and ravaged the valley. The 800–1,500 raiders advanced from the southwest in the night of October 15. They by-passed the Upper Fort (in the vicinity of Toepath Mountain) and approached the Middle Fort (in modern Middleburgh) early in the morning. They besieged the Lower Fort and began firing on it on October 17.

Major Melancthon Woolsey, the commander, was ready to consider terms of surrender when Timothy Murphy (d. 1818), famous for his marksmanship which killed Brigadier General Simon Fraser (1737–1777) at Bemis Heights, fired on the enemy's "flag" each time Major Woolsey tried to receive Sir John's terms of surrender. When the officers of the garrison tried to arrest Murphy, his fellow soldiers rallied around him to prevent the arrest and called Woolsey a coward for wanting to surrender. When Woolsey ordered a white flag to be raised, Murphy threatened to shoot anyone who tried to obey the order. The raiders, unaware of what was happening inside the fort, withdrew because they could not batter the fort. They proceeded down the valley, burning the houses, barns, and crops of the Patriots and killing or taking their domestic animals.

Johnstown (October 25, 1781)

Johnstown has several historic sites, including the Johnstown Battlefield, the site of one of the latter battles of the War for American Independence.
http://www.carogalake.com/Activities/historic_sites/johnstown.htm

Sir William Johnson erected the Fulton County Courthouse (North William and East Main Street) in 1774. It is the only colonial courthouse still standing in New York and still remains in use. The belfry houses a large iron bar that was bent into a triangle and used as a bell to announce the sessions of court. It was also rung in honor of the Declaration of Independence.
http://www.courts.state.ny.us/history/elecbook/fulton/pg1.htm

Johnson Hall State Historic Site (Hall Avenue, west of Route NY 29), a white clapboard Georgian house built in 1763, was the last home of Sir William Johnson.
http://www.thenortherncampaign.org/johnsonsite.htm

St. John's Episcopal Church (North Market Street) was built by Sir William Johnson in 1772. He was buried under the chancel 2 years later. The church burned in 1836 and was rebuilt in a slightly different location in 1840. Johnson's grave was "lost" and discovered later that year. His body, identified by the lead ball in his hip—a souvenir from his victory at Lake George—was reinterred in the rear of the church and is marked by four simple cornerstones.

Sir William Johnson (1715–1774), a British general and Superintendent of Indian Affairs during the mid-1700s, founded the town which is named after him.

Militia Colonel Marinus Willett (1740–1830) led a force of 416 men against a Loyalist and Native American raiding party of 1,000 near Johnson Hall on October 25, 1781. They attacked from the southeast but were repelled by the larger force under Major John Ross. Fighting into the woods in the rainy twilight, Willett believed he had the advantage, but the enemy captured his 1 gun and stripped its ammunition cart before he could retake it. Willett's right flank collapsed in panic, but he managed to rally many of his troops and continue fighting until dusk. The Loyalists and Native Americans withdrew to a nearby hill.

Willett and his men retreated and fled to Fort Johnstown (the old jail located on Montgomery and South Perry streets). Willett reported finding the bodies of 7 enemy and 3 of his own men on the field. He estimated that each side suffered 30–40 wounded and he captured 30 prisoners.

The Battle of Johnstown took place 6 days after Lord Cornwallis had laid down his arms in Yorktown, Virginia.

DOWNSTATE/HUDSON RIVER VALLEY

See the map of Downstate New York.

Fort Montgomery and Fort Clinton (October 6, 1777)

The Fort Montgomery State Historic Site is on U.S. 9W. The site of Fort Montgomery was once covered by a zoo, but the archaeological remains of breastworks and fort structures were excavated and re-dedicated for the 225th anniversary of the battle in 2002.
 http://nysparks.state.ny.us/cgi-bin/cgiwrap/nysparks/historic.cgi?p+41

The site of Fort Clinton is within the confines of Bear Mountain State Park, which is on Route U.S. 9W, 5 miles south of West Point. The fort itself no longer exists.
 http://nysparks.state.ny.us/cgi-bin/cgiwrap/nysparks/parks.cgi?p+131

Fort Clinton should not be confused with Fort Arnold which was later renamed Fort Clinton. Fort Arnold is northeast of West Point whereas the one in this battle is south of West Point. It was destroyed in 1777 and no longer existed when Fort Arnold was renamed Fort Clinton in 1780 after Benedict Arnold's (1741–1801) treason.

The Patriots began work on Fort Montgomery in 1776, south of West Point and located at another narrow point in the Hudson River. The intent was to build a large work of cannons with a "Grand Battery" of six 32-pounders overlooking a long stretch of the river.

When the builders discovered the land on the opposite side of Popolopen Creek was higher and would threaten Fort Montgomery if held by the enemy, they constructed a second fort there and called it Fort Clinton for General George Clinton (1739–1812). These works were completed in 1777. The British attempted to dismantle these defenses a year earlier after they captured forts Washington and Lee.

As upriver at West Point, Fort Montgomery also had a great chain at least 2,100 feet long across the Hudson (see Photo NY-11). Specifications for the rafts that supported the chain called for a "Boom of Pine Logs not less than 50 feet long, placed ten feet apart, and framed together by three cross Pieces; that each Raft be placed 15 feet apart and Connected by strong Chains of 1-$\frac{1}{2}$ inch iron; that the Rafts be anchored with their Butts down the River; that the Butts be armed with Iron."

The boom was supposed to have 40 additional shock-absorbing frames anchored in front of it for further protection. "The points or ends whereof to be shod with Iron so as to answer the double purpose of founding any Ships who may sail up to it, and if that should fail, to Lessen the Shocke of those Vessels when they come to the Boom." The pointed beams were to be about 16 feet long and spaced about 16 feet apart. The boom and frames were never built, so the British broke through the iron chain at Fort Montgomery and sailed past.

Forts Montgomery and Clinton were General Henry Clinton's (1730–1795) objective when he set sail from New York City with 3,000 British, Hessian, and Loyalist troops on October 6, 1777. He landed 2,100 men under the cover of a dense fog on the west shore of the Hudson at Stony Point. They encountered a scouting party of 30 Patriots sent from Fort Clinton to detect any advance by the Crown forces. Sir Henry beat them back and sent 900 men around 1,305-foot Bear Mountain to attack Fort Montgomery. He kept the remaining troops to attack Fort Clinton. In the afternoon, the Crown forces attacked both forts. The 700 defenders fought a bitter defense and refused to surrender. Sir Henry took advantage of the growing dark and the smoky haze of battle to storm both forts which he destroyed after the battle.

The battle delayed the Crown forces from moving north to help Major General John Burgoyne (1722–1792) at Saratoga. General Clinton returned to New York rather than going to Albany. Had this battle not occurred, it is quite possible that Clinton's forces might have changed the outcome of the Battle of Saratoga. Burgoyne surrendered 2 weeks later. The Crown forces never threatened the Hudson Highlands again.

White Plains (October 28, 1776)

The White Plains National Battlefield Site is in White Plains, New York.
            http://www.ohwy.com/ny/w/whplnaba.htm

White Plains is heavily urbanized. There are three markers to commemorate the battle. One is on Chatterton Hill, two are on Battle Avenue.

The Jacob Purdy House (Spring Street, near the intersection with Rockledge Avenue) was Washington's headquarters prior to the battle, October 23-28.
    `http://whiteplainswatch.com/A55866/wpw.nsf/All/Jacob+Purdy+House`

The Elijah Miller House (Virginia Road in North White Plains, at the foot of Miller Hill) was Washington's headquarters for the battle of White Plains. He stayed here for 2 weeks after he left the Jacob Purdy House.
    `http://www.westchestergov.com/history/wash.htm`

On October 12, 1776, General William Howe (1732–1786) embarked 4,000 men in boats at Kip's Bay. He sent them northeastward in a thick fog through the channel known as Hell's Gate. They landed at Throg's Neck which was nearly an island separated from the mainland by a single road that ran through marshes. Howe planned to advance along Throg's Neck over a causeway across swampy ground to attack the Americans from their flank and rear. General George Washington (1732–1799) had the causeway demolished and took a strong position at its far end. A small group of Pennsylvania riflemen under the command of Colonel Edward Hand (1744–1802) defended the bridge. Six days later, Howe embarked his men again and proceeded further up the East River to land at Pell's Point, in Washington's rear, where he marched to New Rochelle.

Howe threatened to cut off the American army on Manhattan from the mainland. Washington had already decided to abandon Manhattan and lower New York via Kingsbridge. He fell back to White Plains (see Photo NY-6 and its caption) on October 18, leaving about 6,000 men behind to man two forts, Fort Washington and Fort Lee, on opposite sides of the Hudson. Colonel Robert Magaw (d. 1789) defended Fort Washington with about 2,800 men, and Major General Nathanael Greene (1742–1786) held Fort Lee with about 3,500 men.

Washington held a good defensive position on the hills of White Plains. If he had to retreat, he could go north into the Hudson Highlands or west to New Jersey. He had over 25,000 men, but more than half were ill or otherwise unfit for duty. As the British advanced north toward him, Washington drew in as many men as he could afford to defend his camp. He fortified Purdy and Hatfield hills, but re-evaluated his position on October 27 and decided to defend Chatterton Hill which sloped 180 feet up from the Bronx River.

Two brigades arrived at the hill to reinforce the Massachusetts militia just as the Crown forces were mustering 13,000 troops including mounted dragoons across the Bronx River for the main attack on Chatterton Hill, the site of the only real fighting of the battle. Howe positioned his artillery (near the present-day railroad station) and began bombarding the Americans on the hill. The Hessians began to cross the Bronx River at the foot of the hills while other forces moved around Chatterton Hill and into the ridges to the west to put the Americans in a crossfire. The Crown forces assaulted the hill twice and were driven back both times (see Photo NY-7). The dragoons attacked a Massachusetts militia unit on one flank and forced them to flee. The rest of the Americans were now vulnerable and were forced to withdraw. The Crown forces took the hill and pushed the defenders off in 50 minutes of heavy fighting.

An American officer described the scene: "They advanced in solid columns . . . The scene was grand and solemn; all the adjacent hills smoked as though on fire, and bellowed and trembled with a perpetual cannonade and fire of field pieces, howitzers and mortars. The air groaned with streams of cannon and musket-shot. The hills smoked and echoed terribly with the bursting of shells; the fences and walls were knocked down and torn to pieces, and men's legs, arms and bodies, mangled with cannon and grapeshot all around us." A Connecticut soldier was appalled by mutilation: "One ball 'first took off the head of Smith, a stout heavy man, and dashed it open, then took Taylor across the bowels. It then struck Sergeant Garrett of our company on the hip [and] took off the point of the hip bone . . . he died the same day . . . Oh! What a sight it was to see within a distance of six rods those men with their legs and arms and guns and packs all in a heap.'"

Washington sent Colonel John Glover (1732–1797) up onto Miller Hill with some artillery. Glover waited until the Crown forces dragged some of their cannon to the top of the lower Travis Hill nearby before opening fire. The Crown forces, caught by surprise, fired 4 shots and withdrew because they found their position too exposed.

Howe waited for reinforcements before undertaking a direct, frontal assault which he planned for October 31. However a heavy rainstorm that lasted for more than 20 hours delayed the attack and gave Washington a chance to withdraw to North Castle. American casualties totaled about 150 men, including 50 dead. Crown forces casualties amounted to 313. Howe received his reinforcements that brought his force to 20,000, but he chose not to pursue Washington. He decided instead to focus on Fort Washington which prevented him from getting supplies overland and forced him to depend on ships traveling the Harlem River and Long Island Sound.

Stony Point and Verplanck's Point (July 15–16, 1779)

The Stony Point Battlefield State Historic Site is in/near Stony Point, New York, 8 miles south of the Bear Mountain bridge off U.S. 9W on Park Road.
`http://nysparks.state.ny.us/cgi-bin/cgiwrap/nysparks/historic.cgi?p+27`

Stony Point became a public park in 1902. There is an elaborate arch over the entrance. A short trail meanders through the remains of the site. (See Photos NY-8 and NY-9.) The park redesigned the exhibit and renovated the museum/Visitor Center for the 225th anniversary of the battle in 2004. See also Photo NY-10, the view of Verplanck's Point from Stony Point.

General Henry Clinton (1730–1795) tried to draw General George Washington (1732–1799) into a general engagement in the summer of 1779. He occupied Stony Point on the west side of the Hudson in May and Verplanck's Point on the opposite shore on June 1. This was an important link between the American forces in New York and New England. Clinton then began to enlarge the earthen forts at these points by cutting down trees and protecting them with an abatis, sharpened stakes made from the tree branches. He left 625 officers and men under Lieutenant Colonel Henry Johnson (1748–1835) to defend them.

Washington sent Brigadier General "Mad Anthony" Wayne's (1745–1796) brigade of about 1,360 light infantry selected from every regiment for their agility, alertness, and daring to retake Stony Point 150 feet above the Hudson River (see Photo NY-8). At first, Wayne was somewhat dismayed by his observations of the position which was practically immune to attack except by a surprise assault. He decided to target specific objectives rather than mount an all-out assault. His men would advance during the night with unloaded muskets to maintain silence. Any man who fired his musket or panicked in the advance would be punished by death.

Major John Stewart (d. 1782) would lead 1 column of 300 men, advancing on Stony Point from the north through the marshes of the Hudson River. Wayne would lead the second column through the waters of Haverstraw Bay on the south. Each column would be preceded by a "forlorn hope" of 20 men to guide the way for the second group of 150 men who would enter enemy lines first, overcome sentries, and sever the abatis.

Meanwhile, Lieutenant Colonel Hardy Murfree (d. 1809) would lead 2 companies in a diversionary attack on the fort's front in the center. They were the only troops allowed to load their muskets to draw the Crown forces from their posts with musket fire. The others would rely only on the bayonet to maintain secrecy. Wayne's brigade began to advance around midnight on July 15, 1779. They only had to travel about a mile and a half to their objective. Wayne's column traveled along Frank Road which becomes Crickettown Road. Stewart's column followed what is now Wayne Avenue toward the river.

The sound of hundreds of men moving waist-deep in the water alerted a British guard who sounded the alarm. The Americans, unable to return fire, hurried to dry ground where they climbed the rocky slope and entered the British earthworks. Colonel Johnson charged down the hill with 6 companies to counter what he thought was the main attack. Wayne's column arrived from the south and cut him off from the central redoubt at the top of a huge outcropping of rocks.

Colonel Johnson was caught between Wayne's men and Murfree's column, unable to get back. The Americans were now in the main redoubt, and he was forced to surrender. The Americans captured the fort at Stony Point in about half an hour with only 15 lives lost, mostly from volunteers in the forlorn hope, and 83 wounded. Casualties might have been higher had the defenders not had to fire downhill in the dark. The British lost 63 killed, 74 wounded, 58 missing, and 472 prisoners including the wounded (see Photo NY-9). One officer escaped by jumping into the river and swimming out to the HMS *Vulture,* the same ship that would carry Major John André (1751–1780) to his rendezvous with Major General Benedict Arnold (1741–1801) 14 months later and take Arnold to safety after his treason. The British occupying Fort Lafayette on Verplanck's Point (see Photo NY-10) probably heard the fighting at Stony Point and wondered who won. When the victors fired their guns at the *Vulture*, they knew.

Wayne offered a $500 prize for the first man into the fort which went to Lieutenant Colonel Francois Louis Teissedre de Fleury (1749–), a French engineer. Fleury was also awarded a silver medal which became a gold when finally awarded in 1783—the only medal awarded to a European volunteer during the war. Wayne also received a gold medal. He continued to lead the charge despite suffering a head wound from grapeshot. He thought he was seriously wounded and asked his men to carry him to the top of the hill so he could die in the redoubt. Major John Stewart (d. 1782), the leader of the second column, was awarded a sliver medal. The action at Stony Point accounted for 3 of the 11 medals Congress awarded during the war.

Washington also planned to take Fort Lafayette at Verplanck's Point after receiving word of Wayne's victory at Stony Point. Wayne wrote to him at 2:00 AM on the morning of July 16: "The fort and garrison with Colonel Johnson are ours. Our officers and men behaved like men who are determined to be free." He dispatched the message immediately, but it went astray. By the time the attack force was in position around Fort Lafayette, Clinton learned of the defeat at Stony Point and sent reinforcements. The Americans abandoned their plans to take Fort Lafayette.

Washington could not spare enough men to defend the fort. He destroyed and abandoned it 2 days later. Clinton reoccupied it the following day, July 19, but withdrew in October. The battle at Stony Point had little tactical importance, but it boosted American morale. This was the last important action fought in the northern states.

West Point (September, 1780)

> The United States Military Academy is in/near Highland Falls, New York, on the west bank of the Hudson River off scenic Old Storm King Highway (NY 218); the academy can also be reached from U.S. 9W.
>
> http://www.usma.edu/
>
> A visitors center (Building 2107) just outside Thayer Gate (South Post) is the starting point for tours of the U.S. Military Academy.
>
> http://www.usma.edu/PublicAffairs/vic.htm
>
> The West Point Museum (Olmsted Hall at Pershing Center, Route U.S. 9W) contains a large collection of military artifacts from antiquity to modern times. It has flags, vehicles, paintings, tanks, uniforms, and weapons, including Revolutionary War uniforms, weapons, and accoutrements. Other galleries feature the history of West Point and the U.S. Military Academy and the story of the founding of the regular army.
>
> http://www.usma.edu/Museum/
>
> The east wall of the Old Cadet Chapel at West Point displays marble shields commemorating the American brigadier and major generals. The space for Benedict Arnold remains empty.
>
> The cemetery behind the chapel contains the grave of Molly Corbin (see Photo NY-14). Molly Corbin was wounded in the assault of Fort Washington when she took her husband's place at the cannon after he fell severely wounded. She is the first woman to be buried at West Point and one of very few Revolutionary War era graves here.
>
> Visitors can view captured weapons from every American war at Trophy Point which also offers a spectacular view of the Hudson Valley and the ruins of Fort Constitution. There is also a display of several links from the great chain that stretched 600 yards across the Hudson to impede British ships (see Photo NY-11).
>
> Fort Arnold remained in use as an arsenal after the war and was closed in 1802 for the creation of the U.S. Military Academy. Only a piece of a parapet remains. A monument on

the east front of Fort Clinton honors Polish Colonel Thaddeus Kosciuszko who planned the defenses at West Point.

Fort Putnam (see Photo NY-12) was first restored as a war monument in 1909 and then again for the Bicentennial in 1975-1976. (The model in Photo NY-13 is from the Fort Putnam museum.)

The Hudson River provided a direct water route to Lake Champlain and to Canada. The British objective was to use the river to split the colonies, so it was important for the Americans to impede British traffic on the river if they couldn't control it. They established a series of forts on opposite sides of the Hudson at points where the river narrows. Guns from these forts could work together firing on passing vessels. These narrow passages in the river also served as ideal spots to block the river with a chain or other obstacles.

Sterling Iron Works (about 25 miles west of West Point) forged the chains. Each link was made of bar iron about 2 inches square with dimensions about 18 inches long and 12 inches wide. The smallest links weighed between 98 and 109 pounds; the largest ones weighed 130 pounds. (See Photo NY-11.) The entire 600-yard chain weighed about 186 tons and floated on log rafts to prevent the passage of enemy ships. Each end was attached to a large block, one in a cove near Constitution Island, the other on the West Point side of the river. It was taken in every winter with a windlass to prevent damage from the ice.

Another strategy was to block the channel with scuttled ship hulks placed end to end. Friendly vessels would find their way through a secret passage while enemy vessels would be lured to an apparent channel protected by a line of chevaux-de-frise. This device consisted of "cassoons" created out of caissons sunken with rocks. The cassoons had pointed spears embedded in them. The iron-tipped pikes were hidden 2 or 3 feet below the water's surface at low tide. Ships striking the chevaux-de-frise would have their hulls punctured. If a ship managed to get past the chevaux-de-frise, it would encounter the great chain and possibly other obstacles.

At West Point, the Hudson makes two turns that almost form a right angle, forcing vessels sailing in either direction to come about to negotiate each turn. A square-rigged warship, with sails slack and the ship not firmly under control, would be particularly vulnerable attempting to maneuver the turn as it came directly under the gun batteries placed on the heights.

Polish engineer Colonel Thaddeus Kosciusko (1746–1817) planned most of the defenses which included 5 forts, 7 redoubts, and a giant iron chain that stretched across the Hudson River. The series of forts included Fort Arnold at the eastern edge (northeast of the parade ground); Sherburne's Redoubt across the river on Constitution Island; Fort Putnam; 3 redoubts covering the southern approaches, named Webb, Wyllis, and Meigs for their commanders under Colonel Rufus Putnam (1738–1824); 4 additional redoubts on the hills; and a number of gun batteries along the shoreline facing upriver from what is now Trophy Point and overlooking the channel between the Point and Constitution Island. The location was so well fortified that it never came under military attack during the war.

The Continental Army built Fort Arnold in 1778. It was constructed of earth and logs and housed 700 men, 12 cannon, and 11 mortars. It was renamed Fort Clinton after Benedict Arnold's (1741–1801) defection and after the fall of Fort Clinton south of West PointFort Putnam, named for Colonel Rufus Putnam (1738–1824) and his soldiers of the 5th Massachusetts Regiment who constructed it, was built 400 feet above the water to the west of Fort Arnold to protect against an overland attack from the mountains (see Photo NY-12).

Fort Montgomery covered the water approach to West Point from the south. And Fort Constitution stood across the river on the high bluffs of an island in the Hudson.

Benedict Arnold, Traitor

General Henry Clinton (1730–1795) could not take West Point by force, so he had to find another way to gain control. He found that way in 1779 when he began a traitorous correspondence with Benedict Arnold, the hero of the march to Quebec and of the battles at Valcour Island, Fort Stanwix, and Saratoga.

In September, 1779, Clinton appointed Captain John André (1751–1780) as his chief of intelligence and promoted him to the rank of major in October. André organized spy rings that extended into Vermont, New Hampshire, Rhode Island, Connecticut, New York, New Jersey, Pennsylvania, Maryland, and Delaware. He ignored Massachusetts because there were very few Loyalists there and because the British did not plan any military operations there.

André promised Arnold lucrative rewards which led to his treason. One of Arnold's enemies had said of him earlier "Money is this man's God," and evidently he was correct. Arnold's treachery may have had its roots in the ingratitude of the Continental Congress that did not recognize him for his heroism in previous battles. Maybe it came from his discontent that the American cause was being supported by a Catholic kingdom against whose soldiers he had once fought. It may also have come from the jealousy of rivals which resulted in many quarrels and grievances, or his second wife, Margaret Shippen, a Loyalist. Shortly after his marriage, he announced that he intended to resign his commission and to obtain land near New York where he would live as a retired country gentleman. He first offered to sell military information to General Clinton a month after his marriage in 1779. The British appointed Arnold a brigadier-general and awarded him £6315 (approximately $894,725) and an annuity of £500 ($70,840) for his wife. His three sons by his first marriage all received commissions, and the two sons of his second marriage later each received pensions of £100 ($14,167) a year.

Arnold also resented the slights Congress had dealt him, and he justified his act by claiming that the Americans were now fighting for the interests of Catholic France and not their own. Arnold obtained an appointment as commander at West Point after insistently lobbying General George Washington (1732–1799) and then entered into a plot to deliver this key post to the British. Washington discovered the plot on September 21, 1780, just in time to foil it, though Arnold himself escaped to become a British brigadier.

André received Arnold's secret correspondence and returned to New York after meeting with him to finalize a deal to surrender to Clinton the American fortress at

West Point and several nearby American strongholds for £20,000 (approximately $2,833,646). Along the way, he visited a British major quartered in Robert Townsend's (ca. 1753–1838) house and aroused the suspicions of Townsend's sister. She overheard the conversation and reported it to her brother. André was caught September 20, 1780, trying to go through the American line with a pass Arnold had issued him.

He also had Arnold's report on Fort Putnam: "F.P., stone, wanting great repairs. Wall on the east side broke down, and rebuilding from the foundation. At the west and south side have been a cheveaux-de-frise; on the west side broke in many places. The east side open; two bombproofs and provision magazine in the fort, and a slight wooden barrack."

On the evening of September 21, 1780, Major Benjamin Tallmadge (1754–1835) happened to be in North Castle, a Continental stronghold in northern Westchester, Connecticut. Here, he learned that three local militiamen had stopped and searched a man by the name of John Anderson whom they encountered near Tarrytown, New York. They found some suspicious papers in his boots. When the man offered to pay for his freedom, the soldiers became even more suspicious, so they brought him to North Castle and turned him over to Lieutenant Colonel John Jameson of the Light Dragoons. Jameson wrote a report of the matter and sent it and Anderson, under guard, to General Benedict Arnold who now commanded West Point. He also sent the papers found on Anderson to General Washington who was on his way to West Point from a meeting with General Donatien Marie Joseph de Vimeur Vicomte de Rochambeau (1750–1813) at Hartford, Connecticut.

Tallmadge persuaded Jameson to have Anderson brought back to North Castle and insisted that the report continue on to Arnold. Arnold, who had already tried unsuccessfully to learn the identities of Washington's spies, issued orders to Tallmadge:

> If Mr. James Anderson, a person I expect from New York should come to your quarters, I have to request that you will give him an escort of two Horse to bring him on his way to this place, and send an express to me that I may meet him.

Tallmadge must have wondered whether the prisoner John Anderson was the same man Arnold wanted to meet with. Tallmadge recalled his impressions on seeing the prisoner:

> As soon as I saw Anderson, and especially after I saw him walk (as he did almost constantly) across the floor, I became impressed with the belief that he had been bred to arms.

Tallmadge got Anderson to admit, on the afternoon of September 24, that he was "Major John André, Adjutant General to the British Army." Lieutenant Colonel Jameson's report of Anderson's arrest reached Arnold at breakfast the following morning. Had Washington not been delayed, he might have been sharing that meal. When Arnold learned of André's capture on the morning of the 25th, he left quickly for the Hudson River where he boarded the HMS *Vulture* (see Photo NY-13) which took him to New York. Jameson's rider, who missed Washington on the road from Hartford, arrived later in the day with André's incriminating papers, making it clear why Arnold left in such a hurry.

Court-Martial of Major John André

Instead of hanging André after a summary hearing, as General William Howe (1732–1786) had done for Nathan Hale (1755–1776), Washington turned the matter over to a 14-member board of general officers which convened at Tappan, New York, on September 29. André admitted the facts but insisted that he did not regard himself as a spy. The British and Americans considered spying something the lowborn were paid to do, so it was difficult for Major André, a British officer and a gentleman, to think of himself as a spy, even if he was caught behind enemy lines in civilian clothes with incriminating information in his shoes.

The board convicted André and recommended the death penalty. Washington sentenced him to hang at 5:00 PM on October 1. He notified General Clinton of his decision. Clinton protested that Arnold, an American general, invited André to meet with him and that André went under a flag of truce. Washington postponed the execution for a day and sent a representative to hear further arguments from a deputation of three British officers at Dobbs Ferry. He finally decided that he would spare André only if Clinton traded Arnold for him. Clinton refused.

André wrote to Washington in an attempt to make him change his mind:

> I trust that the request I make of your Excellency at this serious period, and which is to soften my last moments, will not be rejected. Sympathy towards a soldier will surely induce your Excellency, and a military tribunal, to adapt the mode of my death to the feelings of a man of honour. Let me hope, Sir, that if aught in my character impresses you with esteem towards me, if aught in my misfortune marks me as the victim of policy and not of resentment, I shall experience the operation of these feelings in your breast by being informed that I am not to die on the gibbet.

André was hanged at noon on October 2, just like Nathan Hale.

Brigadier General Oliver de Lancey (1718–1785) succeeded André as chief of intelligence in October, 1780, after André's execution. General Frederick Haldimand (1718–1791), the British commander in Canada, ran his own intelligence operation in Quebec, the Northern Department of the British Secret Service. He also operated in the northern colonies, trying to regain Vermont.

The British had never fully trusted Arnold. He never received a high command and resorted to leading raids along the Connecticut and Virginia coasts. After the American War of Independence, he retired on half pay and lived as a merchant in Canada, the West Indies, and London.

Arnold's treason in September, 1780, marked the nadir of the Patriot cause. In the closing months of 1780, the Americans reorganized the army and its administration and somehow put together the ingredients for a final and decisive burst of energy in 1781. Congress persuaded Robert Morris (1734–1806), a wealthy Philadelphia merchant, to accept a post as Superintendent of Finance, and Colonel Timothy Pickering (1745–1829), an able administrator, to replace Nathanael Greene (1742–1786) as Quartermaster General. Greene, as Washington's choice, was then named to succeed Major General Horatio Gates (1728–1806) in command of the Southern Army. Major General Benjamin Lincoln (1733–1810), exchanged after Charleston, was appointed Secretary at War. Morris took over many of the functions previously performed by unwieldy committees. Working closely with Pickering, he abandoned the old paper money entirely and introduced a new policy of supplying the army by private contracts, using his personal credit as eventual guarantee for payment in gold or silver. It was an expedient but, for a time at least, it worked.

NEW YORK CITY

See the map of Downstate New York.

After the siege of Boston, General George Washington (1732–1799) moved to New York in April, 1776, and turned his attention to the defense of the city and the Hudson Valley. The city at that time extended from the southern tip of Manhattan to Wall Street and had a population of approximately 25,000 people. Defending the city seemed an impossible task, however, as Manhattan was almost surrounded by water and Washington had no navy to contest the British navy that could move men and supplies or bombard the island from three sides. Along with the construction of fortifications at New York City and Long Island, Washington thought it imperative to build new fortifications along the Hudson River (see Photo NY-15 of Fort Lee, New Jersey).

His army of 19,000 men began digging fortifications and creating gun positions all around the city, awaiting a British attack. General William Howe (1732–1786) brought an army of 31,600 men to Staten Island in June and July, 1776. His brother, Admiral Richard Howe (1726–1799), supported him with a flotilla of 280 ships. Washington felt compelled to spread his army to cover the highly vulnerable area. He stationed 4,000 men on Long Island to hold the high ground of Brooklyn Heights overlooking the East River and New York City. He placed most of the rest on Manhattan, at the northern end of the island at Kingsbridge, and at Fort Washington.

Brooklyn Heights (August 27, 1776)
Battle of Long Island (Battle of Brooklyn Heights)

Much of the Battle of Long Island took place in what is now Prospect Park between Prospect Park West and Prospect Park Southwest and Flatbush and Parkside Avenues (see Photo NY-16) (subway: Seventh Avenue/Grand Army Plaza) in Brooklyn, New York.
http://www.prospectpark.org/

Urban development has covered the original sites of the Battle of Long Island. The park contains a Quaker graveyard, gardens, trails, boating facilities, and historic buildings. A semicircular tablet on a boulder near the Grand Army Plaza entrance commemorates the Battle of Long Island.

The Battle Pass Marker (Flatbush Pass) in Prospect Park (near the back of the zoo) was designed by Frederic Wellington Ruckstull and installed in 1923 at the site of a strategic road during the Battle of Long Island. The granite marker with a bronze eagle also marks the site where General John Sullivan was captured.

The Cortelyou House in Brooklyn (see Photo NY-17) was built in 1699 and remained standing until it was demolished in 1897. The reconstruction uses some of the original stones.

The Maryland Monument near Lookout Hill on Third Avenue between 7th and 8th Streets marks the burial site of Lord Stirling's Maryland troops who died attacking the Cortelyou house.

Fort Greene Park (Myrtle and DeKalb avenues and St. Edwards and Cumberland streets, Brooklyn). Sir William Howe hesitated to attack Washington's main army on Brooklyn Heights and began to dig entrenchments for a siege. One of these earthworks was a star fort named Fort Putnam. The fort no longer exists. The site became a park in 1815 and was named for Major General Nathanael Greene. It became Washington Park in 1847 and later renamed Fort Greene Park.

http://www.fortgreenepark.org/

Stanford White designed the "Martyrs' Monument" in the center of Fort Greene Park which is dedicated to the Continental soldiers who died on British prison ships in Wallabout Bay. Ships like the *Jersey,* originally a 64-gun man-of-war, were virtually floating tombs—crowded, filthy, and full of disease. The deceased were often thrown into shallow graves on the shores of Wallabout Bay. The remains of many were collected early in the 19th century and placed in this monument's crypt, dedicated in 1908 and marked by a 145-foot granite column.

http://www.fortgreenepark.org/pages/prisonship.htm

General William Howe (1732–1786) had an army of about 32,000 men supported by a powerful fleet of 280 warships and transports off Staten Island under the command of his brother, Admiral Richard Howe (1726–1799). General George Washington (1732–1799) brought most of his army down from Boston in March and April, 1776, to oppose him. Congress exerted its utmost efforts to reinforce him by raising Continental regiments in the surrounding states and issuing a general call for the militia. Washington was able to muster a paper strength of roughly 28,500 men, but only about 19,000 were present and fit for duty. The larger part of them were raw recruits, undisciplined and inexperienced in warfare, and militia, never to be assuredly relied upon.

Washington and Congress made the same decision the South Carolinians had made at Charleston—to defend their territory in the most forward positions, and this time they paid the price for their mistake. The geography of the area gave the side possessing naval supremacy an almost insuperable advantage.

The city of New York stood on Manhattan Island, surrounded by the Hudson, Harlem, and East Rivers. There was only one connecting link with the mainland, Kingsbridge across the Harlem River at the northern tip of Manhattan. Across the East River on Long Island, Brooklyn Heights stood in a position dominating the southern tip of Manhattan. With the naval forces at their disposal, the Howes could land troops on either Long Island or Manhattan proper and send warships a considerable distance up either the East or Hudson Rivers.

Washington expected Howe to attack him from the western end of Long Island, so he decided to establish a strong position on Brooklyn Heights opposite the southeastern edge of Manhattan (below the Brooklyn side of today's Brooklyn Bridge). If the British captured Brooklyn Heights, they could aim their artillery at New York City and dominate it just as effectively as the Americans had done at Dorchester Heights.

Washington should have considered the city indefensible and abandoned it to take a position farther upriver. But Congress wanted New York defended and losing it without a fight would hurt the morale of the colonists.

Washington divided his army between Manhattan and Brooklyn Heights, separating the two parts by a wide stretch of water which the British could control. Dividing the army was dangerous as it could result in gradual destruction, yet failure to occupy Brooklyn Heights would guarantee the loss of New York City. He also set up a line of defense along the Heights of Guan, a ridge of hills stretching about 5 miles from Gowanus Bay northeast to the Jamaica Pass.

For all practical purposes, command on Long Island was also divided. Major General Nathanael Greene (1742–1786), to whom Washington first entrusted the command, came down with malaria and was replaced by Major General John Sullivan (1740–1795) on August 20, 1776. Greene had a thorough knowledge of the terrain on Long Island but Sullivan did not. Not completely satisfied with this arrangement, at the last moment, Washington placed Major General Israel Putnam (1718–1790) over Sullivan on the 24th, but Putnam hardly had time to become acquainted with the situation before the British struck.

About 3,500 troops defended the line from Gowanus Bay to the Bedford Pass (near where modern Bedford Avenue intersects with Eastern Parkway). They were disposed in fortifications on Brooklyn Heights and in forward positions back of a line of thickly wooded hills that ran across the southern end of the island. Colonel Edward Hand (1744–1802) guarded the Gowanus road with about 550 men. Sullivan commanded 1,000 troops with 4 artillery pieces at the Flatbush Pass over a mile and a half to their left. Lieutenant Colonel Solomon Wills guarded the Bedford Pass a mile to the east with about 880 men and 3 guns. Brigadier General Samuel Miles (d. 1805) with about 400 Pennsylvania riflemen from Brigadier General William Alexander's (Earl of Stirling, 1726–1783) brigade patrolled toward the Jamaica Pass 3 miles northeast of Bedford Pass (approximately at the southern end of today's Cemetery of the Evergreens, just above the intersection of Broadway and Jamaica Avenue). Of the four roads running through the hills toward the American positions, only the Jamaica-Bedford road was left unguarded.

With the rebels entrenched on Brooklyn Heights, General Howe did not want to risk either the heavy loss of life which his army suffered taking Bunker Hill or a possible defeat which would have widespread political consequences. At 8:00 AM on Thursday, August 22, 1776, General Howe sent a force of 4,000 men under General Henry Clinton (1730–1795) and General Charles Cornwallis (1738–1805) to Denyse Point (now occupied by Fort Hamilton; the Verazzano Narrows Bridge connects Brooklyn with Staten Island at this point). The landing boats returned across the Narrows to Staten Island for more troops. These men landed at Gravesend Bay on the southwestern tip of Long Island. By noon, a force of almost 15,000 men, mostly Hessians, (half of Howe's army and twice the size of Washington's army), 40 cannon, and the horses of the dragoons had arrived on Long Island.

Three days later, General Leopold von Heister (1707–1777) landed to the right (southeast) of the previous troops with 2 brigades of German grenadiers. They traveled

4 miles inland to Flatbush to join General Cornwallis's 10 light infantry battalions and Major General Count Karl Emil Kurt von Donop's (1740–1777) jaegers and grenadiers (see Photos VT-1 and VT-2).

Howe led a surprise attack up the unguarded Jamaica-Bedford road about 8:00 AM August 26. He stopped for breakfast before resuming his march west and behind the American left. Brigadier General James Grant (1720–1806) had a brief skirmish with the lower end of the American right (near modern Greenwood Cemetery) around 7:30 AM. German troops distracted the American center at Flatbush. The firing of 2 British cannon at Bedford (near the present intersection of Nostrand Avenue and Fulton Street), about 9:00 AM gave the signal for a general assault.

Howe's column smashed the rear of the American left, crumpling the entire American position. The Germans broke through the center of the American line (at what is now called Battle Pass on East Drive in Prospect Park). Stirling's troops were arrayed in open order, their colors flying about 8:00 AM (see Photo NY-15). He reminded his troops that Brigadier General James Grant (1720–1806), a member of Parliament, boasted in the House of Commons (February 2, 1775) that the Americans would not fight and that he could march from one end of the American continent to the other with 5,000 men. General Alexander's (Lord Stirling) troops, who numbered about 1,600 after the arrival of reinforcements, stood firm for 4 hours enduring artillery fire and light infantry moving to within 150 yards.

Grant's 5,000 men, reinforced to 7,000 with the arrival of the 42nd Highlanders who had been with Heister, attacked the American right flank along Gowanus Bay. Sullivan and some of his men at the Flatbush Pass tried to fight their way to the rear. Sullivan's artillery fired their 3 guns on a light infantry battalion that blocked the way. When Grant's light infantry battalion received reinforcements from the Guards, they attacked. They took heavy casualties but captured Sullivan's guns and drove his troops back to face the bayonets of von Donop's jaegers. The retreating forces met light infantry, dragoons, and jaegers along the way to the fortified camp. These sporadic encounters inflicted most of the American casualties.

The heaviest fighting occurred near Baker's Tavern (near the intersection of Fulton and Flatbush Avenues). This is where Sullivan and most of his troops were captured. Howe and the Germans had routed the American left center by about 11:00 AM.

The Germans, moving along the ridge from the east, attacked the Maryland and Delaware Regiments. Grant's overwhelming numbers, further reinforced by 2,000 marines, attacked and penetrated the American lines where they joined to form a V. Cornwallis and the 71st Regiment (Fraser's Highlanders) blocked the retreat route forcing the Americans across Gowanus Creek—80 yards of water, a swift tide, broad salt marshes on both banks—under fire from musket and artillery fire.

General Alexander led a detachment of 250 Marylanders to attempt to force through the escape route at the stone Cortelyou House (west of Fifth Avenue near 3rd and 8th Streets). (See Photo NY-17.) They attacked the house five times to divert British musket fire, allowing their troops to cross Gowanus Creek west of the house, the only possible escape route to Brooklyn. Many drowned as they fled. British reinforcements stopped Alexander's sixth attack, leaving almost all of his 250 Maryland troops dead.

Howe hoped that the British ships sailing up the East River between Brooklyn and Manhattan would cut off the American retreat, but a violent storm prevented the ships from sailing and flooded both camps. Had Howe pushed his advantage immediately he could have carried the heights and destroyed half the American army then and there. If the British could capture Brooklyn Heights on Long Island, they could aim their artillery at New York City and dominate it just as effectively as the Americans had done at Dorchester Heights overlooking Boston. Instead, Howe halted at nightfall and began to dig trenches signaling his intent to take the heights by "regular approaches" in traditional 18th-century fashion.

Washington managed to evacuate his forces across the East River (around where the Brooklyn Bridge now stands) and retreated into New York on Manhattan Island on the night of August 29. According to one theory, wind and weather stopped the British warships from entering the river to prevent the escape. According to another, the Americans had placed impediments in the river that effectively barred their entry. The skill, bravery, and perseverance of Colonel John Glover's (1732–1797) Marblehead Regiment of Massachusetts fishermen who manned the small fishing boats when the tide was too low for the British fleet to move made the narrow escape possible. They ferried 10,000 or 12,000 troops across the East River in 6 hours, losing only 3 stragglers who stopped to plunder, and 5 cannon which the matrosses could not haul through the hub-deep mud.

As dawn approached on the morning of August 30, a thick fog hid the movements of Washington's men from view. By 7 o'clock, all his men and most of his supplies were safely on the other shore of the East River. His men were exhausted and soaked by the constant rain. They only had pickled pork to eat. Their powder was wet, so they couldn't fire, and their muskets were clogged with mud.

The official British report lists casualties of 89 American officers and 1,097 others. American strength returns of October 8 show a loss of 1,012 men in the campaign for Long Island. The losses of the Crown forces amounted to only 377. The British lost 5 officers and 56 men killed, 13 officers and 275 men wounded and missing. The Germans had 2 men killed, 3 officers and 23 men wounded.

The defeat crushed American morale. Many soldiers thought the war was as good as over and left for home. Others remained behind to plunder. Washington and Greene decided to abandon New York. Greene wanted to burn it to the ground first, as two-thirds of it belonged to Loyalists, but Washington decided against this.

Morale of the British and German troops was high. General Howe knew that Washington could not hold New York and that the Crown forces could take it without losing any more men. General Lord Hugh Percy (1742–1817) thought the campaign would end the war. British ships commmanded both the East River and the Hudson River on the other side of New York.

After the Battle of Brooklyn Heights, the two armies faced each other on Manhattan Island for over 3 weeks. They occasionally shouted good-natured insults across the lines and even exchanged presents. Major General William Heath (1737–1814) recorded that they were so civil to each other, on their posts, that one day, at a part of the creek where it was practicable, a British sentinel asked an American, who was nearly opposite to him, if he could give him a chew of tobacco. The latter, having in his pocket a piece of a thick twisted roll, sent it across the creek to the British sentinel who, after taking off his bite, sent the remainder back again.

Kip's Bay (September 15, 1776)

The area of the Battle of Kip's Bay extends from 32nd Street to 38th Street in Manhattan, but landfill extends the shoreline, obliterating the small inlet where the Crown forces landed on September 15, 1776. The Kip house was located on 35th Street, about 100 feet east of Second Avenue. The Crown forces came ashore just east of that house.

Nathan Hale (1755–1776) is thought to have been hanged as a spy at 46th Street and First Avenue. The spot is part of the plaza surrounding the United Nations building.

General George Washington (1732–1799) had 2 weeks after the Battle of Long Island on August 27, 1776 and his retreat to Manhattan on August 29-30 to prepare his defenses on Manhattan before General William Howe (1732–1786) struck again, landing a force at Kip's Bay above the city of New York (now about 34th Street) on September 15, 1776.

Washington placed 5,000 men in the city and another 5,000 behind earthworks along the East River. He also had 9,000 north of Harlem Heights. They were in a precarious situation. Early on Sunday morning, September 15, 1776, a British naval squadron took a position in the East River about 200 yards from American earthworks at Kip's Bay. The squadron consisted of the *Renown* (44 guns), *Phoenix* (44 guns), *Orpheus* (28 guns), *Rose* (20 guns) (see Photo NY-18), and another 28-gun ship. The warships began a cannonade just before 11:00 AM that continued for over an hour.

Meanwhile 84 flatboats moved from Long Island at 10:00 AM with 4,000 British and Hessian troops. Lord Francis Rawdon (1754–1826) recorded in his diary:

> As we approached [Kip's Bay] we saw the breastworks filled with men and two or three large columns marching down in great parade to support them.
>
> The Hessians, who were not used to this water business and who conceived that it must be exceedingly uncomfortable to be shot at whilst they were quite defenceless and jammed so close together, began to sing hymns immediately. Our men expressed their feelings as strongly, though in a different manner, by damning themselves and the enemy indiscriminately with wonderful fervency.
>
> The ships had not as yet fired a shot but upon a signal from us, they began the most tremendous peal I ever heard. The breastworks were blown to pieces in a few minutes, and those who were to have defended them were happy to escape as quick as possible through the ravines. The columns broke instantly, and betook themselves to the nearest woods for shelter. We pressed to shore, landed, and formed without losing a single man. As we were without artillery, upon an island where the enemy might attack us with five times our number, and as many cannon as he thought proper, it was necessary to attain some post where we might maintain ourselves till we were reinforced, which we knew could not be done quickly. We accordingly attacked and forced a party of the rebels from the Inchenberg, a very commanding height, taking from them a new brass howitzer, some waggons of ammunition, and the tents of three or four battalions who were encamped on it.

Ambrose Serle (1742–1812), secretary to Admiral Richard Howe (1726–1799) wrote: "So terrible and so incessant a roar of guns few even in the army and navy had ever heard before."

The flatboats began to land about 4,000 men on both sides of Kip's Bay at 1:00 PM. Raw Connecticut militia posted at this point abandoned their position, broke and ran north "as if the Devil was in them." Washington himself tried unsuccessfully to halt them and to rally them (near where the New York Public Library stands on Fifth Avenue at 42nd Street). He was reported to have exclaimed as he flung his hat to the ground in despair at the unwillingness of his men to stand their ground: "Good God! Good God! Have I got such troops as these!" or "Are these the men with which I am to defend America?" He even lashed out with his cane at the officers and men of the Connecticut brigade who fled past him in their anxiety to escape the advancing redcoats.

The Crown forces could have destroyed the retreating column very easily had they chosen to do so. Instead, the first division of 4,000 men secured the beachhead and blocked the Boston Post Road (now Lexington Avenue). Here, they seized and held Murray Hill, then called Inclenberg, a mile northwest of Kip's Bay. (It is an area enclosed by 35th and 38th Streets between Lexington and Fifth Avenues.) The Crown forces waited for the second division of 9,000 men to land before advancing any further.

The Boston Post Road which ran the length of Manhattan Island, was the only main road. The Crown forces immediately seized and blocked it, cutting off the escape route. The Americans had to abandon their artillery—more than 70 guns, about half of the artillery in the army—and travel on foot. This allowed them to march faster, as they expected the Crown forces to march quickly across the island to cut their forces in half. Major General Israel Putnam (1718–1790) would have led the retreating Americans into a trap had he not learned from Major Aaron Burr (1756–1836), one of his aides, of a possible alternate route, the Bloomingdale Road which branched off the Boston Post Road. (It followed the route of today's Broadway up the west side of the island, almost up to the location of Grant's Tomb.)

When the Crown forces began advancing up the Boston Post Road, they marched north in parallel with Putnam's column, separated by little more than the width of Central Park, about a mile. Neither column was aware of the existence of the other. They finally met entirely by accident. The Crown forces advance guard on the Post Road reached the point where it entered the east side of present-day Central Park. Here, it came across Colonel William Smallwood (1732–1792) and the remainder of the Maryland regiment. A brief skirmish followed, and the Americans retreated north to join their compatriots in new fortifications on Harlem Heights.

Harlem Heights (September 16, 1776)

The Battle of Harlem Heights took place about 1.5 miles south of Fort Washington near the present day Grant Memorial and Columbia University, off 120th Street, Manhattan.

The site of the Battle of Harlem Heights is covered by urban development. Grant's Tomb occupies the site of the main position of the Crown forces. The heaviest fighting took place in a buckwheat field along 120th Street. The Hollow Way, where the battle started, runs along 125th Street near the location of the 125th Street subway station. The Morris-Jumel Mansion (160th Street and Edgecomb Avenue) was General George Washington's headquarters during the battle and was used by the British and Hessians until their evacuation in 1783.

http://www.morrisjumel.org/

The Americans occupied a strong position on Harlem Heights. Fort Lee and Fort Washington, on opposite banks of the Hudson River, protected them from the British fleet as did batteries commanding Harlem Creek. The Crown forces landed on Manhattan at Kip's Bay on September 15, 1776 and advanced northward to form a line from Horn's Hook on the East River (at 90th Street) across to the Hudson (97th Street and Broadway). The northern outposts extended from McGowan's Pass (near the northeast corner of Central Park at 106th Street) to the Hudson (near 105th Street).

Major General Nathanael Greene (1742–1786) guarded the southern edge of the Harlem Heights plateau with 3,300 men (between Manhattan Avenue and the Hudson overlooking West 125th Street). Major General Israel Putnam (1718–1790) and his 2,500 men were half a mile behind Greene. Major General Joseph Spencer's (1714–1789) 4,200 men were another half mile behind Putnam.

Lieutenant Colonel Thomas Knowlton (1740–1776) with 150 Connecticut rangers set out before dawn on the morning of September 16, 1776, to reconnoiter the enemy position about 2 miles south of the American forward position. They encountered the 2nd and 3rd British light infantry battalions and part of the 42nd Highland Regiment ("Black Watch") about daybreak near Jones's farm (West 106th Street at Broadway). Knowlton's scouts fired about 8 volleys at the light infantry in a $\frac{1}{2}$-hour fire fight and retreated to avoid being flanked after suffering 10 casualties.

The superior Crown forces pursued Knowlton down a depression known as the Hollow Way (south of West 125th Street). General George Washington (1732–1799) rode forward from his headquarters at the Jumel mansion (near West 161st Street) shortly before 9 AM to observe the skirmish when a British Light infantry bugler on the high ground (just north of Grant's Tomb) sounded the hunting call to signal the end of a successful chase.

Washington ordered Lieutenant Colonel Archibald Crary and 150 volunteers from Brigadier General John Nixon's (1727–1815) brigade to counterattack. They advanced across the Hollow Way as Colonel Joseph Reed (1741–1785) led Knowlton's Rangers and 3 rifle companies—about 230 in all—behind the enemy's right flank. Premature musket fire disclosed the flank attack, and the two forces exchanged fire at too great a distance to be effective. Washington sent the rest of Nixon's brigade (about 800) to reinforce Crary.

The Highlanders, realizing the danger, started withdrawing and the rebels pursued. The British reformed behind a fence and began a fire fight. Lieutenant Colonel Knowlton and Major Andrew Leitch (d. 1776) were mortally wounded within 10 minutes, but the fighting continued. Washington reinforced the attack with parts of 2 Maryland regiments and some New Englanders, making sure to include the Connecticut militia who had run from Kip's Bay so that they might redeem themselves.

The British retired south into a buckwheat field (near 120th Street between Broadway and Riverside Drive). They received reinforcements of fresh light infantry troops and Highlanders and formed a line (running just below 119th Street) to take a stand. They held their ground here and engaged in the heaviest fighting of the battle between noon and 1:00 PM. When their ammunition ran low, they retreated again (to present-day 106th Street).

Not wanting to bring on a general engagement, Washington ordered his troops to withdraw about 2:00 PM as large numbers of British reinforcements were arriving. But some Americans did not receive the orders right away and pursued the enemy (as far as 110th Street) before breaking off the action.

The Americans lost 30 killed and 100 wounded and missing out of approximately 2,000 men engaged. The Crown forces probably had about the same number engaged and lost 14 dead and 157 wounded.

This small engagement was a tremendous boost to American morale. It was the first time the American army won a victory in open warfare and showed that troops from the various colonies could work together in harmony. General Howe made no further advances on the American lines in more than a month, but the position on Harlem Heights was basically untenable.

Fort Washington (November 16, 1776)

> Fort Washington Park occupies the site of Fort Washington: Fort Washington Avenue and 183rd Street, Manhattan. Fort Washington Park is also known as Gordon Bennett Park; it is undeveloped as a historical site. The site of Fort Washington has a marker at a rock outcropping which identifies it as the highest natural point on Manhattan, at 265 feet.
> http://www.washington-heights.us/history/archives/000427.html
>
> Fort Tryon Park (192nd Street between Broadway and Riverside Drive, Manhattan) marks the site of the northern redoubt of Fort Washington.
> http://www.nyrp.org/theparks_forttryon.htm

General George Washington (1732–1799), sensing his inability to meet the British in battle on equal terms, moved away to the north toward the New York highlands. Again he was outmaneuvered. General William Howe (1732–1786) quickly moved to Dobb's Ferry on the Hudson between Washington's army and the Hudson River forts. On the advice of Major General Nathanael Greene (1742–1786) (now recovered from his bout with malaria), Washington decided to defend the forts. At the same time, he split his army, moving across the Hudson and into New Jersey with 5,000 men and leaving Major General Charles Lee (1731–1782) and Major General William Heath (1737–1814) with about 8,000 men between them to guard the passes through the New York highlands at Peekskill and North Castle.

After the Battle of White Plains, Howe planned to attack Fort Washington, a pentagonal earthwork built on the highest natural point on Manhattan Island 265 feet above the Hudson, which was now isolated. Colonel Robert Magaw (d. 1789), the commanding officer, held a strong position and believed he and his 1,200 men could hold out for at least a month. He received an additional 1,700 reinforcements in the few days preceding the attack. Although a strong position, the fort had no ditch, no casements, no palisade, no barracks, and weak outworks, making it vulnerable to siege or attack. It also lacked water, food, and fuel. Magaw intended to use the Hudson River to his rear as the escape route if necessary. Steep and densely wooded slopes protected his front. Where natural defenses of rocks and deep ravines did not protect the approaches, he built entrenchments and batteries.

General Howe, now reinforced to 20,000, sent one of his staff to Fort Washington with a drummer and another soldier carrying a white flag on November 15, 1776, to formally invite the American commander to surrender. He gave the traditional warning that, if Magaw failed to surrender, the Crown forces would kill his entire garrison when they took the fort. Colonel Magaw refused to surrender saying that mankind had never fought for a better cause.

The Crown forces began the assault at daybreak the next day as the guns of the *Pearl* in the Hudson River and the batteries on the eastern bank of Harlem Creek opened fire at 7 AM and continued firing until about 11 AM. The army attacked on four fronts. Lieutenant General Wilhelm von Knyphausen (1716–1800) advanced from the north, crossing Kingsbridge about noon with 3,000 Germans, Highlanders, Light Infantry and 9 battalions of the line. (Eighteenth-century soldiers fought shoulder to shoulder in lines. Battalions of the line consist of the companies that remain when the companies of grenadiers and light infantry that protect the flanks are detached.)

The attackers advanced under a heavy fire, scrambling over rocks, dragging cannon up steep, rough roads, clinging to the bushes which sprouted from the crevices. Officers urged their men forward shouting and waving swords.

Brigadier General Edward Mathew (often misspelled Matthews) (1729–1805) and 2 light infantry battalions (3,000 British soldiers) crossed the Harlem River at noon to attack from the east. They landed in a cove or creek near present day 200th Street. Brigadier General William Alexander's (Earl of Stirling, 1726–1783) 42nd Highland Regiment ("Black Watch") crossed the Harlem River below the fort as a feigned attack, but they came under fire from Colonel John Cadwalader's (1742–1786) 3rd Pennsylvania regiment. Magaw reinforced his 150 men with another 100 from the fort.

General Lord Hugh Percy's (1742–1817) column of 2,000 men (1 Hessian brigade and 9 British battalions), originally intended as a diversion, prepared to lead the main assault against the fort from the south. As Percy's column attacked the fort, a little dog would dart out from behind the breastworks and tear the fuses out of shells with its teeth until one exploded in its face.

Washington, Greene, Brigadier General Hugh Mercer (1725–1777), and Major General Israel Putnam (1718–1790) crossed the Hudson from Fort Lee, New Jersey (see Photo NY-15), to Fort Washington for personal reconnaissance. They determined that they could do nothing to help Magaw and returned to Fort Lee. Washington instructed Magaw to fight until dark and then evacuate the fort.

The Americans were soon surrounded by cannon and troops with fixed bayonets. Knyphausen demanded Magaw's surrender about 1 o'clock and gave him 2 hours to make up his mind. Magaw surrendered about 3 PM. Some of the Germans wanted to make good Howe's threat to kill the entire garrison, but they were ordered to take prisoners instead. The Crown forces captured 2,818 American troops and large quantities of valuable munitions, including ammunition and guns. The Americans also suffered 53 killed. The Crown forces lost 458 men killed and wounded, 72 % (330) of them Germans and half of the British casualties from the 42nd Highlanders. Hessian casualties numbered 58 killed and 272 wounded. The British suffered 20 killed, 6 missing, and 102 wounded. Howe renamed the fort Fort Knyphausen to honor his German allies. He now commanded all of Manhattan Island and was in a good position to seize Fort Lee across the Hudson in New Jersey. (See also Fort Lee, New Jersey.)

General Greene hastily evacuated Fort Lee and retreated west to join General Washington at Hackensack on November 20. Washington, with mere remnants of his army, about 3,500 men, was in full retreat across New Jersey with General Charles Cornwallis (1738–1805), detached by Howe, pursuing him rapidly from river to river.

The fall of Fort Washington was another major American defeat, and Washington's army was slowly melting away. Militia left by whole companies, and desertion among the Continentals was rife. When Washington finally crossed the Delaware into Pennsylvania in early December, he could muster barely 2,000 men. The 8,000 men in the New York highlands also dwindled away. Even more appalling, most enlistments expired with the end of the year 1776, and a new army would have to be raised for the following year.

Yet neither the unreliability of the militia nor the short period of enlistment fully explained the debacle that had befallen the Continental Army. Washington's generalship was also faulty. Criticism of the Commander in Chief, even among his official family, mounted, centering particularly on his decision to hold Fort Washington. Major General Charles Lee, the ex-British colonel, ordered by Washington to bring his forces down from New York to join him behind the Delaware, delayed, believing that he might himself salvage the American cause by making incursions into new Jersey. He wrote Major General Horatio Gates (1728–1806), ". . . *entre nous,* a certain great man is most damnably deficient."

Colonel Moses Rawlings (d. 1809) guarded the northern redoubt of Fort Washington (renamed Fort Tryon after the Crown forces captured it) about $\frac{3}{4}$ mile north of Fort Washington. This fort on a 250-foot hill protected the northern end of Fort Washington. Rawlings commanded 250 Maryland and Virginia riflemen and 3 cannon. Margaret Cochran (Molly) Corbin (1751–1800) carried water to the men firing the guns when she saw her husband John fall severely wounded during the bombardment. She caught his rammer staff and took his place at the muzzle. The assault waves continued to advance under the heavy fire. When the British stormed the fort, Molly lay bleeding beside her gun. One arm was nearly severed and part of a breast mangled by three grapeshot. She survived the wagon journey to Philadelphia with other wounded prisoners of war.

Washington issued her a warrant as a noncommissioned officer for her exploits. But, when the commissary at West Point refused to give her the rum portion of her ration because it wasn't customary to give liquor to women, she got angry and began voluminous correspondence to put pressure on him. A higher authority finally ruled: "It appears clearly to me that the order forbidding the issue of Rum to a woman does not apply to Mrs. Corbin." The commandant was directed to issue her the rations and cautioned that "perhaps it would not be prudent to give them to her all in liquor." (The Daughters of the American Revolution verified her records in 1926 and had her remains transferred to the West Point Cemetery, making her the first woman to be buried there. See Photo NY-14.)

4

MASSACHUSETTS

The largest number of troops in the war came from Massachusetts: a total of 83,052 men—15,145 militia and 67,907 Continental Army.

See the Massachusetts map.

Lexington (April 19, 1775)

Minute Man National Historical Park encompasses lands in Concord, Lincoln, and Lexington. The park commemorates the opening battles of America's War for Independence. The majority of the park is a narrow strip of land on either side of Battle Road (State Route MA 2A), with the Minute Man Visitor Center at one end, just off MA 128/I-95, and the North Bridge Visitor Center outside of Concord at the other. The events of April 19, 1775, were not one but many skirmishes along a 20-mile stretch of hilly road between Boston and Concord.

http://www.nps.gov/mima/index.htm

The Lexington Battle Green is at the junction of Massachusetts Avenue, Bedford Street, and Hancock Street in Lexington. The Lexington Battle Green is the site of the first skirmish of the War for American Independence. A boulder inscribed with Captain John Parker's courageous words: "Stand your ground; don't fire unless fired upon, but if they mean to have a war, let it begin here" marks the line where the minutemen formed for battle. The Revolutionary Monument on the Green, surrounded by an iron picket fence, was dedicated in 1799 to the men killed in the first battle of the war (See Photo MA-3).

Those who died on the Green were first buried in the Old Burying Ground and then reinterred behind this monument in 1835. It is considered to be the first monument erected commemorating the American Revolution. The Old Burying Ground, at the far end of the green, next to the Unitarian Church contains the graves of Captain John Parker; Governor William Eustis, who served in the war and then as Secretary of War and ambassador to the Netherlands; Reverend John Hancock; and a British soldier who died in Buckman's Tavern. The oldest stone is dated 1690.

The Buckman Tavern (see Photo MA-2) at 1 Bedford Street is across the street from the Lexington Battle Green. It was built in 1709 and has furnishings of the Revolutionary War period. It was the headquarters of the Lexington Minutemen the night before the first battle. One of the muskets on the wall in the taproom was fired during the battle. A bullet hole from a musket penetrated the original door which is preserved inside the tavern.

http://www.lexingtonhistory.org/buckman_2002.html

The Lexington Visitors Center is nearby at 1875 Massachusetts Avenue.

http://www.lexingtonchamber.org/visitor.html

John Hancock and Samuel Adams stayed at the Hancock-Clark house (see Photo MA-1) at 36 Hancock Street in Lexington on April 17, 1775. Paul Revere headed here on his famous ride to warn them that the Regulars were coming to capture them and the cannon in Concord. The house originally stood across the street. It was moved to its present location in 1896 and restored. Inside, there's a musket used by one of the minutemen, the drum that beat the alarm, and Major Pitcairn's pistols.

The Old Belfry off Clarke Street across the street from the Lexington Green is a reproduction of the original belfry whose bell sounded the alarm that assembled the minutemen. The original was destroyed by wind in 1909. (See Photo MA-4.)

The Muzzie School, on the left side of Massachusetts Avenue has a stone cannon in front of it marking the spot where Lord Percy's relief column of about 1,400 men met the retreating troops about 0.5 mile east of Lexington Green. He put 2 of his 6 cannon into action. One of the cannons fired from here. The other was located at Bloomfield Street farther east on the right side.

The Munroe Tavern at 1332 Massachusetts Avenue, Lexington, served as General Lord Hugh Percy's (1742-1817) headquarters and a hospital during the Battle of Lexington. The 1695 building is restored.
                    http://www.lexingtonhistory.org/munroe_2002.html

The Museum of Our National Heritage at 33 Marrett Road, a short distance from the Munroe Tavern, offers changing exhibits about American history and culture and features exhibits and multimedia presentations about the events of April 19, 1775.

Tensions between Great Britain and her colonies in America continued to mount after the French and Indian War (1757–1763) also called the Seven Years War. A Massachusetts provincial congress, which had superseded the General Court voted money to purchase powder and ball, so the Massachusetts militia collected ammunition and other supplies during the winter of 1774–1775. The militia could obtain limited supplies because of its militia status. Smuggling also brought in a small amount. The military stores in various places along the coast seemed the most obvious sources, and they were usually lightly guarded. The army reinforced some of the garrisons or removed the supplies before the colonials captured them.

The colonials stored their meager supplies under guard at various strategic points throughout Massachusetts. The town of Concord, only 18 miles northwest of Boston, had one of the more important depots. Fearing that the colonials would use the guns and ammunition against them, the army planned to capture them. Paul Revere (1735–1818) brought news of British preparations to John Hancock (1737–1793) and Samuel Adams (1722–1803) who were in Lexington (see Photo MA-1). This warning gave the Committee of Safety time to secure the stores in Concord. They hid the cannon and brought a part of the stores to Sudbury and Groton.

General Thomas Gage (1719–1787) was determined to remove all military supplies from the control of the militia. His troops captured the powder from a magazine at Charlestown, Massachusetts and armaments from a fort at Portsmouth, New Hampshire and from Salem, Massachusetts. He was preparing to raid the store at Concord when the sloop *Nautilus* arrived with a letter from Lord William Legge 2nd Earl of Dartmouth (1731–1801) authorizing him to take stronger action before the colonials could organize armed resistance.

General Gage planned what he hoped would be a secret expedition to seize or destroy the supplies at Concord. But an operation of this magnitude was impossible to keep secret for long. On April 15, Gage relieved the grenadiers and light infantry from duty on the pretence of learning a new military exercise. His intention was simply to overawe the colonials, not to provoke a fight. At night, the boats of the transport ships were launched and moored under the sterns of the men of war. The Sons of Liberty thought these movements looked suspicious.

Militiamen, known as minutemen because they would take up arms at a moment's notice, learned of the army's march to Concord and spread a call to arms from town to town and settlement to settlement. Paul Revere, a master silversmith, who had already carried the Suffolk County Resolves to Philadelphia, Pennsylvania and a warning of the British commander's order to remove military supplies from the fort at Portsmouth, New Hampshire, set out with William Prescott (1726–1795), and William Dawes (1749–1799) on the night of April 18, 1775 to warn Concord that the redcoats were coming to take their military stores.

Since the Sons of Liberty expected that any horseman riding out of Boston that night would be intercepted, they agreed that they would place lanterns briefly in Boston's Old North Church steeple (see Photo MA-12) as a signal of the army movements. One lantern would mean the soldiers left by land across Boston Neck, two that they went out by water across the Charles River.

Lieutenant Colonel Francis Smith (1723–1791) of the 10th Regiment commanded a force of picked companies detached from their regiments for the operation. His second-in-command was Major John Pitcairn (1722–1775). The troops were not told of the operation or their destination until awakened by their sergeants on the night of April 18, 1775. They left the barracks by a back door around midnight and went to boats waiting on a secluded part of the waterfront to take them across the bay. The boats were to be rowed with muffled oars, and the men were to wade ashore.

When the redcoats left the barracks marching to the waterfront, Paul Revere (see Photos MA-11 through MA-13) and William Dawes were sent to Lexington to warn Adams and Hancock that the soldiers were on their way and that the British intended to arrest them. William Dawes, a shoemaker, rode by land across Boston Neck. Paul Revere was rowed across to Charlestown in a boat with oars muffled by the torn-up petticoat of the boatman's girlfriend. They were later joined by William Prescott, a 23-year-old physician.

The Lexington militia, under the command of Captain John Parker (1729–1775), gathered on Lexington Green in front of the meeting-house. A large crowd of spectators stood on the edge of the Green, waiting. After an hour or so, some went home, others went to Buckman's Tavern (see Photo MA-2) which overlooked the Green.

About 4:30 AM, Captain Parker, commander of the Lexington minutemen, ordered the drum beat, alarm guns fired, and Sergeant William Monroe (or Munroe) to form his company in 2 ranks on the green. The officers ordered the redcoats to halt, to prime and load, and then to march forward in double-quick time.

The army detachment of 700 infantrymen encountered about 70–75 minutemen standing on the Green in Lexington. Officers on both sides ordered their men not to fire. Captain Parker supposedly ordered his men: "Stand your ground. Don't fire unless fired upon. But if they mean to have a war, let it begin here." (See Photo MA-3.)

Suddenly a shot rang out, perhaps from the Buckman Tavern or from behind a stone wall beside it. The redcoats opened fire and drove the minutemen from the field, leaving 8 dead and 10 wounded.

Isaac Muzzy (d. 1775), Jonathan Harrington (d. 1775), and Robert Monroe (d. 1775) were killed near the place where the line was formed. Harrington fell near his own house (see Photo MA-3), on the north of the green. His wife saw him fall and then start up, bleeding from his breast. He stretched out his hands toward her and fell again. Rising once more on his hands and knees, he crawled across the road toward his dwelling and died at the door.

The redcoats suffered little: A private of the 10th regiment and probably one other were wounded, and Major Pitcairn's horse was hit. The redcoats then re-formed the column and marched to Concord where they arrived about 8 o'clock in the morning.

Concord (April 19, 1775)

Minute Man National Historical Park encompasses lands in Concord, Lincoln, and Lexington. The majority of the park is a narrow strip of land on either side of Battle Road (State Route MA 2A), with the North Bridge Visitor Center outside of Concord at the west end and the Minute Man Visitor Center at the other.

The North Bridge Visitor Center at 174 Liberty Street, Concord, near the North Bridge exhibits clothed mannequins, artifacts, muskets, and a 12-minute film describing the fight at the North Bridge.
> `http://minuteman.areaparks.com/parkinfo.html?pid=5737`

The North Bridge (Monument Street) in Concord is the sixth bridge on the site since April 19, 1775. It was erected in 1956 and is believed to resemble the original more closely than earlier reconstructions. The bridge itself is not historic, but the site on which it stands is significant due to the associations with the events of April 19, 1775. (See Photo MA-5.)

A short walk from the visitor center, just across the bridge stands Daniel Chester French's Minuteman statue which is engraved with a stanza from Ralph Waldo Emerson's "Concord Hymn."

Emerson spent some of his boyhood at the Old Manse overlooking the bridge. The house was built in 1770 by his grandfather and got the name Old Manse from Nathaniel Hawthorne's "Mosses from an Old Manse" which was written in the study when Hawthorne lived here between 1842 and 1845.
> `http://www.concord.org/town/manse/old_manse.html`

Wright's Tavern on the left as you enter town just before Monument Square served as the headquarters for the army officers. It also served as a military hospital later in the day. Sleepy Hollow Cemetery, on Bedford Street across from Wright's Tavern, contains the graves of the Alcotts, Ralph Waldo Emerson, Daniel Chester French, Nathaniel Hawthorne, and Henry David Thoreau.

Meriam's Corner is at the intersection of Route MA 2A and Old Bedford Road. About 0.5 mile east is Hardy's Hill where the Sudbury militia, under cover along the roadside, fired on troops coming down the hill. A short distance further east is the Hartwell Tavern and Samuel Hartwell farm site. A few hundred yards further down Route 2A is the site where

> Paul Revere was captured on his way to Concord. A plaque and stone marker explain the event.
>
> **http://www.nps.gov/mima/brt.htm**
>
> Traveling eastward toward Lexington, the Minute Man Visitor Center is off State Route MA 2A, near the site of Paul Revere's capture. It serves as a starting point for most visitors, showing a 22-minute film that details the events leading to the battle. A multimedia presentation further recounts the events of April 19, 1775. Ranger programs and exhibits supplement these presentations. Maps are available for tours of the park.
>
> **http://www.nps.gov/mima/index.htm**
>
> Fiske Hill is on the east side of the Minute Man Visitor Center. Here, Colonel Smith tried to re-organize his troops. A walking trail has signs that point out sites like the remains of a stone wall behind which the minutemen took cover and the spot where Pitcairn lost his horse and pistols. A plaque near the Fiske farmhouse and well tells the story of Thomas Heywood, a young minuteman, who encountered one of the King's troops as they both stopped for a drink. One reportedly said, "You're a dead man," and the other responded, "So are you." They both fired at each other. The soldier fell dead and Heywood was mortally wounded. This was the scene of some heavy fighting as Captain Parker and the Lexington Minutemen took fire from the retreating troops who began to run out of ammunition. Colonel Smith was also wounded in one leg here.

The alarm that the redcoats were coming spread through the countryside. Militia companies from the surrounding counties shouldered arms and headed for Concord. One company of about 150 men under Captain William Smith (1728–1793) headed toward Lexington, turned around, and returned to Concord when they saw the approaching column of soldiers. About 300 minutemen gathered at Colonel James Barrett's (d. 1779) farm on Punketasset Hill near the North Bridge (see Photo MA-5), one of two bridges across the Concord River.

When the soldiers arrived in Concord about 8 o'clock in the morning, Colonel Smith sent 3 companies (about 100 men) of light infantry under Captain Lawrence Parsons of the 10th Regiment toward Barrett's farm across the North Bridge past Punketasset Hill where he believed cannon and other arms had been hidden. He posted another 3 companies under Captain Walter Sloan Laurie of the 43rd Regiment on the opposite side of the river. He also ordered the grenadiers to search the buildings in the town for other hidden stores of arms and ammunition.

The grenadiers in town set fire to the courthouse and a blacksmith shop. The militiamen on Punketasset Hill saw the smoke and thought the soldiers were burning the town. The men asked Barrett if they were going to stand by while the soldiers burned the town. Barrett gave the order to advance, but he warned his followers not to fire unless fired upon.

When about 400 militia approached, the redcoats retired over the bridge to the east side of the river, formed as if for a fight, and began to take up the planks of the bridge.

A single shot rang out. The soldiers opened fire on the advancing militia who thought that the redcoats were firing only powder. When a shot whizzed past the ear of one man, he cried out: "God damn it! They're firing ball!" Major John Buttrick (1715–1791), commander of the Concord militia, ordered: "Fire, fellow soldiers! For God's sake, fire!" They did so and wounded 4 officers and killed 3 soldiers in the first volley (see Photo MA-6). Captain Laurie gave the order to retreat.

The colonials held the bridge cutting off the 3 infantry companies at Barrett's farm. But they did not have an organized command, and they divided into 2 groups instead of holding the bridge. About half of the men returned to the north side of the river to tend to their fallen comrades (2 killed and 2 wounded). The rest headed toward town, letting Captain Parsons's 3 companies cross the bridge to rejoin the main body.

Retreat to Lexington

Lieutenant Colonel Francis Smith (1723–1791) ordered a retreat back to Boston around mid-day. When they arrived at Meriam's Corner, about a mile out of Concord (on Route MA 2A 0.4 mile past the Wayside Inn at an intersection with Bedford Road), the redcoats encountered about 1,100 militiamen who gathered here from neighboring communities. The redcoats fired at the militia which returned fire and pursued them back to Boston. The retreat became disorderly as men, tired from a long day's march, plodded back toward Lexington under constant fire from the minutemen. Officers had to stop their troops to form a line across the road. They threatened the soldiers with death unless they pulled themselves together, resumed their proper places in the ranks, and prepared to defend themselves.

Many redcoats had fired all their 36 rounds of ammunition and could not retaliate as the minutemen, hiding behind stone walls and in thick woods, fired on them. The colonials, including women, kept up a steady fire on the troops from farm walls, hedgerows and boulders, from the windows of houses and the roofs of barns. The soldiers tried to find the snipers, raiding houses and taverns along the way.

As the army approached the Hartwell Tavern, scores of minutemen concealed in the woods, opened fire as the column marched past. They killed 8 soldiers, and the location became known as "the bloody angle." The soldiers retaliated by coming up behind the militia and killing 4 of them. The troops tried to keep the sides of the road clear of such sniping attacks, so most of the Patriot casualties resulted from flanking parties.

Additionally, 1,000 relief troops consisting of 3 regiments of infantry and 2 divisions of marines, with two 6-pounder field-pieces, under Brigadier General Hugh Percy (1742–1817) were sent from Boston about 9:00 AM, about an hour after the battle at the North Bridge in Concord, to support the grenadiers and light infantry. This relief force marched 30 miles in 10 hours to cover the retreat. They were intended to relieve the main body who were exhausted from marching all night and from being engaged in combat all day. The Regulars were not supposed to engage the colonials in combat at Lexington; but once gunfire broke out, they were soon outnumbered and under fire all day and many ran out of ammunition, and the relief troops became crucial to their protection.

Retreat to Boston

Massachusetts Avenue continues east into Arlington, then called Menotomy. There are several colonial homes along the way. The heaviest fighting of the retreat occurred in this area, particularly at Peirce's Hill west of town, now called Arlington Heights.

The Jason Russell House and George Abbot Smith History Museum, at 7 Jason Street in Arlington, was the scene of fierce hand-to-hand combat. About 20 minutemen took shelter in the house as the army came down the road. Some of the soldiers fired at the house. Others entered the house bayoneting Jason Russell and 11 minutemen—the largest number of combatants killed in any one place during that day. Eight minutemen held out successfully in the basement, threatening to shoot anybody who came down the stairs. The 1740 house contains some 18th-century furniture and artifacts and still shows evidence of bullet holes. The adjacent Smith Museum features an exhibit about Arlington history.

http://www.arlingtonhistorical.org/house/index.php

The Cooper Tavern is in the heart of Arlington's business section. A small park on the left side of Massachusetts Avenue has a granite marker that says that 80-year-old Samuel Whittmore shot and killed 3 soldiers near this spot. Flankers bayoneted him and left him for dead, but he recovered to live to be 98.

The Black Horse Tavern is across the street from the Cooper Tavern. On their way to Lexington, about 2:00 AM, advancing British troops stormed the Wayside Inn, and surprised the War Planning Council members in session at the Black Horse Tavern across the street. The council members escaped to the cornfields out back and later joined their fellow minutemen up the road in Lexington to join the fighting there.

http://www.arlingtonhistorical.org/battle.php

About 1.25 miles further east, a bridge crosses Alewife Brook, called the Menotomy River in 1775, into North Cambridge. Turn left at the corner at the traffic light at Beech Street in Somerville. At the end of the street where Beech meets Elm, the soldiers came under another attack from militia hidden in a grove of trees.

Beyond Lexington, the infantry column met fierce and bloody resistance in the towns of Menotomy, now Arlington, and Charlestown.

The heaviest fighting of the retreat occurred in Menotony (now called Arlington), where Massachusetts Avenue continues east, particularly at Peirce's Hill west of town.

About 20 minutemen took shelter in the Jason Russell house as the army came down the road. Some of the soldiers fired at the house. Others entered the house bayoneting Jason Russell and 11 minutemen—the largest number of combatants killed in any one place during that day. Eight minutemen held out successfully in the basement, threatening to shoot anybody who came down the stairs.

Fierce fighting continued for another half mile to the Cooper Tavern (in the heart of Arlington's business section). Nearby, 80-year-old Samuel Whittmore shot and killed 3 soldiers. Flankers bayoneted him and left him for dead, but he recovered to live to be 98.

Menotomy had the highest casualty rate of any town in the region—40 British soldiers and 25 Patriots. . Nearly half of the 49 minutemen who were killed in action fell during the Battle of Menotomy. Over half of all the minutemen killed on April 19, 1775 fell at the Jason Russell House.

About a mile and a quarter further east, a bridge crosses Alewife Brook, called the Menotomy River in 1775, into North Cambridge. The fighting began to diminish as darkness was setting in. Here the soldiers came under another attack from militia hidden in a grove of trees. Percy trained one of his guns on them and drove them off.

Lord Percy originally planned to spend the night on Cambridge Commons but decided to go to Charlestown instead where the troops could rest at Bunker Hill, under the protection of navy guns.

At 6:30 PM the soldiers finally reached the safety of Bunker Hill, which was under the guns of the warship *Somerset*. The exhausted redcoats marched nearly 50 miles and had been engaged in action since daybreak, without rest or refreshment. About 10:00 PM, they were ferried back to Boston.

The army suffered heavier casualties on their march back to Boston than they did in the battles at Lexington and Concord. Gage's reinforcements under Lord Percy prevented it from being worse. At the end of the day, out of a total of 1,800 men engaged, they counted 273 casualties: 65 dead, 173 wounded, and 35 missing. Fifteen of the casualties were officers. Of the estimated 3,700 colonials, there were 95 casualties, including those at Lexington: 49 dead and 41 wounded and 5 missing.

News

Post rider Israel Bissel, 23, quickly spread the news of the incidents at Lexington and Concord. He took a note written at 10:00 AM on April 19, rode 36 miles to Worcester in 2 hours, alerted Israel Putnam (1718–1790) at Brooklyn, Connecticut, during the night, and reached Old Lyme at 1:00 AM on April 20. Ferried across the Connecticut River, he reached Saybrook, Connecticut about 4:00 PM and Guilford by 7:00. He arrived at Branford at noon on April 21 and New Haven on the morning of April 22 where apothecary Benedict Arnold (1741–1801) called out his militia company and marched north.

Bissel arrived in New York City on April 23. The news from Boston led New Yorkers to close the port, distribute arms, and burn 2 sloops bound for the army garrison at Boston. Bissel was ferried across the Hudson, arrived at New Brunswick, New Jersey at 2:00 AM on April 24. He reached Princeton by dawn and Trenton by 6:00 AM. He arrived in Philadelphia, Pennsylvania a short while later, having traveled in 5 days a distance the fastest stage would have taken 8 days to cover.

The reports told the story as an unprovoked British attack and of farmers rising in the night to protect their lives, their families, and their property. This provided the emotional impulse for the Patriots to prepare themselves for war.

Charlestown (June 17, 1775)
Bunker Hill

> The Bunker Hill Monument is on Breed's Hill in Monument Square in Charlestown (MBTA subway, Orange Line: Community College). The 221-foot granite obelisk marks the site of the Battle of Bunker Hill (see Photo MA-7). A spiral staircase goes to the top. The lodge at the base of the monument contains dioramas and exhibits about the battle. It includes Israel Putnam's sword and the musket Peter Salem used.
>
> `http://www.nps.gov/bost/bost_lographics/bunkhill.htm`
>
> To the left of the monument is the sculpture of Colonel William Prescott, commander of the redoubt at the Battle of Bunker Hill (see Photos MA-7 and MA-8).

The Massachusetts Provincial Congress called for raising an army of 30,000 from all the colonies on April 23, 1775, 4 days after the battles of Lexington and Concord.

Men came from all over New England. By June, 15,000 militia were camped around Boston.

Two weeks after the surrender of the fort at Ticonderoga, late in May, 1775, the HMS *Cerberus* arrived in Boston with reinforcements that increased General Thomas Gage's (1719–1787) army to 6,500 men. The *Cerberus* also brought three generals—Sir William Howe (1732–1786), Sir Henry Clinton (1730–1795), and Sir John Burgoyne (1722–1792). They found the troops in dismay as a result of being besieged in Boston by what they considered an ill-equipped and amateur force of colonists whom Burgoyne described as "peasants."

The generals all considered that Gage needed more elbowroom. They examined the terrain and decided to attack Cambridge across Boston Neck and the Charles River as soon as possible. They would make diversionary raids on the high ground overlooking Boston: to the north on Charlestown peninsula and to the southeast on Dorchester Heights, a dominant position previously neglected by both sides. Before the redcoats could execute their plan of attacking Cambridge, rebel spies in Boston learned on June 13, probably through careless talk by Burgoyne, that Gage intended to occupy Dorchester Heights 5 days later. The Patriots immediately countered by dispatching a force onto the Charlestown peninsula.

The town of Charlestown lay at the foot of three hills, including Bunker Hill, Moulton's Hill, and Breed's Hill, which overlook Boston from the north. Boston would be in easy range of artillery placed on any of these hills as the Charlestown peninsula is separated from the city by the Charles River, a channel less than half a mile wide. The colonials had evacuated the residents of the town's 300 or so houses because of the threat by the guns of navy warships.

About 1,200–1,400 militiamen fortified Breed's Hill on the night of June 16, 1775, while 2 companies patrolled the empty streets of Charlestown, watching the enemy lines across the water. The colonials originally intended to fortify Bunker Hill, the hill nearest the narrow neck of land connecting the peninsula with the mainland, but, after a 2-hour discussion, the officers decided instead to move closer in and construct works on Breed's Hill which was nearer to Boston. They built a redoubt about 45 yards square in 4 hours. They also planned auxiliary defenses on Bunker Hill. This could have been a tactical blunder as an enemy landing on the neck in their rear could cut off these exposed works and eliminate the retreat route.

The redcoats scorned the colonials, evidently in the mistaken assumption that the assembled "rabble in arms" would disintegrate in the face of an attack by disciplined Regulars. The Patriots held a strong position.

Cannonade

The British had to react to the rebels' occupation of Charlestown. The Mystic River on the north side of the peninsula was too shallow to attack from that route. They had no flat-bottomed boats to navigate the mud flats, so they used the fleet's longboats for landing craft. They decided to make the main landing on the outward side of Moulton's Hill. This landing would give them protection from any rebel artillery, and reinforcements would later land nearby under Breed's Hill.

British sailors aboard the *Lively* which lay at anchor in Boston harbor were astonished to see the fortification complete by dawn. The captain of the *Lively* ordered a broadside against the redoubt, but most of the balls hit the earthen wall and rolled down the slope causing little damage. During the first assault, the fleet fired red-hot shot to burn the town and to protect the army's left flank from snipers in the houses.

General Israel Putnam (1718–1790) said that "The Americans were not afraid of their heads, though very much afraid of their legs; if you cover these, they will fight forever." In the cannonading, a cannon ball killed a young farmhand, tearing off his head. Colonel William Prescott (1726–1795) (see Photo MA-8) commanding the troops at the Breed's Hill redoubt wanted a quick and quiet burial, but the boy got a solemn funeral that demoralized several of his companions who left for home.

In addition to the earthworks on Breed's Hill, the Americans had another 1,000 militiamen on Bunker Hill. More men came over to the Charlestown peninsula from wherever they could be spared. Israel Putnam rode back to Cambridge for reinforcements. He found several hundred Connecticut militiamen. Major General Artemas Ward (1727–1800) sent a messenger to Colonel John Stark's (1728–1822) New Hampshire regiment, renowned as much for their strange clothes as for their marksmanship. A contemporary recorded:

> The arrival of Stark's men brought heart to Prescott's tired Massachusetts militiamen on Breed's Hill, several of whose companions had already had enough of warfare and had decided to follow the example of those who had deserted earlier that day and to go home to their farms and families. Prescott's men were also encouraged when the tall and handsome figure of Dr Joseph Warren appeared amongst them carrying a musket, ready, it appeared to fulfil an earlier promise to die if necessary "up to [his] knees in blood." When Prescott offered to give up his command to him, Warren said he had come not to give orders but to fight.

Assault

Although General Howe was in command of the operation, General Clinton was always second-guessing him. Clinton proposed launching a simultaneous assault behind the main rebel defenses to cut off their retreat across the narrows to the north of Breed's Hill while Howe would land on the southern shore of Charlestown Neck opposite Boston. Howe ignored the advice, preferring a direct attack.

Around noon on June 17, 1775, about 1500 soldiers marched down to the landing craft in their woolen uniforms, carrying rolled blankets on their backs and 3-days' supply of boiled beef and bread in their heavy packs. They boarded 28 barges along with 12 guns.

Clinton and Burgoyne, who directed the artillery on Copp's Hill, watched the first wave of British troops cross the water from Long Wharf as the cannon on Copp's Hill and the guns of the fleet covered them. The barges landed unopposed about 1:00 PM and returned for the next wave. The soldiers formed in lines 3 ranks deep on Moulton's Hill and proceeded to a depression where they were protected from fire from the redoubt (see Photo MA-9). Here they waited for the second wave of troops to arrive.

The Patriots held their fire during the cannonade. The first assault began about 3:00 PM. General Howe led the main assault in person as he had promised to do. He was supported by Brigadier General Sir Robert Pigot (1720–1796) with the 43rd and 52nd Foot. General Pigot's left wing advanced toward the redoubt while Howe's wing assaulted the rebels' left along the Mystic River. Colonel John Stark's New Hampshire soldiers and Captain Thomas Knowlton's Connecticut troops crouched behind a rail fence draped with bunches of grass and a stone wall which they built between the end of the fence and the river.

John Stark ordered his men not to open fire too soon. He reminded them that, with no more than 15 musket balls per man, they were short enough of ammunition. He drove a stake into the earth by the water's edge and ordered the men behind the wall not to open fire until the redcoats had passed it. He told the men behind the fence not to fire until they could see the gaiters of the enemy troops as they came up the hill. They were also to aim low and look for targets with gorgets (a symbol of officer rank).

Howe ordered the 6-pounders to precede the infantry, but the ammunition sent from Boston was for 12-pounders. The mud and soggy ground prevented the guns from getting close enough to fire grapeshot effectively.

The Royal Welch Fusiliers, leading the assault, arrived within 50 yards of the rail fence and prepared for a bayonet charge when Stark gave the order to fire. The survivors advanced immediately and were cut down. The next 2 companies, the 4th and 10th (who were at Lexington), charged into steady fire. Stark had organized his men into 3 ranks. One rank was always ready to fire, so there was no lull between volleys. When the 52nd Regiment reached the front line, they refused to advance. Howe personally led the attack against the rail fence, but rebel fire prevented them from deploying for a bayonet charge. He found himself on three occasions quite alone, all the staff around him lying dead or wounded.

Pigot's redcoats advanced up the slope through the long grass, past clay pits, kilns, and apple trees against the redoubt. Effective musket fire stopped them. When the Patriots fired, they did so in unison, bringing down scores of soldiers in the first volley. As more men were killed in the second volley, whole ranks faltered and retreated as officers and sergeants tried to stop them, prodding the men with halberds, bayonets, and the tips of swords.

Howe regrouped and launched a second attack within 15 minutes. He and Pigot advanced on the redoubt while the light infantry attacked the rail fences. William Prescott ordered the militia on their right to hold their fire until they could see the whites of the soldiers' eyes. Then, they were to fire at the officers. The best shots each had several firearms. Loaders prepared the arms and passed them to the sharpshooters. An army surgeon later testified that many of the colonial muskets were "charged with old nails and angular pieces of iron" so as to occasion "infinite Pain." Another surgeon claimed that many of the balls were encrusted with a white matter "which is supposed to have been some poisonous mixture, for an uncommon rancorous suppuration followed in almost every case."

Twice the redcoats advanced on the front and flanks of the redoubt on Breed's Hill, and twice the Patriots decimated the ranks of the advancing regiments, forcing them to fall back and re-form. Howe regrouped his men. With reinforcements of 400 fresh troops from the 63rd Regiment and the flank companies of the 2nd Marine Battalion from General Henry Clinton, who commanded a supporting force from Copp's Hill across the channel, he attacked the rebel position a third time. This time, the troops dropped their knapsacks and other superfluous accouterments. Some even removed their woolen red coats. The field artillery, which now had the proper ammunition, was ordered to enfilade the breastwork from the rebel left. They accomplished their mission and routed the defenders. Some retreated to the rear, others withdrew to the redoubt.

The British infantry advanced until they were close enough to deploy for a bayonet charge. They encountered devastating musket fire until they were within 10 yards of the redoubt. This time they broke through. The rebels ran out of ammunition and powder and retreated from the troops who advanced steadily with fixed bayonets, shouting and screaming, "stepping over the bodies of their comrades as if they were logs." The redcoats entered the redoubt from two sides and engaged the rebels who, lacking bayonets, defended themselves with rocks and clubbed muskets.

Retreat

The colonials retreated from Breed's Hill shortly before 5:00 PM. The retreat was an orderly one for inexperienced volunteers and militia, but when they reached Bunker Hill and met those who avoided the front line, they all fled. Howe's depleted regiments could not stop the escape.

Dr. Joseph Warren, who had been named general of militia 3 days earlier, on June 14, stood firm in the rear guard, wearing a pale blue coat over a lace-trimmed, satin waistcoat. He was shot in the head and fell into a trench. A soldier plunged a bayonet into his body, then stripped him of his clothes.

The colonials lost about 441 men (140 killed and 301 wounded, of whom 30 were captured) while the redcoats lost 1,053 (226 killed and 827 wounded)—almost half the force engaged. This included 63 officers wounded and 27 killed. Peter Salem, an African American, distinguished himself by shooting Major John Pitcairn (1722–1775) through the head. Salem Poor, a freeman who served in the militia under Benjamin Ames, is credited with shooting Lieutenant Colonel James Abercrombie (d. 1775). Most of men wounded at Bunker Hill were not brought to the hospitals in Boston until evening. Many died of shock or by hemorrhaging before then. Others developed gangrene.

Bunker Hill was a Pyrrhic victory, its strategic effect practically nil since the two armies remained in virtually the same position they had held before. Its consequences, nevertheless, cannot be ignored. A force of farmers and townsmen, fresh from their fields and shops, with hardly a semblance of orthodox military organization, had met and fought on equal terms with a professional British army. This astonishing feat had a sobering effect on the British, for it taught them that Patriot resistance was not to be overcome easily. Never again would British commanders lightly attempt such an assault on rebels in fortified positions. Bunker Hill, along with Lexington and Concord, went far to create the American tradition that the citizen soldier, when aroused, is more than a match for the trained professional, a tradition that was to be reflected in American military policy for generations afterward.

Boston (June 17, 1775 to March 17, 1776)

There are many historic sites in Boston, Massachusetts.
http://www.nps.gov/bost/index.htm

Among them is Boston's Old North Church with a sculpture of Paul Revere on horseback (see Photo MA-12) nearby.

Paul Revere lived in a house (see Photo MA-11) in Boston's North End, which lies at the bottom of a hill. The dominant structure at the top of the hill, a short distance away, is his parish church, the Old North Church.

The rear of the Old North Church can be seen in the background of Photo MA-12. Paul Revere arranged to have lanterns hung in the church's steeple as a signal to alert the Patriots which route the British Regulars would take to Lexington and Concord. The front of the church faces the Charles River and Charlestown. The lanterns were hung in this part of the steeple. The original steeple was destroyed in a gale in 1804, rebuilt in 1806, and repaired in 1834 and 1847. Descendants of Paul Revere restored it to its original lines in 1912. It was repaired again in 1934, but Hurricane Carol destroyed it again in August, 1954. The current steeple, erected in 1955, follows the lines and the height (190 feet) of the original.
http://www.oldnorth.com/

Paul Revere is buried in the Old Granary burial ground in Boston. His grave (see Photo MA-13) is aside that of John Hancock. Other nearby residents include Samuel Adams, Crispus Attucks and other victims of the Boston Massacre, and the parents of Benjamin Franklin. The grave is about 0.5 mile away from Revere's house, near the Boston Common which, ironically, is where the Regulars were camped.

Boston had a population of about 16,000 people in 1775. It was situated on a peninsula with a very narrow neck of land at its base, called Boston Neck. General Thomas Gage (1719–1787) protected the city from a land attack by fortifying Boston Neck, but artillery on the hills on the Charlestown peninsula or on Dorchester Heights on a much wider peninsula to the south (South Boston) would definitely threaten the city.

Gage had an army of only 3,500 men in January, 1775. He waited in vain for reinforcements and sent out officers in civilian clothes to make maps of the surrounding countryside and to draw plans of places likely to be centers of resistance. By the end of April, an estimated 10,000 men gathered on the hills overlooking Boston, causing General Gage to become increasingly concerned. He could see the rebels gathering in ever-increasing numbers on the hills around him. Their fires could be seen burning at night, as they made encampments, dug entrenchments, and collected supplies by cart and carriage. Dr. Joseph Warren (1741–1775), who was now President of the Massachusetts Provincial Congress appealed for even more men as the provincials began an 11-month siege of the city.

The appeal brought hundreds of men to the camps around Boston. After the battle of Bunker Hill, neighboring towns sent their minutemen or militia to help in the siege of Boston. Within a few weeks, the number had grown to about 15,000. Artemas Ward, a major-general of the Massachusetts militia, commanded them.

As the Patriots dug themselves in, they sniped at the enemy sentries and fired on their guard ships. John Trumbull (1756–1843), the 19-year-old son of the Governor of Connecticut, described the situation:

> The entire army, if it deserved the name, was but an assemblage of brave, enthusiastic, undisciplined country lads; the officers in general, quite as ignorant of military life as the troops, excepting a few elderly men, who had seen some irregular service among the provincials, under Lord Amherst. Our first occupation was to secure our positions, by constructing fieldworks for defense.
>
> Nothing of military importance occurred for some time; the enemy occasionally fired upon our working parties, whenever they approached too nigh to their works; and in order to familiarize our raw soldiers to this exposure, a small reward was offered in general orders, for every ball fired by the enemy, which should be picked up and brought to head-quarters. This soon produced the intended effect—a fearless emulation among the men; but it produced also a very unfortunate result; for when the soldiers saw a ball, after having struck and rebounded from the ground several times (*en ricochet*) roll sluggishly along, they would run and place a foot before it, to stop it, not aware that a heavy ball retains a sufficient impetus to overcome such an obstacle. The consequence was, that several brave lads lost their feet, which were crushed by the weight of the rolling shot. The order was of course withdrawn, and they were cautioned against touching a ball, until it was entirely at rest.

Major General John Thomas (1724–1776), Ward's most trusted senior officer, commanded one of the 2 brigades on the American right wing at Roxbury opposite Boston Neck. Most of the rest remained in reserve at Cambridge. These units included some African-American men. Three "slaves—Inlisted with the Consent of their Masters" came in Colonel John Nixon's (1727–1815) regiment from New Hampshire, camping on Winter Hill in September, 1775. Another New Hampshire company stationed at Winter Hill in late 1775 included 2 African Americans. General Thomas wrote:

> In the regiments at Roxbury, we have some Negroes; but I look on them, in General, Equally Serviceable with other men, for Fatigue & in action; many of them have proved themselves brave.

General George Washington (1732–1799) organized his army and maintained a siege around Boston with his limited supplies. Congress and the individual colonies sponsored voyages to the West Indies, where the French and Dutch had conveniently exported quantities of war materials. Washington put some of his troops on board ship and with an improvised navy succeeded in capturing numerous British supply ships. He sent Colonel Henry Knox (1750–1806), later to be his Chief of Artillery, to Fort Ticonderoga. In the winter of 1775–1776, Knox brought some 50 pieces of captured cannon (see Photo MA-10) to Cambridge over poor or nonexistent roads in icebound New York and New England. By March, 1776, despite deficiencies in the number of Continentals, Washington was ready to close in on Boston.

In addition to the problems brought about by the war and the occupation, Boston spent a difficult winter of 1775–1776. The winter was very cold and wet. The rebels cut off supplies, creating a severe fuel shortage. The army demolished a number of houses, wharves, stores, and vessels belonging to rebels, using the wood to heat their living quarters until a coal ship finally arrived in January. They tore down the "useless houses" in Charlestown—the few that were not destroyed in the Battle of Bunker Hill—dividing them into lots and assigning portions to each regiment. The supply was so scarce that the soldiers disobeyed orders and ignored severe prohibitions and demolished houses and fences. On December 5, General William Howe (1732–1786) directed "the provost to go his rounds, attended by the executioner, with orders to hang up on the spot the first man he should detect in the fact, without waiting for further proof for trial." When no fuel supply had arrived by the 14th, he authorized working parties to take down the Old North Church and 100 old wooden houses.

An account written on December 14 says: "The distress of the troops and inhabitants in Boston is great beyond all possible description. Neither vegetables, flour, nor pulse for the inhabitants; and the king's stores so very short, none can be spared from them; no fuel, and the winter set in remarkably severe. The troops and inhabitants absolutely and literally starving for want of provisions and fire. Even salt provision is fifteen pence sterling per pound." When ships brought fresh provisions, the prices were so expensive that most of the soldiers couldn't afford them.

Epidemics of scurvy, dysentery, and other diseases broke out. Smallpox spread through the troops, who were generally inoculated. Military commanders thought this disease alone would give them sufficient protection against an enemy assault. Many men died, and funerals became almost as common as punishments for stealing. Some of the offenders were hanged, some were sentenced to receive 400, some 600, some 1,000 lashes on the bare back with a cat-o'-nine-tails (see Photo MA-14). This punishment was extended to those who received stolen goods.

Discipline was necessary to preserve order in the military and punishment was common. The usual penalty was a whipping with a small whip called a cat-o'-nine-tails, or "cat" for short. In the navy, the cat-o'-nine-tails was kept in a bag aboard ship. If the captain did not know who to punish for an offense he would threaten to punish several sailors, hoping that one would reveal the true culprit. When a sailor told the captain the offender's identity, he had "let the cat out of the bag" for punishment—a phrase which today means revealing a secret.

Along with the scarcity of heating fuel, a severe epidemic of dysentery broke out. It attacked the soldiers first in their cramped quarters. It then spread to the inhabitants in and around the city. Abigail Adams and her children all became ill, but they recovered. Her mother, her husband's brother, and a domestic servant all died from the disease. Abigail could do nothing to prevent the deaths from dysentery, but smallpox was another matter. Soldiers returning from the army that had invaded Canada and ill Bostonians would probably spread the disease across New England. She began making arrangements to have herself and her children inoculated. This was a difficult decision for an 18th-century person. Inoculation was a new and emerging medical technique that required being deliberately infected with the disease.

The risk of getting smallpox "in the natural way" could result in death. It was quite another matter to expose oneself knowingly and willingly to the disease, so no parents wanted to expose their children to the disease and risk death or serious disfigurement. Consequently, people refused inoculation or postponed it as long as possible. The war forced them to face the issue because smallpox followed the armies. Some colonials even charged the army with intentionally spreading the disease. Many wives, like Abigail

Adams, had to make these life-or-death decisions on their own, in the absence of their husbands, whenever a large number of soldiers from either side arrived in a given area.

The British soldiers slept in leaky tents and built huts during the day. They believed the rebels besieging them lived more comfortably in barracks and in the entrenchments they were constructing so quickly. They feared that the rebels would open fire on them at any moment. The soldiers may have been lions, but they were lions confined in a den, and the provincial rebels were their keepers.

Dorchester Heights (March 4–17, 1776)

Thomas Park, at the end of Telegraph Street off Dorchester Street in South Boston, is named for Major General John Thomas (1724–1776) who commanded the operations on Dorchester Heights.

The topography of Dorchester Heights has changed considerably since 1776. Some of the hills have been leveled, and landfill has pushed the shoreline further away. The Boston skyline and harbor can be seen over the roofs of the houses surrounding Thomas park. The north-south streets provide restricted views that evoke the hill's strategic importance, but there are no redoubts or cannon on Dorchester Heights. A 115-foot white marble monument, commissioned in 1898 and dedicated in 1902, marks what remains of the heights. The steeple, in the style of a colonial meetinghouse, can be seen from quite a distance. Stone markers identify the approximate locations of the redoubts (see Photo MA-15).

While the effort to conquer Canada was moving toward its dismal end, General George Washington (1732–1799) finally took the initiative at Boston. The Patriots captured over 100 iron cannon and several mortars at Fort Ticonderoga in a surprise attack on May 10, 1775. In the winter, Henry Knox (1750–1806), a former bookseller and now Chief of Artillery in the Continental Army, brought about 50 of the best artillery pieces to Cambridge over poor or nonexistent roads in icebound New York and New England (see Photos MA-10 and MA-15).

On March 4, 1776, Major General John Thomas (1724–1776) directed 2,000 men and 360 oxcarts to the top of Dorchester Heights to mount the cannon aimed at the troops in Boston and their ships in the harbor. As the ground was still frozen, the men used pre-cut heavy timbers to build fortifications above ground.

Sir William Howe (1732–1786), who had succeeded General Thomas Gage (1719–1787) in command, planned to capture Dorchester Heights on the night of March 5–6 but called it off when he saw the fortifications on the hill (see Photo MA-15). He reportedly said that the rebels had done more work in one night than his troops could have done in months. He blamed a storm that began a few hours after the attack would have begun for altering his decision. A few days later, Washington fortified Nook's Hill, also known as Dorchester Hill, about half a mile north and closer to Boston.

By March 7, Howe had already decided to move his army out of Boston. It would be presumptuous to say that their exit was solely a consequence of rebel pressure. Howe had concluded long since that Boston was a poor strategic base and intended to stay only until the transports arrived to take his army to Halifax in Nova Scotia to regroup and await reinforcements. Nevertheless, Washington's maneuvers hastened his departure. The troops boarded their ships on March 17 and sailed for New York. The re-occupation of Boston was an important psychological victory for the Patriots, balancing the disappointments of the Canadian campaign. The stores of cannon and ammunition General Gage was forced to leave behind were a welcome addition to the meager rebel arsenal.

5

RHODE ISLAND

Rhode Island contributed 10,192 men to the war effort—4,284 militia and 5,908 Continental Army.

See the Rhode Island map.

Newport

As in Philadelphia, there was no battle fought in Newport itself, although there was a naval battle on August 10. Newport was headquarters for the British, then the French, and it served as one of Rhode Island's five capitals that rotated every few months. The Battle of Rhode Island was fought just outside of Newport (in Portsmouth—see below), but there are still fortifications in Newport.

Newport has many colonial homes and other 18th-century properties of interest. Many of them housed French or British officers during the War for American Independence.

The Colony House (1739), the seat of the General Assembly, Rhode Island's first state house, and the nation's second oldest Capitol, still stands. General Jean Baptiste Donatien de Vimeur Comte de Rochambeau (1725–1807) greeted Washington here. The Declaration of Independence was read from its balcony, and the Federal Constitution was ratified in the building in 1790.

`http://www.newporthistorical.com/the2.htm`

The British had a fort and batteries at the site of Fort Adams (off Harrison Avenue). The remains of earthen redoubts built and occupied by the British can still be seen at Castle Hill, Miantonomi Hill (Admiral Kalbfus Road and Hillside Avenue), and Sunset Hill.

Green End (Bliss Hill) Fort on Vernon Avenue in Newport is probably the hardest site to find. Coming south on RI 214, at the intersection of RI 214 and Green End Avenue, go right. When Green End Avenue bears to the left, continue straight on Miantonomi Avenue to the second left (Boulevard Avenue), turn left onto Vernon Avenue which is a dead end. A short distance down the street, there's a clearing on the left that looks like a park. This is the site of a half-acre redoubt which anchored the eastern end of the British fortifications protecting Newport from a land attack. It is important because it allows locating other fortifications which no longer exist. When the British left Newport, the redoubt was occupied by the French. A 7-foot granite marker identifies the landmark. The ramparts are overgrown with trees and shrubs.

One or more British warships patrolled the mouth of Narragansett Bay from the arrival of HMS *Squirrel* in the autumn of 1763 until the beginning of the War for American Independence. The animosity engendered by their presence and the enforcement of the Navigation Laws which required stopping, searching, and seizing vessels caused frequent quarrels in Newport streets.

The bitterness increased with the beginning of the war, and the townspeople refused to supply British ships, considering it as aiding and supporting the enemy. The Royal Navy retaliated by robbing supply ships and threatening to fire on the town. As the preservation of the town depended upon supplying the British fleet with provisions, the General Assembly exempted the town from the penalties prescribed by the act of October, 1775.

When the British fleet evacuated Boston on March 17, 1776, the vessels in Newport also left, probably to go to Halifax. Narragansett Bay was now free of the annoyances of the British navy for the first time in over 10 years. But the respite was brief.

Admiral Sir Peter Parker (1721–1811) sailed up the west passage of Narragansett Bay with a fleet of 7 ships of the line, 4 frigates, and 70 transports on December 7, 1776 after feigning an attack on Connecticut. The following day, between 5,000 to 8,000 British and Hessian troops landed on Aquidneck Island, also called Rhode Island, without resistance. The Patriots could only muster 600 men to oppose them and had to withdraw. This gave the British control of Newport, Rhode Island's capitol and its most prosperous town, and all of Aquidneck Island. They used Newport as a base to harass American shipping. British occupation adversely affected the recruitment of soldiers for the Continental Army. Newport was now the second largest British stronghold in the American colonies after New York and would remain so until October 25, 1779.

Recruiting

The Rhode Island General Assembly voted to raise 2 regiments of infantry and 1 of artillery for a duration of 15 months "for the defense of the United States in general, and this State in particular." The State offered a bounty of £16 (approximately $2,150 in today's currency) in addition to what Congress granted in an attempt to stimulate recruitment for the Continental Army. It also promised each enlistee arms, accouterments, a blanket, and a knapsack. Increasing the bounty to £22 (approximately $2,955) in April did not prove any more successful, nor did fining towns £10 (approximately $1,420) for every soldier that they fell short of their quota.

Rhode Island, as most other states, still could not meet its quota for the Continental Army, leaving General George Washington (1732–1799) with a shortage of troops. James Mitchell Varnum (1748–1789), a brigadier general of the Continental troops from Rhode Island, suggested to General Washington, on December 29, 1776 that the "deficiencies in the Rhode Island battalion be made up by enlisting Negroes." Washington reversed his earlier decision to prohibit African Americans from serving in the army and wrote a letter to Governor Nicholas Cooke (1717–1782) of Rhode Island recommending their recruitment.

In 1778, faced with the difficulties of recruiting soldiers, Rhode Island and Massachusetts voted to recruit regiments of colored men. Rhode Island was the first to do so in February, 1778, when it enacted "that every able-bodied negro, mulatto or Indian man slave, in the State, may enlist into either of the two said battalions to serve during the continuance of the present war with Great Britain." No records exist of the debates in the General Assembly over their recruitment, but the important point is that the legislators decided to free these slaves before enlisting them in the Continental Army.

Not everybody agreed to arm African Americans. Some members of the Assembly signed a "Protest Against Enlisting Slaves to Serve in the Army." They argued that the state did not have enough slaves who would be likely to enlist and the project should be abandoned. They may also have feared that creating a regiment of men of color might also give the British the idea of using men of color against the Patriots or that it might appear that the state had purchased a band of slaves to defend the country.

Three months after the Rhode Island General Assembly voted to enlist slaves in the Continental Army, it rescinded its order. Three-fifths of the members of the newly elected assembly had not sat in the previous assembly. This body voted in May, 1778, not to allow slaves to join the army after June 10, 1778, stating that "it is necessary for answering the purposed intent by said act that the same should be temporary." Even though the Assembly reversed itself, African Americans continued to enlist after the June 10 deadline. Records of the State Treasurer indicate that 44 slaves enrolled in the regiment between June 12 and October 13.

Estimates of the number of African Americans who joined the 1st Rhode Island Regiment run from 100 to 300. The weekly returns of the Regiment indicate that "the new rais'd regiment of blacks," commanded by Colonel Christopher Greene (1737–1781) consisted of 197 men, excluding commissioned and non-commissioned officers" by June 10, 1778.

The French Fleet

After the signing of the Treaty of Alliance with France on February 6, 1778, France openly allied itself with the American cause. Admiral Comte Jean-Baptiste-Charles-Henri-Hector d'Estaing (1729–1794) sailed from Toulon on April 13, 1778, with 12 ships of the line, 4 frigates, and 1,000 troops. His fleet carried Monsieur Gerard, the first Minister from France to the United States and the first minister from any foreign power to come to the new nation. Five or six officers of the Continental Navy were also on board as was Silas Deane, returning from diplomatic service.

Eighty days of storms delayed the fleet which arrived in Delaware Bay on July 7, 10 days after Admiral Richard Howe's (1726–1799) fleet, which d'Estaing planned to attack, had sailed for New York. D'Estaing proceeded to New York, but the water around the harbor was too shallow for his largest ships; so he sailed to Newport, after 11 days, to support the attack on the Crown forces based there. He anchored his fleet in a wide crescent commanding the entrance to Narragansett Bay on July 29.

While d'Estaing waited for the Continental Army to assemble under Major General John Sullivan (1740–1795), he worked at destroying British vessels in Narragansett Bay. In doing so, he rendered 212 guns inactive. The Americans recovered some of these guns and used them against their former owners.

The French fleet proposed to cannonade the town of Newport while General Sullivan attacked it by land. However, Sullivan, convinced that his troops were not yet ready, asked for a few days' delay, followed by similar requests until 9 days had elapsed.

Major General Marie Jean Paul Joseph du Motier Marquis de Lafayette (1757–1834) arrived in Providence on Sunday, August 2—ahead of the troops he was bringing from General George Washington (1732–1799). The following morning at 9:00 AM, he was on board d'Estaing's flagship, *Languedoc*.

The 2 Continental brigades and 2 companies of the train of artillery from the Grand Army at White Plains, New York, reached Providence on August 3. Brigadier General James Mitchell Varnum (1748–1789) commanded one of the brigades and Brigadier General John Glover (1732–1797) commanded the other.

Uniting the French and Americans proved difficult. The French officers considered the American officers as social inferiors. They viewed the soldiers more as an armed rabble than as an army because of their lack of rigid discipline, their varied clothing, and heterogeneous weapons. The Americans also had their prejudices against the French derived from the Seven Years War (also known as the French and Indian War). They considered the officers proud, excitable, and jealous of glory.

General Sullivan and Major General Nathanael Greene (1742–1786) wanted to land the American troops followed by the French troops at a single point under the protection of d'Estaing's fleet. They would then attack Newport by land while the fleet attacked it by sea. d'Estaing disagreed, insisting that the French and Americans land simultaneously at two points. Negotiations went on for several days. It was finally agreed, at d'Estaing's suggestion, that the American forces would be divided. General Greene would cross from Tiverton to Portsmouth while Lafayette would cross simultaneously from Conanicut (Jamestown Island) to Portsmouth with the French marines, sailors, and infantry along with some Continental troops and militia.

General Lafayette left Providence for Tiverton on August 6 with General Varnum's and General Glover's brigades. General Sullivan transferred his headquarters to the same place and took command of the army the next day. The combined attack was set for Monday, August 10.

Count d'Estaing brought 8 of his ships through the main channel of Narragansett Bay and anchored off Gould Island about noon on August 8 in preparation for landing the marines and soldiers the next day on Conanicut. The Crown forces evacuated the fort at Butts Hill in Portsmouth late in the afternoon and withdrew within the outer line of defenses at Newport. These defenses extended from Coddington's Cove to Easton's Pond.

When General Sullivan learned of the evacuation of the fort at Butts Hill on the morning of August 9, he ordered that it be occupied at once. The French regarded this action as a deliberate breach of the agreement for a simultaneous landing and as an attempt to deprive the French of the glory of equal participation in the first landing. They also considered it an insult to the dignity of France and began to be suspicious of the Americans.

When d'Estaing received a message from General Sullivan announcing that a portion of his troops had already landed and he needed artillery support, d'Estaing stopped drilling his troops and arranging for their transportation the next day. He ordered the troops already landed on Conanicut to go to General Sullivan's assistance, but, as the fog lifted, he saw Lord Howe's fleet of 36 ships carrying 4,000 troops to reinforce General Sir Robert Pigot (1720–1796) at Newport. Taken completely by surprise, d'Estaing's fleet was distributed in the three channels of Narragansett Bay and a large portion of his troops was on shore. He re-embarked his troops immediately and gathered his ships together during the night to prepare for action.

At 8:30 Monday morning, August 10, d'Estaing's fleet set sail to attack the British fleet, promising to return as soon as possible. He left 3 frigates in the East Channel and a galley in the West Channel to assist General Sullivan. D'Estaing's ships were larger and had more firing power than Howe's, but a ferocious gale on the night of August 11 dispersed and battered both fleets. Howe returned to New York to refit. D'Estaing returned to Narragansett Bay on August 19 and 20, but he refused to cooperate with Sullivan whom he disliked. He sailed to Boston at midnight on August 21 to refit his ships. General Marie Joseph de Motier Marquis de Lafayette (1757–1834) rode to Boston to entice the Frenchman and his 4,000 soldiers back into the fray but to no avail. (For the rest of the story about the Battle of Rhode Island, see Portsmouth below.)

The French returned to Newport in the summer of 1780 when Admiral Charles Louis d'Arsac Chevalier de Ternay (1722–1780) arrived with a fleet of 7 ships of the line, 3 frigates, and transports carrying General Jean Baptiste Donatien de Vimeur Comte de Rochambeau (1725–1807) and 4,000 troops. They occupied the vacated British base.

When Admiral Louis, Comte de Barras (d. ca. 1800) reached Boston in early May, 1781, he brought news that Admiral François Joseph Paul Comte de Grasse (1722–1788) was headed for the West Indies with instructions to cooperate in North America. Rochambeau met with General Washington in Wethersfield, Connecticut, on May 21, 1781 to plan their strategy for the Yorktown campaign.

Portsmouth (August 28–29, 1778)
Butts Hill
Battle of Rhode Island

> The Battle of Rhode Island is the only major land battle fought in the state. Butts Hill Fort, Patriots Park, and the Portsmouth Town Hall are historical sites related to this battle in Portsmouth, Rhode Island.
>
> Some earthworks of Butts Hill Fort (see Photo RI-1) remain (Butts Street off Sprague Street in Portsmouth, behind the high school).
>
> Patriots' Park (RI 114 northbound and U.S. 24) commemorates the contributions of the 1st Rhode Island Regiment (comprised of approximately 95 former slaves and 30 free African Americans) which earned accolades for bravery for repulsing a Hessian attack three times (see Photo RI-3).
>
> The Portsmouth Town Hall occupies the top of Quaker Hill on RI 138. A cannon recovered from the HMS *Flora* and placed in front of the Portsmouth Town Hall marks the site of the British position during the battle. The Quaker Meeting House that gives the hill its name still stands at Hedley Street and Middle Road. A marker at the corner of Union Street and East Main Road identifies where the first shots were fired.

Fort Barton (Highland Road at Lawton Avenue, Tiverton), an earthen fort, remains in fairly complete shape as does another round earthwork just to the north on private land. Fort Barton was the launching point for General John Sullivan's invasion force for the battle and their refuge after the retreat.

A statue in Fall River, Massachusetts (in North Park at President Avenue [RI 6] and Rock Street) commemorates Lafayette's ride to Boston in an attempt to convince Admiral d'Estaing to return to Rhode Island.

Admiral Comte Jean-Baptiste-Charles-Henri-Hector d'Estaing (1729–1794) arrived off the coast of Delaware with 12 ships of the line and some 4,000 French soldiers in late June, 1778. He proceeded to New York to try to capture Sir Richard Howe's fleet of 9 ships in New York harbor. However, when he arrived off Sandy Hook on July 9, he discovered that the water was too shallow for his ships to get at the British fleet. General George Washington (1732–1799) and d'Estaing decided instead to attack the British at Newport, Rhode Island, the second largest British seaport at the time. The British had held Newport since December, 1776. General Sir Robert Pigot (1720–1796) now defended it with only 3,000 men.

Major General John Sullivan (1740–1795) commanded about 1,000 Continental soldiers. He called out about 6,000 militia; General George Washington (1732–1799) sent him 3,000 more Continentals under Major General Marie Jean Paul Joseph du Motier Marquis de Lafayette (1757–1834), bringing the total American force in Rhode Island to 10,000 troops in July, 1778. In the first week of August, Sullivan's army was camped at Tiverton, Rhode Island. The French landed on Conanicut Island (Jamestown Island) in Narragansett Bay. The Americans planned to cross at Tiverton and move down the east side of Rhode Island (now called Aquidneck Island) while the French would land on the western side, hoping to trap General Sir Robert Pigot (1720–1796) on the island.

Admiral Richard Howe (1726–1799) had received a squadron of 13 vessels from England bringing his fleet to 36 warships. He came north to challenge Admiral Comte Jean-Baptiste-Charles-Henri-Hector d'Estaing (1729–1794) who sailed out to meet him with his 12 ships which were larger and had more firing power than Howe's. A ferocious gale on the night of August 11 dispersed both fleets. Howe returned to New York to refit. D'Estaing's fleet returned to Narragansett Bay on August 19 and 20, but d'Estaing refused to cooperate with Sullivan whom he disliked and sailed to Boston at midnight on August 21 to refit his ships.

The Crown forces evacuated the forts opposite Sullivan, inducing him to land on August 9, 1778, instead of the 10th. He established his camp on the northern part of the island at Butts Hill Fort (see Photo RI-1). His army extended across the island from shore to shore. He then advanced to within a mile of the British fortifications on August 15 and began to establish siege lines. He concentrated on the eastern side of the island, expecting the French to take the western side. However, when d'Estaing left, so did many of the militia. Sullivan's army dropped to fewer than 5,000 men in a few days. Moreover, a large part of that army consisted of the Rhode Island militia which had been called out on August 1 to serve 20 days and only had 5 more days to serve, so

Sullivan asked Governor Greene (William Greene, Jr., Governor from May, 1778, to May, 1786) for the other half of the militia. He realized that, without the protection of the French fleet, he would be vulnerable to fire from British ships in Narragansett Bay.

Work on the American batteries proceeded during August 17 and 18 despite cannon fire from the British batteries across the valley. The first American battery opened on the morning of the 19th, and 300 cannonballs had been fired by 10:00 AM. The British evacuated one redoubt by 1:00 PM. The incessant cannonade between the two armies lasted 2 days, causing the British to abandon their outer line of defense.

D'Estaing's fleet returned to Narragansett Bay on August 19, but it was so battered by the storm that the Count sent an officer to inform Sullivan that he returned as promised but could not remain to assist him. He sailed to Boston around midnight to refit his ships.

Even though the Crown forces withdrew their artillery from the outer defenses, Sullivan felt too weak to attack because the "volunteers which composed a greater part of my army had returned [home] and reduced my numbers to little more than that of the enemy. Between two and three thousand returned in the course of 24 hours and others were still going off upon a supposition that nothing could be done before the return of the French fleet." Sullivan started removing his heavy baggage to the north of the island during the night of Sunday, August 23 and continued the following nights.

The arrival of 3 British frigates on August 27 brought news that Major General Charles Grey (1729–1807) had already sailed from New York with 3,500 men bound for Newport. The following day, convinced that a crisis was developing, Sullivan requested Lafayette to ride to Boston to urge d'Estaing to hurry the repairs to his ships and to beg that he would send his 4,000 troops overland to join the Americans on Rhode Island (Aquidneck Island). Meanwhile, Sullivan began to withdraw to the north of the island where he would hold the ground until he received definite information about the French fleet. Lafayette's trip proved fruitless.

Sullivan placed his best unit, the Continental troops with some militia, in the first line in front of Butts Hill. The militia formed the second and third lines. The second line took position in line with or slightly forward of Fort Butts while the third line was placed behind Butts Hill. The 1st Rhode Island Regiment, the black regiment, with its core of 95 ex-slaves and 30 freedmen, most of them raw recruits, protected the right flank (see Photo RI-3).

When General Pigot awoke on August 29 and found the American batteries silent, he ordered an attack. There were two main roads running north and south on either side of the island. (They correspond roughly to East Main Road [RI 138] and West Main Road [RI 114].) The British troops advanced along East Main Road while the Hessians marched up West Main Road. They encountered little opposition until they reached Union Street, about 2.5 miles south of Quaker Hill.

Pigot anchored his right flank on Quaker Hill (RI 138 and Crossing Street) and his left flank on Turkey Hill (in the vicinity of Cory's Lane and Hedley Street). He advanced toward Butts Hill Fort but could not break through Sullivan's left flank defended by Brigadier General James Mitchell Varnum (1748–1789) and Brigadier General John Glover (1732–1797).

The Hessians (see Photo RI-2) attacked Sullivan's right where they made 3 charges and experienced stiffer resistance than they had expected. They found large bodies of troops behind earthworks "chiefly wild looking men in their shirt sleeves, and among them many negroes." The Rhode Islanders fought exceptionally well and maintained their ground for an hour. The arrival of reinforcements helped to prevent the Hessians from breaking through and inflicting heavy losses on the Americans and the defenders forced them back to Turkey Hill.

Colonel John Trumbull (1756–1843), Sullivan's aide-de-camp, carried an order to retire to Colonel Edward Wigglesworth (d. 1826) who commanded the rear guard on Quaker Hill. He describes the scene:

> I had to mount the hill by a broad, smooth road, more than a mile in length from the foot to the summit where was the scene of conflict . . . At first I saw a round shot or two drop near me and pass bounding on. I met poor Colonel Toussard, who had just lost one arm blown off by the discharge of a field piece, for the possession of which there was an ardent struggle. He was led off by a small party. Soon after, I saw Captain Walker of H. Jackson's regiment, who had received a musket ball through his body, mounted behind a person on horseback. He bid me a melancholy farewell and died before night. Next grapeshot began to sprinkle around me and soon after musket balls fell in my path like hailstones. This was not to be borne. I spurred on my horse to the summit of the hill and found myself in the midst of the melee. "Don't say a word, Trumbull," cried the gallant commander. "I know your errand but don't speak; we will beat them in a moment."
>
> "Colonel Wigglesworth, do you see those troops crossing obliquely from the west road towards your rear?"
>
> "Yes, they are Americans coming to our support."
>
> "No Sir, those are Germans; mark, their dress is blue and yellow not buff; they are moving to fall into your rear, and intercept your retreat. Retire instantly—don't lose a moment or you will be cut off."

The gallant man obeyed reluctantly and withdrew the guard in fine style slowly, but safely.

About 4 o'clock, the Crown forces withdrew to Quaker Hill and Turkey Hill. Sullivan also withdrew when he learned that 5,000 fresh British troops were on their way. Brigadier General John Glover (1732–1797) directed sailors to successfully ferry the troops across the Sakonnet River and evacuated the army to Fort Barton in Tiverton during the night of August 31. The Americans were safely in Tiverton by midnight. General Lafayette called the battle of Rhode Island "the best fought action of the war."

General Sullivan reported the Americans suffered only 211 casualties. Colonel Christopher Greene's regiment had a total of 22, of which 2 were killed, 9 wounded, and 11 missing. Of the 138 African Americans engaged, only 1 was killed and 7 were wounded, none seriously. General Pigot reported his losses to General Clinton as 260 killed, wounded, and missing. Many accounts report much larger figures. The *Providence Gazette* of September 5, 1778 supposed British casualties at "upward of 700." A week later, it reported from "an officer who arrived on Wednesday in a Flag of Truce from Newport we learn that the Enemy acknowledged that they lost 1,023 men killed, wounded, and taken in the late action on Rhode Island."

The day after the battle, the Hessian colonel "applied to exchange his command and go to New York, because he dared not lead his regiment again to battle, lest his men shoot him for having caused so much loss." General Sir Henry Clinton (1730–1795) arrived in Newport on the morning of September 1 with 72 ships and 4,500 men.

During the battle, the African-American soldiers generally fought side by side with whites, but the Battle of Rhode Island is probably the only one in which African Americans played a conspicuous role as a racial group, even though they were still in the ranks at Yorktown, Virginia. A rumor began to spread through the American camp the day after the battle that the African American troops did not perform well. General Sullivan quickly stopped the rumor by circulating a statement that the reports were false and that "by the best Information the Commander-in-Chief thinks that the Regiment will be intituled to a proper share of the Honours of the day." (See Photo RI-3.) The regiment was then stationed in East Greenwich where it protected the West coast of Narragansett Bay for a little more than a year. When the British left Newport, the Rhode Island Continental Regiments moved in. The 1st and 2nd Rhode Island Regiments were combined in January, 1780, and served in the Yorktown campaign.

This first effort at French and American cooperation resulted in a fiasco that produced a great deal of ill feeling. Admiral d'Estaing left Boston for the West Indies. General Clinton also sent a large force there. Washington's army spent the winter in comparative quiet, except for several small raids near New York City which kept the inhabitants frightened.

6

CONNECTICUT

Connecticut contributed the second largest number of troops to the war: a total of 39,177 men—7,238 militia and 31, 939 in the Continental Army. All three of the Purple Hearts awarded by George Washington went to Connecticut men.

See the Connecticut map.

Danbury and Ridgefield (April 26–27, 1777)

> The David Taylor House on the left side of Main Street in Danbury, part of the Danbury Scott-Fanton Museum, has a good diorama with scale-model homes. It shows how this part of town was laid out and how the Crown forces destroyed it, virtually unopposed.
>
> The Keeler Tavern, 132 Main Street in Ridgefield, which is now a museum has a cannon-ball from the battle wedged in a wooden beam behind a panel on the exterior of the building.
>
> **http://www.keelertavernmuseum.org/**
>
> A sign on North Salem Road, a short distance from the fork at Ridgebury Road, near Titicus marks the site of the first engagement in the Battle of Ridgefield, where General Wooster (1711–1777) attacked the rear guard.
>
> A monument that appears like a tall, narrow tombstone, on Route CT 116, about a mile south of the intersection with Route CT 35 marks the site of a second encounter where Wooster was mortally wounded.
>
> At Compo Beach, southeast of Westport, two mounted cannon identify a driveway going to the beach. A tablet on the other side of a low stone wall commemorates the action at Compo Hill where Governor Tryon disembarked his men before the raid and where he returned to embark for New York.

Danbury, Connecticut was a manufacturing center and a storage supply depot for the Patriots in 1777. It was an obvious target for the Crown forces. New York Governor William Tryon (1729–1788) led 2,000 Loyalist and British troops against the town on Wednesday, April 23, 1777. They disembarked 2 days later near Fairfield and marched about 23 miles to Danbury to destroy a supply depot there. They also destroyed most of the town as well. They began late in the afternoon of Saturday, April 26, 1777 and continued the following day, burning 41 homes, barns, and warehouses.

On the night of April 26, an exhausted messenger arrived from Danbury to report that the Crown forces were burning the city and to ask Colonel Henry Ludington (d. 1817), of Fredericksburg, New York, to call out the militia and come defend the city. Colonel Ludington's 16-year-old daughter, Sybil, volunteered to spread the alarm. She rode her horse, Star, to Carmel, New York and on to Mahopac and Mahopac Falls, knocking on the door of each house. She continued over Barret Hill to Kent Cliffs, Peekskill, and Farmers Mill, then home through Stormville, covering 40 miles.

Governor Tryon left Danbury and headed west to Ridgebury before turning south to Ridgefield, 15 miles south of Danbury. A large number of men gathered at the Ludington home and marched to Ridgefield to block the Crown forces from returning to their ships in Long Island Sound on April 27. Brigadier General Benedict Arnold (1741–1801), who had been in nearby New Haven on personal business and brooding about Congress passing him over for promotion for his military exploits, assumed command of the American forces.

Brigadier General David Wooster (1711–1777) pursued Governor Tryon with 200 militia. Tryon and his men camped near the intersection of North Salem Road (Route CT 116) and Barlow Mountain Road (which no longer exists). General Wooster attacked the rear guard either around 8:00 AM or between 11:00 AM and noon. He captured 40 prisoners and withdrew quickly.

The militia had been firing at the redcoats constantly for more than an hour when they turned their 3 cannon against the militia. Wooster led his men forward to try to capture one of the guns. He had one horse killed beneath him and another wounded before getting shot in the spine with a musket ball. Paralyzed, he was taken to a nearby meetinghouse and then to Danbury by litter. He died 6 days later on May 2.

By this time, Arnold arrived with about 400 militia and organized a defense of the town by 11:00 AM about 1.2 miles south of where Wooster was wounded. They erected a barrier of farm carts, logs, and other impediments on a ridge at the narrowest part of Main Street. Here, they awaited Tryon's men who approached in 3 columns about 2:00 PM. Tryon reorganized his troops, putting 200 men on each flank and his 3 field pieces in the center. The cannon fired at the barricade while Tryon attacked Arnold's left. The superior numbers of the Crown forces compelled Arnold to withdraw, and he narrowly avoided capture. The British reported 27 men killed, 15 officers and 104 men wounded, and 29 men missing. The Americans lost General Wooster, 6 other officers, and 100 privates. The wounded comprised 3 officers and 250 privates. They also lost 50 privates captured.

Arnold prepared another defense across Governor Tryon's expected route to his ships, but a Loyalist guide led Governor Tryon and his men around the American lines to their fleet in Long Island Sound the next morning. Before Arnold could mount an attack, the redcoats made a diversionary attack which surprised the militia and allowed the army to embark for New York City.

Arnold was promoted to major general for his courage on the battlefield at Ridgefield. General David Wooster was buried in Wooster Cemetery in Danbury.

New Haven (July 5, 1779)

Black Rock Park or Nathan Hale Park (Woodward Avenue) overlooks New Haven harbor from the east. It contains a reconstruction of Black Rock Fort which was called Fort Rock before being renamed in honor of Nathan Hale after the War for American Independence. Most of the skirmishing occurred here.

http://www.forttours.com/pages/fortnathanhale.asp

East Rock Park, about 7 miles north of Black Rock, was a place Native Americans used for signaling. Many of the inhabitants of New Haven took refuge here during the raid by the Crown forces. The park covers 647 acres and contains a rock that is 359 feet high and 1.5 miles long.
http://cityofnewhaven.com/parks/eastrockpark.htm

Captain Benedict Arnold (1741–1801) mustered his 2nd Company, Connecticut Governor's Foot Guard, on New Haven Green on April 22, 1775. They forced the New Haven selectmen to surrender the keys to the municipal powder house and headed to Massachusetts. Too late to assist Lexington and Concord, this company helped fortify Bunker Hill.

New Haven, a notorious center for illicit trade in the mid-18th century, became General Henry Clinton's (1730–1795) prime objective in July, 1779, when he began a punitive expedition along the Connecticut coast. Clinton sent Brigadier General George Garth's (d. 1819) division to attack New Haven on July 5. Garth encountered little opposition until he reached a bridge across the West River. Here, a small band of about 25 volunteers, including Yale students, delayed the advance by taking up the planks of the bridge and mounting 2 guns and some earthworks there. The Crown forces detoured along Milford Hill to the Derby Road and entered the town about noon.

A second division under General William Tryon (1729–1788), former royal governor of New York, landed on the east side of the harbor and attacked Black Rock, a small garrison with 3 guns. The defenders annoyed the Crown forces considerably as they landed a short distance south of them. Garth's division joined with Tryon's division the next day. After securing his position, Garth planned to burn New Haven. However, the local militia were gathering in such numbers that Garth withdrew from the town after a certain amount of murder, rape, and pillage. The Crown forces and 30 or 40 prisoners re-embarked at Black Rock on the July 6 and continued their raids to the south. New Haven was spared the fate of Fairfield, Green Farms, and Norwalk which were burned during the next few days.

Wethersfield (May 21, 1781)

The Webb-Deane-Stevens Museum is at 211 Main Street in Wethersfield.
http://www.webb-deane-stevens.org/

The Joseph Webb House contains a mural of the Battle of Yorktown painted in 1916. Contrary to popular belief, the actual strategy for the final battle of the war was not formulated in this house. The generals only discussed their initial strategy here. The house is furnished as it supposedly looked when Washington and Rochambeau met here.

General George Washington (1732–1799) had been trying to persuade the French to cooperate in a combined land and naval assault on New York in the summer of 1781. General Jean Baptiste Donatien de Vimeur Comte de Rochambeau (1725–1807), commander of the French army in America, brought his 4,000 troops from Newport, Rhode Island in April and placed them under Washington's command. The prospects were still bleak since the combined Franco-American force numbered but 10,000 against General

Henry Clinton's (1730–1795) 17,000 in well-fortified positions. The two generals met in the Joseph Webb House in Wethersfield, Connecticut on May 21, 1781 to plan their strategy.

Rochambeau knew that 3,200 troops were on the way from the West Indies, but he had instructions not to disclose the information. He proposed attacking General Charles Cornwallis (1738–1805) in Virginia, but Washington thought it more prudent to attack New York, as it might draw enemy troops from the South. The two leaders continued a heated discussion, after which Rochambeau accepted Washington's plan but sent the French fleet to the Chesapeake anyway.

On August 14, Washington learned that the French fleet in the West Indies, commanded by Admiral François Joseph Paul Comte de Grasse (1722–1788), would not come to New York but would arrive in the Chesapeake later in the month and remain there until October 15. He saw immediately that, if he could achieve a superior concentration of force on the land side while de Grasse still held the bay, he could trap Cornwallis on the Virginia coast and destroy the British army at Yorktown before Clinton had a chance to relieve it.

Even without unified command of Army and Navy forces, Franco-American cooperation this time was excellent. Admiral Louis, Comte de Barras (d. ca. 1800) immediately put out to sea from Newport to join de Grasse. Washington sent orders to General Marie Joseph de Motier Marquis de Lafayette (1757–1834) to contain General Charles Cornwallis (1738–1805) at Yorktown. He then made a feint in the direction of New York to deceive Clinton. On August 21, he started the major portion of the Franco-American Army on a rapid secret movement to Virginia, via Chesapeake Bay, leaving only 2,000 Americans behind to watch Clinton.

Clinton heard that Washington met with the Comte de Rochambeau at Wethersfield, Connecticut and that Rochambeau offered to join him with 4000 French soldiers encamped around Newport. Clinton also feared that the Comte de Grasse was on his way from the West Indies with a large French fleet and more French troops to attack him. Since Cornwallis's force was almost four times as strong as Lafayette's, Clinton thought it reasonable to ask Cornwallis to send 3000 troops to New York as soon as possible. With his remaining troops, Cornwallis was to take a defensive position. (See also Yorktown, Virginia.)

Groton/New London (September 6, 1781)
Fort Griswold

Fort Griswold is on the east bank of the mouth of the Thames River at Monument Street and Park Avenue in Groton, Connecticut (see Photo CT-2).
> `http://dep.state.ct.us/stateparks/parks/fort_griswold.htm`

The Groton Monument rises 134 feet from the hilltop at Fort Griswold. It was dedicated in 1830 to the victims whose names appear on a tablet on the monument. The 17-acre park preserves portions of the earth and stone fortifications where a plaque commemorates Jordan Freeman (d. 1781) at the point where he impaled Major William Montgomery (see Photo CT-1).

Other buildings on the property include the Ebenezer Avery House, where the wounded were treated, and the Monument House which contains relics of the Fort Griswold massacre. Originally located on Thames Street, the house was moved here in 1971.

Fort Trumbull is on the west bank of the mouth of the Thames River in New London.
http://dep.state.ct.us/stateparks/parks/fort_trumbull.htm

General George Washington (1732–1799) was headed to Virginia in late August, 1781 when Benedict Arnold (1741–1801) proposed a diversionary strike on New London, a major storage depot in Connecticut. General Henry Clinton (1730–1795) gave him a command of 1,700 men. Arnold, who grew up in New London and knew the terrain well, set sail on September 6, 1781.

Two forts protected New London at the mouth of the Thames River: Fort Trumbull on the west bank and Fort Griswold (see Photo CT-2) on the east bank in what is now Groton, Connecticut. Arnold split his forces. He led the attack against the sparsely garrisoned Fort Trumbull on the west bank and Lieutenant Colonel Edmund Eyre (d. 1781) commanded the assault on Fort Griswold.

Stephen Hempstead, one of the survivors of the battle, records in his diary that Fort Griswold had stone walls 10 or 12 feet high surrounded by a ditch. It also had a wooden palisade 12 feet high and a parapet with gun embrasures. Platforms for cannon and a firing step were immediately behind the wall. A triangular breastwork and a redoubt with a 3-pounder protected a gate on one side. The southwest bastion had a flagstaff and 3 guns facing the river. The other bastion had 4 guns, 2 facing the river and 2 facing the opposite direction to cover the nearby gate.

Sergeant Rufus Avery (1752–1842), on guard duty at Fort Griswold, spotted Arnold's fleet about daybreak and had 2 of the fort's guns fired as a signal to the local militia that an attack was imminent. Arnold, expecting the signal, had a third gun fired immediately afterward, turning the alarm signal into a "good news" message. This prevented the militia in the neighboring towns from reinforcing the forts.

Arnold landed about 9:00 AM and easily routed the two dozen men at Fort Trumbull, who fired one volley, spiked their cannon and fled across the river to Fort Griswold which occupied the stronger position. Arnold destroyed about 150 buildings. The townspeople reported that he stood in the cemetery at Hempstead Street north of Bulkeley Square viewing the flames "with the apparent satisfaction of a Nero." Arnold claimed that accidental fires caused most of the destruction. (The cemetery is the final resting place of some 100 Revolutionary War veterans.) Arnold achieved no military objective in burning New London, the last important battle in the North. He further discredited his once outstanding record.

Lieutenant Colonel Edmund Eyre assaulted Fort Griswold about noon. His men advanced from behind some rocky ledges more than 2,000 feet away. Major William Montgomery (d. 1781) led another column behind a hill about 2,500 feet away. The fort was defended by Lieutenant Colonel William Ledyard (d. 1781) and about 140 men. Eyre attacked from three sides but had to retreat under heavy fire. A second assault was also repulsed. The British stormed the walls in desperate fighting.

Sergeant Avery recalls:

> I was at the gun with others when it was discharged into the British ranks and it cleared a very wide space in the solid columns. It has been reported by good authority that about twenty were killed and wounded by that one discharge of grapeshot. As soon as the column was broken by loss of men and officers they were seen to scatter and trail arms coming on with a quick step towards the fort and climbing to the west (the side facing the Thames). We continued firing but they advanced on the south and west side of the fort. Colonel Eyre was mortally wounded. Major Montgomery now advanced with his men coming on in solid columns bearing around to the north until they got east of the . . . battery which was east of the fort, then marching with a quick step into the battery. Here we sent among them large and repeated charges of grapeshot which destroyed a number as we could perceive them thinned and broken. Then they started for the fort a part of them in platoons discharging their guns, and some of the officers and men scattering they came around on the east and north side of the fort . . . Here Major Montgomery fell near the northeast part of the fort.

George Middleton, an eye-witness, recorded that Jordan Freeman, an African American and Ledyard's orderly, was one of two men responsible for fatally stabbing Major Montgomery with a spear in hand-to-hand combat when the British scaled the fort's walls. (See Photo CT-1.) He also reports Montgomery's last words were an order to put the garrison to death.

Despite losing their commanding officers, the attackers surrounded the fort and tried to open the gate, but were repulsed. Avery continues: "There was hard fighting and shocking slaughter and much blood spilled before another attempt was made to open the gates which was this time successful."

After 40 minutes of bloody fighting, the outnumbered Americans finally surrendered. Ledyard offered his sword to Lieutenant Colonel Abram Van Buskirk of the 3rd Battalion of New Jersey Volunteers. American accounts of the battle report that Van Buskirk accepted the sword and thrust it through Ledyard's body and that the British then began bayoneting and shooting the surrendered men. Benson J. Lossing says Major Bromfield, another Loyalist officer, killed Ledyard while Stephen Hempstead identifies the man as Colonel Beckwith. Sergeant Avery was distracted at that moment, but he reports:

> I noticed Colonel William Ledyard on the parade stepping toward the enemy and Bloomfield [probably Bromfield] generally raising and lowering his sword in a token of bowing in submission. He was about six feet from them when I turned my eyes off from him and went up to the door of the barracks and looked at the enemy who were discharging their guns through the windows. It was but a moment that I had turned my eyes from Colonel L. and saw him alive and now I saw him weltering in his gore.

Avery recalls that the British put their own wounded in the shade and left the American wounded and dying out in the hot sun, refusing to give them water. Casualty reports vary. One source says that 70 to 80 were killed, all except 3 after the surrender. Arnold's report to Clinton claims 85 were found dead in the fort and 60 wounded, many of them dying later. Total losses seem to be about 240 killed and another 70 taken prisoner. The British lost 48 killed and 145 wounded, including Eyre who received a mortal wound.

Avery records that the wounded were loaded into an ammunition wagon and brought to the top of the hill before being brought to the ships below for loading. The men pulling the cart lost control of the cart which rolled down the hill and struck a tree, adding to the suffering. Avery was taken to New York as a prisoner and exchanged a short while later.

The spot where Montgomery was impaled was the location of the heaviest fighting of the battle. Many of the British casualties occurred here. One account reports the British buried their dead in a mass grave in the ditch of the ravelin which protected the gate, but there is no marker to indicate this.

7

NEW JERSEY

New Jersey contributed a total of 15,174 men to the war effort—4,448 militia and 10,726 Continental Army.

See the New Jersey map.

Fort Lee (November 18, 1776)

Fort Lee Historic Park is on Hudson Terrace south of the George Washington Bridge (on its New Jersey side) in Palisades Interstate Park.
                    http://www.fieldtrip.com/nj/14611776.htm

Fort Lee Historic Park is on the site of the northern redoubt of Fort Lee, about 0.5 mile northeast of the main fort. The reconstructed fort has a cannon battery overlooking the Hudson and the Manhattan skyline and parapets with embrasures and firing steps. (See Photos NJ-1 and NY-15.) The visitor center shows a 12-minute film every hour, and lighted displays depict the campaign. Exhibits include models, miniature scenes, and pictures accompanied by descriptive text.

Fort Lee, which was called Fort Constitution in 1776, was built 300 feet above the Hudson River in September, 1776, by General George Washington's (1732–1799) troops as a link in fortifications defending New York and the Hudson River against British warships (see Photos NJ-1 and NY-15). It was across the Hudson from Fort Washington. (See also Fort Washington, New York.) Colonel Robert Magaw (d. 1789) was in command at Fort Washington and Major General Nathanael Greene (1742–1786) at Fort Lee. Greene crossed the Hudson on occasion for consultations.

General Charles Cornwallis (1738–1805) led 4,500 men (2 battalions of Hessian grenadiers, 2 companies of jaegers, and 8 battalions of British reserves) across the Hudson 5 miles north of Fort Lee, on November 16, 1776. They assembled on the east shore opposite Closter's Landing and moved south to attack Fort Lee so quickly that the Americans barely had time to escape. When the British entered the fort, they found only 12 men, all of them drunk. They took about 150 other prisoners captured in the vicinity. In the Americans' hurried retreat from Fort Lee, tents remained unfolded, pots were left boiling on camp fires, and tables prepared for the officers' dinner and loaded guns were abandoned.

After General Greene's hasty evacuation of Fort Lee he retreated west to join General Washington at Hackensack on November 20. Washington led his demoralized army on a retreat through New Jersey during the last weeks of 1776. The Crown forces pursued the Americans "always keeping a day's march out of reach." Cornwallis and General William Howe (1732–1786) joined forces on December 6 and continued advancing together as Washington's army seemed to disintegrate. General Henry Clinton (1730–1795) occupied Rhode Island, using it as a base to harass American shipping. The British seemed ready to end the war as soon as spring returned.

Washington Crossing (December 25, 1776)
Titusville

Washington Crossing State Park is in/near Titusville, New Jersey. From Trenton go 8 miles northwest on State Route NJ 29, then northeast on County Road 546 to the entrance (355 Washington Crossing–Pennington Road).
> http://www.state.nj.us/dep/parksandforests/parks/washcros.html

Washington Crossing State Park is an 800-acre park which runs along the Delaware River. The visitor center/museum contains a large collection of Revolutionary War artifacts. An interpretive center contains exhibits. Continental Lane (see Photo NJ-3), over which the Colonial troops marched on Christmas night in 1776, extends nearly the length of the park.

The Ferry House (see Photo NJ-2) in Washington Crossing State Park at the south end of Continental Lane is across the Delaware River from McConkey's Ferry, Pennsylvania. George Washington stayed here until all his men had crossed the Delaware on the night of December 25, 1776. It has been restored as a Dutch farmhouse. A taproom, a kitchen, and a bedroom contain period furniture which was probably not in the building in 1776.

The Nelson House, across NJ 29 near the river bank, is a small museum that has historical exhibits. There is a separate Washington Crossing Park on the Pennsylvania side of the river. (See also Washington Crossing, Pennsylvania.)

General George Washington (1732–1799) formulated a bold plan to strike the Hessian garrisons at Trenton and Bordentown by surprise early in the morning the day after Christmas, 1776, when the troops might be expected to relax their guard for holiday revelry. He had all the boats on the river removed to escape into Pennsylvania and to prevent General William Howe's (1732–1786) further advance. This was the only time in the war that Washington commanded naval superiority over the British.

George Washington personally commanded his force of 2,400 men across the Delaware River on the night of December 25, 1776. They crossed from Pennsylvania to New Jersey at McConkey's Ferry, Pennsylvania, 9 miles upstream from Trenton. Washington stayed at the Ferry House (see Photo NJ-2) on the New Jersey side until all his men had crossed.

The troops would then proceed in 2 columns by different routes, converging on the opposite ends of the main street of Trenton in the early morning of December 26, 1776. A second force of about 1,900 men, mainly militia, under Colonel John Cadwalader (1742–1786) was to cross south of Trenton near Bordentown to attack the Hessian garrison there; a third force of 700 men, also militia, under Brigadier General James Ewing (1736–1805), was to cross directly opposite Trenton to block the Hessian route of escape across Assunpink Creek.

Elisha Bostwick recalled the difficulties of crossing and re-crossing the Delaware:

> When crossing the Delaware with the prisoners in flat bottom boats the ice continually stuck to the boats, driving them down stream; the boatmen endevering to clear off the ice pounded the boat, and stamping with their feet, beconed to the prisoners to do the same, and they all set to jumping at once with their cues flying up and down, soon shook off the ice from the boats, and the next day re-crossed the Delaware again and returned back to Trenton, and there on the first of January 1777 our yeers service expired, and then by the pressing solicitations of his Excellency a part of those whose time was out consented on a ten dollar bounty to stay six weeks longer, and altho desirous as others to return home, I engaged to stay that time and made every exertion in my power to make as many of the soldiers stay with me as I could, and quite a number did engage with me who otherwise would have went home.

Christmas night was cold, windy, and snowy and the Delaware River was filled with blocks of ice. It took 9 hours for the 2,400 men to make the crossing from Pennsylvania to New Jersey. Neither Cadwalader nor Ewing was able to fulfill his part of the plan. Driven on by Washington's indomitable will, the main force did cross as planned and the 2 columns, commanded respectively by Major General Nathanael Greene (1742–1786) and Major General John Sullivan (1740–1795), converged on Trenton at 8 o'clock in the morning of December 26, taking the 1,400 Hessians, commanded by Colonel Johann Gottlieb Rall (1720–1776), largely by surprise.

Trenton (December 26, 1776)

The Old Barracks Museum (see Photo NJ-4) on Barrack Street in Trenton, New Jersey is the only surviving colonial barracks in the United States. Constructed in 1758, it was occupied at various times by British, Hessian, and Continental troops and by Loyalist refugees. Colonel Johann Gottlieb Rall and 1,400 Hessians, including elements of Knyphausen's and von Lossberg's regiments, were quartered here. These barracks were Washington's objective at the Battle of Trenton. A cultural history museum includes a restored officers' quarters with 18th-century furnishings and permanent and changing exhibits. The history laboratory provides interactive experiences.

                              http://www.barracks.org/

The Sons of the American Revolution erected 12 stone obelisks, in 1914, to mark Washington's retreat route from Trenton to Princeton.

- Number One is at the southwest corner of South Broad Street and Hamilton Avenue.

- Number Two is 0.7 mile east of Number One on the left side of Hamilton Avenue.

- Number Three is in Hamilton Township in the vicinity of the intersection of Greenwood and Ward Avenues near the northwest side of Greenwood Cemetery.

- Number Four is near the Mercer County Geriatric Center at Jencohallo Avenue and Chewalla Boulevard (off Nottingham Way) in Hamilton Township.

- Number Five is near the Veterans of Foreign Wars Post on Christine Avenue off Klockner Avenue.

- Number Six is about 2 miles away from Number Five on the left side of Quaker Bridge Road.

- Number Seven is 1 mile north of Number Six off Youngs Road east of Quaker Bridge Road.

■ Number Eight is 0.5 mile north on Hughes Drive in the Van Nest Refuge, just west of Quaker Bridge Road.

■ Number Nine is on Quaker Bridge Road in the Mercer Mall just north of the intersection with Route U.S. 1.

■ Number Ten is almost 2 miles north of Number Nine on Quaker Bridge Road in a wooded area owned by the Institute for Advanced Study in Princeton Township.

■ Number Eleven is in a field on the right side of Quaker Bridge Road 1 mile north of Number Ten.

■ Number Twelve is in the woods behind the Clark House at Princeton Battlefield State Park.

The British and Hessian troops went to winter quarters on December 14, 1776. Major General Count Karl Emil Kurt von Donop (1740–1777) based half of his 3,000 men in Trenton (a small town of about 100 houses) and the other half at Bordentown and Burlington, respectively 7 and 17 miles downstream to the southeast. Headquarters was located at New Brunswick, 27 miles north. General William Howe (1732–1786) settled in New York and General Charles Cornwallis (1738–1805) prepared to return to England.

While Howe rested comfortably in New York, General George Washington (1732–1799) desperately sought to reconcentrate his forces and redeem the defeat in New York. Major General Charles Lee (1731–1782) had the misfortune of getting captured by the British on December 12, 1776 and his 2,000 remaining men then made haste to join Washington. Eight decimated regiments were also pulled from the Northern Army, and with some Pennsylvania militia, Washington was able to assemble a force totaling about 7,000 by the last week of December, 1776. If he was to use this force, he would have to do so before the enlistments expired on December 31.

Thus, General Washington formulated a plan for a surprise dawn strike on the Hessian garrisons at Trenton (see Photo NJ-4) and Bordentown, on December 26, 1776, when the troops might be expected to relax their guard for holiday revelry. (Washington had all the boats on the river removed in order to escape into Pennsylvania and to prevent General William Howe's (1732–1786) further advance. This was the only time in the war that Washington commanded naval superiority over the British.) Under his personal command, Washington's force of 2,400 men was to cross the Delaware upstream from Trenton, then proceed by different routes in 2 columns, converging on the opposite ends of the main street of Trenton.. A second force, mainly militia, of about 1,900 men, under Colonel John Cadwalader (1742–1786) was to cross farther south and attack the Hessian garrison at Bordentown. A third force under Brigadier General James Ewing (1736–1805), of 1,000 men, also militia, was to cross directly opposite Trenton to block the Hessian route of escape across Assunpink Creek.

American troops lost the cover of darkness because of the time it took to cross the Delaware and march to Trenton (see Photo NJ-3, the road to Trenton), arriving in Trenton after daybreak. Cadwalader got some of his men across but not his artillery, so the attack on Bordentown never occurred. Ewing could not get his men across, leaving the Hessians with an escape route to the south.

First Battle

On the morning of December 26, Washington surprised the Hessian soldiers at Trenton. Even though Loyalist sympathizers had warned Colonel Johann Gottleib Rall (1720–1776) that the colonials were planning an attack and even gave him the day and time, Rall ignored them because the patrol activities of the colonials on December 25 convinced him that he need not fear a general attack but only a patrol. The Hessians celebrated all Christmas day and into the night. Rall did not get to bed until about 6:00 AM, drinking and playing cards at the home of a Loyalist townsman. A farmer named Wall delivered a message concerning the movements of the enemy troops, but Rall put the note in his pocket and forgot about it.

The guard on duty the following morning consisted of hung-over pickets and their officers who did not expect anything out of the ordinary. When Washington attacked, the Hessians tried to form for battle, but they faced artillery batteries, commanded by Captain Thomas Forrest (d. 1825) and Captain Alexander Hamilton (1755–1804), firing down the streets. The Hessians withdrew in disorder as Brigadier General William Alexander's (Lord Stirling, 1726–1783), men charged down the streets to capture 2 guns that had been hastily emplaced.

The Americans had superior numbers and the advantage of surprise. The artillery under Colonel Henry Knox (1750–1806) was placed at the end of King and Queen Streets, dominating the town. Firing as rapidly as possible, they kept the Hessians from forming to defend themselves.

Colonel Rall rallied his troops for a charge, but the American infantry now occupied houses along both sides of the street, firing on the Hessians. Colonel Rall ordered a retreat and was mortally wounded. The Hessians surrendered about 9:30 after a fight that lasted either 35 minutes or 1 hour and 45 minutes, depending on which account of the battle you read. American casualties totaled 4 killed, 3 of whom supposedly froze to death during the withdrawal, and 3 wounded. General Howe reported Hessian casualties as 40 men killed and wounded besides officers and 918 prisoners, including 30 officers. About 500 escaped over the Assunpink to Bordentown because Ewing was not in place to block their escape. Washington reported, on December 28, the total number of prisoners numbered about 1,000.

Second Battle

Washington met with his senior officers and decided not to defend Assunpink Creek and risk losing most of his army. Cornwallis ceased attacking when it became too dark to see, deciding to wait until the following day to capture Washington who was cornered with the river behind him.

Since there were not enough boats around Trenton to cross into Pennsylvania, trying to retreat across the Delaware would risk losing most of the army. Instead, Washington slipped away during the night, moving in the opposite direction. He left a group of some 400 men to keep the campfires burning brightly, guard the creek, work noisily at digging entrenchments, then slip away at daybreak.

The Americans muffled the gun wheels with old rags and marched quietly across Cornwallis's front. A cold northwest wind froze the roads, so the army did not encounter the mud which slowed the Crown forces during the day. They followed deserted and little known back roads toward Princeton. At daybreak, Brigadier General Hugh Mercer (1725–1777) and a brigade of 350 men seized the Stony Brook Bridge 2 miles from Princeton to delay Cornwallis's pursuit, while the main body under Washington and Sullivan continued the retreat from Trenton to Princeton.

Princeton (January 3, 1777)

Princeton Battlefield State Park is at 500 Mercer Road, south of town.
`http://www.state.nj.us/dep/parksandforests/parks/princeton.html`

A monument at Mercer, Nassau, and Stockton streets commemorates the battle. A tile map on the battlefield interprets the action.

The Thomas Clark House (see Photo NJ-5) still stands on the crest of the battlefield and British and American graves lie in the distance marked by the Ionic columns from the portico of an 1836 Philadelphia mansion (see Photo NJ-6).

Princeton University's Nassau Hall (see Photo NJ-7), completed in 1756. was the university's only building. It housed classrooms, dormitories, teachers' quarters, and dining rooms. Both sides used it as barracks and as a military hospital during the War for American Independence. The Continental Congress met in Nassau Hall in 1783 when mutinous American soldiers drove its members from Philadelphia. The Congress also received the news of the treaty of peace with Great Britain here.
`http://alumni.princeton.edu/~ptoniana/nassauhall.asp`

Encouraged by his success at the Battle of Trenton on December 26, 1776, General George Washington (1732–1799) determined to make another foray. By an impassioned appeal to the patriotism of the men, supplemented by an offer of a $10 bounty in hard money, he was able to persuade at least part of his old army to remain for 6 more weeks. With a force of around 5,000 Washington crossed the Delaware River again on the night of December 30, 1776.

When General William Howe (1732–1786) heard the news of the Battle of Trenton, he canceled General Charles Cornwallis's (1738–1805) leave and ordered him to take command in New Jersey. He hurried south from New York City, reaching Princeton on the evening of January 1, 1777. The next morning, he marched toward Trenton with 5,500 men to confront Washington.

Heavy rain during the night filled the roads with mud, slowing Cornwallis's travel. Large bands of American troops commanded by Colonel Edward Hand (1744–1802) and Major General Nathanael Greene (1742–1786) delayed him further. The British had reached Washington's main line of defense south of Assunpink Creek late in the afternoon of January 1. Cornwallis decided to wait until daylight the next morning to cross the creek, believing that he had the Americans in an inescapable trap: Washington had his back to the river and no apparent line of retreat.

That night Washington met with his senior officers and decided not to defend Assunpink Creek and risk losing most of his army. As there were not enough boats around Trenton to cross into Pennsylvania, trying to retreat across the Delaware River was also deemed to be risky. Instead, Washington devised a plan to slip away during the night, moving toward New York, the opposite direction from that which the British expected. At daybreak, Brigadier General Hugh Mercer (1725–1777) and a brigade of 350 men seized the Stony Brook Bridge 2 miles outside Princeton to delay Cornwallis's pursuit, while the main body under Washington and Major General John Sullivan (1740–1795) continued toward Princeton itself, planning to outflank the Crown forces, destroy a rear guard, and capture a vital supply depot in Brunswick, even though his troops had little food and some lacked shoes.

While Washington closed on Princeton, a regiment of British infantry reinforced by some dragoons and a part of another regiment (800 men in all) commanded by Lieutenant Colonel Charles Mawhood (d. 1780) was marching toward Trenton to join Cornwallis. Mawhood had just crossed the Stony Brook Bridge when he discovered Mercer's force behind him. He turned his men around and crossed back over the bridge in double-time. Both Mercer and Mawhood recognized the tactical value of a hill on the east side of the brook and raced toward it.

Mercer, realizing he could not reach the heights first, turned to join Sullivan's men who were coming down a road (no longer in existence) that cut across the battlefield at a diagonal toward Nassau Hall in town. A small detachment of redcoats fired on Mercer's men from behind a fence, so Mercer led a charge that drove them back up the slope. Mawhood now realized how small a force Mercer had. He turned and charged across the field from the other side of present Mercer Road. The Continentals could not re-load fast enough to fire another volley before they received Mawhood's bayonet charge that drove them back in confusion. General Mercer tried to rally his men but was bayoneted seven times and left for dead near the Thomas Clark house. According to legend, Mercer refused to be removed from the field and was placed under a white oak tree. He died of his wounds in the Clark house 9 days later (see Photo NJ-5).

As Mercer's and Colonel John Cadwalader's (1742–1786) troops were retreating under Colonel Mawhood's advance, General Washington galloped onto the field. Disregarding his personal safety, he rode within 30 yards of the British line, calling the retreating men to return to the fight. A volley rang out filling the air with smoke and hiding Washington from view. When it cleared, the men saw him on his white horse, encouraging them to go forward (see Photo NJ-6).

Continental troops from Sullivan's column arrived, formed a line, and advanced. With the reinforcements, the Continental troops outnumbered the British and drove them into Princeton where some took refuge in Nassau Hall (see Photo NJ-7) of the College of New Jersey (the original name of Princeton University). Captain Alexander Hamilton brought an artillery piece, fired 2 shots into the building. The first glanced off. The second went through the main room on the ground floor. Hamilton then ordered a charge, and about 200 redcoats promptly surrendered. Colonel Mawhood abandoned his guns, ordered a charge, and personally led it straight through the American ranks. He then turned about and gained the road to Trenton. Washington pursued Mawhood for several miles and captured about 50 prisoners.

The battle lasted less than half an hour. The Americans lost 23 killed, including General Mercer, and 20 wounded. The Crown forces lost 28 killed, 58 wounded, 187 missing, and 323 captured. Washington wanted to continue on to the main British supply base at New Brunswick, but his troops were exhausted. They had been under arms for 40 hours in bitterly cold weather with practically no food. He did not want to risk a pitched battle with Cornwallis's fresh troops marching back from Trenton.

Cornwallis's soldiers marched into Princeton at the same time that the American rearguard marched out, ending Howe's campaign to destroy the Continental Army, capture Washington, and take Philadelphia. Washington proceeded toward Morristown, New Jersey where his army went into winter quarters on Howe's flank, threatening any move the British might make through New Jersey or up the Hudson.

The British had had enough of winter warfare. Howe drew in his outposts in New Jersey to New Brunswick and Perth Amboy and settled in for the winter. Sir William Howe found that, despite his smashing rout of the Americans in New York, he was left with little more than that city, a hold in New Jersey, and the port of Newport, Rhode Island.

The battles of Trenton and Princeton saved the American army and temporarily saved Philadelphia, the capital of the colonies. They also cleared most of the enemy out of New Jersey, except for New Brunswick and Amboy (now Perth Amboy) where they posed no threat. These battles against an army of professional, trained, and battle-tested soldiers offset the worst effects of the disastrous defeats in New York and restored Washington's prestige as a commander with both friend and foe alike. In the execution of the two strokes east of the Delaware, Washington had applied the principles of offense, surprise, and maneuver with great success and finally achieved stature as a military commander. If these victories did not assure him that he could recruit such an army as Congress had voted, they did at least guarantee that he would be able to field a force the following year.

National Park (October 22, 1777)
Red Bank Battlefield
Fort Mercer

Red Bank Battlefield Park, location of Fort Mercer, is in National Park, New Jersey, at 100 Hessian Avenue, 2 miles west at the Delaware River.

`http://www.co.gloucester.nj.us/parks/red.htm`

Visitors to the reconstructed parts of Fort Mercer enjoy sweeping views of the Delaware River and can appreciate the strength of its position. A nearby exhibit of chevaux-de-frise shows a rarely seen underwater obstruction salvaged from the Delaware River after about 170 years of immersion. The logs on display, retrieved in 1936, are about 30 feet long and have attached to them portions of the chain that held them together.

The obstacle, fully assembled, consists of a large coffer filled with long heavy poles from which two to four heavy timbers, each tipped or sheathed in iron, extend outward at 45-degree angles to impale enemy ships. Each section was about 65 feet long and 20 inches square. The entire obstacle was lined with 30,000 feet of 2-inch plank. It was floated into the river and then sunk by using stones to fill the coffers to weight it down. Anchors held it in place keeping the points of the protruding timbers about 4 feet below the low-water mark. Ships coming toward the city would get impaled. Those traveling away from the city would depress the timbers with no adverse effect.

The exhibit also includes boxes of grapeshot found around the old breastworks.

The house of James and Ann Whithall (see Photo NJ-8), also in Red Bank Battlefield Park, was commandeered by the Continental Army in April, 1777. The apple orchard was destroyed to build Fort Mercer, and the house was used as a field hospital during the Battle of Red Bank. Major General Karl von Donop died here. He was interred on the battlefield on October 28, 1777. The house is open to the public.

Fort Mercer was named for Brigadier General Hugh Mercer (1725–1777) who died at Princeton. Together with Fort Mifflin near Philadelphia across the Delaware River, it presented a deterrent for any force planning a water approach to Philadelphia. The fort occupied a bluff above the river. Colonel Thaddeus Kosciusko (1746–1817) forti-fied it with 9-foot high earthen walls with sharpened tree branches, called fraise, embedded in it. Colonel Christopher Greene (1737–1781) commanded the garri-son of 400 of his fellow Rhode Islanders and a few New Jersey militia with 14 cannons.

The Crown forces needed to eliminate the fort to open the Delaware River to keep supplies flowing to the army. Major General Count Karl Emil Kurt von Donop (1740–1777) and his 1,200 Hessians crossed the Delaware at Cooper's Ferry, now Camden, to the north on October 21, 1777. They camped at Haddonfield that night. A young apprentice blacksmith named Jonas Cattell ran 5 miles from Haddonfield to Fort Mer-cer during the night to warn Greene that the Hessians were camped to his north, a lightly protected side of Fort Mercer.

Greene moved his men away from the river to the northern face. When von Donop arrived, he demanded surrender, but Greene refused. The Hessians attacked Fort Mer-cer from the north and south. The Hessians advanced up the steep slopes twice under heavy fire from the smaller American force. Losing nearly half their men, the Hessians retreated to Philadelphia. Von Donop was one of the 400 battlefield casualties. Two British warships sent to support von Donop ran aground and had to be abandoned. The Americans set one of them, the 64-gun *Augusta*, afire with hot shot (heated cannon balls) from Fort Mifflin. The warship blew up on October 23; the British burned the other, the 16-gun frigate *Merlin*. The explosion caused a soldier at Fort Mifflin, across the river near Philadelphia, to write that it "seemed to shake the earth to its center." Tom Paine, who was several miles west of Philadelphia, was "stunned with a report as loud as a peal from a hundred cannon at once."

The Americans captured, court-martialed, and hanged two of their countrymen— one white, one black—who had guided von Donop to Fort Mercer. When the defend-ers of Fort Mifflin were forced to abandon the fort during the night of November 15, Fort Mercer became untenable. Greene abandoned the fort during the night of Novem-ber 20 as Cornwallis advanced with 2,000 troops for another assault.

Freehold (June 28, 1778)
Monmouth

Monmouth Battlefield State Park in/near Freehold, New Jersey, 3 miles west on Business Route NJ 33 (1.5 miles west of the Freehold Circle). (See Photos NJ-9 and NJ-10.)
`http://www.state.nj.us/dep/seeds/monbat.htm`

The visitor center features displays that trace the troops' movements during the battle. On the grounds is the Craig House, built in 1710 and restored to its 18th-century appearance.

As General Henry Clinton (1730–1795) prepared to depart Philadelphia in 1778, General George Washington (1732–1799) had high hopes of winning the war by a cooperative effort between his army and the French fleet. Admiral Comte Jean-Baptiste-Charles-Henri-Hector d'Estaing (1729–1794) with a French naval squadron of 11 ships of the line and transports carrying 4,000 troops left France in May to sail for the American coast. D'Estaing's fleet was considerably more powerful than any Admiral Richard Howe (1726–1799) could immediately concentrate in American waters. For a brief period in 1778, the strategic initiative passed from British hands, and Washington hoped to make full use of it.

Sir Henry Clinton had already decided, before he learned of the threat from d'Estaing, to move his army overland to New York, largely because he could find no place for 3,000 horses on the transports along with his men and stores and the hundreds of Loyalists who claimed British protection. He began evacuating Philadelphia on June 18, 1778. At the same time, he sent 5,000 men to attack St. Lucia, an important French harbor in the West Indies. He also sent 3,000 men to Florida and smaller detachments to Bermuda and the Bahamas.

Clinton headed toward New York with 10,000 to 17,000 men in very hot and humid weather with frequent downpours. His men carried 80-pound packs, and their heavy woolen uniforms were soggy and painful to wear. He also had an immense baggage train of 1,500 wagons and 5,000 horses. The wagon train stretched 12 miles along the road. Lieutenant General Wilhelm von Knyphausen (1716–1800) commanded the guard which required almost half the army. Washington's much less heavily encumbered army moved faster, closing in on his left flank and harassing him, threatening to overtake him. Patrols demolished bridges ahead of him. The Americans were close to trapping Clinton who covered less than 30 miles in 5 days when he turned northeast toward Monmouth Courthouse on June 25, 1778. The mid-day heat grew more intense. The soldiers, in their thick woolen uniforms and weighed down by their heavy packs, became more exhausted and ill-tempered.

Washington had gathered about 12,000 men by the time Clinton left Philadelphia. He immediately occupied the city and began to pursue Clinton, undecided as to whether he should risk an attack on the British column while it was on the march. His Council of War was divided, though none of his generals advised a "general action." The boldest, Brigadier General "Mad Anthony" Wayne (1745–1796), and the young major general, Marie Joseph de Motier Marquis de Lafayette (1757–1834), urged a "partial attack" to strike at a portion of the Crown forces while they were strung out on the road; the most cautious, Major General Charles Lee (1731–1782), who had been exchanged and had rejoined the army at Valley Forge, advised only guerilla action to harass the enemy columns.

At the same time, Major General Horatio Gates (1728–1806) advanced from the north to prevent Clinton from crossing the Raritan River to Amboy. Clinton, taking personal command of the rearguard, turned right and headed toward Sandy Hook at the mouth of the Hudson River where ships were waiting to carry them to New York.

On June 23, Washington sent an additional 1,500 men to help the New Jersey militia harass the British troops. Later in the day, he sent another 1,400 men and Colonel Daniel Morgan's (1736–1802) 600 riflemen, bringing the number of men pursuing Clinton to over 5,000.

On June 26, Washington decided to take a bold approach, though he issued no orders indicating an intention to bring on a "general action." He sent forward an advance guard composed of almost half his army to strike at the rear of the Crown forces when Clinton moved out of Monmouth Courthouse on the morning of June 27. Washington met with Lee, Lafayette, Wayne, and others on Saturday afternoon, June 27. They decided to move against the enemy. Lee claimed the command from Lafayette when he learned the detachment would be so large. He was to attack east of the town while Washington supported him with the main body of the army.

At 4:00 A.M June 28, Clinton sent Von Knyphausen's division ahead with the baggage train. Cornwallis would follow with a larger force of 3 brigades: the Guards, 2 battalions of British grenadiers and the Hessian grenadiers, 2 battalions of British light infantry, the 16th Dragoons, and Colonel John Graves Simcoe's (1752–1806) Queen's Rangers, a Loyalist unit.

Washington received a report of enemy movements by 5:00 AM, but Lee wasn't ready to move until 7:00 AM. As the British passed Monmouth County Courthouse on that hot Sunday, General Charles Lee's 5,000 men advanced over rough ground that had not been reconnoitered and made contact with Clinton's rearguard. Clinton outnumbered Lee by about 3 to 2. He sent an urgent message to Knyphausen for reinforcements and ordered an attack, hoping to gain the advantage before Washington arrived. Lee's 12 guns (see Photo NJ-9) opened artillery fire. Clinton reacted quickly and maneuvered to envelop the American right flank. Lee, feeling that his force was in an untenable position, began a retreat that became quite confused in the appalling heat. The British grenadiers pressed hard against the American front, while the light infantry and 16th Light Dragoons raced round their left flank.

There was much confusion among Lee's commanders and aides. Lafayette withdrew from one position to take another. The other commanders, uninformed of the order, interpreted this action as a retreat and ordered their units back as well. This caused a general withdrawal which Lee could not stop. Washington rode up amidst the confusion and, exceedingly irate to find the advance guard in retreat, exchanged harsh words with Lee. Washington then assumed direction of what had to be a defense against a counterattack. He rallied the disorganized troops and formed a new line (along the road that now borders the cemetery, just past the intersection of County Road 522 and U.S. 9). He held his position until the main body arrived to take up positions a half mile to the west. The Americans met the attacking Crown forces with vollies of musketry and artillery. The battle that followed in the afternoon heat involved the bulk of both armies and lasted until nightfall with both sides holding their own in one of the longest battles of the War for American Independence.

When Lee ordered a retreat, Mary Ludwig Hays's husband John served on the gun crew. The temperature was around 100 degrees. Molly brought pitcher after pitcher of cool water from a spring to the troops, earning her nickname Molly Pitcher. She also tended the wounded and once hoisted a disabled soldier on her shoulders and carried him to safety. On one of her water trips, Molly found her husband with the artillery, replacing a casualty. John fell wounded, leaving the gun crew with too few men to serve it. They were about to drag it to the rear when Molly took the rammer staff from her husband's hands and joined the crew, swabbing the barrel under heavy fire. (See Photo NJ-10.)

Joseph Plumb Martin (1760–1850) recorded the event:

> While in the act of reaching for a cartridge and having [one foot] as far from the other as she could step, a cannon shot from the enemy passed directly between her legs without doing any damage than carrying away all the lower part of her petticoat. Looking at it with apparent unconcern, she observed that it was lucky that it did not pass higher, for in that case it might have carried away something else, and then she continued upon her occupation.

Clinton sent strong forces to attack both of Washington's flanks. One column marched up Wemrock Road to attack Greene who turned his artillery on Comb's Hill against them. The troops that attacked the left flank were beaten back by a wild bayonet charge that some historians believe was the turning point of the battle. Meanwhile, the British grenadiers tried to break the center of the line with repeated assaults. Eyewitnesses reported an entire line of grenadiers collapsed from exhaustion in the intense heat as they charged up the slope.

The Continentals pushed the Crown forces back and pursued them. Washington urged them on riding up and down encouraging his men, seemingly unconcerned for his safety. He was only 30 or 40 feet from the enemy at times.

For the first time the American troops, trained by Major General Friedrich Wilhelm von Steuben (1730–1794), fought well with the bayonet as well as with the musket and rifle. Their battlefield behavior generally reflected the Valley Forge training. Nevertheless, Washington failed to strike a telling blow at the Crown forces for Clinton slipped away in the night and in a few days completed the retreat to New York. General Charles Lee demanded and got a court-martial at which he was judged guilty of disobedience of orders, poor conduct of the retreat, and disrespect for the Commander in Chief. He was suspended from command for 12 months. Congress later approved the sentence which prompted Lee to write an insulting letter to the Congress, which expelled him from the army and ended his career.

The Americans lost about 369 men (76 killed, 161 wounded, and 132 missing). The Crown forces lost about 358 killed and wounded. Many of the missing dropped because of heat exhaustion and later rejoined their units. About 37 Americans and 60 British died of sunstroke (or heat exhaustion). Washington recorded that his men buried more than 249 enemy dead. Some historians believe the Crown forces lost more than 1,200 men in this one battle—about one-quarter of the troops involved in the battle if half of Clinton's army of 10,000 was occupied protecting the wagon train. The Americans almost lost some people who would become notable. Alexander Hamilton almost got killed when his horse got shot out from under him. Lieutenant Colonel Aaron Burr (1756–1836) recklessly pursued the enemy until their guns began killing the men around him.

Jersey City (August 19, 1779)
Paulus Hook Fort

> Paulus Hook Fort Site: A park now occupies the site at the intersection of Washington and Grand Streets in Jersey City.
>
> Commercial development has long since obliterated the site of "Light-Horse Harry" Lee's victory. The site of the main British fortification is believed to be in the vicinity of the park.

General George Washington (1732–1799) ordered 2 forts built at Paulus Hook (also spelled Powles Hook and pronounced Poole's Hook) early in the war. The hook was a large spit of land jutting out into the Hudson River. Washington saw this site as a crucial location for defending the Hudson or launching an attack into New York, as it was the closest point in New Jersey to New York City. However, the Americans abandoned the fort in September, 1776 when the Continental Army retreated through New York. The British took it over and occupied it for the rest of the war.

Captain Henry "Light-Horse Harry" Lee (1756–1818) led an American assault on the fort in the early morning of August 19, 1779. The 200 soldiers garrisoning the fort were asleep when Lee's force of 400 men stormed the fortifications. A small group of soldiers managed to escape into a redoubt in the center of the fort. Lee, fearing reinforcements from New York City would trap him, hastened to depart. Moreover, the soldiers in the redoubt would be able to fire grapeshot at the Americans at dawn. The Americans got their powder wet crossing the water-filled moat in the assault, so they could not fire back. They left without forcing the Crown forces out of the redoubt. Nor did they spike the cannon or destroy the powder magazine, but they took 159 prisoners.

Lacking boats, the tired Americans had to march overland. Along the way, they met some 50 soldiers who may have been stragglers from Lee's command who had become lost during the earlier night march to Paulus Hook. The retreating troops received some dry ammunition from these stragglers.

Just as Crown forces were about to overtake the American column, Virginia Continentals arrived to reinforce them. As the British soldiers opened fire, Lee quickly dispatched two groups of soldiers who caused the Crown forces to withdraw.

The Americans lost 2 dead and 3 wounded. Although there are no reports of British casualties, we know they lost 159 prisoners. The raid suffered many setbacks, but it disrupted the British fortification at Paulus Hook and helped raise American morale. The Second Continental Congress awarded Lee a gold medal for his exploits. Major William Sutherland, the British commander, was court-martialed.

Morristown (January 6, 1776 to May 28, 1777; December 1, 1779 to June 22, 1780)

Morristown National Historical Park consists of several units. Washington's Headquarters and the Historical Museum and Library are at 230 Morris Avenue, in Morristown. Fort Nonsense is off Ann Street behind the Morris County Courthouse, in Morristown. Jockey Hollow (north entrance off Western Avenue in Morris Township, south entrance off Tempe Wick Road in Harding Township) is about 5 miles southwest of the city.
http://www.nps.gov/morr/index.htm

Washington's headquarters (see Photo NJ-13) during the winter encampment at Morristown was the house of Jacob Ford, Jr. (230 Morris Avenue) . The weather was so cold that the ink froze in the inkwells. This is where Washington wrote his appeals for men and supplies and issued orders for recruiting officers to help raise the 88 battalions Congress had authorized.
http://www.nps.gov/morr/morr1.htm

Reproductions of soldier's huts (see Photos NJ-11 and NJ-12) can be seen at the Jockey Hollow site of Morristown National Historical Park.

General George Washington (1732–1799) selected the easily defensible site of Morristown for his military headquarters (see Photo NJ-13) and the main encampment of his Continental Army in the winter and spring of 1777 and again during the bitter winter of 1779–1780. Although there were no battles fought in Morristown, the army struggled for its survival here, particularly during the second encampment. Despite starvation, disease, and mutiny, Washington reorganized his weary and depleted forces almost within sight of strong British lines in New York.

In the winter of 1779–1780, the army suffered worse hardships than at Valley Forge. It was the coldest winter of the war, leaving the half-starved army shivering most of the time. The men lacked clothing and proper huts (see Photos NJ-11 and NJ-12). The Hudson River had frozen so solidly between New York and the fort of Paulus Hook (about $\frac{3}{4}$ mile away) that even the most heavily laden carts could be driven across it, a circumstance never known before. Four feet of snow fell over 4 days. Private Joseph Plumb Martin recorded:

> At one time it snowed the greatest part of four days successively, and there fell nearly as many feet of snow . . . We were absolutely, literally starved: I do solemnly declare that I did not put a single morsel of Victuals into my mouth for four days and as many nights, except a little black birch bark which I gnawed off a stick of wood, if that can be called victuals. I saw several of the men roast their old shoes and eat them, and I was afterwards informed by one of the officers' waiters, that some of the officers killed

and ate a favourite little dog that belonged to one of them . . . The fourth day, just at dark, we obtained a half pound of lean beef and a gill of wheat for each man. Whether we had any salt to season so delicious a morsel, I have forgotten, but I am sure we had no bread . . . When the wheat was so swelled by boiling as to be beyond the danger of swelling in the stomach, it was deposited there without ceremony.

Congress could do little but attempt to shift its responsibilities onto the states, giving each the task of providing clothing for its own troops and furnishing certain quotas of specific supplies for the entire army. The system of "specific supplies" did not work at all. Not only were the states laggard in furnishing supplies, but, when they did, it was seldom at the time or place they were needed. The breakdown in the supply system was more than even Quartermaster General Nathanael Greene (1742–1786) could cope with. In early 1780, under heavy criticism in Congress, he resigned his position as Quartermaster.

Under such difficulties, Washington had to struggle to hold even a small army together. Recruiting of Continentals, difficult to begin with, became almost impossible when the troops could neither be paid nor supplied adequately and had to suffer such winters as those at Morristown. Enlistments and drafts from the militia in 1780 brought less than half as many men for one year of service as had enlisted in 1776 for 3 years or the duration of the war.

While recruiting lagged, morale among those men who had enlisted for the longer term naturally fell. Desertion became common again. Mutinies became common and usually had the same causes: bad winter quarters, the inadequacy of food and clothing, no pay, and long enlistments. The mutinies in 1780 and 1781 were suppressed only by measures of great severity. The arrival of warmer weather did little to alleviate the army's suffering.

The Pennsylvania Line mutiny at Jockey Hollow in 1781 was the most serious. The troops marched on Philadelphia with the intent of confronting the Congress. Brigadier General "Mad Anthony" Wayne (1745–1796) tried unsuccessfully to stop them. The troops marched into Princeton, where Congress had fled to avoid them, and occupied the city. Negotiations went on for days in Nassau Hall (see Photo NJ-7) before an agreement was reached to allow the soldiers who had served for most of the war to leave if they so desired. Congress promised to address the other grievances as best it could. During the mutiny, the British sent two agents to try to persuade the mutineers to desert. The two agents were arrested, handed over to the army, and executed.

The Jersey Line mutiny at Pompton Lakes was suppressed with the force of arms and the execution of three of the ringleaders. The mutiny of several Connecticut militia units during the 1779–1780 encampment was also suppressed.

Discipline was hard to maintain. Desertion, drinking, gambling, and plundering became common problems and were punishable by fines, whippings, imprisonment, and death. Desertion, more than any other crime, was punished by execution. Washington's general orders of May 25, 1780, condemned 11 convicted deserters to be hanged at 11:00 AM the following day. Wagons brought the men to the Grand Parade in Jockey Hollow. They stopped near a scaffold and 11 freshly dug graves. Just before the execution of the sentence, an officer read a reprieve for 10 men. James Coleman, a frequent deserter and the only one remaining, was resigned to his fate. He helped tighten the rope around his neck, but when the trap was sprung, the rope broke. He remounted the platform and reputedly said to the executioner, "I told you the rope was not strong enough; do get a stronger one." The executioner complied.

The army also had to face another serious attack in Morristown. Smallpox spread like wildfire in the army camps and infected the civilian population. Washington instituted a program of inoculations. This was a difficult decision for an 18th-century person. Inoculation was a new and emerging medical technique that required being deliberately infected with the disease. The risk of getting smallpox "in the natural way" could result in death. It was quite another matter to expose oneself knowingly and willingly to the disease.

The inoculation program began in secret and eventually was extended to the civilian population in the Morristown area when the results seemed favorable. Parents were reluctant to expose their children to the disease and risk death or serious disfigurement. But the war forced them to face the issue because smallpox followed the armies. Many wives had to make these life-or-death decisions on their own in the absence of their husbands whenever a large number of soldiers from either side arrived in a given area.

Springfield/Union/Elizabeth (June 7–23, 1780)
Battle of Springfield
Battle of Connecticut Farms

A curbside marker in Union reads: "Connecticut Farms—Settled by Yankees 1667—Scene of Hardest Fighting Against Invading British and Hessians June 6, 1780. Became Union in 1880."

Another plaque on the front of the Connecticut Farms Presbyterian Church, built in 1791, identifies it as standing on the site of a former church "where was fought a battle on June 7, 1780, between American forces under General Maxwell and Colonel Dayton and the British army in its advance to Springfield. The church and the village were burned by the British during their retreat on June 23, 1780. The British second advance here formed into 2 columns and advanced to Springfield where they were repulsed." The plaque also lists the names of 72 men who served in the militia and army during the War for American Independence and are buried at Connecticut Farms.

Reverend James Caldwell lived in the Hutching House (126 Morris Avenue [NJ 82], Springfield, New Jersey), built about 1750 and better known as the Cannonball House because it was struck in the side by a cannonball. It is one of the four surviving buildings in Union and headquarters of the Springfield Historical Society. Visitors can see the cannonball among the exhibits. Despite the devastation of this portion of New Jersey in 1780, several important structures of the Revolutionary and earlier period remain, particularly in Elizabeth.

`http://www.unioncountynj.org/togotodo/4centwk/4crev.html`

Lieutenant General Wilhelm von Knyphausen (1716–1800) was in temporary command in New York City while General Henry Clinton (1730–1795) was in Charleston, South Carolina. He ordered 5,000 men from British, Hessian, and New Jersey Loyalist units to march toward the American army encamped at Morristown, New Jersey on

June 7, 1780. Some historians do not know why he launched this large raid, but some think that Knyphausen planned to exploit the news of mutinies among the Continentals. Others think he believed Loyalist sympathies were increasing and that the local populace would greet his men with open arms. Others think it was to draw General George Washington (1732–1799) and his army out of Morristown.

Knyphausen realized his error when he got to Elizabethtown (now Elizabeth) where local militia and farmers rushed to block his advance. Colonel Elias Dayton (1737–1807), in command of a regiment of 2,500 men including local militia, prevented Knyphausen from crossing the bridge over the Rahway River at Springfield. The strong American resistance surprised the Crown forces who retreated to the high ground just to the northwest of Connecticut Farms, now Union, in a heavy thunderstorm during the night of June 7 and entrenched. The Patriots received reinforcements and pursued the Crown forces who burned most of the homes at Connecticut Farms as they continued retreating to De Hart's Point near Elizabethtown on June 9. His operation a failure, Knyphausen evacuated part of his force to Staten Island and then lay on his arms waiting for Sir Henry Clinton to return to New York from Charleston, where he had beaten the Continentals under Major General Benjamin Lincoln (1733–1810).

Meanwhile, Washington moved the main body of his army from Morristown to Short Hills, just to the northwest of Springfield. Delighted with the performance of Dayton and the New Jersey militia, he was unsure of Knyphausen's intent. He thought the Crown forces might be planning a major march up the Hudson River Valley, so he scattered his troops throughout the area to prepare for any eventual attack.

Clinton returned to New York City on June 17. He examined the situation and feared that Washington might head north to join a French force on its way across the Atlantic headed for Newport, Rhode Island. Clinton planned a second strike toward Springfield with another column marching on the main objective: Morristown. Both sides were considerably reinforced as the Crown forces approached Springfield on June 23, 1780, but this time they met a well-organized opponent.

The Crown forces now numbered about 6,000 men while the Americans had about half that number. Major General Nathanael Greene (1742–1786) commanded about 1,000 American regulars and militia at Springfield while Washington moved his main force to Pompton because British ships moving up the Hudson on June 20 threatened West Point. Mounted troops, including Captain Henry "Light-Horse Harry" Lee's (1756–1818) Legion screened the country between Springfield and Elizabethtown while Brigadier General Edward Hand (1744–1802) commanded a task force of 500 men to harass the beachhead at De Hart's Point.

Knyphausen approached the Raritan River just east of Springfield with half his army while the other half proceeded (along what is now Vauxhall Road to envelop the Americans). Here, they encountered Lee's dragoons, reinforced with 2 regiments of New England regulars and militia who prevented them from attaining their objective.

Colonel Israel Angell's (1740–1832) Rhode Island Continentals defended the Springfield Bridge preventing Knyphausen's troops from crossing for 40 minutes. Angell and the Rhode Islanders then withdrew through the village to join Colonel William Shreve's New Jersey militia around the "Second Bridge," just west of the village while Greene concentrated the rest of his force on the high ground around the Connecticut Farms Presbyterian Church.

The formidable American force caused Knyphausen to discontinue the action. His troops burned all but four of the buildings in Springfield before withdrawing to Staten Island, leaving only their dead, wounded, some stragglers, and some prisoners of war. Washington had already ordered the evacuation of supplies from Morristown and proceeded to support Greene when he received news that no help was needed at Springfield.

The Americans lost 13 killed, 61 wounded, and 9 missing. British losses are not reported but contemporary journalists estimated them at about 150.

The *"Fighting Parson"*

Reverend James Caldwell, pastor of the First Presbyterian Church in Elizabeth, had delivered a memorable series of sermons at Connecticut Farms in 1774 and became known as the "high priest of the Revolution" by the Loyalists and as the "fighting parson" by the Patriots. Caldwell's wife Hannah and their children took refuge in the parsonage at Connecticut Farms as the Crown forces advanced on June 7. She was killed on that day and became a martyr. The inscription on the monument in Elizabeth to Reverend Caldwell and his wife reads: "killed . . . by a shot from a British soldier, June 25th, 1780, cruelly sacrificed by the enemies of her husband and of her country."

Not only is the date wrong, but some of the other details may be questioned. While we can never know for certain what really happened, there is evidence that she may have been murdered by a former servant for revenge (Lossing, Benson. *Pictorial Field Book of the Revolution* I, 325 n.).

After the first skirmish in Springfield, Reverend Caldwell went to Connecticut Farms to serve Colonel Dayton's regiment as chaplain when he learned of his wife's death. During the battle of June 23, Patriot soldiers reportedly had run out of wadding for their muskets and Caldwell is said to have gone into the church to get an armful of Watts' hymnals to give to the men. He reportedly encouraged them by yelling "Give 'em Watts, boys—give 'em Watts!" as they tore pages out, but primary sources make no mention of this.

Reverend Caldwell was shot dead by James Morgan, an American sentry, in Elizabethtown on November 24, 1781. The apparent cause was an argument over the soldier's strict interpretation of the special orders prescribed for his guard post. However there was evidence that Morgan had been bribed to kill Caldwell whenever he found an opportunity. Morgan was tried in a building where the Presbyterian Church now stands at Broad Street and Mountain Avenue in Westfield, New Jersey. He was found guilty of murder and hanged at Morgan's or Gallows Hill on Broad Street at the northeast side of town.

8

PENNSYLVANIA

Pennsylvania contributed 33,035 men to Washington's army—7,357 militia and 25,678 in the Continental Army.

See the two Pennsylvania maps: Eastern Pennsylvania; Southeastern Pennsylvania/ Philadelphia vicinity.

PHILADELPHIA

Independence National Historical Park is in downtown Philadelphia.
`http://www.nps.gov/inde/index.htm`

Independence National Historical Park includes buildings in Independence Square and others throughout the city that are closely associated with the Colonial period, the founding of the nation and Philadelphia's early role as national capital. These buildings include the visitor center (at 3rd and Chestnut Streets), Independence Hall, Congress Hall, the old City Hall, the Liberty Bell Pavilion, the Second Bank of United States (an 1824 structure that now houses Independence National Historical Park's National Portrait Gallery) and Washington Square.

Other interesting sites include the Declaration (Graff) House (a reconstruction of the dwelling in which Thomas Jefferson drafted the Declaration of Independence in June 1776), the Betsy Ross House (where the Colonial seamstress supposedly stitched the first American flag in 1777), Franklin Court (once owned by Benjamin Franklin, who lived in Philadelphia from 1722 until his death in 1790). The complex encompasses an underground theater and museum as well as five houses, the exteriors of which have been restored to their Franklin era appearances), and the Thaddeus Kosciuszko National Memorial (exhibits and audiovisual displays in English and Polish describe Thaddeus Kosciuszko's contributions to the American Revolution).

Famous churches include St Peter's Church (erected in 1761, where 4 signers of the Declaration of Independence worshiped) and Christ Church, the house of worship of 15 signers of the Declaration of Independence. Brass plaques mark the pews once occupied by George Washington, Benjamin Franklin and Betsy Ross. The 1727 structure typifies early Georgian architecture. It has one of the oldest Palladian windows in North America. It also contains the font from which William Penn was baptized in 1644. The church's burial ground contains the graves of Benjamin Franklin and 4 other signers of the Declaration of Independence. Old St Joseph's Church was the first Roman Catholic church in Philadelphia. The Marquis de Lafayette and Comte de Rochambeau worshiped here.

Elfreth's Alley is one of many narrow streets lined with quaint restored houses that have stood since the days of the city's founding.

Because of their significance, Carpenters' Hall, Independence Hall, the Declaration (Graff) House, and Washington Square merit further discussion below.

Although no military battles were fought in Philadelphia, the city was the seat of Congress. Many of the ideological battles that preceded the war and then gave it direction were fought here.

Carpenters' Hall (September 5 to October 26, 1774)

Carpenters' Hall (see Photo PA-1), a site in the Independence National Historical Park, is at 320 Chestnut Street, Philadelphia, Pennsylvania. Built in 1771, it was the site of the First Continental Congress in 1774 (September 5, 1774 to October 26, 1774). The building houses a collection of early carpentry tools as well as chairs used by the Congress, flags, and other artifacts of the Revolution (see Photo PA-2). An 11-minute videotape presentation chronicles the history of the Carpenters' Company, the nation's oldest trade guild, which still owns and operates the hall.

First Continental Congress

Shortly after news of the Coercive Acts reached America, colonists wanted to stop importing British goods. Others wanted to convene a congress of all the colonies to decide what action they should take. Providence, Rhode Island, first called for such a congress on May 17, 1774. Other colonies soon followed suit and selected delegates to participate in this meeting.

The First Continental Congress met at Carpenters' Hall (see Photos PA-1 and PA-2) in Philadelphia on September 5, 1774. A privately owned building, it offered the delegates greater secrecy than the Pennsylvania State House. Fifty-six delegates represented 12 of the colonies. Georgia and the other mainland British colonies of Quebec, East Florida, and West Florida, which remained loyal to King George III, did not send any representatives. The members adopted the title of "The Congress," but popular usage added the word "Continental" to distinguish it from various provincial congresses.

The Congress elected Peyton Randolph (1721–1775) of Virginia as its presiding officer and Charles Thomson (1729–1824) ("The Sam Adams of Philadelphia") as secretary, even though he was not officially a delegate. The Congress served as the "national government" from 1774 until 1781 when the Articles of Confederation established the Confederation Congress. The delegates pledged themselves to secrecy and decided to vote by provincial units, with each province having one vote. Many colonies chose moderate men as their representatives, but almost all of them seemed to vote like radicals once they settled down to business.

The delegates had no intention of gaining independence from Great Britain. Nor did they come merely to register their protests against the Coercive Acts. Rather, the question was how to avert the threat represented by those Acts. The instructions they had received from the various legal and quasi-legal bodies that elected them plainly charged the delegates to find a way to reestablish the harmony that had characterized colonial relations with Britain before 1763.

Suffolk Resolves

On September 17, 1774, just 12 days after convening, the delegates endorsed the Suffolk Resolves, the work of Joseph Warren (1741–1775) which a convention in Suffolk County, Massachusetts adopted on September 9 and sent to Philadelphia by Paul Revere (1735–1818). The resolutions:

1. declared the Coercive Acts unconstitutional and not worthy of obedience;
2. urged the people of Massachusetts to form a government to collect taxes and withhold them from the royal government until the repeal of the Coercive Acts;
3. advised the people to arm and form their own militia;
4. recommended strong economic sanctions against Britain.

On September 27, Congress adopted a resolution banning imports from Great Britain and Ireland after December 1, 1774.

Galloway's Plan of Union

Conservative Joseph Galloway (1731–1803) of Pennsylvania introduced his famous Plan of Union on September 28 to offset the endorsement of the Suffolk Resolves.

Declaration of Colonial Rights and Grievances

On October 14, 1774, the delegates adopted a series of resolutions that came to be known as the Declaration of Colonial Rights and Grievances. These resolutions stated the rights to which the colonists thought they were entitled "by the immutable laws of nature, the principles of the English constitution, and the several charters or compacts." They included a clause written by John Adams (1735–1826) that proclaimed the colonists' right to govern themselves in matters of taxation and internal law. The resolution acknowledged that Parliament, by consent not by right, might regulate the commerce of the Empire to Britain's advantage, provided it made no attempt to raise a revenue in doing so.

The Declaration also stated that all acts of Parliament that taxed the colonists, including the remaining Townshend duty on tea, were infringements on American rights. Finally the Congress demanded the repeal of the Coercive Acts, the Quebec Act, and several other laws it deemed unconstitutional.

The Association

On October 20, 1774, the Congress accomplished its most important work by adopting unanimously the Association (or Continental Association). This document, modeled upon a Virginia Association framed August 1–6, 1774, began with a statement of the grievances of the colonies and listed 9 acts of Parliament which it demanded be repealed, either entirely or in part. It then outlined a plan of non-importation of British goods to take effect on December 1. The delegates, more out of self-interest than from a difference in policy, found it more difficult to agree about non-exportation of American goods since the crops had already been harvested. After considerable debate the delegates incorporated non-exportation into the Association but delayed its effective date until September 1, 1775.

The Association called for totally discontinuing the slave trade beginning on December 1 and banning consumption of British products and various foreign luxury products effective March 1, 1775. The Association provided for establishing committees in each county, town, and city to assure that everyone complied with the provisions of the Association. The primary method of enforcement was community condemnation. Violators would be punished by publicity and boycott. Any province which failed to keep the Association would also be boycotted. By April, 1775, the Association was in operation in 12 colonies. Even Georgia adopted a modified version on January 23, 1775.

Before adjourning on October 26, the First Continental Congress approved, on October, 22, a resolution that called for another meeting to be held on May 10, 1775, if Parliament did not redress their grievances before then. The timing allowed for news of the Congress's actions to arrive in England and to receive a response.

There was little chance that the colonists would take the first step toward reconciliation. Most of them hoped the King and Parliament would make some move toward compromise upon receiving the results of the Continental Congress. The Patriots made their demands; they adopted a policy of commercial warfare to coerce Great Britain into compliance; they only needed to rally public opinion behind their cause.

Independence Hall
(May 10, 1775 to September 17, 1787)

Independence Hall (see Photo PA-3) is on Chestnut Street in Independence Square between 5th and 6th Streets in Philadelphia. It is in Independence National Historical Park.

Independence Hall, originally the Pennsylvania State House, built in 1732, is the site where the Second Continental Congress met in 1775 and decided to resist the King and Parliament, where the Declaration of Independence and Constitution were debated and signed, and where George Washington (1732–1799) accepted the role of Commander in Chief of the Continental Army.

The Assembly Room (see Photo PA-5) has been restored to look as it did when the founding fathers debated here from 1775–1787. Some of the furniture, including Washington's "rising sun" chair (see Photo PA-4) are original. Across the hallway is the restored Pennsylvania Supreme Court Chamber. Upstairs, the Governor's Council Chamber, Long Room, and Committee Room have been restored and furnished in period style.

Second Continental Congress

The Second Continental Congress assembled in Philadelphia on May 10, 1775, the same day the rebels captured Fort Ticonderoga, which opened the road to Canada. The Congress found itself forced to turn from embargoes and petitions to the problems of organizing, directing, and supplying a military effort.

Before Congress could assume control, the New England forces assembled near Boston, Massachusetts fought another battle on their own at Breed's Hill, the bloodiest single engagement of the entire Revolution. After the Battle of Lexington and Concord, at the suggestion of Massachusetts, the New England colonies moved to replace the militia gathered around Boston with volunteer forces, constituting what may be loosely called a New England army. Each state raised and administered its own force and appointed a commander for it. Discipline was lax and there was no single chain of command. Though Major General Artemas Ward (1727–1800), the Massachusetts commander, exercised overall control by informal agreement, it was only because the other commanders chose to cooperate with him, and decisions were made in council. While by mid-June, 1775 most of the men gathered were volunteers, militia units continued to come and go. The volunteers in the Connecticut service were enlisted until December 10, 1775, those from the other New England states until the end of the year.

The Continental Congress authorized the establishment of the Continental Army on June 14, 1775, 3 days before the Battle of Bunker Hill. The next day, it appointed George Washington (1732–1799) Commander in Chief.

Declaration of Independence

The provincial Congress of North Carolina authorized its delegates to the Continental Congress to support "Independency" on April 12, 1776, making it the first colony to do so. These instructions took several weeks to reach the Continental Congress. Meanwhile, on May 10, the Continental Congress adopted a resolution introduced by John Adams (1735–1826) urging the colonies to form their own governments. The preamble called for the full exercise of local government and the suppression of all royal authority. This caused more heated debate than the resolution itself. Delegates from the middle colonies had objections, but the resolution passed 5 days later. Adams interpreted it to mean independence and regarded it as "the most important Resolution that ever was taken in America."

The day after Thomas Jefferson (1743–1826) returned to the Congress, his countrymen in Williamsburg authorized their representatives in Philadelphia to vote for and sign a declaration that the colonies were free and independent states. They also instructed the delegates to propose that Congress draft a declaration of independence.

Congress received the Virginia resolution, along with the earlier one from North Carolina, on May 27. Congress tabled the resolution for 10 days while the delegates debated other matters. Richard Henry Lee (1732–1794) changed the wording on June 7 and resubmitted it as three propositions:

> That these United Colonies are, and of right ought to be, free and independent States, that they are absolved from all allegiance to the British Crown, and that all political connection between them and the State of Great Britain is, and ought to be, totally dissolved.
>
> That it is expedient forthwith to take the most effectual measures for forming foreign Alliances.
>
> That a plan of confederation be prepared and transmitted to the respective Colonies for their consideration and approbation.

John Adams of Massachusetts seconded the motion, but Congress deferred action on it until July 1. On June 11, Congress appointed a committee comprising Thomas Jefferson (1743–1826), Benjamin Franklin (1706–1790), John Adams, Roger Sherman (1721–1793), and Robert R. Livingston (1746–1813), to prepare a declaration in line

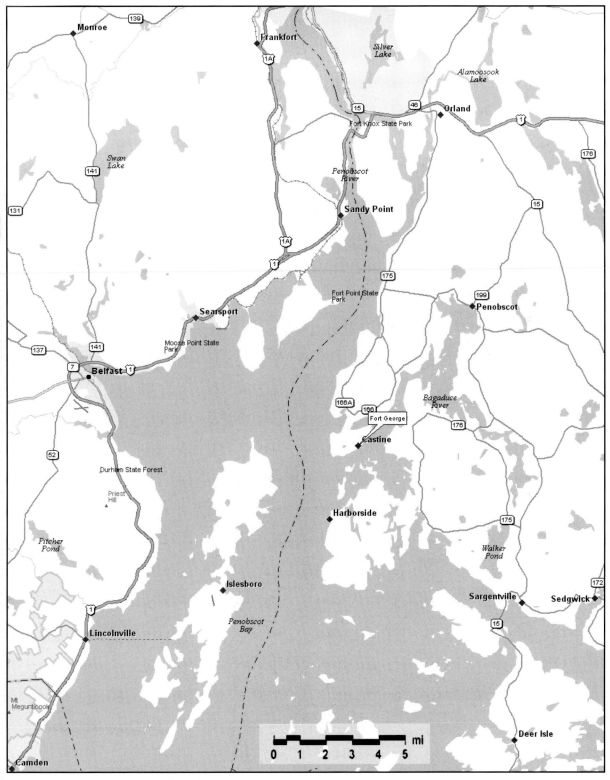

Maine, Map for *Battlegrounds of Freedom*

© 2003 DeLorme (www.delorme.com) Street Atlas USA® Plus

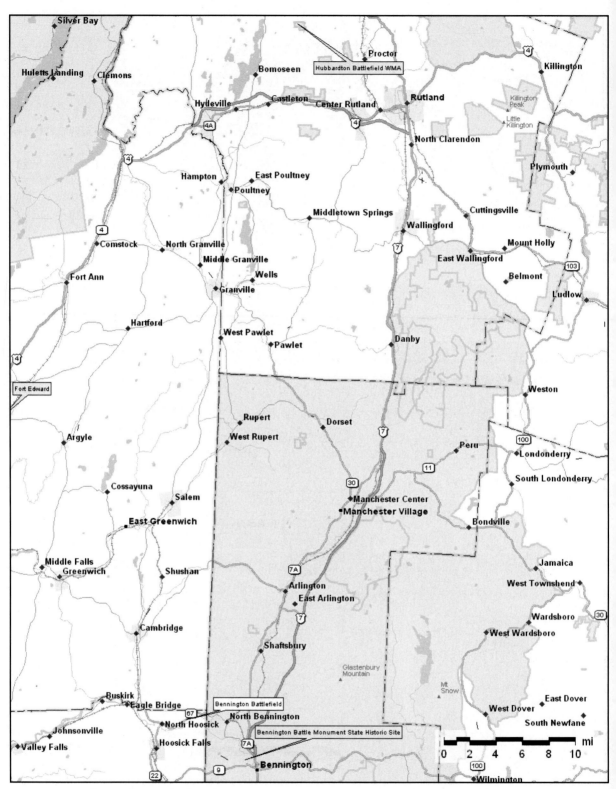

Silver Bay

Huletts Landing   Clemons   Bomoseen   Proctor   [4] Killington

Hydeville   Castleton   Center Rutland   Rutland   Killington Peak

[4A]   [4]   Little Killington

North Clarendon

Hampton   East Poultney   Plymouth
Poultney

Middletown Springs   Cuttingsville
Wallingford

[4]   Comstock   North Granville   Mount Holly
Middle Granville   [7]   East Wallingford   [103]
Fort Ann   Wells   Belmont
Granville   Ludlow

Hartford   West Pawlet   Danby
Pawlet

[4]   Weston

Fort Edward   Rupert   Dorset   [100]
West Rupert   [7]   Peru   Londonderry

Argyle   South Londonderry
Cossayuna   [30]   [11]
Salem   Manchester Center   Bondville
East Greenwich   Manchester Village

Middle Falls   Jamaica
Greenwich   Shushan   [7A]   West Townshend
Arlington   Wardsboro   [30]
East Arlington
Cambridge   [7]   West Wardsboro
Shaftsbury

Glastenbury Mountain
Mt Snow
East Dover
Buskirk   Bennington Battlefield   West Dover
Eagle Bridge   [67]   North Bennington   South Newfane
Johnsonville   North Hoosick   Bennington Battle Monument State Historic Site
Valley Falls   Hoosick Falls   [7A]
[22]   [9]   Bennington   mi
0 2 4 6 8 10
[100]   Wilmington

Hubbardton Battlefield WMA

Vermont, Map for *Battlegrounds of Freedom*   © 2003 DeLorme (www.delorme.com) Street Atlas USA® Plus

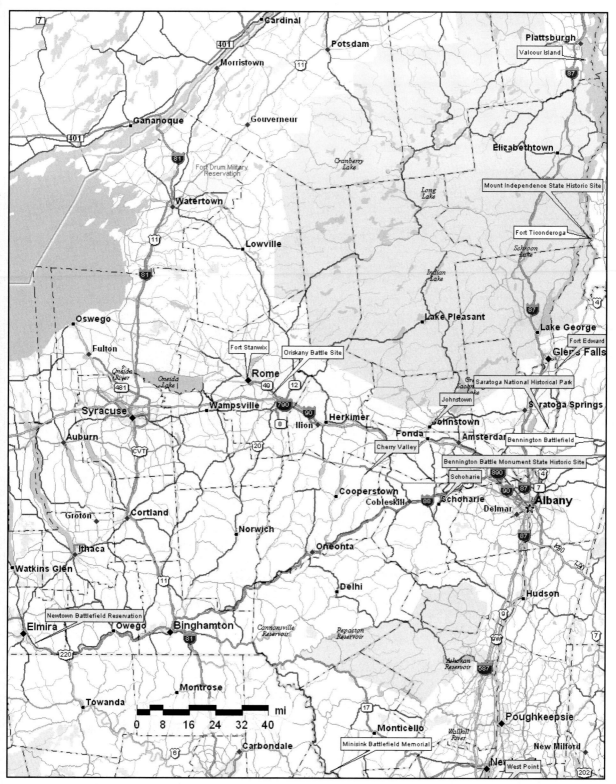

Upstate New York, Map for *Battlegrounds of Freedom*

© 2003 DeLorme (www.delorme.com) Street Atlas USA® Plus

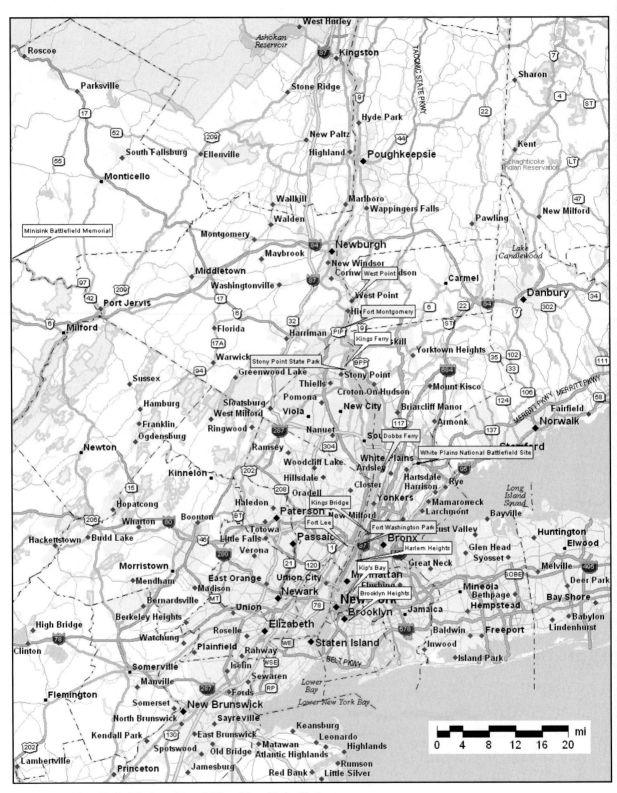

Downstate New York (Hudson River Valley, New York City),
Map for *Battlegrounds of Freedom*

© 2003 DeLorme (www.delorme.com) Street Atlas USA® Plus

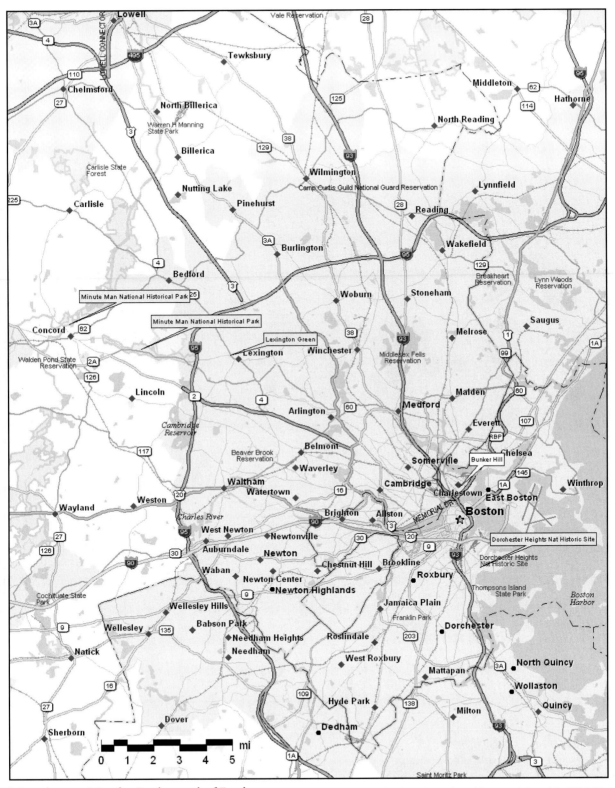

Massachusetts, Map for *Battlegrounds of Freedom*

© 2003 DeLorme (www.delorme.com) Street Atlas USA® Plus

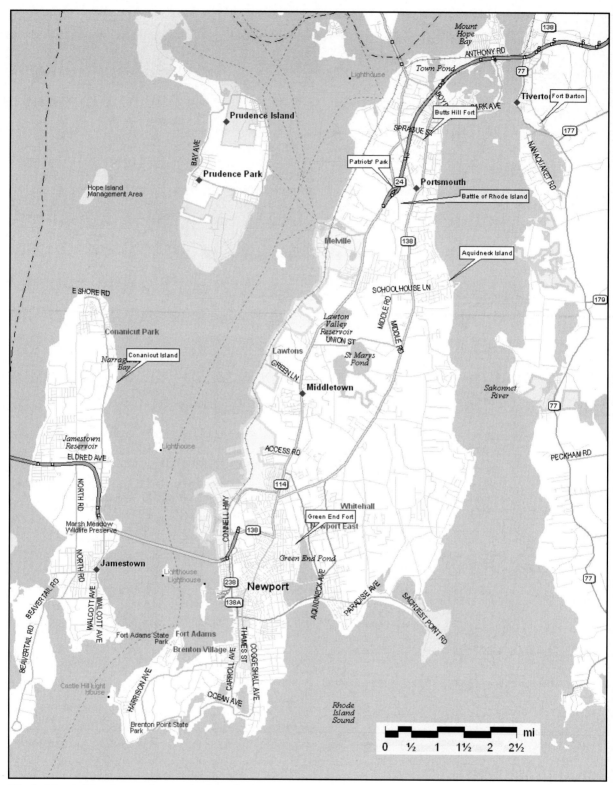

Rhode Island, Map for *Battlegrounds of Freedom*

© 2003 DeLorme (www.delorme.com) Street Atlas USA® Plus

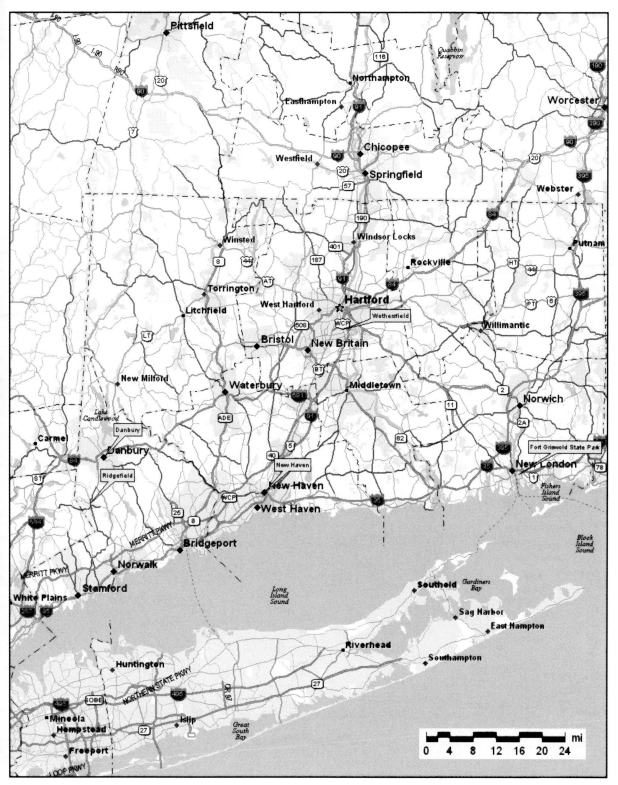

Connecticut, Map for *Battlegrounds of Freedom*

© 2003 DeLorme (www.delorme.com) Street Atlas USA® Plus

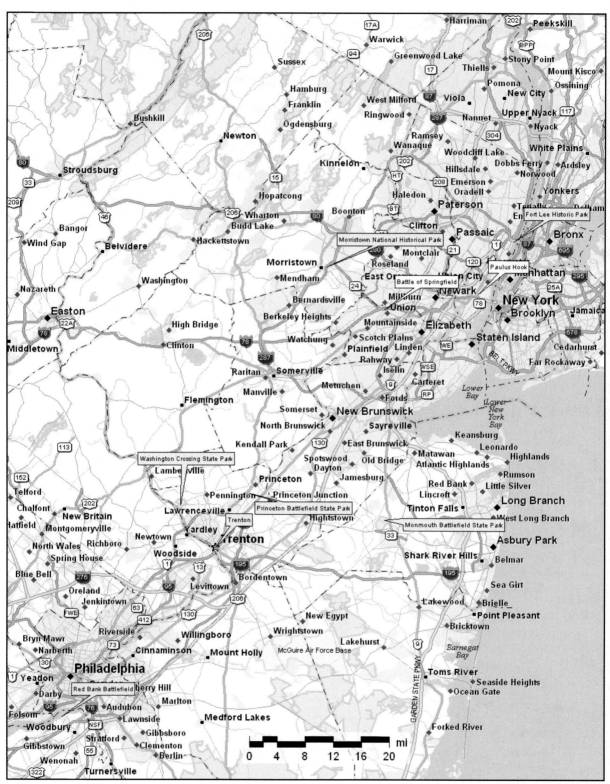

New Jersey, Map for *Battlegrounds of Freedom*

© 2003 DeLorme (www.delorme.com) Street Atlas USA® Plus

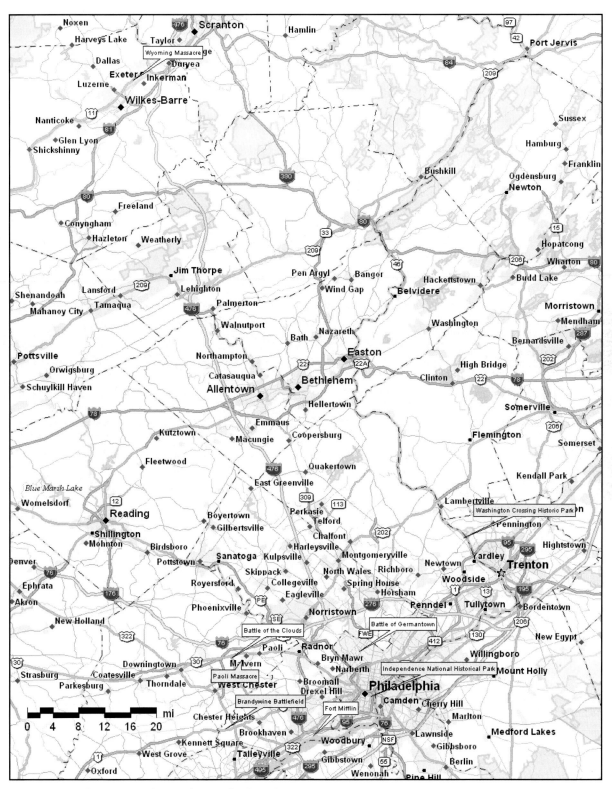

Eastern Pennsylvania, Map for *Battlegrounds of Freedom*

© 2003 DeLorme (www.delorme.com) Street Atlas USA® Plus

Southeastern Pennsylvania/Philadelphia area,
Map for *Battlegrounds of Freedom*

© 2003 DeLorme (www.delorme.com) Street Atlas USA® Plus

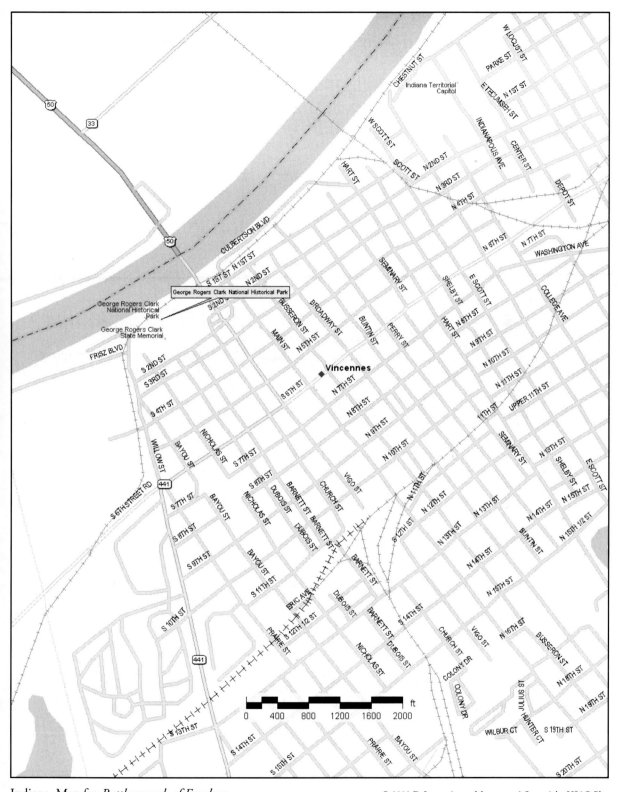

Indiana, Map for *Battlegrounds of Freedom*

© 2003 DeLorme (www.delorme.com) Street Atlas USA® Plus

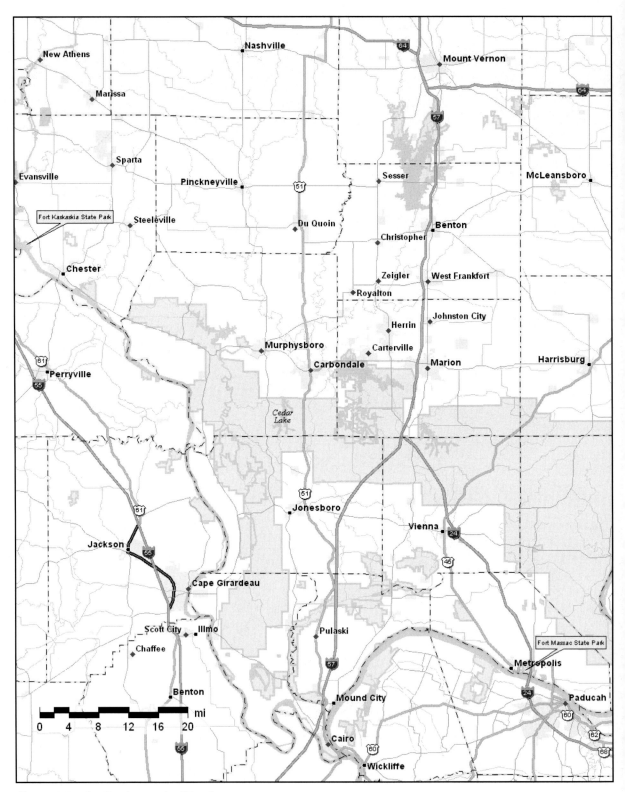

Illinois, Map for *Battlegrounds of Freedom*

© 2003 DeLorme (www.delorme.com) Street Atlas USA® Plus

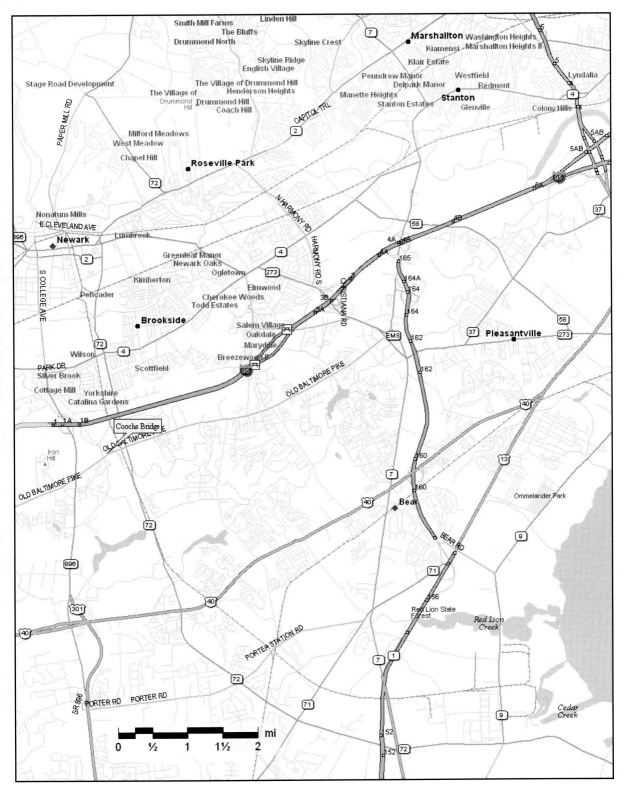

Delaware, Map for *Battlegrounds of Freedom*

© 2003 DeLorme (www.delorme.com) Street Atlas USA® Plus

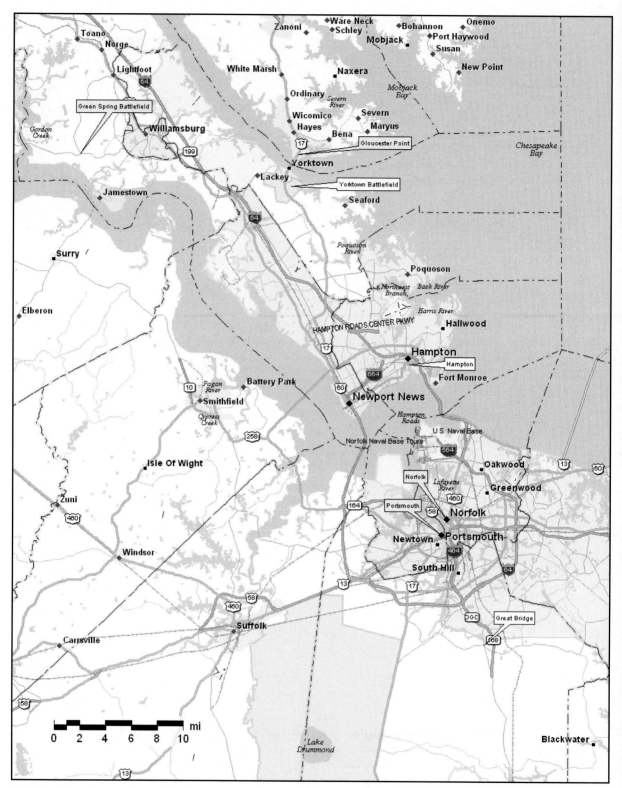

Virginia, Map for *Battlegrounds of Freedom*

© 2003 DeLorme (www.delorme.com) Street Atlas USA® Plus

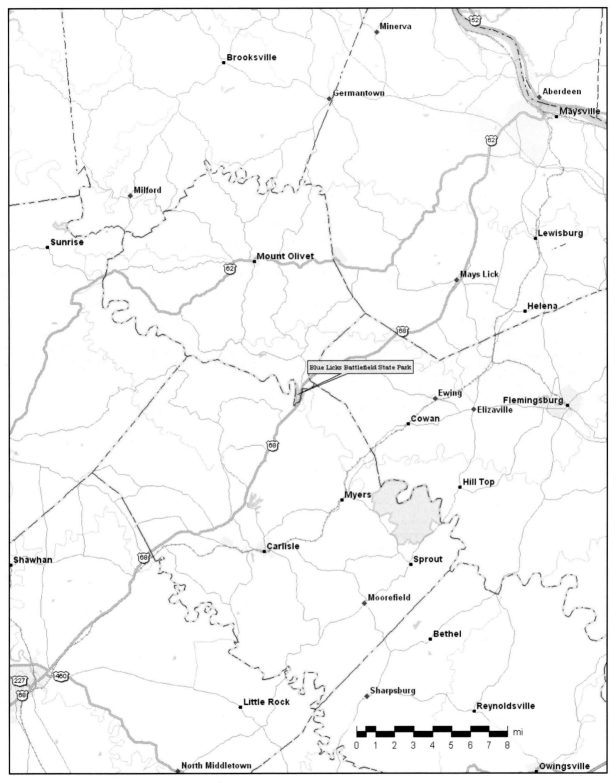

Minerva

Brooksville

Germantown

Aberdeen

Maysville

Milford

Lewisburg

Sunrise

Mount Olivet

Mays Lick

Helena

Blue Licks Battlefield State Park

Ewing

Flemingsburg

Elizaville

Cowan

Hill Top

Myers

Carlisle

Sprout

Shawhan

Moorefield

Bethel

Little Rock

Sharpsburg

Reynoldsville

North Middletown

Owingsville

mi
0 1 2 3 4 5 6 7 8

Kentucky, Map for *Battlegrounds of Freedom*

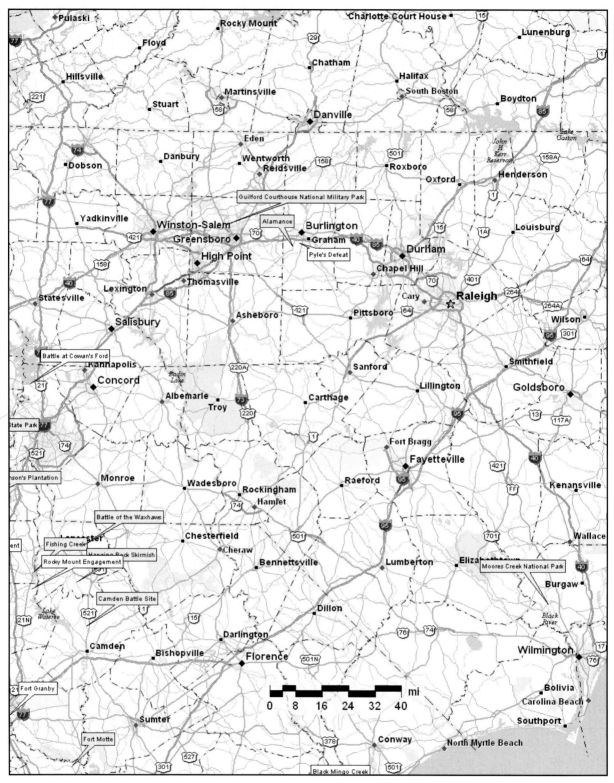

North Carolina, Map for *Battlegrounds of Freedom*

© 2003 DeLorme (www.delorme.com) Street Atlas USA® Plus

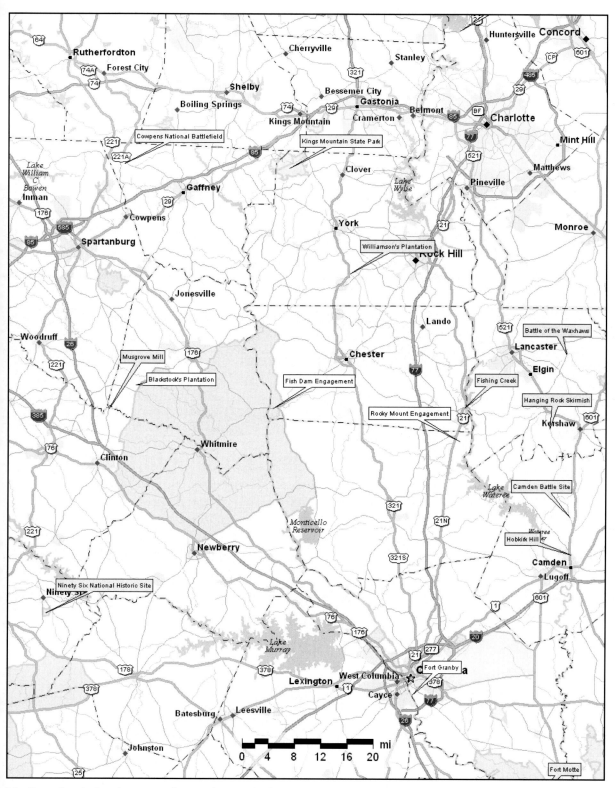

Northern South Carolina, Map for *Battlegrounds of Freedom*

© 2003 DeLorme (www.delorme.com) Street Atlas USA® Plus

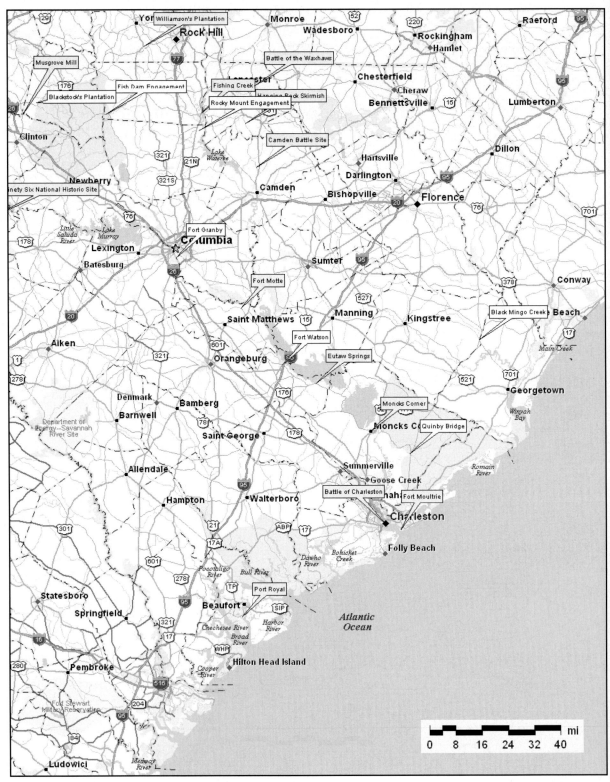

Southern South Carolina, Map for *Battlegrounds of Freedom*   © 2003 DeLorme (www.delorme.com) Street Atlas USA® Plus

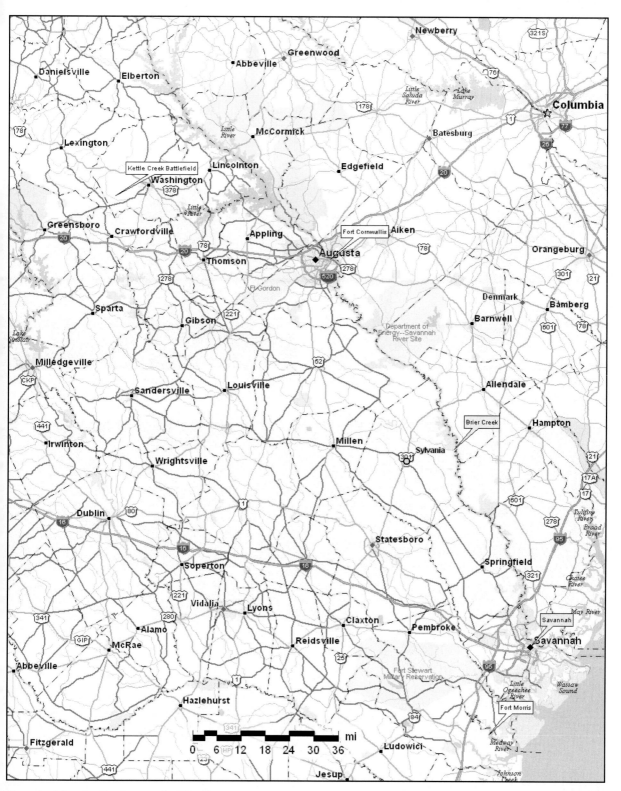

Georgia, Map for *Battlegrounds of Freedom*

© 2003 DeLorme (www.delorme.com) Street Atlas USA® Plus

Photo VT-1: Re-enactors wearing Hessian uniforms. The Hessian jackets are dark blue. The front of the hats bears an engraved brass plate.

Photo VT-2: Re-enactor wearing a jaeger uniform. The uniform is dark green with red trim. The hat is dark blue.

Photo VT-3: Re-enactors portray British and Hessian troops on the march. The small group in the foreground is comprised of British soldiers wearing bright red jackets. On the left are marching Hessians; their jackets are blue.

Photo NY-1: Fort Ticonderoga, New York. The sally port, the entrance to Fort Ticonderoga, is protected by two howitzers. The tripod to the right of the sally port is a cannon gin, used to raise and lower gun barrels onto the carriage.

Photo NY-2: The Northeast bastion of Fort Ticonderoga. Mount Independence is in the background.

Photo NY-3: Musket fire from a re-enactment emanates from inside the palisade of Fort Stanwix.

Photo NY-4: Reconstruction of the Balcarres redoubt on the occasion of the 225th anniversary of the Battle of Saratoga.

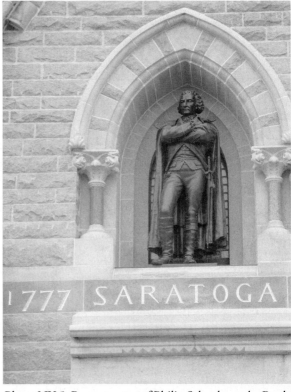

Photo NY-5: Bronze statue of Philip Schuyler at the Battle Monument in Schuylerville commemorating the victory at Saratoga.

Photo NY-6: Elijah Miller House, White Plains. General George Washington selected the Elijah Miller House as his headquarters for the Battle of White Plains. He stayed here for 2 weeks after he left the Purdy House (Spring Street, near the intersection with Rockledge Avenue) where he stayed October 23–28.

Photo NY-7: Assault on hill (re-enacted) by Crown forces, who are at the top of the hill pushing the Patriots into the woods.

Photo NY-8: One of the gun batteries at Stony Point as it appears today.

Photo NY-9: This marker honors those British soldiers who died at Stony Point.

Photo NY-10: View of Verplanck's Point from Stony Point.

Photo NY-11: Links from the second great chain that stretched across the Hudson River at Trophy Point. Each link was made of bar iron about 2 inches square with dimensions about 18 inches long and 12 inches wide. The smallest links weighed between 98 and 109 pounds; the largest ones weighed 130 pounds.

Photo NY-12: Inspection of troops at Fort Putnam (re-enacted).

Photo NY-13: Model of HMS *Vulture* in the collection of the Fort Putnam museum.

Photo NY-14: Molly Corbin's grave marker in the cemetery behind the Old Cadet Chapel at West Point. Molly Corbin was wounded in the assault of Fort Washington when she took her husband's place at the cannon after he fell severely wounded.

Photo NY-15: Fort Lee, New Jersey. This view of the reconstructed northern redoubt of Fort Lee shows a façade of the fort protected by fascines with two gun emplacements.

Photo NY-16: Prospect Park, Brooklyn. This section of Prospect Park, called Longmeadow, was probably where General William Alexander (Earl of Stirling) positioned his troops at the beginning of the Battle of Brooklyn Heights.

Photo NY-17: The Cortelyou House in Brooklyn was built in 1699 and remained standing until it was demolished in 1897. This reconstruction uses some of the original stones. The Maryland state flag hangs from the window in the center to honor the Maryland troops who fought and died here.

Photo NY-18: Replica of the HMS *Rose* built for the nation's Bicentennial, shown under sail. The *Rose's* main mission was to patrol the coast of New England to enforce the navigation laws and to prevent piracy.

Photo MA-1: The Hancock-Clark House, Lexington, Massachusetts. John Hancock and Samuel Adams stayed at the Hancock-Clark House at 36 Hancock Street on April 17, 1775.

Photo MA-2: The Buckman Tavern overlooks the Lexington Green. The minutemen gathered in the taproom before dawn on April 19, 1775.

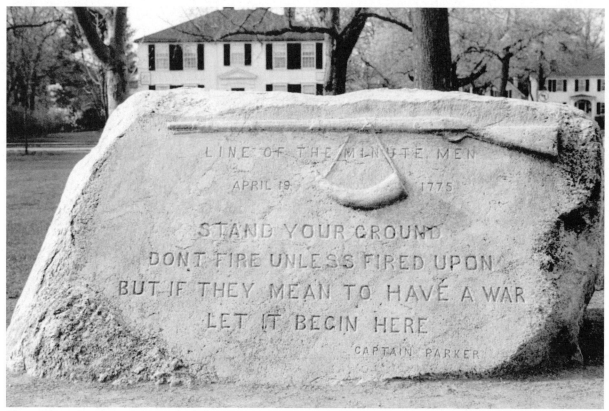

Photo MA-3: Lexington Monument. The monument on Lexington Green, Bedford and Harrington streets, marks the battle line of the minutemen on April 19, 1775. The Harrington house is in the background.

Photo MA-4: The Old Belfry, Lexington. This photo shows a reproduction of the original belfry, whose bell sounded the alarm that assembled the minutemen.

Photo MA-5: The North Bridge in Concord. This is the sixth bridge on the site since April 19, 1775. It was erected in 1956 and is believed to resemble the original more closely than earlier reconstructions.

Photo MA-6: The grave of British Soldiers who died at the North Bridge in Concord.

Photo MA-7: The Bunker Hill Monument, Charlestown, Massachusetts. The sculpture to the left of the monument is of Colonel William Prescott, commander of the redoubt at the Battle of Bunker Hill.

Photo MA-8: This sculpture of Colonel William Prescott stands at the base of the Bunker Hill Monument.

Photo MA-9: British forces (re-enactors) prepare to attack the rebels entrenched on top of the hill. The artillery is behind the troops.

Photo MA-10: Fort Ticonderoga, New York, with its cannons.

Photo MA-11: Paul Revere's house, Boston. Paul Revere lived in this house in Boston's North End.

Photo MA-12: Sculpture of Paul Revere on horseback, Boston. The rear of the Old North Church is in the background.

Photo MA-13: Paul Revere's grave. Paul Revere is buried in the Old Granary burial ground in Boston.

Photo MA-14: Cat-o'-nine-tails. The usual penalty in the military was a whipping with a small whip called a cat-o'-nine-tails, or "cat" for short.

Photo MA-15: This monument marks the site of one of the redoubts constructed on Dorchester Heights. The inscription commemorates the feat of General Henry Knox who brought the cannon from Fort Ticonderoga in New York to this site. The water of Boston harbor is clearly visible behind the row of houses.

Photo RI-1: Butts Hill Fort, inside of moat. This is one of 18 forts constructed in Rhode Island, and is undeveloped. This view shows the moat overgrown with trees. The inside of the fort is to the left of the picture. Notice the steepness of the moat walls. They would have been even steeper and more difficult to climb over 225 years ago.

Photo RI-2: Hessian troops (re-enactors) ready for battle. The coats, which can weigh 10–15 pounds, are dark blue with yellow facings. The (tall) mitre caps bear an engraved brass plate. The Hessian flag is mostly gold and blue.

Photo RI-3: The Memorial to Black Soldiers in Patriots' Park (RI 114 and U.S. 24 northbound (from Portsmouth) commemorates the contributions of the 1st Rhode Island Regiment comprised of approximately 95 former slaves and 30 free African Americans.

Photo CT-1: This memorial plaque at Fort Griswold commemorates Jordan Freeman, an African American and Lieutenant Colonel William Ledyard's orderly. It is located at the point where Freeman fatally stabbed Major William Montgomery.

Photo CT-2: Fort Griswold as seen from the top of the Groton Monument. The fort's classic star shape is clearly visible. The fortifications and gun emplacements at the bottom of the hill in the upper right quadrant of the photo date from the Civil War.

Photo NJ-1: Fort Lee, New Jersey, was an earthen fort. This is a view of one of the reconstructed bastions with a fraise, sharpened stakes built into the exterior wall to deter attackers.

Photo NJ-2: The Ferry House in Washington Crossing State Park (in/near Titusville, New Jersey).

Photo NJ-3: The road to Trenton: Continental Lane, over which the Colonial troops marched on Christmas night in 1776 after crossing the Delaware River. Many of the men had no shoes or boots and left bloody footprints in the snow.

Photo NJ-4: The Old Barracks in Trenton was the focal point of the Battle of Trenton. Colonel Johann Gottleib Rall and 1,400 Hessians, including elements of the Knyphausen and von Lossberg regiments, were quartered here.

Photo NJ-5: The Thomas Clark house, Princeton, New Jersey, where General Hugh Mercer died of his wounds 9 days after the Battle of Princeton.

Photo NJ-6: The Princeton battlefield. The Ionic columns in the distance mark British and American graves.

Photo NJ-7: Princeton University's Nassau Hall, completed in 1756, was the university's only building. It housed classrooms, dormitories, teachers' quarters, and dining rooms. Both sides used it as barracks and as a military hospital during the War for American Independence.

Photo NJ-8: The house of James and Ann Whithall was commandeered by the Continental Army in April, 1777. The apple orchard was destroyed to build Fort Mercer, and the house was used as a field hospital during the Battle of Red Bank. Major General Karl von Donop died here. He was interred on the battlefield on October 28, 1777. The house is open to the public.

Photo NJ-9: Monmouth: Battlefield from Comb's Hill, location of American cannon at the battle of Monmouth. Re-enactors (British troops, those in the foreground wearing the "traditional" red coats) prepare for the 225th anniversary of the battle. A cherry orchard lies at the top of the ridge and a split-rail fence borders the path to the orchard. Cornfields cover the lower part of the hill.

Photo NJ-10: Cannon crews at the 225th anniversary of the Battle of Monmouth. Careful examination of the photo will reveal a couple of women assisting the crews, recalling the story of Molly Pitcher.

Photo NJ-11: Morristown, soldiers' houses. The soldiers lived in tents until they could build more durable huts such as these for shelter.

Photo NJ-12: Interior of a soldier's hut at Morristown.

Photo NJ-13: George Washington's headquarters, Morristown. The house of Jacob Ford, Jr. (230 Morris Avenue) was Washington's headquarters during the winter encampment at Morristown. Even though the weather was so cold that the ink froze in the inkwells, the officers' quarters were still more comfortable than those of the soldiers.

Photo PA-1: Carpenters' Hall, Philadelphia, site of the First Continental Congress September 5, 1774 to October 26, 1774.

Photo PA-2: The interior of Carpenters' Hall shows a table and chairs that the delegates might have used in their deliberations.

Photo PA-3: Independence Hall, originally the Pennsylvania State House, was built in 1732. It is where the Second Continental Congress met in 1775 and where the Declaration of Independence and Constitution were debated and signed.

Photo PA-4: Witnesses to independence, Independence Hall. The Syng inkstand was used to sign the Declaration of Independence on August 2, 1776. John Hancock presided over the Second Continental Congress from the Rising Sun Chair. It was also used by George Washington when he presided over the Constitutional Convention in 1787.

Photo PA-5: The Assembly Room of Independence Hall has been restored to look as it did when the founding fathers debated here from 1775–1787. Some of the furniture, including Washington's "rising sun" chair (on the dais in the background), is original.

Photo PA-6: The Tomb of the Unknown Soldier of the American Revolution is on the western edge of Washington Square in Philadelphia.

Photo PA-7: Re-creation of one of the rooms Thomas Jefferson rented upstairs in Jacob Graff's house where he drafted the Declaration of Independence.

Photo PA-8: Durham boat. Washington and his men crossed the Delaware River in Durham boats such as the one shown here.

Photo PA-9: Raft for horses and cannon. The horses and 18 cannon were ferried across the Delaware on rafts such as this one.

Photo PA-10: McConkey's Ferry Inn. Nine miles upstream from Trenton, this is where General George Washington's troops boarded the Durham boats to cross the Delaware into New Jersey.

Photo PA-11: A reproduction of the farmhouse used by George Washington as his headquarters at the Battle of the Brandywine.

Photo PA-12: The original farmhouse which served as the Marquis de Lafayette's headquarters at the Battle of the Brandywine.

Photo PA-13: Re-enactors executing a British bayonet charge.

Photo PA-14: Cliveden/Chew Mansion (6401 Germantown Avenue in Germantown) was the summer home of Benjamin Chew. It was the center of much of the Battle of Germantown and still bears evidence of cannon and musket fire.

Photo PA-15: Fort Mifflin. President John Adams ordered Fort Mifflin rebuilt in 1798. The riverside is original, and the reconstruction used much of the 1770s foundation. The bunks are believed to date from 1812. The fort remained in use until 1962.

Photo PA-16: Valley Forge, outer defenses.

Photo PA-17: Valley Forge. Reconstructions of log cabins built for housing soldiers.

Photo PA-18: George Washington's headquarters at Valley Forge.

Photo PA-19: Grand Parade, Valley Forge. During the 6 months at Valley Forge, the Continental Army was reorganized and drilled to fight on equal terms with British Regulars in the open field. The Grand Parade is where Baron Friedrich Wilhelm von Steuben trained the troops.

Photo PA-20: One of the redoubts protecting Valley Forge. Some of the reconstructed soldiers' huts can be seen in the valley below the cannon which overlooks the Grand Parade.

Photo VA-1: This re-enactor portrays a rifleman, probably a Pennsylvania rifleman. Note the leggings and the moccasins. General Washington adopted the fringed linen hunting shirt for many of his troops early in the war because it was relatively easy to make and it made it difficult for the enemy to distinguish riflemen from musketeers. (The rifle had an effective range three times greater than the musket.)

Photo VA-2: During the siege of Yorktown, General Cornwallis used the home of Thomas Nelson, Governor of Virginia, as his headquarters. This photo shows a cannonball lodged in the wall of the third floor (between the two windows).

Photo VA-3: Redoubt Number 9, Yorktown. This photo shows the exterior of reconstructed Redoubt Number 9 with openings for gun emplacements to the left. (Photo VA-7 is a view from inside Redoubt Number 9.)

Photo VA-4: The Fusiliers' Redoubt (Yorktown) was named for the Royal Welch Fusiliers who manned it.

Photo VA-5: Allied line, grand French battery, Yorktown.

Photo VA-6: French artillery park, Yorktown.

Photo VA-7: Inside Redoubt Number 9, Yorktown. (See also Photo VA-3, redoubt exterior.)

Photo VA-8: Communicating trench linking the second siege line to Redoubt Number 9, Yorktown. The zigzag pattern provides added protection to the attackers

Photo VA-9: The Moore House, Yorktown, where the surrender documents were signed.

Photo VA-10: Surrender field at Yorktown. The split rail fence marks the route that the defeated army supposedly took to lay down their arms. The soldiers then assembled in the open field.

Photo VA-11: A few representative pieces of artillery surrendered by the Crown forces at Yorktown. This exhibit borders Surrender Field.

Photo NC-1: The monument marks the site of the Battle of the Alamance. The flags denote the relative positions of both sides.

Photo NC-2: Continental troops (re-enactors) positioned behind a split-rail fence await attack by the Crown forces.

Photo NC-3: Guilford Courthouse main battlefield with American guns pointed toward the Crown forces' line of advance. Lord Cornwallis placed one of his guns just behind the tree line in the background. William Washington's cavalry was held in reserve on the ridge marked by the Cavalry Monument at the left. The Stuart Monument, in the ravine at the center of the photo, honors Colonel James Stuart of the Queen's Guard. (Photo NC-4 shows the view from the British cannons.)

Photo NC-4: British cannon facing American cannon, Guilford Courthouse, with one of Cornwallis's 3 cannon positioned along the edge of the woods. Note the distance between the two forces. The 2 guns in the background mark the position of the Continental forces (see Photo NC-3).

Photo NC-5: The Turner monument, Guilford Courthouse. When Kerenhappuck Norman Turner learned that her son was badly wounded in the battle at Guilford Courthouse, she rode 300 miles on horseback to nurse him and the other soldiers. Her son had a fever, so she made holes in a tub, suspended it from the rafters, and filled it with water. The cool water dripping slowly on her son's wounds and body acted like a modern ice pack and lessened the fever.

Photo NC-6: The Hoskins/Wyrick House served as Cornwallis's headquarters during the battle of Guilford Courthouse. It also served as a field hospital for both sides.

Photo SC-1: Captured British prisoners flanked by American troops (re-enactors). The British prisoners wear red coats and carry their muskets clubbed (inverted), while the blue-coated Americans have bayonets fixed to their muskets.

Photo SC-2: The Joseph Kershaw house at the Historic Camden Revolutionary War site. General Cornwallis used the house as his headquarters prior to and during the Battle of Camden.

Photo SC-3: The uniforms of the British army were not all red. Tarleton's Legion, as most dragoons of the period, wore green regimental coats like the one shown here.

Photo SC-4: Terrain of King's Mountain.

Photo SC-5: The Memorial to Major Patrick Ferguson at Kings Mountain marks the spot where he was wounded.

Photo SC-6: Battlefield of Cowpens.

Photo SC-7: Fort Ninety-Six with remains of siege lines. A cannon is visible left of center as is a Maham gun tower (see Photo SC-11) toward the rear of the picture. (For more on the Maham gun tower, see the account of Fort Watson in Santee, South Carolina.)

Photo SC-8: Reconstruction of Fort Sullivan, renamed Fort Moultrie after the 1776 battle, with palmetto trees on either side. The structure supported by the brick columns is the firing platform. The cannon on the ground behind it date from the Civil War, as does the fort structure in the right background of the photo. Fort Moultrie was used through World War II. Courtesy of Carl Becker.

Photo SC-9: Hornwork, Charleston. This tabby block on the west side (King Street side) of Marion Square is all that remains of the hornwork which stood at the center of Charleston's inner defenses during the siege of 1780. Courtesy of Paul Bazin.

Photo SC-10: The Old Exchange and Provost Dungeon was built by the British in 1771 as the Customs House and Exchange for the prosperous city of Charles Towne.

Photo SC-11: The Maham gun tower was first used at the Battle of Fort Watson. It stood about 60 feet high. The reconstruction seen here is from Ninety-Six National Historic Site. The remains of the zigzag siege lines are clearly visible at the base of the tower in the foreground.

Photo SC-12: A British camp (of re-enactors) protected by chevaux-de-frise. The small circular bell tent to the left of the chevaux-de-frise is to store muskets and to protect them from the weather.

Photo RLH-1: This cornfield served as the site for much of the 225th anniversary re-enactment of the Battle of Monmouth. Note the short distance between the opposing forces.

Photo RLH-2: Lean-to, re-enactors' camp. Most Native Americans sided with the British. This photo shows the Native American portion of the camp with two men sharing a lean-to.

Photo RLH-3: Re-enacting has activities for the entire family to enjoy and share. Here, children help with the cooking.

Photo RLH-4: Equipment. Riflemen or rangers occupy this tent. A canteen and a variety of powder horns and shot pouches are draped over the support. The powder horn is used for priming the firing pan of the rifle.

Photo RLH-5: Laundry, 18th-century style, at re-enactors' camp.

Photo RLH-6: Changing of the guard at the Patriot artillery park, re-enactment of the Battle of Monmouth. The artillerists are members of the United Train of Artillery. Note the sponge, worm, and rammer crossed over the gun barrels. These are the tools the artillerists use to clean and load the cannon. The brown coats with red trim are called "lottery coats." They were given to the army by the French government. Because they were insufficient in number to clothe all the troops, the soldiers drew lots to determine who got one, hence the name.

with Lee's resolution. Jefferson was given the task of preparing the draft. Adams and Franklin made several minor changes to Jefferson's draft before the committee submitted it to Congress on June 28.

July 1

When Congress convened on July 1, it constituted itself into a committee of the whole to resume discussion of Lee's resolution of June 7. John Hancock (1737–1793) gave the chair to Benjamin Harrison (1726?–1791) of Virginia, and the delegates pledged to keep the proceedings secret. The committee of the whole would then report back to the Congress which alone could take formal action.

John Dickinson (1732–1808) and the Pennsylvania delegation, while not exactly Loyalists, were loyal to the King. They preferred to blame Parliament for past injustices rather than King George III (1738–1820). The colonists had always asked that matters be restored to the way they were before 1773. When the King and Parliament and the Prime Minister ignored their pleas and sent soldiers and ships against them, they felt forced into forming a separate nation.

When John Adams referred to the Pennsylvania delegation as "puling, pusillanimous cowards," the delegates became agitated to the point of standing, stomping, waving their arms for recognition from the chair, shouting at each other, arguing, and interrupting the speaker with sarcasm.

New Jersey had a new group of delegates sitting for the first time. These 5 members wanted a summary of the arguments on both sides of the issue. The delegates hoped that debate on the measure would be limited to John Adams (for) and John Dickinson (against).

John Dickinson argued that the Colonies were too weak to fight the Crown. George Washington was in New York commanding 25 regiments totaling 9,000 men. Six days earlier, lookouts at Gravesend had spotted a few masts anchored inside Sandy Hook. The next day, more arrived. By the third day, lookouts saw "a forest of masts" between Staten Island and the New Jersey coast. Dickinson questioned whether the untrained men of the Continental Army could fight against the tremendous fleet that Admiral Richard Howe (1726–1799) had standing off New York or whether they could win against General William Howe's (1732–1786) army of highly skilled and trained British soldiers and Hessians.

Adams argued that the Americans were already fighting for their freedom. Would they let the British army gobble up the colonies one by one? They had to fight and win to survive. They would have to get help from France which had a long-standing antipathy for the British and which lost large tracts of land after the Seven Years' War.

The delegates decided that each delegation would vote as a unit, regardless of the number of members in each one. Those who saw a vote going against them insisted that the clerk regard it as "unanimous." Hancock prepared to call a roll of the colonies, but it was getting close to dinner time. Vote counters such as Franklin and John Adams tallied 7 in favor to 6 against at the end of the first day of debate. New Hampshire, Massachusetts, Rhode Island, Connecticut, Virginia, North Carolina, and Georgia favored independence. Pennsylvania, New York, New Jersey, Delaware, Maryland, and

South Carolina were still against it. Seven to six was considerably less than the unanimity that Congress wanted, so it adjourned to resume the following day.

July 2

When the Congress convened on July 2, the members were still far from unanimous in their desire for independence. John Dickinson and Robert Morris (1734–1806), who commanded the majority vote in Pennsylvania's 7-member delegation, did not attend the meeting that day. Dickinson could not sign a declaration of independence in good conscience. Robert Morris decided that if the delegates passed a declaration, he would sign it when the time came. He gave his reasoning: "I think that the individual who declines the service of his country because its councils are not comfortable to his ideas, makes but a bad subject; a good one will follow if he cannot lead." These absences gave the majority vote to the pro-independence members of the delegation.

Caesar Rodney (1728–1784) of Delaware was in Dover on the evening of July 1, having just returned from investigating Loyalist agitations in Sussex County. He received a dispatch from Thomas McKean (1734–1817), his fellow delegate, that the Delaware delegation was deadlocked, and they needed his vote to break the tie. Rodney, who had skin cancer on his face and covered it with a green silk cloth, could have gone to England to be treated by the finest physicians and surgeons. As he was opposed to the King and Parliament, he would not go. Instead, he risked his health further that night by riding the 80 miles from Dover, Delaware to Philadelphia in a thunderstorm. He arrived just in time to cast his and Delaware's vote for independence.

The Committee of the Whole considered Richard Henry Lee's three resolutions as one. Everyone knew that this vote would indicate how the vote on the declaration would go. The vote was as close to unanimous as the delegates could get—12 to 0, with one abstention. Overnight, the radicals obtained 3 votes. South Carolina switched position; Caesar Rodney broke Delaware's tie; and Dickinson's and Morris's absence changed direction for Pennsylvania. New York was inclined to vote for the Lee resolutions, but an order from New York not to vote for independence still bound them. They hoped for a change of orders, but it had not arrived, so they abstained.

John Adams was excited by the proceedings of July 2. Writing to his wife, Abigail, in Boston, he said:

> The Second Day of July 1776, will be the most memorable Epocha in the history of America—I am apt to believe that it will be celebrated by succeeding Generations, as the Day of Deliverance by solemn Acts of Devotion to God Almighty. it ought to be solemnized with Pomp and Parade, with Shews, Games, Sports, Guns, Bells, Bonfires and Illuminations, from one End of this Continent to the other, from this Time forward, forevermore.

The delegates seemed to have ignored General Washington's letter that morning reporting that his spies counted 140 ships in Lower New York Bay. A more accurate count totaled 400 transports, 52 ships of the line, and 27 armed sloops and cutters—the greatest war fleet ever assembled. Another 39 ships of war and 2,500 men were on their way north from Charleston, South Carolina where General Henry Clinton (1730–1795) and Lord General Charles Cornwallis (1738–1805) had been defeated attempting an amphibious landing. These forces would arrive within a week or two to further strengthen General Howe's army of 32,000 soldiers on Staten Island.

July 3

The discussion of July 3 and 4 turned to the Declaration of Independence and the form of the announcement. Benjamin Harrison called for a full reading of Jefferson's draft of the declaration without interruption. If any members wanted to make revisions, it would be read again, slowly, paragraph by paragraph. After editing the document in its final form, the Committee of the Whole would vote whether or not to adopt it. If a favorable vote prevailed, the declaration would go to a public printer before returning to the Congress, sitting as a congress, for signing by the president and clerk. Those who opposed the declaration tried to procrastinate or fight for time. Congress refused to delay and began to edit the declaration, making more than 80 modifications.

Thomas Jefferson was a private person who did not appreciate criticism. He was also too proud to stand to defend his draft. Instead, he squirmed under his portable desk, making notes and changing his copy as delegates made amendments.

July 4

On July 4, 1776, Congress made several small alterations; deleted several sections, including one condemning black slavery; incorporated Lee's resolution; and issued the whole as the Declaration of Independence. Jefferson never commented publicly on what Congress did, but he always considered the changes as "mutilations."

Because of the abstention of the New York delegates from the final vote, the declaration could not yet be called the "Unanimous Declaration" of the 13 states, so it was entitled "A Declaration by the Representatives of the United States in General Congress Assembled." It carried only the names of John Hancock, the president of the Congress, and John Thomson, the clerk. It did not acknowledge Jefferson or the committee.

The preamble explains why the Continental Congress drew up the declaration and why the members felt it necessary to break their ties with England. A brief philosophical passage proclaims the universal rights of human beings. It follows John Locke's (1632–1704) philosophy of government that states that men are, by nature, free, equal, and independent of each other. They agree, in a social compact, to limit complete independence and to form a society under the supervision of government in order to protect themselves and their possessions. The consent of the governed creates government for a definite purpose. If any particular government fails to fulfill its purpose, it should be replaced by one that will.

The members of the Congress wanted to show that they were justified in seeking independence. They drew up a list of complaints against the King's acts in general terms. They wrote this list of complaints in the form of a legal indictment that intended to absolve them from any responsibility and to put all the blame on the King. This would give the Americans moral and legal justification for rebellion. This section assumes that the King acted intentionally and in bad faith in each instance, and it is the King's bad general purpose, rather than his bad acts, that makes the indictment so effective.

Because the declaration focuses on the King's bad intention, it does not mention Parliament. This is a significant change because the colonists debated Parliament's authority in all the controversy during the preceding decade, and they always dealt with Parliament rather than with the King.

Nor does the declaration speak of the "rights of British subjects." The colonists were now declaring their independence from Britain, and they could not present a convincing argument from the point of view of the rights of British subjects. They had to justify their separation from Great Britain on more general grounds. They focused on the natural rights of man. Because the King violated those basic human rights, they were no longer bound by the legal obligations of British subjects. They explained that the connection between the colonies and Great Britain was never very strong but only one entered into voluntarily by a free people.

Jefferson's underlying ideas built upon the generally accepted philosophy of the period that God established a "natural order" of things for the guidance of mankind. Human reason could discover the "laws" of this natural order; these laws govern human ideas, conduct, and institutions.

Hancock knew that Congress would adjourn late. It was getting close to supper time when the final changes were made. The Committee of the Whole voted on the Declaration of Independence and sent it to the Congress. Benjamin Harrison left the presiding officer's chair and gave it to John Hancock. Hancock made no speech, saying that he was prepared to accept the will of the Congress. Clerk Thomson called the roll. The colonies adopted the declaration unanimously. New York abstained because its delegates were still not authorized to vote for independence. However, the New York Provincial Congress voted to endorse the declaration on July 9.

Congress resolved on July 19 to have the Declaration of Independence engrossed on parchment. On August 2, the 53 members present signed it; the 3 absentees signed later. The members of Congress did not have to sign the Declaration of Independence to make it valid, but they knew that, within a few days, everybody would want to know who signed it. John Hancock signed his name with a large and flourishing hand. He said later that the King would not have to squint to find out whom he would hang first. The names of the signers were kept secret until January 18, 1777, after the battles of Trenton and Princeton.

Twenty-four of the signers of the Declaration of Independence were lawyers and jurists. Eleven were merchants, 9 were farmers and large plantation owners, men of means, well educated. They signed the Declaration knowing that the penalty would be death if they were captured. They had to expect success, and they knew that they and their countrymen would have to defeat the world's most formidable military and naval power at the time. In July, 1776, this might have seemed an impossible task with the greatest fighting force ever assembled gathering in New York.

Constitution

Congress organized a committee to cope with the matter of confederation. That committee produced a draft report, "Articles of Confederation and Perpetual Union," which Congress debated intermittently for nearly a year before adopting it as the first constitution of the United States on November 15, 1777. Ratified on March 1, 1781, the Articles of Confederation were more a "league of friendship" among independent states than a true act of union, but they governed the United States from the final years of the war, through the peace negotiations, and into the early years of the nation.

The Articles of Confederation failed to provide for a strong central government which led to the calling of a "Grand Convention" in Philadelphia in the summer of 1787 to revise the document. Revision proved impossible and the 55 convention delegates created an entirely new charter that would supplant the Articles as the law of the land. The result was the Constitution of the United States which was adopted on September 17, 1787 and ratified the following year.

Washington Square

> Washington Square is 1 block southwest of Independence Hall. The Tomb of the Unknown Soldier of the American Revolution (see Photo PA-6) is on the western edge of Washington Square, which is the site of other 18th-century burials.

Thomas Holme, William Penn's surveyor, plotted the city of Philadelphia as five squares in 1682. What is now Washington Square was then called Southeast Square because Quakers did not believe in naming places after people. The square soon came to be used as a burial ground for strangers in the city and continued to serve as a cemetery from 1704 to 1794.

Troops from General George Washington's army were already being buried in the square in 1776. About 4,000 soldiers were buried in several mass graves 20 feet by 30 feet along 7th and Walnut Streets (western side of the square). This is also the site of the Tomb of the Unknown Soldier of the American Revolution (see Photo PA-6). Another 4,000 soldiers were buried on the south side of the square. When the British occupied Philadelphia in 1777, the Walnut Street Jail, facing the Square, was used to hold prisoners of war. Conditions were so poor that an average of 12 people died each day. About 2,000 such prisoners were buried along the Walnut Street side. When Yellow Fever broke out in the city in 1793, about 5,000 of Philadelphia's 50,000 residents died of the disease. Many of them were buried along the 6th Street side of the square.

Declaration (Graff) House (June, 1776)

> The Declaration (Graff) House, on the southwest corner of 7th and Market Streets, is a reconstruction of the dwelling in which Thomas Jefferson drafted the Declaration of Independence in June, 1776. We don't know what the house looked like when Jefferson occupied it, so the reconstruction tries to evoke Jefferson's life, representing his passion for music, for instance, with a violin. (See Photo PA-7.)
> `http://www.ushistory.org/declaration/graff/`

Jacob Graff, a modest stonemason, rented the second floor of his townhouse (see Photo PA-7) to 33-year-old Thomas Jefferson (1743–1826), the second youngest delegate to the Second Continental Congress in 1776. Congress appointed Jefferson to a committee, along with Benjamin Franklin (1706–1790), John Adams (1735–1826), Roger Sherman (1721–1793), and Robert R. Livingston (1746–1813) to prepare a declaration of independence in line with Richard Henry Lee's (1732–1794) resolution of June 7, 1776.

Jefferson was given the task of preparing the draft because John Adams considered him best suited for the task of authorship as he was a Virginian and the declaration should come from a Virginia man. Adams also thought Jefferson was a better writer than he. Jefferson worked on his draft from June 11 until June 28, 1776, writing completely from memory, borrowing phrases and ideas, and adding his own ideals. Adams and Franklin made several minor changes to Jefferson's draft before the committee submitted it to Congress on June 28.

British Occupation

After the defeat at Brandywine, General George Washington (1732–1799) continued to attempt, unsuccessfully, to block General William Howe's ((1732-1786) march on Philadelphia. The Continental Congress fled to York (PA) in anticipation the occupation of Philadelphia on the same day as the Paoli Massacre. General William Howe's troops moved into Philadelphia on September 26, 1777 and spent the winter in Philadelphia. Washington's winter quarters were at Valley Forge, from which he was to emerge with an army equivalently trained to that of the enemy.

General William Howe's first task upon occupying Philadelphia was to open the Delaware River to British shipping so he could supply his army. Until then, he would have to bring his supplies overland from the Chesapeake River and escort them safely. He assigned 3,000 men for this duty. He began by trying to remove the booms and other obstacles which the Americans had sunk from one side of the river to the other and to capture the forts and redoubts whose guns covered them. He fortified Webb's Ferry and built a bridge to the south bank of the Schuylkill River onto Province Island. Here, he established a battery in the marshy ground and began to bombard Fort Mifflin on October 11, 1777. American guns were too small or improperly placed to respond effectively.

After the Battle of Germantown (October 4, 1777), Howe concentrated his army and moved to confront General George Washington (1732–1799) at Whitemarsh but withdrew to winter quarters in Philadelphia without giving battle. He dallied in Philadelphia, forfeiting whatever remaining chance he had to win a decisive victory before the effects of the French alliance were felt. He had had his fill of the American war and the King accepted his resignation from command, appointing General Henry Clinton (1730–1795) as his successor.

The British Army and the Philadelphia Loyalists said goodbye to their old commander in one of the most lavish celebrations ever held in America, the *Mischianza,* a veritable Belshazzar's feast organized by Captain John André (1751–1780). The handwriting on the wall appeared in the form of orders already in Clinton's hands, to evacuate the American capital (Philadelphia). With the French in the war, England had to look to the safety of the long ocean supply line to America and to the protection of its possessions in other parts of the world. Clinton's orders were to detach 5,000 men to the West Indies and 3,000 to Florida and to return the rest of his army to New York by sea.

David Bushnell, inventor of the submarine, devised a plan to try to sink British ships in the Delaware River. On January 5, 1778, the Americans floated explosive and incendiary mines down the Delaware in kegs. This "Battle of the Kegs" did no damage, but it caused the British to panic. Francis Hopkinson satirized the event in the *New Jersey Gazette* on January 21.

General Sir Henry Clinton (1730-1795), now in command of the Crown forces in America, decided to evacuate Philadelphia and go to New York. He and his army left Philadelphia on June 18, 1778 and marched overland because the Royal Navy could not provide enough transports to convey 10,000 to 17,000 men, 3,000 horses, supplies, and the hundreds of Loyalists who claimed British protection. General George Washington (1732–1799) and his army left Valley Forge, Pennsylvania the following day, June 19, in pursuit of the redcoats. The two armies engaged each other at the Battle of Monmouth (New Jersey) on June 25, 1778.

CONTINENTAL ARMY

The late arrival of General William Howe's (1732–1786) reinforcements and stores ships in 1777 gave General George Washington (1732–1799) time that he sorely needed. Men to form the new Continental Army came in slowly, and the Americans did not have a force of 8,000 until June, 1778. The defenses were even more thinly manned on the northern line. Supplies for troops in the field were also short, but the arrival of the first 3 ships bearing secret aid from France vastly improved the situation. They were evidence of the covert support of the French government, a mission sent by Congress to France was working diligently to enlist open aid and to embroil France in a war with England. The French Foreign Minister, the Comte de Vergennes (1719–1787), had already decided to take that risk when and if the American rebels demonstrated their serious purpose and ability to fulfill it by some major victory in the field.

With the first foreign material aid in 1777, the influx of foreign officers into the Continental Army began. These officers were a mixed blessing. Most were adventurers in search of fortune or of reputation with little facility for adjusting themselves to American conditions. Few were willing to accept any but the highest ranks. Nevertheless, they brought with them professional military knowledge and competence that the Continental Army badly needed. When the misfits were culled out, this knowledge and competence were used to considerable advantage. Brigadier General Louis Lebeque de Presle Duportail (1743-1802), a Frenchman, and Colonel Engineer Thaddeus Kosciuszko (1746–1817), a Pole, did much to advance the art of engineering in the Continental Army; Brigadier General Casimir Pulaski (1747–1779), another Pole, organized its first genuine cavalry contingent; Major General Baron Johann de Kalb (1721–1780) and Friedrich Wilhelm Ludolf Gerhard Augustin Baron von Steuben (1730–1794), both Germans, and General Marie Joseph de Motier Marquis de Lafayette (1757–1834), an influential French nobleman who financed his own way, were all to make valuable contributions as trainers and leaders. These foreign volunteers had little effect on the Continental Army of 1777, however, and it remained much as it had been before, a relatively untrained body of inexperienced enlistees.

When Howe finally began to stir in June, 1777, Washington posted his army at Middlebrook, New Jersey, in a position either to bar Howe's overland route to Philadelphia (then the Continental capital) or to move rapidly up the Hudson to oppose an advance northward. Washington confidently expected Howe to move northward to join with Major General John Burgoyne (1722–1792) but decided he must stay in front of the main British army wherever it went. He disposed a small part of his army under General Rufus Putnam (1738–1824) in fortifications guarding the approaches up the Hudson and, at a critical moment, detached a small force to aid Major General Philip Schuyler (1733–1804) against Burgoyne. He kept the bulk of his army in front of Howe in an effort to defend Philadelphia. He had forts built along the Delaware River and took other steps to block the approach to the Continental capital by sea.

Washington Crossing (December 25, 1776)

Washington Crossing Historic Park is a 500-acre park divided into two areas. The Thompson's Mill section is 1.5 miles southeast of New Hope via State Route PA 32. The McConkey's Ferry section is 5 miles farther south on PA 32. A bridge connects the park with New Jersey's Washington Crossing State Park. (See also Washington Crossing, New Jersey.)

`http://www.phmc.state.pa.us/bhsm/toh/washington/washingtoncrossing.asp`

The army camped at Bowman's Hill about 4 miles north of the site of the actual crossing. A memorial flagpole marks the graves of the troops who died during the encampment. A visitor center and several 18th-century buildings dominate the site of the crossing. One of these is the brown fieldstone McConkey's Ferry Inn (see Photo PA-10) where Washington dined before the crossing.

Another is the Durham Boat House which houses replicas of the boats the troops used to cross the river (see Photos PA-8 and PA-9). The boats were first built in 1750 to carry iron ore and pig iron down the Delaware to Philadelphia. They remained in operation until about 1860 with as many as 300 boats manned by more than 2,000 men carrying iron ore, iron, whiskey, and grain from Easton to Philadelphia in their heyday. The boats varied in length from 40 to 60 feet. An empty boat had a draft of about 5 inches; fully loaded with 15 tons, it could float in only 30 inches of water. The Durham boats depended on the current to travel downstream. A crew of 6 men and a captain used poles and oars to travel against the current and through the rapids. A stern-sweep oar 25 to 30 feet long guided the boats.

General George Washington (1732–1799) formulated a bold plan to strike the Hessian garrisons at Trenton and Bordentown (New Jersey) by surprise on Christmas night, 1776, when the troops might be expected to relax their guard for holiday revelry. He had all the boats on the river removed and hidden behind Malta Island in the Delaware to escape into Pennsylvania and to prevent General William Howe's (1732–1786) further advance. This was the only time in the war that Washington commanded naval superiority over the British. His force of 2,400 men under his personal command was to cross the Delaware at McConkey's Ferry (see Photo PA-10), 9 miles upstream from Trenton then proceed in 2 columns by different routes, converging on the opposite ends of the main street of Trenton in the early morning of December 26. A second force of about 1,900 men, mainly militia, under Colonel John Cadwalader (1742–1786) was to cross below near Bordentown to attack the Hessian garrison there as a diversion to prevent the reinforcement of the Trenton garrison. A third column of 1,000 men, also militia, under Brigadier General James Ewing (1736–1805), was to cross directly opposite Trenton at the Trenton Ferry to block the Hessian route of escape across Assunpink Creek.

The 2,400 men started ferrying across the river about 6:00 PM Christmas Day. Washington expected to have all his men across the river by midnight, but the last men did not cross until about 3:00 AM, 9 hours after the first men crossed. They used specially designed Durham boats (see Photo PA-8) that were wide and flat and capable of handling heavy loads. The horses and 18 cannon were ferried across on rafts (see Photo PA-9).Colonel John Glover's (1732–1797) Marblehead regiment ferried the troops across the Delaware, just as they had done in evacuating Long Island.

Elisha Bostwick recalled the difficulties of crossing and re-crossing the Delaware:

> When crossing the Delaware with the prisoners in flat bottom boats the ice continually stuck to the boats, driving them down stream; the boatmen endevering to clear off the ice pounded the boat, and stamping with their feet, beconed to the prisoners to do the same, and they all set to jumping at once with their cues flying up and down, soon shook off the ice from the boats, and the next day re-crossed the Delaware again and returned back to Trenton.

Christmas night was cold, windy, and snowy, and the Delaware River was filled with blocks of ice. The temperature was well below freezing and snow became mixed with sleet. Washington marched into Trenton from the north intending to take the Hessians by surprise. Neither Cadwalader nor Ewing was able to fulfill his part of the plan. Driven on by Washington's indomitable will, the main force did cross as planned and the 2 columns, commanded respectively by Major General Nathanael Greene (1742–1786) and Major General John Sullivan (1740–1795), converged on Trenton at 8 o'clock in the morning of December 26. Washington's plan depended on secrecy, darkness, and the enemy's underestimating the capabilities of his army. He took the 1,400 Hessians, commanded by Colonel Johann Gottlieb Rall (1720–1776), completely by surprise.

Chadd's Ford (September 11, 1777)
Battle of the Brandywine

Brandywine Battlefield Park is in/near Chadd's Ford, Pennsylvania, along the north side of U.S. Route 1, 1 mile east of State Route PA 100.

        `http://www.ushistory.org/brandywine/brandywine.htm`

The Battle of the Brandywine covered over 10 square miles, but the state park only encompasses 50 acres. The visitor center contains exhibits about the battle. A reproduction of the farmhouse used by Washington as a headquarters is on the grounds (see Photo PA-11), as is the original preserved farmhouse where the Marquis de Lafayette was quartered (see Photo PA-12). A scenic driving tour of the area has a few interpretive signs and memorials.

        `http://www.thebrandywine.com/attractions/battle.html`

General William Howe (1732–1786) left New York on July 23, 1777, with an army of 13,000 men on about 260 ships. After maneuvering in New Jersey, he sailed down the coast and up the Chesapeake Bay to Head of Elk (now Elkton, Maryland, a small town at the head of the Elk River), arriving on August 25.

General George Washington (1732–1799) planned a general engagement to defend the city of Philadelphia in 1777. He placed his army at Chadd's Ford on Brandywine Creek on September 9, 1777 in an attempt to block General Howe's probable route from the Chesapeake Bay to Philadelphia. Because he did not have an accurate map of the area, he relied on erroneous information that there was no ford across the creek immediately to the north of his position.

The Crown forces began to advance on Chadd's Ford shortly after dawn on September 11, 1777. Lieutenant General Wilhelm von Knyphausen (1716–1800) led 5,000 men to attack the center of the American line. General Lord Charles Cornwallis (1738–1805) led the larger main force of 12,500 men about 6 miles north, across the Brandywine, and then 3 miles east, following Great Valley Road (no longer in existence). He circled around the American right flank in a maneuver similar to the one Howe used on Long Island, attacking Major General John Sullivan (1740–1795) from the rear.

Knyphausen's Hessian troops met constant fire from Washington's sharpshooters opposite the ford. British cannons opened fire at 4:00 PM. Cornwallis drove the Americans back to Dilworth where Sullivan regrouped his men. Cornwallis also regrouped his men to keep up his attack, even though 4 of his battalions had lost their way in the thick woods between Birmingham Meeting House and Dilworth. He forced Sullivan out of Dilworth, but Washington brought his reserve under Major General Nathanael Greene (1742–1786) to cover Sullivan's retreat to Chester. Fighting continued until dark.

Knyphausen took advantage of the withdrawal of the American troops to cross Chadd's Ford and come to Cornwallis's assistance. After crossing the Ford, Knyphausen's men encountered Cornwallis's 4 battalions and took them along. The 2 British columns met after nightfall but were too exhausted to pursue the Americans any further. They had lost 577 killed and wounded and 6 missing. Hessian casualties accounted for only 40 of the total.

Washington suffered a serious defeat but not as bad as at New York where he nearly lost his army. He had lost 11 guns, and between 1,200 and 1,300 casualties: 400 as prisoners, 300 dead, and about twice as many wounded, including General Marie Joseph de Motier Marquis de Lafayette (1757–1834). It could have been worse. The casualties could have included Washington.

Major Patrick Ferguson (1744–1780, of the Royal Welch Fusiliers, scouting ahead of his men, heard the sound of horses' hooves and took cover. He records:

> We had not lain long . . . when a rebel officer, remarkable by a hussar dress, passed towards our army within a hundred yards of my right flank, not perceiving us. He was followed by another dressed in dark green or blue, mounted on a bay horse, with a remarkably large cocked hat.
>
> I ordered three good shots to steal near . . . and fire at them, but the idea disgusted me. I recalled the order. The hussar in returning made a circuit, but the other passed again within a hundred yards of us, upon which I advanced from the woods towards him.

On my calling, he stopped, but after looking at me, proceeded. I again drew his attention and made signs to stop but he slowly continued his way. As I was within that distance at which in the quickest firing I could have lodged half-a-dozen of balls in or about him before he was out of my reach, I had only to determine. But it was not pleasant to fire at the back of an unoffending individual, who was acquitting himself very coolly of his duty, so I let him alone.

The day after, I had been telling this story to some wounded officers who lay in the same room with me, when one of our surgeons, who had been dressing the wounded rebel officers, came in and told us they had been informing him that General Washington was all the morning with the light troops and only attended by a French Officer in a hussar dress, he himself dressed and mounted in every point as above described. I am not sorry that I did not know at the time who it was.

Major Ferguson might have shot Washington and perhaps ended the war at Brandywine; but he himself would have his right elbow shattered in the battle.

Howe went on to capture Philadelphia on September 26.

Frazer (September 16, 1777)
Battle of the Admiral Warren Tavern
Battle of White Horse Tavern
Battle of the Clouds

> The Battle of the Admiral Warren Tavern or the Battle of White Horse Tavern, called the Battle of the Clouds by local residents, was fought north of the historical marker in front of Villa Maria Hall, the administration building of Immaculata College, Route PA 352, a little more than 1 mile south of Route U.S. 30 (3.5 miles west of Paoli).
>
> The Admiral Warren Tavern is near the intersection of Lancaster Road (now Lincoln Highway, Route U.S. 30) and Warren Avenue in Malvern, Pennsylvania. The White Horse Tavern is a private residence on Swedesford Road near the intersection with Boot Road in the village of Planebrook.
>
> General Washington's headquarters during the battle were at Malin Hall on a side road off Swedesford Road. The American line of defense generally followed King Road, which was then called Indian King Road. A plaque on the west side of PA 352, about 0.2 mile north of Goshenville, identifies the house that Cornwallis used before the battle.

General George Washington (1732–1799) retreated across the Schuylkill River after the Battle of Brandywine (September 11, 1777). He still wanted to block General William Howe's (1732–1786) march on Philadelphia. He crossed the Schuylkill again and took a position on the Swedesford Road (No. 15023, running into PA 401, then U.S. 30 near Malvern). The two armies clashed on September 16, 1777, near White Horse Tavern, Pennsylvania, 5 days after the Battle of Brandywine.

A torrential rainstorm ruined nearly all of the 40,000 musket cartridges issued to the Continental Army. The British had properly designed cartridge boxes that kept their powder dry, so they forced Washington to retreat again.

The engagement is usually known as the battle of "Admiral Warren Tavern" or "White Horse Tavern." The name "Battle of the Clouds" is local, derived from the ridge, the highest ground between Philadelphia and Harrisburg. The Admiral Warren Tavern is in Malvern, Pennsylvania, and the White Horse Tavern in the village of Planebrook. Contemporary accounts refer to the taverns as being about 3 miles apart.

General Washington's headquarters during the battle were at Malin Hall. Neither Boot Tavern, where General Knyphausen's advance guard routed Washington's right (west) flank, nor the Three Tuns Tavern and Hershey's Mill, where General Cornwallis's vanguard struck the opposite flank are still standing. The American line of defense generally followed King Road, then called Indian King Road.

Malvern (September 20, 1777)
Paoli Massacre

The Paoli Massacre Site is in Malvern Memorial Park, Monument Road, Malvern. Go 0.5 mile west from Warren Avenue on Monument Road. The junction of these streets is 0.4 mile east of King Street and 0.8 mile north of a traffic light on the Paoli Pike.

Malvern Memorial Park near the massacre site contains a mass grave of about 53 of the dead. A polished granite obelisk nearby commemorates the "massacre."

The day after the Battle of Brandywine (September 11, 1777), the British headed toward the Schuylkill River, near Philadelphia. General George Washington (1732–1799) sent 1,500 Pennsylvania Continentals under Brigadier General "Mad Anthony" Wayne (1745–1796) against their left flank and rear to delay their advance.

General William Howe (1732–1786) learned of Wayne's encampment from captured messages and Loyalist spies. He ordered Major General Charles Grey (1729–1807) to put an end to this tiresome harassment. Grey ordered the 5,000 men of the 3 battalions assigned to him to remove the flints from their muskets so they would not be tempted to open fire and betray their advance. He was later known as "No Flint" Grey for this action. Grey's battalions set out on September 19, 1777 and caught Wayne with a sudden surprise attack near an inn known as the Paoli Tavern about 1 o'clock in the morning of September 20.

The British drove off Wayne's pickets and charged into the camp before the Continentals could defend themselves. They used only bayonets (see Photo PA-13). However, most of the Americans did not have bayonets, and they had no time to reload in the confusion and close quarters of hand-to-hand combat. Many men were killed as they ran in front of their campfires. Those who tried to hide in the darkness were hunted down and bayoneted. Wayne lost 53 men killed and 100 wounded. The rest fled to the west. The British reported 6 men killed and 22 wounded.

One of Grey's officers described what happened:

> The enemy . . . some with arms, others without, [ran] in all directions with the greatest confusion. The light infantry bayoneted every man they came up with. The camp was immediately set on fire, and this, with the cries of the wounded, formed altogether one of the most dreadful scenes I ever beheld. Every man that fired was instantly put to death. Captain Wolfe was killed, and I received a shot in my right hand, soon after we entered the camp. I saw the fellow present at me, and was running up to

him when he fired. He was immediately killed. The enemy were pursued for two miles. I kept up till I grew faint from loss of blood and was obliged to sit down. Wayne's brigade was to have marched at one in the morning to attack our battalion while crossing the Schuylkill river, and we surprised them at twelve. Four hundred and sixty of the enemy were counted the next morning, lying dead, and not one shot was fired by us—all done with the bayonet. We had only twenty killed and wounded.

The battle got the epithet of "massacre" from the mangled condition of the bodies and the lopsided casualty figures; but the British were not guilty of any offense—they just enjoyed a one-sided victory. The term "massacre" also fails to account for the 71 prisoners Grey captured.

The next day, Grey rejoined Howe marching to the Schuylkill, plundering farms along the way. Washington had moved into position to prevent the British crossing the river, so Howe tricked Washington by marching upriver to the west. Washington marched parallel to Howe who countermarched at night and crossed the Schuylkill at Flatland Ford near Valley Forge on September 23. This put him between Washington and Philadelphia. The British army arrived in Germantown on September 25 and entered Philadelphia the next day behind a parade of heavy guns with bands playing triumphant airs and Loyalist cheering.

On the same day as the Paoli Massacre, the Continental Congress fled from Philadelphia to York, Pennsylvania, about 85 miles to the west. Despite heavy casualties at Brandywine and Paoli, Washington soon replaced his losses, but Howe could not.

Germantown (October 4, 1777)

Much of the Battle of Germantown was fought around Cliveden at 6401 Germantown Avenue in Germantown. (See Photo PA-14.)

http://www.cliveden.org/

Cliveden/Chew Mansion was the summer home of Benjamin Chew whose daughter Peggy was escorted to the *Mischianza* by Captain John André. Ironically, she later married John Eager Howard in 1787. He commanded the 4th Maryland Regiment at Germantown and later became Governor of Maryland and a U.S. Senator.

Upon entering Philadelphia on September 26, 1777, General William Howe (1732–1786) dispersed his forces, stationing 9,000 men north of the city at Germantown, America's first German settlement, 3,000 in New Jersey, and the rest in Philadelphia.

General George Washington (1732–1799) took advantage of Howe's temporarily reduced numbers. He had recently received reinforcements and now had an army totaling about 8,000 Continentals and 3,000 militia, outnumbering the British. His army was encamped 16 miles from Germantown, along the Skippack Road (which coincides almost exactly with the present-day Germantown Avenue). He decided to make a surprise attack on the main British camp at Germantown just as he had done at Trenton. The plan was much like that used at Trenton but involved far more complicated movements by much larger bodies of troops.

Four columns—2 of Continentals under Major General John Sullivan (1740–1795) and Major General Nathanael Greene (1742–1786) and 2 of militia—moving at night over different roads were to converge on Germantown simultaneously at dawn on October 4, 1777. The 2 columns of Continentals arrived at different times. A thick fog reduced visibility to a few yards, making a difficult plan even more so. Even though the troops wore pieces of white paper in their hats to identify themselves, they sometimes fired on their own men in the fog and smoke. The thick fog also caused the gunpowder smoke to hang in the air, further reducing visibility. The 2 militia columns never arrived at all.

Most of the fighting took place around the mansion of Benjamin Chew (see Photo PA-14), former chief justice of Pennsylvania. About 120 British troops occupied the stone summer house and began firing on the Continentals, holding up the advance while American generals argued whether they could leave a fortress in their rear. Brigadier General Henry Knox (1750–1806) prevailed on Washington to force the defenders to surrender before allowing the reserve to proceed. They opened fire with artillery, broke the front door, smashed the windows, destroyed the statuary and vases in the yard, but could not penetrate the thick, stone walls. Nor were they able to burn it. The Continentals then assaulted the house but suffered heavy casualties from a well-positioned opponent firing at point-blank range.

In the fog and the confusion of fighting, 2 American brigades began to fire at each other. The word spread through the ranks that the British were attacking from behind, and the retreat turned into a rout. The officers could not stop it and had to call off the attack when General Charles Cornwallis (1738–1805) arrived with fresh troops. The battle lasted nearly 3 hours, and the Americans retreated about 9:00 AM, leaving Howe's troops in command of the field.

Both sides suffered heavy losses. The British had 537 casualties, the Americans had 652 and lost 438 more as prisoners. Neither commander had much to show for his efforts. Washington lost his chance of retaking Philadelphia; Howe withdrew there for the winter. He found no swarms of Loyalists rallying to the British standards, and he had left Major General John Burgoyne (1722–1792) to lose a whole British army in the north.

Even though the Americans lost the battle, leading statesmen and generals of Europe, particularly the French, were impressed with Washington's boldness and the fighting ability of an army which could recover quickly from a defeat at Brandywine to take the offensive and come so close to a victory. When the French government later learned of Burgoyne's surrender at Saratoga, the ministers remembered Germantown which helped them decide to form an alliance with the Americans.

Fort Mifflin (October 10–15, 1777)

Fort Mifflin is on Fort Mifflin Road at the foot of Island Avenue off I-95 (in Philadelphia).
`http://www.thebrandywine.com/photoop/fort_mifflin.html`

President John Adams ordered Fort Mifflin rebuilt in 1798. The riverside is original, and the reconstruction used much of the 1770s foundation. The bunks are believed to date from 1812. The fort remained in use until 1962. The 13 restored buildings mostly interpret the Civil War era but the tours and demonstrations also cover its Revolutionary origins. (See Photo PA-15.)

British engineer Captain John Montresor (1736–1799) laid out stone walls on the western shore of the Delaware River south of Philadelphia to defend the city in 1771. The fortification, known as Fort Mud or Mud Island, became an American stronghold in the fall of 1777, garrisoned by Lieutenant Colonel Samuel Smith (1752–1839) and renamed for Major General Thomas Mifflin (1744–1800).

General George Washington (1732–1799) kept General William Howe (1732–1786) besieged in Philadelphia by controlling the roads in and out of the city and holding 2 forts that commanded the Delaware River: Fort Mercer, on the New Jersey side at Red Bank, and Fort Mifflin, on Mud Island in the river itself. This broke Howe's communications and supply routes by sea. Howe needed to eliminate the forts to allow his supplies to come up the river. He entrusted Captain Montresor with the task of dismantling the fortifications he had once built.

Montresor began bombarding Fort Mifflin every half hour on October 15, 1777. Red-hot cannonballs set fire to the barracks, but they did not silence the guns at the fort. Reinforcements managed to sneak in at night, and the attackers laid siege to the fort. Heavy rains deterred Montresor's efforts further as he prepared batteries to assault Fort Mifflin's unprotected land side.

He attacked again on October 22 and was repulsed even though the navy had joined the bombardment. The squadron included the 64-gun *Augusta,* the *Roebuck* (44-guns), the frigates *Pearl* and *Liverpool,* the sloop of war *Merlin* (18-guns), and the galley *Cornwallis.* That night, the *Augusta* and the *Merlin,* ran aground on the mud flats in the river near the second line of chevaux-de-frise. The next morning, the guns of both Fort Mifflin and Fort Mercer opened upon them setting the *Augusta* afire. Ambrose Serle (1742–1812), secretary to Admiral Richard Howe (1726–1799), claims that the fire started when a flaming wad from a musket fired by a marine struck a hammock. The flames spread almost instantly to the dry, tar-coated rigging and spread quickly. The crews abandoned the ships, but the *Augusta*'s second lieutenant, chaplain, gunner, and 40 seamen confined to sick bay burned to death. On October 23, the *Augusta* blew up. The explosion caused a soldier at Fort Mifflin to write that it "seemed to shake the earth to its center." Tom Paine, who was several miles west of Philadelphia, was "stunned with a report as loud as a peal from a hundred cannon at once." The British burned the *Merlin.*

Washington ordered 2 Connecticut regiments to Mud Island to help Fort Mifflin. Private Joseph Martin (1760–1850) recalls the hardships:

> Here, without winter clothing, not a scrap of either shoes or stockings to my legs or feet, I endured hardships sufficient to kill half a dozen horses.

On November 10, 1777, the Crown forces had completed their batteries on nearby Province Island. They consisted of two 32-pounders, six 24-pounders, one 18-pounder, and many lesser guns as well as the guns from ships in the Delaware. The artillery also launched 2 floating batteries to bombard Fort Mifflin. The bombardment was increased on November 15 and continued for 6 days. It was one of the most terrible of the war with cannons firing at the fort at a rate of 50 shots a minute.

Joseph Plumb Martin reports:

We had, as I mentioned before, a thirty-two pound cannon in the fort, but had not a single shot for it. The British also had one in their battery upon the Hospital Point, which, as I said before, raked the fort, or rather it was so fixed as to rake the parade in front of the barracks, the only place we could pass up and down the fort. The artillery officers offered a gill [a half pint] of rum for each shot fired from that piece, which the soldiers would procure. I have seen from twenty to fifty men standing on the parade waiting with impatience the coming of the shot, which would often be seized before its motion had fully ceased and conveyed off to our gun to be sent back again to its former owners. When the lucky fellow who had caught it had swallowed his rum, he would return to wait for another, exulting that he had been more lucky or more dexterous than his fellows.

Seven British ships joined the assault by November 15 and silenced the American guns. The defenders fought valiantly but evacuated Fort Mifflin a week later after one of the most memorable defensive stands ever made on American soil. It took more than a month to capture this poorly manned, undergunned little fort. The Americans lost an estimated 250–400 men killed while the Crown forces had only 13 dead and 24 wounded in addition to the casualties from the *Augusta*.

The loss of Fort Mercer and Fort Mifflin meant that Washington could not starve the British out of Philadelphia. The first British supply ship reached Philadelphia on November 23. The Americans needed some kind of victory to boost morale. They had a brief skirmish in what is called the Battle of Edge Hill, in early December, before going into winter quarters at a place called Valley Forge, 20 miles northwest of Philadelphia.

Howe had gained his objective but it proved of no lasting value to him. No swarms of Loyalists rallied to the British standards. He had left Major General John Burgoyne (1722–1792) to lose a whole army in the north. And, with winter setting in, prolonged campaigning was out of the question. He settled comfortably in Philadelphia. Seven months later, Clinton replaced him and evacuated Philadelphia to fortify New York City and Staten Island.

See also National Park, New Jersey (Fort Mercer).

Valley Forge (December 19, 1777 to June 19, 1778)

Valley Forge National Historical Park comprises 3,600 acres extending east from the village of Valley Forge along State Route PA 23.
                    http://www.nps.gov/vafo/index.htm

A self-guiding tour visits the reconstructed huts of Muhlenberg's Brigade (Photo PA-17), Washington's Headquarters (Photo PA-18), the Memorial Arch, and the original entrenchment lines and fortifications. (See Photos PA-16, PA-19, and PA-20.)

There were no battles fought at Valley Forge. Despite the hardships the soldiers endured, they received the training they needed to form them into an army capable of meeting the enemy on equal terms.

Six thousand Continentals stayed with General George Washington (1732–1799) (see Photo PA-18 of Washington's Valley Forge headquarters) during the bitter winter of 1777–1778 (from December 19, 1777 to June 19, 1778) and suffered much. The wintry winds penetrated the tattered tents that were the only shelter at first. Some men had no shoes, no pants, no blankets. Weeks passed when there was no meat and men were reduced to boiling their shoes and eating them.

To provide adequate rations for the 16 brigades of 800 men in the army required 34,577 pounds of meat and 168 barrels of flour per day. Food was in short supply, and foraging parties had to be formed frequently. Brigadier General "Mad Anthony" Wayne (1745–1796), who lived near Valley Forge, led many of these foraging parties and was so successful that he became known as "the drover." Local residents would hide their best horses and cattle when the army was nearby. The army endured hunger and cold in the tents and roughly built log cabins (see Photo PA-17) for weeks.

Major General Baron Johann de Kalb (1721–1780) wrote to a friend on Christmas Day, 1777 about the difficulties:

> It is certain that half the army are naked, and almost the whole army go barefoot. Our men are also infected with the itch, a matter which attracts very little attention either at the hospitals or in camp. I have seen the poor fellows covered over and over with scab . . . We have hardly been here more than six days, and are already suffering from want of everything. The men have had neither meat nor bread for four days, and our horses are often left without any fodder. What will be done when the roads grow worse, and the season more severe?

The soldiers looked like scarecrows as they paraded in tattered uniforms and even in torn blankets. Many had no boots and had to stand on their hats when on sentry duty. They lived mostly on "fire cakes," lumps of flour baked on stones. Most men slept on the ground since straw, like everything else, was in short supply. During that terrible winter some 2,000 troops died from disease brought on by supply shortages, exposure, and poor sanitation.

The suffering was largely unnecessary. While the soldiers shivered and went hungry, food rotted and clothing lay unused in depots throughout the country. True, access to Valley Forge was difficult, but little determined effort was made to get supplies into the area. The supply and transport system broke down. In mid-1777, both the Quartermaster and Commissary Generals resigned along with numerous subordinate officials in both departments, mostly merchants who found private trade more lucrative.

Congress, in refuge at York, Pennsylvania, and split into factions, found it difficult to find replacements. If there was not, as most historians now believe, an organized cabal seeking to replace Washington with Major General Horatio Gates (1728–1806), there were many, both in and out of the army, who were dissatisfied with the Commander in Chief, and much intrigue went on. Gates was made president of the new Board of War set up in 1777 and at least two of its members were enemies of Washington. In the administrative chaos at the height of the Valley Forge crisis, there was no functioning Quartermaster General at all.

Washington weathered the storm and the Continental Army was to emerge from Valley Forge a more effective force than before. With his advice, Congress instituted reforms in the Quartermaster and Commissary Departments that temporarily restored the effectiveness of both agencies. Washington's ablest subordinate, General Nathanael

Greene (1742–1786), reluctantly accepted the post of Quartermaster General and things began to improve. He was efficient and sent foraging parties through the surrounding area as well as into New Jersey and Delaware. He also knew how to influence Congress to provide some of the things it had promised. The Continental Army itself gained a new professional competence from the training given by the Prussian, Friedrich Wilhelm von Steuben (1730–1794).

Steuben appeared at Valley Forge in February, 1778, arrayed in such martial splendor that one private thought he had seen Mars, the god of war, himself. He represented himself as a baron, a title he had acquired in the service of a small German state, and as a former lieutenant general on the staff of Frederick the Great, though in reality he had been only a captain. The fraud was harmless, for Steuben had a broad knowledge of military affairs, and his remarkable sense of the dramatic was combined with the common touch a true Prussian baron might well have lacked.

Washington had long sensed the need for uniform training and organization, and after a short trial he secured the appointment of Steuben as Inspector General in charge of a training program. Steuben carried out the program during the late winter and early spring of 1778, teaching the Continental Army a simplified but effective version of the drill formations and movements of European armies, proper care of equipment, and the use of the bayonet, a weapon in which British superiority had previously been noted. He attempted to consolidate the understrength regiments and companies and organized light infantry companies as the elite force of the army. He constantly sought to impress upon the officers their responsibility for taking care of the men. (See Photo PA-19 for the Grand Parade where Baron Friedrich Wilhelm von Steuben trained the troops.)

While Steuben trained the infantry, French Brigadier General Louis Lebeque de Presle Duportail (1743–1802) restructured the Corps of Engineers and trained the artillery, miners, and sappers. (See Photos PA-16 and PA-20 for artillery at Valley Forge.)

Steuben never lost sight of the difference between the American citizen soldier and the European professional. He noted that American soldiers had to be told why they did things before they would do them well, and he applied this philosophy in his training program. His trenchant good humor and vigorous profanity, almost the only English he knew, delighted the Continental soldiers and made the rigorous drill more palatable. After Valley Forge, Continentals would fight on equal terms with British Regulars in the open field.

Wyoming Valley (July 3–4, 1778)
Wyoming Massacre

The Wyoming Massacre site is on Wyoming Avenue (Route PA 11 and Susquehanna Avenue) in Bloomsburg, Pennsylvania.

The remains of 166 victims from the massacre were buried in a mass grave in the fall of 1778. A 63-foot granite monument, erected in the 1840s, at 4th Street and Wyoming Avenue marks the grave site. The inscription lists the names of some 40 survivors. The 2 guns that stand guard date from the Civil War and were mounted in the casemates of Fort Hancock at Sandy Hook and used in the defenses of New York Harbor. The Bloody Rock is preserved in a small memorial down the road on 8th Street. Urbanization has obliterated the pine woods, swamps, and fields, leaving no reminder of the bloody events that occurred around present Wyoming Avenue and the surrounding area.

With the outbreak of the War for American Independence, the Wyoming Valley's importance as a granary led to a number of attacks by Loyalist and Native American forces. Connecticut and Pennsylvania both claimed land in the area and attempted to secure their claims in bloody conflicts. Both sides reorganized and aligned themselves with the Loyalists or the Patriots when the war began.

John Butler (1728–1796), the 53-year-old Loyalist leader, led 200 British troops, 200 Loyalists, and 700 Native Americans, mainly Senecas and Cayugas, in an attack in the Wyoming Valley on July 3, 1778. They marched 200 miles from Fort Niagara against 300 confused Pennsylvania militia and 60 regulars 4 miles north of Kingston near Forty Fort. They routed the defenders and essentially wiped them out. Only 60 men were able to escape. This left settlements of the Wyoming Valley unprotected. Two prisoners who managed to escape told the story of a Native American woman killing 14 prisoners at a site now known as "The Bloody Rock."

The following day, July 4, the Seneca and Cayuga warriors traveled through the valley in a series of raids looting, killing 300 people, and destroying more than 1,000 homes. Butler also took a large quantity of livestock. Some accounts report the Seneca and Cayuga warriors chased the survivors as they tried to escape through the swamps and woods along the river as they fled to Forty Fort. Reports of the massacre of men, women, and children, including the torture and burning to death of many of the rebels, spread up and down the valley. The incident became known as the Wyoming Massacre.

Other accounts claim that John Butler did his best to limit punishment only to those who had actively resisted. Still others say that the Loyalists in the Wyoming Valley seized an opportunity to take revenge for the treatment they had received from the Whigs. The survivors accepted John Butler's terms of surrender the next day in which they agreed to lay down their arms for the remainder of the war, destroy their fortifications, and stop persecuting their Loyalist neighbors.

Major General John Sullivan (1740–1795) led an expedition up the Susquehanna River in reprisal. His army destroyed their farms and orchards so thoroughly that the Seneca and Cayuga were forced to move to Fort Niagara and live off British charity for the rest of that year and most of the next. They never recovered from this devastation.

9

INDIANA

Indiana was part of the colony of Virginia during the War for American Independence. See the Indiana map.

Vincennes (February 25, 1779)

The George Rogers Clark National Historical Park is located on Barnett Street within the city of Vincennes along the Wabash River in the southwestern part of Indiana. From Highway U.S. 50 east and west or from Highway U.S. 41 from the north, use the 6th Street exit. Stay on 6th Street to the intersection with Barnett Street (approximately 2.5 miles). Turn right on Barnett and follow it to the park. On Highway U.S. 41 from the south, use the Willow Street exit. Turn right on Willow Street for approximately 2 miles to the intersections with South 6th Street, turn right. Travel 4 blocks and turn left on Barnett Street which will lead to the park.

http://www.nps.gov/gero/index.htm

The George Rogers Clark Memorial, built in 1931–1932, is a Doric temple surrounded by a 20-acre plaza. The memorial contains seven large murals which depict Clark's life and the conquest of the Old Northwest. The rotunda houses a bronze statue of Clark. The memorial commemorates the capture of Fort Sackville from British Lieutenant Governor Henry Hamilton and his soldiers by Lieutenant Colonel George Rogers Clark and his frontiersmen on February 25, 1779. The heroic march of Clark's men from Kaskaskia on the Mississippi in mid-winter and the subsequent victory over the British remains one of the great feats of the American Revolution. Adjacent to the memorial there is a visitor center where one can see interpretive programs and displays.

The exact location of Fort Sackville is not known, but it is believed it was located in the present-day George Rogers Clark National Historical Park. Archaeological evidence suggests that the fort's front wall was roughly between the Clark Memorial and the Lincoln Memorial Bridge in Vincennes. Fort Sackville was renamed for Patrick Henry, and Vincennes served as the capital of the Indiana Territory from 1800 to 1813.

The French built a series of military posts between the Great Lakes and the Louisiana territory. The one built in Vincennes was constructed in 1731 and named for the builder and first commander, François Marie Bissot, Sieur de Vincennes (1700–1736). A permanent settlement grew up around the post in the next few years. The British acquired the post from France after the Seven Years War (French and Indian War) (1756–1763) and renamed it Fort Sackville for a British government official.

The British dominated a large portion of the Trans-Appalachian frontier. The Proclamation of 1763 which officially ended the Seven Years War forbade the settlement of lands west of the Appalachian Mountains. There were many Native American tribes located between the Appalachian Mountains and the Mississippi River. Although never unified, the warriors from these tribes greatly outnumbered both the British and the Americans and constituted a strong military force on the western frontier. American settlement west of the Appalachian Mountains posed a threat to their way of life and caused most of them to favor the British.

British officials actively encouraged the Native Americans to attack American frontiersmen beginning in 1777. The British supplied the warriors with weapons and ammunition and rewarded them with gifts when successful war parties returned with scalps and prisoners. From their posts north of the Ohio River, the British sent Native American war parties against those settlers who ignored the proclamation line, including those in Kentucky (also a part of Virginia at that time).

Colonel George Rogers Clark (1752–1818) organized the Kentucky militia to defend against these raids. Not content to wait for the attacks, he took his plan to Patrick Henry (1736–1799), governor of Virginia, and gained approval for a major offensive campaign. He planned to lead a force of frontiersmen into the Illinois country and strike at the source of Native American raids.

Clark led his army down the Ohio River with fewer than 200 men, called the Kentucky Long Knives, during the summer of 1778. He then proceeded overland, covering approximately 120 miles in 5 days. He captured the British posts at Kaskaskia and Cahokia along the Mississippi River, near St. Louis. French settlers occupied these posts after the Seven Years War. They disliked living under British rule, so Clark quickly gained their support. Father Pierre Gibault (1737–1814) and Dr. Jean Laffont volunteered to travel to Vincennes on behalf of the Americans. That settlement also gave its support to Clark, but the French at Detroit and other northern posts continued to support the British.

British Lieutenant Governor Henry Hamilton (d. 1796) (The "Hair Buyer") received news about the fall of the 3 outposts by August 6. He left Detroit in early October, 1778, with a mixed force of English soldiers, French volunteers and militia, and Native American warriors, intending to retake Fort Sackville in Vincennes. Picking up Native American allies along the way, his force numbered about 500 when he arrived at Vincennes 71 days later (December 17).

Clark left Captain Leonard Helms in charge at Vincennes. With only a few men on whom he could depend, Helms had no hopes of defending the fort against Hamilton's force. Hamilton recaptured the fort on December 17, and the French settlers, faced with overwhelming force, returned to British allegiance.

Hamilton allowed most of his force to return home for the winter, as was customary in 18th-century warfare, postponing his intended invasion of the Illinois country. He planned to muster his forces in the spring for an attack on Clark's posts on the Mississippi River. Victories there would pave the way for a joint effort with tribes from south of the Ohio River to drive all American settlers from the Trans-Appalachian frontier.

Francis Vigo (Joseph Maria Francesco Vigo) (1747–1836), a merchant and supporter of the American cause, left his home in St. Louis and headed for Vincennes, unaware that the fort was in British hands. He was taken prisoner near the settlement, held for several days, and released, his captors not realizing Vigo's involvement with the

Americans. Vigo returned to St. Louis and then went to Kaskaskia, 50 miles south, where he provided Clark with valuable information concerning the military situation in Vincennes and Hamilton's intent to attack in the spring.

Clark, determined to capture Hamilton, set out from Kaskaskia on February 6, 1779, with his force of approximately 170 Americans and Frenchmen. They covered the distance in 18 days. About 10 miles from Vincennes, they found themselves in country flooded with icy water which they had to wade through—sometimes shoulder-deep. They arrived in Vincennes after nightfall on February 23, 1779.

The French citizens greeted Clark's men warmly and provided them food and dry gunpowder. Clark's men surrounded the fort which was now defended by approximately 40 British soldiers and a similar number of French volunteers and militia from Detroit and Vincennes. The French troops were not inclined to fire on the enemy when they realized that the French inhabitants of the town again sided with the Americans.

Clark brought from Kaskaskia flags sufficient for an army of 500. He had them unfurled and carried within view of the fort, giving the impression of having a much larger army. His American soldiers, experienced woodsmen, could maintain a rate of fire that convinced the British that they indeed faced a large army. The woodsmen were armed with the famed long rifle which was accurate at longer ranges than the defenders' muskets. (See Photo VA-1, rifleman.)

Clark ordered the construction of tunnels, from behind the riverbank a short distance from the fort, to plant explosive charges under fort walls or beneath powder magazines. His men also built barricades and entrenchments to provide additional cover.

Hamilton considered surrendering and requested Clark meet with him at the nearby church, St. Francis Xavier Catholic Church. He tried to get liberal conditions, but Clark insisted on unconditional surrender. After a long and heated discussion, they failed to agree upon acceptable terms and each commander returned to his respective post.

A Native American raiding party which Hamilton sent out to attack American settlers along the Ohio River returned to Vincennes at this time, during a lull in the battle. They saw the British flag flying as usual from the fort and began yelling and firing their weapons in the air. They realized their mistake too late, when the frontiersmen killed or wounded several of them and captured others.

Clark ordered 5 of the captured warriors to be tomahawked in full view of the fort in retaliation for the raids in which numerous men, women, and children had been slaughtered. The executions were intended to demonstrate to Native American observers that the redcoats could no longer protect those tribes who made war on the Americans and to put pressure on the British who sensed they could suffer the same fate.

Hamilton reluctantly agreed to Clark's final terms which were just short of unconditional surrender. He described his thoughts at having to surrender: "The mortification, disappointment and indignation I felt, may possibly be conceived . . ." The defeated British army marched out of Fort Sackville and laid down their arms at 10 AM on Thursday, February 25, 1779. Clark had the American flag raised above the fort and 13 cannon shots fired in celebration. An accident during the firings severely burned several men, including American Captain Joseph Bowman who died 6 months later and was buried in the church cemetery adjacent to the fort. The surrender of Fort Sackville marked the beginning of the end of British occupation and control of the western frontier of America.

Even though he was unable to achieve his ultimate objective of capturing Detroit, Clark successfully prevented the British from achieving their goal of driving the Americans from the Trans-Appalachian frontier. His brilliant military activities caused the British to cede to the United States a vast area of land west of the Appalachian Mountains. That territory now includes the states of Ohio, Indiana, Illinois, Michigan, Wisconsin, and the eastern portion of Minnesota.

10

ILLINOIS

Illinois was part of the colony of Virginia during the War for American Independence. See the Illinois map.

Ellis Grove (July 4, 1778)
Fort Kaskaskia

Fort Kaskaskia State Historic Site is off Route IL 3, 10 miles north of town on the Mississippi River.

`http://www.state.il.us/hpa/hs/Kaskaskia.htm`

The original site of Fort Kaskaskia has been obliterated by the Mississippi River, but a 275-acre park, which contains the Garrison Hill Cemetery, preserves the history of the area.

Fort Kaskaskia was built by the French along the Kaskaskia River in 1736 before the French and Indian War. The settlement of 80 stone houses became the largest French colonial settlement in the Illinois region. The townspeople partially destroyed the fort to keep it out of British hands. The British took it over in 1763 and fortified a Jesuit mission in the village which they called Fort Gage.

The British left many of the former French outposts lightly defended during the War for American Independence, for they had gathered their western forces in Detroit. Twenty-three-year-old George Rogers Clark (1752–1818), an explorer of the Ohio Valley, had secret orders from Patrick Henry (1736–1799), governor of Virginia, to capture the town of Kaskaskia and nearby Fort Gage. They expected that this might lead to the capture of the entire Northwest and open the Mississippi and Ohio rivers to Spanish supplies from New Orleans. Spain was an American ally at the time.

Clark sailed down the Ohio River with fewer than 200 men, called the Kentucky Long Knives, in the summer of 1778. He covered 120 miles in 5 days, landing at the site of Fort Massac where he planned a surprise overland attack on Kaskaskia. After a night crossing of the Kaskaskia River, Clark surrounded the town. When the French commander learned of Clark's approach, he mustered the militia, but he surrendered on July 4, 1778 without firing a single shot.

Although the British were fairly tolerant of the inhabitants and their cultural and religious beliefs, the former French citizens disliked living under British rule. They much preferred Clark's benevolent leadership which won their allegiance to the state of Virginia. These new allies would become valuable in Clark's conquest of the region.

Metropolis (Summer, 1778)

Fort Massac

Fort Massac State Park is at 1757 Fort Massac, west off I-24 via U.S. 45, 2 miles east of town.

```
http://www.free-attractions.com/sg/illinois/
       fort%20massac%20state%20park.htm
```

A reconstructed fort of 1796 and a statue of Clark mark the site. A plaque near the monument reads: "In memory of George Rogers Clark—and his faithful companions in arms who by their enterprise and courage won the Illinois country for the Commonwealth of Virginia and so for the American Union."

The French built Fort Massac in 1757 but abandoned it long before George Rogers Clark (1752–1818) arrived in the summer of 1778. Clark and his Kentucky Long Knives rested at the site before the arduous overland march to capture Fort Kaskaskia.

11

DELAWARE (AND MARYLAND)

Delaware contributed a total of 2,762 men to the Continental Army—376 militia and 2,386 Continental Army. Delaware provided the Continental Army with only a single regiment, but that unit fought with distinction in many battles of the war. They earned the nickname the "Blue Hen Chickens" after a particularly fierce breed of fighting gamecock—a nickname that still survives.

Maryland saw no military action during the War for American Independence, but its troops fought in almost every major engagement. The colony contributed 3,919 militia and 13,912 to the Continental Army—a total of 17,831 men.

See the Delaware map.

Newark (September 3, 1777)
Cooch's Bridge

Cooch's Bridge Battlefield is on Old Baltimore Pike, off Route DE 896.
`http://www.sar.org/dessar/coocgift.htm`

The Battle at Cooch's Bridge was the only fighting on Delaware soil. The only display commemorating the battle is a small memorial of 4 small cannons and a descriptive plaque. A 90-foot observation tower in nearby Iron Hill Park offers a view of the terrain.

The British planned to move their main forces from New Jersey to Delaware in the summer of 1777 in preparation for an assault on the colonial capital of Philadelphia, Pennsylvania. They went by sea around the Delmarva Peninsula and disembarked at Head of Elk, now Elkton, Maryland, on August 28, 1777. After 33 days, they were only 20 miles closer to Philadelphia than they were at Perth Amboy, New Jersey earlier in the summer.

Brigadier General William Maxwell (1733–1796) positioned his light infantry near Cooch's Bridge in Delaware to block General William Howe's (1732–1786) advance on Philadelphia. Lieutenant Colonel von Wumb led Howe's advance column on September 2, 1777. His Hessians enveloped the Americans and followed with a bayonet charge. Maxwell's light infantry performed a series of delaying actions until the Hessians broke their line. The infantry fled to General George Washington's (1732–1799) main line north of Cooch's Bridge.

There is great discrepancy in the casualty reports. The Americans lost approximately 30 killed and an undetermined number of wounded while the Crown forces suffered between 20 and 30 total casualties. The Battle of Cooch's Bridge accomplished little more than delaying the British advance on Philadelphia. The newly formed American light infantry saw their first action here, and legend has it that the Betsy Ross flag flew for the first time at Cooch's Bridge.

12

VIRGINIA

Virginia contributed more than 30,678 men to the war effort—more than 4,000 militia and 26,678 in the Continental Army.

See the Virginia map.

Hampton (September 2 and October 24, 1775)

> Nothing remains of the original 18th-century Hampton, Virginia waterfront. Commercial fishing companies now occupy the waterfront area on the Hampton River at the foot of King Street. The wharf on which Squires's men hoped to land has long since been replaced by a terminal for fishing boats. The brick homes and willow trees that sheltered the town's defenders have been replaced by more recent and less attractive structures.

The first armed confrontations between Crown forces and rebels in Virginia occurred in Hampton when the weather forced Captain Mathew Squires in command of the British sloop *Otter* to seek shelter in the James River near the town on September 2, 1775. Some local Whigs saw an opportunity to capture the ship's guns and burn one of her small boats while a local Patriot entertained Squires at his home.

Squires returned to Hampton on Tuesday, October 24, 1775, under orders from Lord John Murray, 4th Earl of Dunmore (1732–1809), the Royal Governor of Virginia. The residents, expecting his return, had sunk 5 sloops across the entrance to Hampton Creek, now called Hampton River, and had sent a message to Williamsburg requesting reinforcements.

Unable to sail the *Otter* into Hampton Creek, Squires sailed 6 tenders into it and began firing on the town. He also sent a landing party to burn the town; but they never reached the shore, as the residents were waiting for them, sheltered behind the brick homes and willow trees that then lined the waterfront.

Unable to get his men ashore, Squires moved his ships into positions from which he could enfilade the town. He waited through the night as 100 militiamen rode from Williamsburg. They arrived by daybreak when Squires resumed the bombardment. The musket fire from the shore was so effective that Squires ordered his fleet to withdraw. The attackers inflicted minimal damage to the town, burning only St. John's Church and one other building. Squires lost 2 men killed and 2 wounded while the Virginians reported no casualties.

Great Bridge (December 9, 1775)

Great Bridge, Virginia is located 12 miles south of Portsmouth at the intersection of Routes VA 165 (Mt. Pleasant Road) and VA 168 (Battlefield Boulevard).

Nothing remains of the site of the first battle of the Revolution in Virginia. Highway markers indicate the general location of the earthworks on both sides of the causeway.

Lord John Murray, 4th Earl of Dunmore (1732–1809) had placed the colony under martial law on November 7, 1775.

Dunmore needed men badly as he had fewer than 300 British troops in Virginia when the hostilities began. Most of the Regular troops had been sent to the North to keep the peace. He began recruiting a Loyalist army on November 17, 1775.

Lord Dunmore offered freedom to all African Americans who joined "His Majesty's Troops . . . for the more speedily reducing the Colony to a proper sense of their duty, to His Majesty's crown and dignity." Five hundred African Americans offered their services within a week. Dunmore formed them into the Ethiopia Regiment, giving them guns as fast as they arrived and outfitting them in uniforms that had the words "Liberty to Slaves" inscribed across their breasts. This action raised the army Dunmore needed, but lost the support of almost every plantation owner.

Dunmore saw recruitment of African Americans as a quick way to build his army. He also knew that his proclamation attacked his enemies' economic system. Without slaves, many southern Patriots could not run their plantations successfully.

Plantation owners saw Dunmore's "Ethiopian Regiment" as a nightmare come true: Their own slaves were now given guns and turned against them. The *Virginia Gazette* published frantic appeals that the slaves remain loyal to their masters and ignore Dunmore's offers: "be not then, ye negroes, tempted by this proclamation to ruin your selves" ran one article, implying that awful punishments awaited any slave who was caught trying to join the Crown forces. Patrick Henry (1736–1799) wrote that Dunmore's action was "fatal to the publick safety" and called for "early and unremitting Attention to the Government of the Slaves."

British Regulars did not meet the American rebels in battle again for nearly 6 months after the battle at Bunker Hill. The next engagement occurred in a tidal swamp around the Elizabeth River, 12 miles south of Norfolk. Dunmore's (1732–1809) 600-man army constructed a small earthworks at the east end of a 120-foot bridge by early December, 1775.

Colonel William Woodford (1734–1780) commanded a force of about 900, made up of 400 Virginia Continentals, local militia, and North Carolinians. They camped at the west end of the bridge, rather than risk a costly assault across the narrow causeway and bridge. Woodford had his own redoubt constructed on the west end of the bridge and defended it with 90 men. He supposedly used an African-American servant of John Marshall's father who pretended to be a deserter to trick Lord Dunmore into thinking he had weak defenses.

The Ethiopia Regiment (a core of Regular soldiers, some 60 Loyalists, a band of mariners, and more than 200 African-American troops) made two assaults against

Colonel William Woodford's 2nd Virginia Regiment shortly after daybreak on Saturday, December 9, 1775. The colonials defeated the first assault. Dunmore's troops advanced across the causeway a second time with the support of 2 cannon. The Virginians held their fire until the attackers rushed forward, thinking the redoubt had been abandoned. They ran right into a volley that drove them back again. The rebels attacked Dunmore's flank, forced them back to their redoubt, and captured both guns and a number of prisoners. In less than a half-hour of fighting, Dunmore's 62 casualties included 13 deaths while the colonials numbered only 1 wounded. This victory over a better-trained enemy cleared the way for the colonials to move into Norfolk as Lord Dunmore and his small armed force took refuge on board warships in Norfolk harbor.

Norfolk (January 1, 1776)

Blue "Norfolk Tour" signs lead visitors to points of interest in the city. An information center on VA 192 features an orientation film.

The only structure to survive the destruction of early 1776 is St. Paul's Church (St. Paul's Boulevard and City Hall Avenue), built in 1739 on the site of a chapel that had been there almost a century. The south wall still has a cannonball embedded in it. A stone tablet says it was fired by Lord Dunmore on January 1, 1776.

Lord John Murray, 4th Earl of Dunmore (1732–1809), the royal governor of Virginia, fled Williamsburg in 1775 and established a base at Norfolk, which shortly became the only city in Virginia remaining under British control. He threatened to free the slaves and reduce Williamsburg to ashes in April, 1775, if the colonists rebelled against British authority.

After skirmishing at Great Bridge in December, 1775, Dunmore realized that he would not be able to hold Norfolk. He, the Loyalists, and his small army of Regulars, militia, and slaves boarded Royal Navy ships anchored offshore. American Colonel William Woodford (1734–1780) occupied the city on December 13. The rebels refused to supply Dunmore's fleet and fired on the ships with rifles. (See Photo VA-1, American rifleman.) Negotiations with rebel leaders to allow foraging in Norfolk proved fruitless.

Dunmore retaliated at 4:00 AM on January 1, 1776, by bombarding the city. He also sent landing parties to burn waterfront warehouses. The militia responded by torching the homes of prominent Loyalists. The conflict soon got out of control, and the militia destroyed the entire town to prevent its use by the Crown forces.

Dunmore moved back to Norfolk and had temporary barracks built. He departed soon afterward and the rebels reoccupied the city in February. They completed the destruction of the town, rendering it practically useless as a base of operations. It would not revive until after the war.

There are no records of casualties, but several noncombatants were killed or wounded. The battle is significant because it ended British rule in Virginia early in the war.

Portsmouth (May 10, 1779)

Fort Nelson

> Highway markers explain the events that took place in Portsmouth, Virginia. A monument on the grounds of the U.S. Naval Hospital (established in 1827), on the peninsula at the north end of Green Street, marks the site of Fort Nelson. In front of the entrance to the Portsmouth Shipyard Museum on Crawford Parkway, there's a little park at the edge of the U.S. Naval Shipyard. General Charles Cornwallis (1738–1805) embarked his troops for Yorktown from this point.

Portsmouth was a strategic military objective in early U.S. conflicts. Major General Edward Mathew (often misspelled Matthews) (1729–1805) landed here with a force of 1,800 men on Monday, May 10, 1779. He sent some troops to the town of Gosport where they encountered a force of 100 men who offered resistance from a redoubt north of the town called Fort Nelson. Mathew's men seized supplies and weapons and captured or destroyed about 130 vessels without any casualties. After 7 British vessels bombarded and set fire to the city and the surrounding Tidewater areas, Benedict Arnold (1741–1801) set up headquarters and the British line of defense at Fort Nelson (which is now called Hospital Point).

Green Spring (July 6, 1781)

> The Green Spring Battlefield is between Williamsburg and Jamestown, near the junction of VA 5 and County Road 614. The site has become part of the Colonial National Historical Park.
>
> There are no markers to interpret the action that occurred here.

As British General William Howe (1732–1786) and Major General John Burgoyne (1722–1792) went their separate ways in 1777, seemingly determined to satisfy only their personal ambitions, so General Henry Clinton (1730–1795) and General Charles Cornwallis (1738–1805) in 1781 paved the road to Yorktown by their disagreements and lack of coordination. Clinton was Cornwallis's superior in this case, but the latter enjoyed the confidence of Colonial Secretary Sir George Germain (1716–1785) to an extent that Clinton did not. Clinton, believing that without large reinforcements the British could not operate far from coastal bases, had opposed Cornwallis's ventures in the interior of the Carolinas, and, when Cornwallis came to Virginia, he did so without even informing his superior of his intention.

Since 1779, Clinton had sought to paralyze the state of Virginia by conducting raids up its great rivers, arousing the Loyalists, and establishing a base in the Chesapeake Bay region. He thought this base might eventually be used as a starting point for one arm of a pincers movement against Pennsylvania for which his own idle force in New York would provide the other. A raid conducted in the Hampton Roads area in 1779 was highly successful, but when Clinton sought to follow it up in 1780, the force sent for the purpose had to be diverted to Charleston, South Carolina to bail Cornwallis out after Kings Mountain. Finally in 1781, he got an expedition into Virginia, a contingent of 1,600 under the American traitor, Benedict Arnold (1741–1801). In January, 1781, Arnold conducted a destructive raid up the James River all the way to Richmond. His presence soon proved to be a magnet drawing forces of both sides to Virginia.

Then, on May 20, Cornwallis arrived from Wilmington, North Carolina and took over from Major General William Phillips (1731–1781). With additional reinforcements sent by Clinton, he was able to field a force of about 7,000 men, approximately a quarter of the British strength in America.

Cornwallis and Clinton were soon working at cross-purposes. Cornwallis proposed to carry out major operations in the interior of Virginia, but Clinton saw as little practical value in this tactic as Cornwallis did in Clinton's plan to establish a base in Virginia for a pincers movement against Pennsylvania. Cornwallis at first turned to the interior and engaged in a fruitless pursuit of General Marie Joseph de Motier Marquis de Lafayette (1757–1834) north of Richmond. Then, on receiving Clinton's positive order to return to the coast, establish a base, and return part of his force to New York, Cornwallis moved back down the Virginia peninsula to take a position at Yorktown, a small tobacco port on the York River just off the Chesapeake Bay. In the face of Cornwallis's insistence that he must keep all his troops with him, Clinton vacillated, reversing his own orders several times and in the end granting Cornwallis's request.

Cornwallis was also confused by Clinton's letters. Not only did they use convoluted and ambiguous wording but they did not arrive in the order in which they had been written. Cornwallis received one letter on July 8 followed 4 days later by three other letters, all written before it. Another letter arrived on July 20 countermanding previous instructions and advising contradictory measures.

Major General Marie Jean Paul Joseph du Motier Marquis de Lafayette (1757–1834) followed General Charles Cornwallis (1738–1805) as he traveled down the peninsula to Williamsburg, intending to cross the James and establish a base near Portsmouth. Lafayette was looking for an opportunity to catch the Crown forces in a vulnerable position crossing the river. Brigadier General "Mad Anthony" Wayne (1745–1796), leading an advance guard of about 500 men, later reinforced to 900, thought he was attacking Cornwallis's rear guard near Green Spring. He soon found himself engaged with Cornwallis's main force of 7,000. Lafayette could not get to Wayne in time to provide much support.

Cornwallis hoped to draw Lafayette's main force into battle and deliver a decisive blow by extending his line in both directions beyond Wayne's flanks. Wayne charged, catching Cornwallis by surprise. They attacked through grapeshot and musket fire to within 70 yards and stopped the British advance for 15 minutes. Lafayette arrived in time to support the Pennsylvanians' withdrawal. He had two horses shot from under him in the action. Cornwallis reported to General Henry Clinton (1730–1795) that he waited until "near sunset" to attack. With only about an hour of daylight for the entire action, he was unable to pursue the retreating enemy who attained the reserve line at the Green Spring Plantation. They remained there for a few hours and withdrew to Chickahominy Church during the night. Of the 900 troops engaged, Wayne lost 28 killed, 99 wounded, and 12 missing. He also lost 2 guns. Cornwallis had 75 killed and wounded.

YORKTOWN

Yorktown is one part of Colonial National Historical Park which is on the peninsula between the York and James rivers. The park covers 9,000 acres and includes Yorktown Battlefield; Jamestown, the Original Site; the Colonial Parkway; and the Cape Henry Memorial at Cape Henry. Park headquarters is in the Yorktown Visitor Center.

`http://www.nps.gov/colo/index.htm`

The Yorktown Visitor Center/Yorktown Battlefield is 0.75 mile south of Yorktown, Virginia on the edge of town, at the east end of the Colonial Parkway. The center includes parts of Washington's campaign tents, an observation deck, a reconstructed section of a gun deck, and a British frigate captain's cabin. A 16-minute film relates the events of the siege. Automobile tours begin at this point as do self-guiding and taped tours of the battlefield. Tour leaflets and tape rentals are available in the center.

`http://www.nps.gov/colo/Yorktown/ythomevc.htm`

The Yorktown Victory Center, off I-64 exit 247 on Old State Route VA 238 near the Colonial Parkway and U.S. 17, is a museum of the War for American Independence. "Road to Revolution," an open-air walkway, chronicles the events that led to the colonies declaring independence from Great Britain. "Witnesses to Revolution," the first in a series of themed indoor galleries, presents the stories of a representative group of 10 people whose lives were affected by the Revolution.

The "Converging on Yorktown" gallery has exhibits that tell how Yorktown became the setting for the decisive battle of the War for American Independence and describe the multinational nature of forces that converged there in 1781. "Yorktown's Sunken Fleet" reveals the story of the *Betsy* and other British ships scuttled or lost in the York River during the siege of Yorktown. Other exhibits relate the experiences of ordinary soldiers and describe the final step in America's journey to nationhood—the development of the Constitution and Bill of Rights.

Daily life during and just after the Revolution is re-created outdoors in a Continental Army encampment and an 18th-century farm where costumed interpreters demonstrate firing muskets and a cannon, discuss 18th-century medical practices, prepare meals, plant and cultivate crops, and process fiber into cloth.

The Yorktown Monument, between the battlefield and the entrance into town, commemorates the victory in 1781.

Visitors may view redoubts, trenches, and artillery on the Yorktown Battlefield. (See Photos VA-3 through VA-8.)

Grace Episcopal Church/Yorktown Battlefield was built of native marl (mixture of clay and limestone) about 1697. The British used it as a magazine during the siege of Yorktown. It was partially burned in 1814 but rebuilt later. General Thomas Nelson, Jr. is buried in the churchyard.

Moore House/Yorktown Battlefield is accessible from the battlefield tour route. The commissioners from the combined American and French armies met in the house with British representatives on October 18, 1781, and drafted the terms of General Charles Cornwallis's surrender. (See Photo VA-9.)

`http://www.nps.gov/colo/Ythanout/Moore%20House.htm`

Surrender Field (see Photos VA-10 and VA-11) is south of the battlefield on U.S. 17. A split-rail fence marks the route the Crown forces followed to lay down their arms in the formal surrender ceremony. Interpretive markers tell the story, and there's a display of some of the artillery surrendered at that time.

Nelson House is at the southwest corner of Main and Nelson streets in downtown Yorktown. The Georgian style house built about 1711 was the home of General Thomas Nelson, Jr., Governor of Virginia and a signer of the Declaration of Independence, who commanded the Virginia militia during the battle. General Cornwallis used it as his headquarters during the siege; General Nelson is reported to have told General Washington to fire on the house. A cannonball is still embedded in a wall on the third floor. (See Photo VA-2.)

General George Washington (1732–1799) had been trying to persuade the French to cooperate in a combined land and naval assault on New York in the summer of 1781. General Jean Baptiste Donatien de Vimeur Comte de Rochambeau (1725–1807), commander of the French army in America, brought his 4,000 troops from Newport, Rhode Island in April and placed them under Washington's command. The prospects were still bleak since the combined Franco-American force numbered but 10,000 against General Henry Clinton's (1730–1795) 17,000 in well-fortified positions.

Then, on August 14, Washington learned that the French fleet of 29 ships and over 3,000 troops in the West Indies, commanded by Admiral François Joseph Paul Comte de Grasse (1722–1788), would not come to New York but would arrive in the Chesapeake later in the month and remain there until October 15. He saw immediately that if he could achieve a superior concentration of force on the land side while de Grasse still held the bay he could destroy the British army at Yorktown before Clinton had a chance to relieve it.

Even without unified command of Army and Navy forces, Franco-American co-operation this time was excellent. Admiral Louis, Comte de Barras (d. ca. 1800), immediately put out to sea from Newport to join de Grasse. Washington sent orders to General Marie Joseph de Motier Marquis de Lafayette (1757–1834) to contain General Charles Cornwallis (1738–1805) at Yorktown. He then made a feint in the direction of New York to deceive Clinton. On August 21, he started the major portion of the Franco-American Army on a rapid secret movement to Virginia, via the Chesapeake Bay, leaving only 2,000 Americans behind to watch Clinton. Washington kept his plans secret from the entire army so Clinton would not learn of his plans from deserters or prisoners. He arrived in Philadelphia, Pennsylvania on September 2; at Head of Elk, Maryland on September 6; and in Williamsburg, Virginia on the 14th with Lafayette.

Chesapeake Bay (September 5, 1781)
Battle of the Chesapeake

On August 30, 1781, while General George Washington (1732–1799) was on the move southward, Admiral François Joseph Paul Comte de Grasse (1722–1788) arrived in the Chesapeake with his entire fleet of 24 ships of the line and a few days later debarked 3,000 French troops to join General Marie Joseph de Motier Marquis de Lafayette (1757–1834).

General Charles Cornwallis (1738–1805) wrote a coded message to General Henry Clinton (1730–1795) on August 31, 1781, telling him that he could clearly see the sails of about 40 enemy vessels between Cape Charles and Cape Henry off the Virginia coast, "mostly ships of war and some of them very large." Clinton responded that he would try to help Cornwallis, either by sending reinforcements or by mounting a diversion. Clinton decided he could not send reinforcements until the Royal Navy could transport them or protect them on the long march overland. He decided to mount a diversion instead. He sent Benedict Arnold (1741–1801) on a raid on Fort Griswold in New London, Connecticut.

Admiral Thomas Graves (1725–1802), the British naval commander in New York, meanwhile had put out to sea in late August with 19 ships of the line, hoping either to intercept Admiral Louis, Comte de Barras's (d. ca. 1800), squadron or to block de Grasse's entry into the Chesapeake. He failed to find Barras, and, when he arrived off Hampton Roads on September 5, he found de Grasse already in the bay.

When Graves saw the French ships coming out past Cape Henry, he ordered his fleet to reverse their order in the battle line. Admiral Samuel 1st Viscount Hood (1724–1816), who preceded the fleet, now occupied the rear. He assumed that Graves would attack the French who had not yet formed for battle. Graves delayed for an hour, giving de Grasse time to finish drawing up his battle line. Around mid-afternoon, Graves ordered the attack.

De Grasse knew that Admiral de Barras was on his way from Newport, Rhode Island to the Chesapeake with General Jean Baptiste Donatien de Vimeur Comte de Rochambeau's (1725–1807) siege artillery. He could not let the British fleet intercept him, but he had to wait for the tide to turn. When the tide turned around noon, de Grasse ordered his ships to prepare for battle.

The French, who had more ships and greater firing power, sallied forth to meet Graves. Both fleets were badly damaged in the inconclusive engagement off the Virginia capes that lasted $2\frac{1}{2}$ hours. The British suffered more damage because the French had greater gun power. The British lost the only vessel sunk in the battle—the 74-gun *Thunderer* which sank 2 days later.

For all practical purposes the victory lay with the French for, while the fleets maneuvered at sea for 5 days following the battle, de Barras's squadron slipped into the Chesapeake, and the French and American troops got past the British fleet into the James River. Then de Grasse returned to the Chesapeake on September 10 where he joined with de Barras's squadron, with several heavy cannon and tons of salt beef aboard his ships. The combined French fleet now numbered 35 ships of the line.

Graves thought the enemy now had "so great a naval force in the Chesapeake that they [were] absolute masters of its navigation." He turned to Hood, his second-in-command, for advice. Hood replied, "Sir Samuel would be very glad to send an opinion, but he really knows not what to say in the truly lamentable state we have brought ourselves." Graves decided his only alternative was to bring his "shattered fleet" to New York to refit. The Battle of the Chesapeake confirmed French command of the Chesapeake and sealed the fate of Cornwallis's army.

Siege of Yorktown (September 28 to October 19, 1781)

General Charles Cornwallis (1738–1805) set off for Yorktown intending to fortify it and Gloucester, on the northern bank of the York River opposite Yorktown. Both places were on low ground and would require building exceptionally strong fortifications to make them safe as naval stations. Cornwallis thought that the men's time and energy could be better employed in other ways. Even using as many African Americans as he could muster, Cornwallis would have to put the whole army to work either building the fortifications with the few entrenching tools with which his army was supplied or in guarding the working parties.

Yorktown had some natural advantages as a naval station. Gloucester lay less than a mile to the north, and swamps were on the east and west. A strong British squadron was expected to sail by October 5, 1781, to take a position between the two towns. An American force coming by sea would have to come from the south.

When Cornwallis occupied Yorktown, he planned to obtain a good seaport and harbor, never thinking that he would have to defend it against a siege from the land. He used the home of Thomas Nelson, Governor of Virginia, as his headquarters during the siege of Yorktown (see Photo VA-2 of Nelson House). General Cornwallis began constructing an outer line of redoubts and an inner line of earthworks, redoubts, and batteries around the town. Two redoubts, Numbers 9 (see Photo VA-3) and 10, strengthened the east end of the line. Two ravines in the rear of the town, Yorktown Creek and Wormley Creek, offered a little protection against an attack. Cornwallis also constructed a series of outworks on both sides of Wormley Creek northwest of Yorktown near the river. This star-shaped redoubt became known as the Fusiliers' Redoubt because some of the Royal Welch Fusiliers manned it (see Photo VA-4).

When General George Washington's (1732–1799) army arrived in Yorktown on September 26, 1781 the French fleet was in firm control of the Chesapeake Bay, blocking General Cornwallis's sea route of escape. A decisive concentration had been achieved. Counting 3,000 Virginia militia, Washington had a force of about 8,850 Americans and 7,800 French troops—a far greater number than Cornwallis had expected. Cornwallis had an army of only about 7,400 men, including about 2,000 German troops, to defend Yorktown and Gloucester. He concentrated on Yorktown from the beginning.

Gloucester Point

Gloucester was defended by a line of entrenchments across the Point and by about 700 British infantry commanded by Lieutenant Colonel Thomas Dundas (1750–1794). Lieutenant Colonel Banastre Tarleton (1744–1833) and his cavalry joined him, raising his strength to 1,000. They faced 1,500 Virginia militia under Brigadier General George Weedon (1734–1793) who were stationed there to check foraging expeditions and to close a possible escape route for the British army. The Americans were joined later by 600 French dragoons and 800 French marines.

Another force of American and French troops formed an arc across the interior of the point. (A French map of the Yorktown campaign shows the British fort on Gloucester Point as a semicircular structure with its broad, open end on the southeast shore of the point and extending across most of the point. A National Park Service booklet on the siege says the fortifications enclosed the village of Gloucester Point and consisted of a single line of entrenchments with 4 redoubts and 3 batteries. Nothing appears to remain of the structures, and U.S. 17 cuts right through the area it encompassed. Most of the French troops were probably placed east of U.S. 17, extending several miles to the northwest.)

The only skirmish here occurred on October 3 when the Americans drove back a foraging party. Afterward, the Allies established their camps closer to the British camp and contained them until the end of the siege. Closing the siege lines around the Gloucester Point fort, the Americans forced Tarleton to surrender. The Crown forces were paroled in 1782. Tarleton returned to England and never returned to America.

Preparations

The Americans and French prepared for the siege of Yorktown that proceeded in the best military traditions of Sebastien Le Prestre de Vauban (1633–1707) under the direction of French engineers. Cornwallis soon realized that he could not hold Yorktown without reinforcements. Even though Clinton promised to send help, Cornwallis knew he could not count on him.

Major Generals Marie Joseph de Motier Marquis de Lafayette (1757–1834), Benjamin Lincoln (1733–1810) (who had been exchanged after his capture at Charleston), and Friedrich Wilhelm von Steuben (1730–1794) each commanded 2 brigades of Continental troops. General Thomas Nelson (1738–1789), Governor of Virginia and a native of Yorktown commanded the militia. General Jean Baptiste Donatien de Vimeur Comte de Rochambeau (1725–1807) commanded the French wing which consisted of 7 regiments organized into 3 brigades. Both armies also had their own complements of engineers, cavalry, and artillery. Brigadier General Henry Knox (1750–1806) commanded the American artillery brigade.

On September 27, Washington ordered his troops to encircle Yorktown within a mile of the British fortifications. The troops encountered no opposition until midday when they came close to Yorktown where they met a few enemy pickets. On September 29, the American wing on the right or east side of the line tightened the circle by moving farther to the right and nearer the enemy. The Allied (American and French) army established permanent camps that formed a 6-mile-long curve extending from the York River, northwest of the town, around to the south through woods and fields, then east to Wormley Creek. The swamps and marshes of Beaverdam Creek separated the American wing on the right and the French wing on the left (see Photos VA-5 and VA-6).

Cornwallis abandoned his forward position during the night of September 30 except for the Fusiliers' Redoubt (see Photo VA-4) northwest of Yorktown and Redoubts 9 (see Photos VA-3 and VA-7) and 10 close to the river on the east side of the town. The day before, he received information from Clinton that a large fleet and 5,000 men would sail to reinforce him within a few days. He decided that he only needed to hold out for a few days and that he could do so more easily by occupying the inner defense line. As delays inevitably occur in war, Clinton's fleet waited for a favorable wind and tide and actually sailed from New York on the day of Cornwallis's surrender.

The Americans and French immediately occupied the abandoned fortifications and began additional construction, including a new redoubt. The French advanced against the Fusiliers' Redoubt on the left and drove in the pickets, but the position was too strongly defended. British guns in the main fortifications maintained a heavy and sustained fire on the Allies, but they continued to work on new construction, completing it in about 4 days.

Siege

The Allies completed preparations for the siege during the first days of October. They surveyed and planned, collected and constructed their siege material, and brought up the heavy guns which had been landed at the James River, 6 miles to the southwest. The French (see Photo VA-6) made a diversionary attack against the Fusiliers' Redoubt early in the evening of October 6 as 4,300 men began digging the first parallel trench between the lines. This trench extended about 2,000 yards and ran approximately parallel to the British inner defense line. The average distance of the line from the British defenses was only 800 yards except opposite Redoubts 9 and 10. The officers put 1,500 men to work digging, while 2,800 men guarded them. By morning, the trenches were deep enough to protect the sappers digging the next day (see Photo VA-8).

The Allies placed artillery along the trench and began an immense cannonade on October 9. The French constructed a small defense opposite the Fusiliers' Redoubt from which they could fire their guns against the British ships anchored in the harbor. That battery opened fire first, driving the frigate *Guadeloupe* across the river to Gloucester Point. Two hours later an American battery joined in the bombardment. George Washington fired the first shot. Forty cannon and 16 mortars continued, firing 3,600 shots on the first day. The French and American artillery nearly silenced the British guns. Red-hot shot from the French battery set the frigate *Charon* on fire and destroyed it.

Food supplies, even of putrid meat and worm-holed biscuits, were running so low that the British drove African Americans out of the town. The numbers of sick and dead increased daily. A German soldier noted the bodies lying unburied in the town, some of them with "heads, arms and legs shot off."

Stephen Popp in the British lines remembered:

> We could find no refuge in or out of the town. The people fled to the waterside and hid in hastily contrived shelters on the banks, but many of them were killed by bursting bombs. More than eighty were thus lost, besides many wounded, and their houses utterly destroyed. Our ships suffered, too, under the heavy fire, for the enemy fired in one day thirty-six hundred shot from their heavy guns and batteries. Soldiers and sailors deserted in great numbers. The Hessian Regiment von Bose lost heavily, although it was in our rear in the second line, but in full range of the enemy's fire. Our two regiments lost very heavily too. The Light Infantry posted at an angle had the worst position and the heaviest loss. Sailors and marines all served in defending our lines on shore.

Cornwallis was forced to conclude that "against so powerful an attack, [he could] not hope to make a very long resistance." He had about 3,250 men fit for duty and faced an Allied army of about 16,000 men.

Colonel Philip van Cortlandt, of the 2nd New York Regiment later recalled:

> The first gun which was fired I could distinctly hear pass through the town . . .
> I could hear the ball strike from house to house, and I was afterwards informed that it
> went through the one where many of the officers were at dinner, and over the tables,
> discomposing the dishes, and either killed or wounded the one at the head of the
> table. And I also heard that the gun was fired by the Commander-in-Chief, who was
> designedly present in the battery for the express purpose of putting the first match.

The sappers finished digging a zigzag connecting trench (see Photo VA-8) 200 yards forward by October 11. About dusk on October 11, they began work on a second parallel, completing about 750 yards that night. They continued working for the next 3 days, but they could not complete the line to the York River on the right because of the two British redoubts, Numbers 9 and 10.

The Allies decided to capture the two redoubts on the night of October 14. The French were to attack Redoubt Number 9, the stronger of the two forts with 120 British and Hessians, and the Americans would take Redoubt Number 10, defended by 70 men. This would be the last infantry assault of the war. Each force consisted of 400 men. Lieutenant Colonel Guillaume Comte de Forbach Comte de Deux Ponts (1754–1813) led the French, and Lieutenant Colonel Alexander Hamilton (1755–1804) commanded the Americans.

Both columns began their assault at 8:00 PM. A "forlorn hope" preceded each column to cut through the abatis. The Americans advanced with unloaded muskets and fixed bayonets and took Redoubt Number 10 in about 10 minutes. They did not wait for the sappers to chop through the abatis and lost fewer men. The French encountered some difficulties but captured their objective in less than half an hour. Sergeant Joseph Plumb Martin (1760–1850) recorded his observations of the assault on Redoubt Number 10:

> We arrived at the trenches a little before sunset. I saw several officers fixing bayonets
> on long staves. I then concluded we were about to make a general assault upon the
> enemy's works, but before dark I was informed of the whole plan . . .
>
> The sappers and miners were furnished with axes and were to proceed in front
> and cut a passage for the troops through the abatis . . . At dark the detachment . . .
> advanced beyond the trenches and lay down on the ground to await the signal for . . .
> the attack, which was to be three shells from a certain battery . . . All the batteries in
> our line were silent, and we lay anxiously waiting for the signal . . . Our watchword
> was, "Rochambeau" . . . Being pronounced, "Ro-sham-bow," it sounded when pro-
> nounced quick like, "Rush on boys."
>
> We had not lain here long before the . . . signal was given for us and the French . . .
> the three shells with their fiery trains mounting the air in quick succession. The word,
> 'up up' was then reiterated through the detachment. We . . . moved toward the re-
> doubt we were to attack with unloaded muskets.

The French had 15 men killed and 77 wounded taking Redoubt Number 9, the stronger of the two. The Americans lost 9 killed and 25 wounded. The sappers continued digging the trenches immediately after the capture of the two redoubts, incorporating both into the second parallel by morning.

Cornwallis attempted a sortie with 350 men near the center of the line just before daybreak of the 16th. They spiked a few guns before being driven back, but the disabled guns were repaired and soon resumed firing on Yorktown. Cornwallis was in a hopeless situation. He hoped to get some of his troops across the river, break through the Gloucester lines, and escape to New York. He embarked some of his men in small boats and landed them on the opposite shore before midnight of October 16. A storm scattered the boats and prevented a second trip across.

Surrender (October 19, 1781)

At 10:00 AM on October 17, the fourth anniversary of Major General John Burgoyne's (1722–1792) surrender at Saratoga and the very day that Admiral Thomas Graves (1725–1802) set sail from New York with a reinforced fleet and 7,000 troops for the relief of Yorktown, a drummer began to beat a "parley." The guns ceased fire; a British officer appeared, was blindfolded and taken into the American lines where he asked for an armistice. General Charles Cornwallis (1738–1805) began negotiations on terms of surrender. Graves arrived 5 days too late.

The officers met at the Moore House (see Photo VA-9) on October 18, 1781, to settle the terms of surrender.

Cornwallis requested that the Loyalist civilians and American army deserters at Yorktown and Gloucester not be punished for supporting the British. He also asked permission for his troops to return to Europe as Major General Horatio Gates (1728–1806) had done with General Burgoyne's army at Saratoga. General George Washington (1732–1799) would not comply with these requests. Because Sir Henry Clinton (1730–1795) did not allow Major General Benjamin Lincoln (1733–1810) to march out with drums beating and flags flying at the surrender at Charleston, South Carolina, the British army would endure the same humiliation at Yorktown.

Cornwallis protested that he was not responsible for Clinton's harshness at Charleston. One of the American negotiators replied, "It is not the individual that is here considered. It is the nation." Washington later agreed to let the British parade to music, provided it was not a parody of any American tunes which the British bands enjoyed playing. During the negotiations, soldiers on both sides rested in the sun, and bands entertained each other with music.

At 2:00 PM on October 19, 1781, the defeated British army marched out from Yorktown dressed in new uniforms so they would not have to surrender them to the Americans. The Allies formed 2 lines with the French on one side and the Americans on the other. The French wore white uniforms with black gaiters and their white standards with gold fleurs-de-lis flew above their heads. The Americans wore darker, drabber clothes; the British turned their gaze away from them. The British army marched between these 2 lines to a tune called "When The King Shall Enjoy His Own Again." Someone later switched the name of the piece to "The World Turned Upside Down" to make a political statement. (See Photo VA-10.)

Cornwallis pleaded illness and did not attend. He sent Brigadier General Charles O'Hara (1740–1802) of the British Guards, his second-in-command and the only other general officer on the British side, in his place. General O'Hara tried first to give Cornwallis's sword to General Jean Baptiste Donatien de Vimeur Comte de Rochambeau (1725–1807), acknowledging that the British were surrendering to the French rather than to the Americans. Rochambeau motioned him toward Washington who indicated that he should hand the sword to General Lincoln who had surrendered to the British under similar circumstances at Charleston, South Carolina. Lincoln accepted the sword and then returned it. The troops then marched to the surrender field where they laid down their arms.

Mathieu Dumas who met the troops and directed them recalls:

> I placed myself at General O'Hara's left hand . . . He asked me where General Rochambeau was. "On our left," I said, "at the head of the French line." The English general urged his horse forward to present his sword to the French general. Guessing his intention, I galloped on to place myself between him and M. de Rochambeau, who at that moment made me a sign, pointing to General Washington who was opposite to him.
>
> "You are mistaken," said I to General O'Hara. "The commander-in-chief of our army is on the right." I accompanied him, and the moment that he presented his sword, General Washington, anticipating him said, "Never from such a good hand."

The British soldiers passed between the 2 lines of Allied troops and laid down their arms. Some of them threw their weapons down angrily, as though they wanted to smash them on the ground until General O'Hara prevented them from doing so. As they marched away, some appeared drunk and many were close to tears, biting their lips or weeping.

Lieutenant Colonel Banastre Tarleton (1744–1833) surrendered the troops in the Gloucester lines across the river. Before doing so, he told Brigadier General Marquis de Choisy, the Allied commander, that, because of his evil reputation, he feared for his life if left in the hands of the militia. De Choisy excluded some of the militia from the surrender ceremony and everything proceeded smoothly.

The British surrendered 7,247 officers and soldiers and 840 seamen at Yorktown and Gloucester. They also gave up 264 cannon (see Photo VA-11), 6,658 muskets, 457 horses and over £2,000 (approximately $288,200) in cash. Ironically, there were still 30,000 British and American troops fit for duty in America. Casualties during the siege were fewer than expected. The British and Hessians lost 156 killed and 326 wounded. The Americans lost only 20 killed and 56 wounded; the French 52 killed and 134 wounded.

So far as active campaigning was concerned, Yorktown ended the war, even though the Crown forces still held New York City and the main port cities of the South. Both General Nathanael Greene (1742–1786) and General Washington maintained their armies in position near New York and Charleston for nearly 2 more years, but the only fighting that occurred was some minor skirmishing in the South, in South Carolina and Georgia, and on the Ohio frontier. King George III wanted to continue the war, but the British people were overwhelmingly opposed. The ministry fell, and a new cabinet that decided the war in America was lost was appointed. General Sir Guy Carleton (1724–1808) succeeded General Henry Clinton (1730–1795) in the spring of 1782. Shortly after assuming command in New York, he wrote Washington to ask for a cessation of hostilities. With some success, Britain devoted its energies to trying to salvage what it could in the West Indies and in India.

Peace negotiations began in 1781 and dragged on until 1783. The British finally declared an end to hostilities in February, 1783. Congress did the same in April. The treaty of peace, The Peace Treaty of Paris, acknowledging the independence of the United

States of America was formally signed on September 3, 1783 and ratified by Congress in January, 1784. The treaty also defined the boundaries of the new nation, settled fishing rights, and made arrangements for the payment of debts, the treatment of Loyalists, and the evacuation of Crown forces.

13

KENTUCKY

Kentucky was part of the colony of Virginia during the War for American Independence. It became a state in 1792.

See the Kentucky map.

Mount Olivet (August 19, 1782)
Blue Licks

Blue Licks Battlefield State Park is near Mount Olivet, Kentucky, on U.S. 68 at the crossing of Licking River near the village of Blue Lick Springs in Nicholas County. It is the site of the last Revolutionary War engagement fought in Kentucky.

The 100-acre Blue Licks Battlefield State Park covers most of the battlefield. The park offers beautiful scenery and marked landmarks of the battle. A granite obelisk commemorates those who died in the conflict and are interred in the burial grounds. It was dedicated on August 19, 1928 and bears a statement by Daniel Boone: "So valiantly did our small party fight, that, to the memory of those who unfortunately fell in the battle, enough of honor cannot be paid." A museum displays Native American and pioneer relics, bones of prehistoric animals found nearby, old gun and glassware collections, and a small relief model of the field. It also shows a 10-minute audiovisual program. Recreational facilities include campsites, picnic areas, a playground, and a community pool.

British captain William Caldwell and Simon Girty (1741–1818) led a band of Loyalists and Native Americans against Wheeling, in what is now West Virginia, in July, 1782. They then attempted a surprise raid on the unprotected outpost settlement of Bryan's Station, 5 miles northeast of modern Lexington, Kentucky on August 16. After 2 days of futile fighting, Caldwell began a slow retreat northeast to the Ohio border. He and his men made it easy for the Kentuckians to follow their trail.

Daniel Boone (1734–1820), Benjamin Logan (1743–1802), and about 180 frontiersmen started converging on Bryan's Station a few hours after Caldwell had left. The Kentucky volunteers rode in pursuit of Caldwell and Girty's force until dawn Monday, August 19. They stopped to rest 4 miles from the lower Blue Licks, about 40 miles from Bryan's Station, when they saw about 30 Native Americans remaining in plain view. The remaining force of 50 Butler's Rangers (a Loyalist regiment recruited and commanded by John Butler (1728–1796)), and more than 300 Wyandot, Ottawa, Ojibwa, Shawnee, Mingo, and Delaware warriors hid in the dense ravines, ready for an ambush. Lieutenant Colonel John Todd (1750–1782) asked Daniel Boone his opinion. He knew the area well and sensed an ambush. He replied:

> You see the Indians have shown themselves on the hill beyond the river, loitering, as if
> to invite pursuit—there are two ravines there, filled with brush and timber for their
> protection; it is not wise to heedlessly run into the trap set for us.

He advocated waiting until Logan arrived with a large force, but if the men insisted on fighting, he suggested that half of them should cross the Licking River several miles north and flank the enemy to prevent a possible ambush. The ford was narrow, but the water was deep and fast. Ravines and cliffs surrounded the north and sides, making it the worst possible place to launch an attack.

At a council of war, some of the men were convinced the Native Americans were on the run and could be defeated. If they waited, they might be attacked. Some accused Boone of cowardice. They decided to cross the river and attack. Boone commanded the left with about 70 men, including his son Israel. Todd took the center, and Lieutenant Colonel Stephen Trigg commanded the right. Major Hugh McGary led an advance party of about 25 men. The 3 divisions advanced about a mile and came within 60 yards of the enemy before the first shot was fired about 7:30 AM. The blistering volley from the woods left only McGary and two other men in the vanguard alive. Trigg and his men were annihilated; a few minutes later, the middle line collapsed.

Todd wrote later: "Several efforts were made to rally, but all in vain . . . Our men suffered much in the retreat, many Indians having mounted our men's horses, having open woods to pass through to the river, and several were killed in the river."

The 15-minute battle cost the frontiersmen about 70 killed and 7 captured, including Daniel Boone's son, Israel. Logan's force had proceeded 6 miles beyond Bryan's Station when it encountered the first band of men fleeing from the battle. Logan and his men prepared to fight, but they only encountered more survivors. Logan returned to the lower Blue Licks on August 24, 1782 with 470 men. Boone recalled the event to his biographer, John Filson (ca. 1747–1788), the following year:

> Being reinforced, we returned to bury the dead, and found their bodies strewed every
> where, cut and mangled in a dreadful manner. This mournful scene exhibited a horror
> almost unparalleled: Some torn and eaten by wild beasts; those in the river eaten by
> fishes; all in such a putrefied condition that none could be distinguished from an-
> other.

Many settlers returned East after the battle. Boone wrote to the governor of Virginia on August 30 for an additional 500 militia to defend the frontier.

14

NORTH CAROLINA

North Carolina contributed 11,238 men to the war—3,975 militia and 7,263 in the Continental Army.

See the North Carolina map.

Alamance (May 16, 1771)
Burlington Vicinity

Alamance Battleground is near Burlington, North Carolina, exit 143 off I-85, then 6 miles southwest on Highway NC 62. It commemorates the 1771 battle between Loyalist governor William Tryon's (1729–1788) militia and an inexperienced army of Colonial reformers known as the "Regulators."
    http://www.ah.dcr.state.nc.us/sections/hs/alamance/alamanc.htm

There's not a strong link between the Regulators' movement and the War for American Independence, but the context is important and the battle site is interesting. A plaque map and text explain the Regulators and the battle. A monument on the battle site is accompanied by flags marking the positions of the opposing forces (see Photo NC-1).

The John Allen house, a log home typical of 1780s North Carolina, is on the battlefield near the visitor center which offers a 25-minute audiovisual presentation about the battle.

Another battle that took place in the Burlington vicinity is Pyle's Defeat (1781). See below. To reach the site of Pyle's Defeat from Alamance, retrace your route back about 0.7 mile along Route SC 62 to Anthony Road (SC 1147). Take a right on Anthony Road and proceed about 1.25 miles to the intersection with Old Trail Road.

Although there is not a strong link between the Regulators' movement and the War for American Independence, the event provides insights into the Southern mindset and gives some background as to why the British lost their Loyalist support later in the war.

Loyalist Governor Tryon (1729–1788) saw the "Regulators," a leaderless mob of colonial reformers, as a threat to the authority of royal governors, and the Regulators' protests against the Stamp Act and Townshend Act were merely surface manifestations. On the one side, the Governor considered it his duty to defend the mother country against dangerous rebels; the militia took up arms to defend their homes from a western invasion (the Regulators lived in the more rural western part of the state). On the other side, the Regulators supposedly fought for better local government.

Rumors began to spread that the Regulators were preparing to march to the coast. The citizens of New Berne, North Carolina began preparing the capital for an attack. Governor William Tryon ordered a moat built between two rivers bordering the town.

He stopped the sale of arms to prevent them from getting to the Regulators. He cancelled the spring, 1771, session of the Hillsborough court and called out the militia on March 19, 1771. However, the soldiers did not want to take arms against their fellow countrymen, so Tryon offered a 40s bounty (almost $300) to stimulate recruitment.

Tryon and about 1,000 men marched west with swivel guns, in late April, to meet the Regulators while Loyalist general Hugh Waddell commanded a secondary troop of about 300 men in the back country. The Governor and his army encountered only minor difficulties, but a large force of Regulators blocked Waddell's path near Salisbury, forcing the Loyalists to turn back. Regulator commandoes disguised as slaves also captured and destroyed a large supply of gun powder being rushed from South Carolina.

Governor Tryon and a militia of about 1,200 men, mostly those whose privileges were involved, met about 2,000 Regulators about 5 miles from the Great Alamance River on May 16, 1771. The Regulators were an unorganized, leaderless mob with no tactical strategy. They came armed with muskets and rifles, but most of them believed that a compromise would make fighting unnecessary. They thought their presence would give the westerners an appearance of strength. Tryon refused to negotiate and demanded total and immediate surrender from the Regulators, giving them a 1-hour time limit to comply.

In the tension, shots rang out and the battle began. The Regulators were routed after several hours. Tryon ordered the forest containing rebel snipers set on fire. The Regulators lost an estimated 200 men killed or wounded while the Governor's troops suffered only 70 casualties. The Regulators dispersed, and Tryon offered rewards for each horse, gun, and saddle taken from the Regulators to make counterattack impossible; but this action only resulted in widespread looting. Over 6,000 men were granted amnesty after taking an oath of allegiance to the King. Later 12 Regulators were tried for treason and 6 were hanged.

Radicals in other colonies used reports of the battle to incite the people against the King. The Battle of Alamance destroyed the Regulator movement. Many of the people who belonged to the movement decided to leave North Carolina for unsettled territory across the Blue Ridge Mountains. As many as 1,500 families may have departed the Piedmont during 1772 alone.

Only a minority of the people in the Regulator counties seem to have sided with the Patriots in the Revolutionary War because they hated the Revolutionary leaders who fought against them near the Alamance River. Most of them probably remained neutral. Nonetheless, neighbors in the interior of the Carolinas settled their grudges or took revenge, as Loyalists fought against Whigs.

Four days after returning to his palace, Governor Tryon set sail for Manhattan to assume his duties as the new royal governor. Josiah Martin (1737–1786), Tryon's replacement, tried to reconcile the rebels. After a visit to the Piedmont, he became convinced that necessity forced the Regulators to revolt.

North Carolina recognized the importance of the interior and made some concessions to the region in the convention of 1776. Thirteen of the 44 sections of North Carolina's Constitution come from reforms sought by the Regulators.

Currie (February 27, 1776)

Moores Creek

Moores Creek National Battlefield lies near the town of Currie at 200 Moores Creek Road about 20 miles northwest of Wilmington and 4 miles west of U.S. 421, off NC 210.
http://www.nps.gov/mocr/index.htm

Moores Creek National Military Park, established in 1926, contains 50 acres of land. A visitor center near the park's entrance offers explanatory exhibits, displays, and an audio-visual program that depict the battle. It is also the starting point of two self-guiding trails with interpretive exhibits. The Patriot earthworks and the bridge have been reconstructed. A plaque shows the earthworks were in the shape of a horseshoe with a 2-foot high parapet and a ditch 3 feet below.

The park is a comparatively small, self-contained area that is excellent for walking and reconstructing the events. There are 2 guns placed approximately where the Patriot guns pointed at the creek. They represent the 2 guns the Patriots called "Old Mother Covington and her daughter". One is a cast-iron British cannon dated 1750. The other is a small brass swivel gun which fired a $\frac{1}{2}$-pound ball 750 to 900 yards. Old Mother Covington was a 2-$\frac{1}{2}$-pound cannon mounted on a galloper carriage. The Daughter was a $\frac{1}{2}$-pound swivel gun. Swivel guns were usually mounted on tree stumps and were easy to move and set up.

The park includes several monuments. The Heroic Women Monument was erected in memory of Mary Slocum and other women of the Cape Fear region. Mary, the wife of a militiaman, rode 65 miles to help the wounded. The James Moore Monument honors the commander of the 1st North Carolina Regiment. The Grady Monument marks the grave of private John Grady, the only Patriot to die in the battle. A picnic area is available.

Loyalties were sharply divided among the population of North Carolina after the Battle of Lexington and Concord, Massachusetts. The Patriots forced the royal governor into exile. However, many inhabitants remained loyal to the Crown but were very slow to become organized and challenge their Patriot counterparts. Commander-in-Chief General Thomas Gage (1719–1837) was convinced that there was strong support in the South, so he organized a strong expeditionary force under General Charles Cornwallis (1738–1805), General Henry Clinton (1730–1795), and Admiral Sir Peter Parker (1721–1811) to go to Brunswick Town, North Carolina.

Clinton sailed from Boston on January 20, 1776, planning to meet Cornwallis's force arriving from Ireland. Clinton arrived at Cape Fear, near Wilmington, North Carolina, in March, 1776. However, Clinton was forced to wait until the end of May before all of Cornwallis's troops arrived due to a terrible storm in the North Atlantic.

Gage planned for the Loyalists to join the British forces near Cape Fear. By February 18, 1776, approximately 1,500 Loyalists, consisting mostly of recently immigrated Highland Scots and about 130 ex-Regulators gathered to march toward the coast. Colonel James Moore (1737–1777), commanding 650 men of the 1st North Carolina Regiment, left Wilmington to oppose them. Three groups of Patriot militia joined them bringing the force to 1,100 men.

The Loyalists maneuvered past the Patriots but lost the race to Moores Creek Bridge, the only way to cross Moores Creek, a dark, sluggish stream 50 feet wide and 5 feet deep about 40 miles from Brunswick Town. The bridge probably consisted of two logs across the creek with planks nailed across them. The Patriots erected earthworks on the east side of the bridge and defended it with 150 men on February 25. They also placed two guns there to cover the bridge. The remaining force guarded the western banks but later withdrew to the eastern bank. The Patriots also removed many of the planks of the bridge and greased the bridge stringers to discourage any attempt at crossing.

The Loyalists arrived the next day and camped on the bridge's upper side until evening when they left to join another group of Loyalists. When they returned about dawn the next day, they expected to catch the enemy by surprise, but they found them entrenched on the other side of the bridge. The Loyalists decided to take it on February 27, 1776. About an hour before dawn, a party of 75 Highlanders charged out of the woods with their broadswords raised and bagpipes playing. They found their way over the bridge in the fog and met a withering volley of musket and cannon fire at a range of 30 yards before they reached the earthworks on the opposite bank. The volley, combined with the grease, left many of the attackers struggling in the creek where many drowned. The others turned and fled. Some Patriots rushed forward, replaced the planks, and crossed the creek in a counterattack that confused and demoralized the Loyalists and sealed the victory. The fight lasted only 3 minutes.

The Patriots lost 1 man killed and 1 man wounded; the Loyalists lost 30 killed and 40 wounded and 850 prisoners. The Patriots also captured the Loyalists' baggage which included 350 guns and shot bags, 1,500 muskets, 150 swords and dirks, 2 medicine chests, 13 wagons and their horses, and $75,000 in gold.

The Battle of Moores Creek Bridge demonstrated the surprising Patriot strength in North Carolina and eliminated any chances of Loyalist militia joining the British in North Carolina. The British departed the area and sailed to Charleston, South Carolina, where they were defeated at the Battle of Sullivan's Island several months later. They would not return to North Carolina until 1780 during the pursuit of the American army after the Battle of Cowpens. In retaliation for the Loyalist defeat, General Henry Clinton (1730–1795) burned the town of Brunswick, North Carolina and the plantation of Colonel Robert Howe (1732–1786). Brunswick was not rebuilt and remains in ruins to this day.

Cornelius (February 1, 1781)
Cowan's Ford

> Battle at Cowan's Ford: Route NC 73 at Lake Norman, 8 miles west of town of Cornelius.
>
> Lake Norman covers the site of the battle, but a monument nearby commemorates the event.

After the Americans defeated the Crown forces at the Battle of Cowpens (in South Carolina) on January 17, 1781, Lord General Charles Cornwallis (1738–1805) wanted to defeat the forces commanded by Major General Nathanael Greene (1742–1786) and Brigadier General Daniel Morgan (1736–1802). When Cornwallis reached the

Catawba River at Cowan's Ford, he had the option of taking a straight route suitable for wagons or a shallower one for horses, that turned and crossed a small island before reaching the east bank some distance south of the other ford.

General William Lee Davidson (1746–1781), a Patriot militia commander, and his force of about 300 men defended the shorter, but harder horse route which Cornwallis took across the river. Dick Beale, Cornwallis's Loyalist guide, deserted without warning them about the two fords. Many deserted and fled under enemy fire as they crossed the 500-yard-wide ford on February 1, 1781. They inadvertently took the wagon route that made tougher going in the water but led to the more lightly defended route. Cornwallis's troops scrambled up the lightly defended banks and defeated Davidson before he could move reinforcements from the horse ford. As 34-year-old Davidson was forming his men along the high bank to delay Cornwallis as long as possible, a Loyalist fired from the middle of the stream and killed him. His men withdrew, leaving Cornwallis securely established on Greene's side of the Catawba.

Robert Henry, a local schoolboy posted at the wagon ford, thinks Davidson's militia inflicted many more casualties in the river crossing than they have been given credit for. He says that the swift current carried away most of the wounded who fell into the stream when they were hit.

Burlington Vicinity (February 25, 1781)
Pyle's Defeat

> To get to the site of Pyle's Defeat, from I-85/40, take exit 145. Anthony Road (State Route NC 1148) is a little over 0.2 mile south of the exit. Take this for about 1.2 miles to get to Old Trail Road to the state historical marker, which is the only identification for the battle site.
>
> The Battle of Alamance (above) also took place near Burlington. To get to the Alamance site from Pyle's Defeat, continue along Anthony Road to the intersection with Route NC 62. Turn left on Route NC 62 and continue on this route until you come to the Alamance.

Major General Nathanael Greene (1742–1786) sent Major General Henry "Light-Horse Harry" Lee (1756–1818) from Virginia to North Carolina on February 18, 1781 with orders to harass the Crown forces. Lee crossed the Dan River with his Legion and Brigadier General Andrew Pickens's (1739–1817) South Carolina militia. He tried to surprise Lieutenant Colonel Banastre Tarleton (1744–1833) on the morning of February 25. However, Tarleton had already broken camp.

As Lee pursued Tarleton, the front of Lee's Legion encountered two mounted Loyalists who mistook the Americans for Tarleton's Legion, probably because they wore green coats similar to those worn by Tarleton's men (see Photo SC-3). The Loyalists were taken to Lee who took advantage of their mistake by posing as Tarleton. He learned that Colonel John Pyle had recruited about 400 Loyalists and that they were on their way to join Tarleton. Lee sent one of the men back to Pyle to congratulate him on raising his force, directing him to ask Pyle if "he would be so good as to draw out on the margin of the road, so as to give convenient room for his much fatigued troops to pass without delay to their night position."

Lee then ordered riflemen into the woods to cover his left flank while the messenger brought the dispatch to Pyle and returned. Lee took the lead of his column and soon saw Pyle's men lined up on the right side of the road. He rode toward Pyle, speaking occasionally to the Loyalists, complimenting them on their "good looks and commendable conduct." The South Carolina militia exposed themselves prematurely and shooting broke out as Lee was shaking hands with Pyle, intending to identify himself and to offer the Loyalists safety if they would go home or join his men.

Lee's Legion immediately wheeled to their right and charged the Loyalists with drawn sabers. Lee recorded "The conflict was quickly decided, and bloody on one side only." Many of the Loyalists, thinking a mistake had been made, shouted "You are killing your own men!" or "I am a friend to his Majesty!" or "Hurrah for King George!" At least 90 Loyalists were killed in the brief skirmish and most of the rest wounded, including Pyle who was left for dead.

The action is called a "defeat," but it resembles British victories by Tarleton at the Waxhaws and Major General Charles "No Flint" Grey (1729–1807) at Paoli which were called "massacres." The importance of this skirmish is that it destroyed any hopes Cornwallis had of getting help from the Loyalists of North Carolina at a time when he needed all the help he could get.

Greensboro (March 15, 1781)
Guilford Courthouse

Guilford Courthouse National Military Park covers 220 acres in northwest Greensboro, off U.S. 220 (Battleground Avenue) 6 miles north of the city.

`http://www.nps.gov/guco/index.htm`

Guilford Courthouse National Military Park includes wayside exhibits throughout the battlefield (see Photos NC-3 and NC-4) and a visitor center with displays, films, and brochures. A 2.5-mile auto tour leads to many of the monuments, including the graves of John Penn (1740–1788) and William Hooper (1742–1790), signers of the Declaration of Independence.

The Cavalry Monument honors all American cavalry, including Virginian Peter Francisco, known as "The Goliath of the Revolution." At the Battle of Guilford Courthouse, Francisco—who weighed 260 pounds and stood 6 feet 6 inches tall—supposedly used a 5-foot sword to kill 11 men. It was given to "the strongest man in Virginia" by George Washington.

The Stuart Monument (see Photo NC-3) honors Colonel James Stuart of the Queen's Guard. It marks the spot where Stuart fell in hand-to-hand combat and where his sword was found in 1866.

The Turner monument honors Kerenhappuck Norman Turner (see Photo NC-5). When she learned that her son was badly wounded in the battle at Guilford Courthouse, she rode 300 miles on horseback to nurse him and the other soldiers. Her son had a fever, so she made holes in a tub, suspended it from the rafters, and filled it with water. The cool water dripping slowly on her son's wounds and body acted like a modern ice pack and lessened the fever.

> Tannenbaum Park is 0.25 mile west on U.S. 220 at 103 Green Acres Lane. The park contains picnic areas, two log cabins, and a former British military hospital built in 1778. The Hoskins/Wyrick House (see Photo NC-6) served as British headquarters during the battle of Guilford Courthouse. It also served as a field hospital for both sides.

The war reached a stalemate in the North in 1778. The British shifted their attention to the South, conquering South Carolina and Georgia by 1780.

General Nathanael Greene (1742–1786) was appointed to replace Major General Horatio Gates (1728–1806) after the defeat at Camden, South Carolina on August 16, 1780. When Greene arrived at Charlotte, North Carolina, on December 2, 1780, he found a command that consisted of 1,500 men fit for duty, only 949 of them Continentals. The army lacked clothing and provisions and had little systematic means of procuring them. Greene decided that he must not engage General Charles Cornwallis's (1738–1805) army in battle until he had built up his strength and that he must instead pursue delaying tactics to wear down his stronger opponent. The first thing he did was to take the unorthodox step of dividing his army in the face of a superior force, moving part under his personal command to Cheraw Hill and sending the rest under Brigadier General Daniel Morgan (1736–1802) west across the Catawba over 100 miles away. Greene wrote:

> I am well satisfied with the movement. . . . It makes the most of my inferior force, for it compels my adversary to divide his, and holds him in doubt as to his own line of conduct. He cannot leave Morgan behind him to come at me, or his posts at Ninety-Six and Augusta would be exposed. And he cannot chase Morgan far, or prosecute his views upon Virginia while I am here with the whole country open before me. I am as near to Charleston as he and as near Hillsborough as I was at Charlotte; so that I am in no danger of being cut off from my reinforcements.

Divided forces could live off the land much easier than one large force and constitute two rallying points for local militia instead of one. Greene was, in effect, sacrificing mass to enhance maneuver.

Cornwallis, an aggressive commander, had determined to gamble everything on a renewed invasion of North Carolina. Ignoring General Henry Clinton's (1730–1795) warnings, he depleted his base in Charleston, South Carolina by bringing almost all his supplies forward. In the face of Greene's dispositions, Cornwallis divided his army into not two but three parts. He sent a holding force to Camden, South Carolina to contain Greene, directed Lieutenant Colonel Banastre Tarleton (1744–1833) with a fast-moving contingent of 1,100 infantry and cavalry to find and crush Morgan, and, with the remainder of his army moved cautiously up into North Carolina to cut off any of Morgan's force that escaped Tarleton.

General Nathanael Greene's strategy was to defend North Carolina and harass General Charles Cornwallis as he moved northward. General Cornwallis still had two armies left which were larger than Greene's and Brigadier General Daniel Morgan's , and he was uniting them and placing them between the American forces.

Lieutenant Colonel Banastre Tarleton moved with his contingent to find and crush Morgan, but, as it turned out, it was Morgan who defeated Tarleton at Cowpens, South

Carolina on January 17, 1781. When Cornwallis learned of the defeat at Cowpens, he himself set out after Morgan, determined to crush the Americans and release their 525 prisoners. Morgan had to move fast to escape Cornwallis. Although he was encumbered with both his own and the Crown forces wounded plus all his prisoners, Morgan covered 100 miles and crossed 2 rivers in 5 days. He stayed a day's march ahead of Cornwallis and eventually rejoined Greene at Guilford Courthouse on February 8. Greene continued to retreat northward through North Carolina up to the Dan River, just over the Virginia border, then back into North Carolina again, keeping just far enough in front of his adversary to avoid battle with Cornwallis's superior force.

Cornwallis was too heavily committed to the campaign in North Carolina by now to withdraw. Hoping to match the swift movement of the Americans, he destroyed all his superfluous supplies, baggage, and wagons but lost time in doing so. He set forth in pursuit of Greene's army but could get nothing from the countryside. He lacked food and boats to follow the Americans across the river, so he returned to Hillsboro, North Carolina, hoping to enlist Loyalists in the area. He found very few. One group that responded to his call mistook a party of American cavalry for Tarleton's British Legion. They were soon surrounded and slaughtered. This discouraged other Loyalists from joining Cornwallis.

Finally on March 15, 1781, at Guilford Courthouse in North Carolina, on ground he himself had chosen (he surveyed it weeks before during the retreat), Greene halted and gave battle. By this time he had collected 1,500 Continentals and 3,000 militia to the 1,900 tired, ill-clothed, and hungry Regulars the British could muster.

Greene hid his troops in the woods on either side of the road and kept a reserve immediately in front of the courthouse. He used Morgan's tactic and placed the inexperienced North Carolina militia in the front line behind a rail fence with the woods at their back. Here, they could fire at the Crown forces crossing the open fields (see Photo NC-2). He then placed the Virginia militia a quarter mile further east in heavy woods which would break up the tight enemy formations at the same time they protected the militia. Greene then placed his 1400 Continentals about 500 yards away on a slight rise and behind another cleared field.

Cornwallis placed his men on either side of the road, just as Greene had done. He left 3 guns in the road and held a corps of German jaegers, the light infantry and the cavalry of the British Legion, all under the command of Banastre Tarleton, in reserve. (See Photo NC-3.)

The Crown forces, tired from a 12-mile march that morning to reach the battlefield, began the attack at about 1:00 PM after a brief artillery duel. They met heavy and continuous fire, but they came on steadily. The North Carolina militia fired 2 rounds and retreated into the woods. The sharpshooters on either side of them also withdrew from tree to tree, while the cavalry under Lieutenant Colonel William Washington (1752–1810) and Lieutenant Colonel Henry "Light-Horse Harry" Lee (1756–1818) moved slowly back with them. Lee's Legion and supporting troops on the American left, or south flank, were forced up a hill so far from the army that they were engaged in a separate battle until the main action was almost over.

The north flank on the right fell back to the second line, 350 yards to the rear in the woods, and formed on their right flank. When the North Carolina militia broke and fled, "throwing away arms, knapsacks, and even canteens [as] they rushed like a torrent headlong through the woods," the Crown forces encountered the Virginia militia in the second line. The Americans allowed the British light infantry, with the 23rd Foot and the jaegers under Colonel James Webster (ca. 1743–1781) to get within a few yards, and then charged with the bayonet, driving the Crown forces back in confusion. The redcoats rallied and eventually forced the second line to give way and seek cover behind the Continental troops or in the woods.

The Crown forces came out of the woods, after fighting two battles, to find another open field with 1,400 Continental regulars on the other side. The third line included Greene's best infantry: Brigadier General Isaac Huger's (1743–1797) 2 regiments of Virginia militia on the right and Colonel Otho Holland Williams's (1749–1794) 2 Maryland regiments on the left. This line was drawn up on the hill in front of and northwest of Guilford Courthouse about 350 yards behind the second line. They saw the Crown forces break through the right half of the second line, but they held their fire until the enemy came within 100 feet (about 100 yards past the Visitor's Center building).

The 1st Maryland fired a volley and charged the Crown forces with bayonets across a ravine and up an adjacent slope where they eventually rallied. Colonel Washington saw this and drove his dragoons forward into the midst of the enemy and scattered them. Peter Francisco (ca. 1760–1831), a 6-foot-6-inch giant, swinging a 5-foot saber given to him by George Washington killed 11 men before falling wounded.

Cornwallis sent his 3 guns to the edge of the woods where they soon opened fire (see Photo NC-4). Brigadier General Charles O'Hara's (1740–1802) grenadiers and battalion of Guards charged. The 2nd Maryland Regiment broke under the pressure, when Colonel Washington's cavalry struck the Guards in the rear, while the 1st Maryland Regiment turned to attack their flank in savage fighting.

Cornwallis's 3 field guns, firing grapeshot, halted the massacre but killed as many British guardsmen as American cavalry. Greene ordered a retreat, and the Americans left the field, abandoning their guns and marching northward.

Greene might have been able to destroy Cornwallis's army before these troops rallied, but if a counterattack failed, he might lose the army, the last organized force in the south. So he relented. The Americans lost 79 killed and 185 wounded. Cornwallis lost over 500 killed and wounded—between a third and a quarter of the force engaged. His army, already outnumbered by more than 2 to 1 before the battle, could hardly afford such heavy losses. The Guards alone had 11 of its 19 officers fall as casualties and more than 200 of the 462 men. The survivors, who had eaten nothing since their 4 ounces of flour and 4 ounces of dry beef the previous afternoon, lay down in the steady rain without food or shelter.

The British held the field after a hard-fought battle, but, like Bunker Hill, it was a Pyrrhic victory. When Colonial Secretary Sir George Germain (1716–1785) announced the victory to Parliament, Charles James Fox (1749–1806) remarked: "Another such victory would ruin the British army." His ranks depleted and his supplies exhausted,

Cornwallis withdrew to Wilmington on the coast, and then decided to move north-ward to join the British forces General Henry Clinton (1730–1795) had sent to Virginia.

After the Battle of Guilford Courthouse, General Greene recorded his observations in a letter:

> The battle was fought at or near Guilford Court-House, the very place from whence we began our retreat after the Light Infantry joined the army from the Pedee. The battle was long, obstinate and bloody. We were obliged to give up the ground and lost our artillery, but the enemy have been so soundly beaten that they dare not move towards us since the action, notwithstanding we lay within ten miles of him for two days. Except the ground and the artillery, they have gained no advantage. On the contrary, they are little short of being ruined. The enemy's loss in killed and wounded cannot be less than between six and seven hundred, perhaps more.
>
> Victory was long doubtful, and had the North Carolina militia done their duty, it was certain. They had the most advantageous position I ever saw, and left it without making scarcely the shadow of opposition. Their general and field officers exerted themselves, but the men would not stand. Many threw away their arms and fled with the utmost precipitation, even before a gun was fired at them. The Virginia militia behaved nobly and annoyed the enemy greatly. The horse, at different times in the course of the day, performed wonders. Indeed, the horse is our great safeguard, and without them the militia could not keep the field in this country . . . Never did an army labour under so many disadvantages as this; but the fortitude and patience of the officers and soldiery rise superior to all difficulties. We have little to eat, less to drink, and lodge in the woods in the midst of smoke. Indeed, our fatigue is excessive. I was so much overcome night before last that I fainted.
>
> Our army is in good spirits, but the militia are leaving us in great numbers to return home to kiss their wives and sweethearts.
>
> I have never felt an easy moment since the enemy crossed the Catawba until since the defeat of the 15th, but now I am perfectly easy, being persuaded it is out of the enemy's power to do us any great injury. Indeed, I think they will retire as soon as they can get off their wounded.

After the Battle of Guilford Courthouse, Cornwallis spent 2 miserable, rain-soaked days on the field tending to the wounded of both sides and burying his dead (See Photo NC-6). He realized he could not afford to risk another battle in an unfriendly country with his small force. He was so short of supplies and had so little transportation that he had to leave several of his wounded in Greene's care when he left the field. He found few committed Loyalists and many determined rebels in the south. Many rivers obstructed the army, and he found it virtually impossible to find adequate provisions and forage in that inhospitable land. So, he decided to abandon the Carolinas and go to Virginia.

Cornwallis left Lord Francis Rawdon (1754–1826) in command in the Carolinas and headed to Wilmington, North Carolina where his army could get supplies by sea. Greene pursued for a short distance until April 8, then turned south into South Carolina. Without consulting General Clinton, Cornwallis left Wilmington for Virginia on the morning of April 25 with no more than 1,435 men fit for duty. Although defeated in battle, Greene won his objective and Cornwallis moved to Virginia, where he finally surrendered his army at Yorktown on October 19, 1781.

15

SOUTH CAROLINA

South Carolina had more than 6,000 men serve in the Continental Army. It probably has more Revolutionary War sites than any other state (see Appendix 1). Each of the state's 46 counties has sites. A visitor cannot hope to see them all in a brief time. However, one can visit all the sites that commemorate the events that affected the outcome of the war. One can also see enough significant local spots to understand how the people of South Carolina coped with the War for American Independence.

General Henry Clinton (1730–1795) captured Charleston in May, 1780. He left General Charles Cornwallis (1738–1805) in charge when he returned to New York. Cornwallis established a series of forts from Charleston to Ninety-Six on the Georgia border. He placed them at Camden, Rocky Mount, Hanging Rock, Fort Watson, Fort Motte, and Fort Granby.

Cornwallis defeated Major General Horatio Gates (1728–1806), commanding the American army in the South, at Camden in August, 1780. Major General Nathanael Greene (1742–1786) replaced Gates as commander in December, 1780, and divided his army into several smaller groups. This forced Cornwallis to deal with many opposing units. Unable to risk a general engagement, Greene kept out of Cornwallis's reach.

Because of the number of sites included in this chapter, the state is divided into three sections: Northern, Charleston area, and Southern. There are two maps: Northern South Carolina and Southern South Carolina.

NORTHERN

See the map of Northern South Carolina.

Lancaster (May 29, 1780)
Battle of the Waxhaws

To get to the Battle of the Waxhaws site, take Route SC 522, south of Route SC 9, 9 miles east of town.

Colonel Buford's men are buried in a common grave in a grove alongside SC 522. A 2-foot high wall of white rocks surrounds the grave and a 7-foot obelisk serves as the common headstone. The site looks like a little roadside park and is easy to ignore.

The British began to establish a ring of posts across the northern part of South Carolina after the fall of Charleston on May 12, 1780. The main one was at Camden, with others to the north, east, and west. Lieutenant Colonel Banastre Tarleton (1744–1833) and his cavalry eliminated the last organized resistance in the state on May 29, 1780 at the Waxhaws, a district near the North Carolina border.

Colonel Abraham Buford (1749–1833) with 350 Virginians was moving south to reinforce Charleston when Tarleton's 170 cavalry and 100 infantry (the infantrymen were mounted behind the cavalrymen) overtook him after riding 105 miles in 54 hours. Tarleton formed his men on a nearby hill only 300 yards away in full view of Buford who formed a line facing him. Even though exhausted, they attacked immediately in three groups, one on each flank, and one at the center. Buford's men obeyed his strict orders to hold their fire. Buford had several artillery pieces, but they were up front with the baggage and were never brought into action.

The Americans opened fire at close range, but they didn't have enough time to reload. The British infantry charged the American center while Tarleton circled around the American position with a cavalry unit. A bayonet charge destroyed Buford's line, and he decided to surrender. The ensign who raised the flag of truce was "instantly shot down." Tarleton slaughtered all but 100 of Buford's 350 Virginians. Tarleton lost only 3 killed and 12 wounded. The battle produced the phrase, "Tarleton's quarter," meaning massacre of defenseless men.

Robert Brownfield, a surgeon on the scene, wrote:

> The demand for quarters, seldom refused to a vanquished foe was at once found to be in vain. Not a man was spared . . . (Tarleton's dragoons) went over the ground plunging their bayonets into everyone that exhibited any signs of life, and some instances, where several had fallen over the others, these monsters were seen to throw off on the point of the bayonet the uppermost, to come at those underneath.

General Henry Clinton (1730–1795) returned to New York on June 8, leaving General Charles Cornwallis (1738–1805) in command in the South with about 8,300 British and Loyal American troops. Cornwallis established his main seaboard bases at Savannah, Beaufort, Charleston, and Georgetown, and in the interior extended his line of control along the Savannah River westward to Ninety-Six and northward to Camden and Rocky Mount. However, his force was too small to police so large an area, even with the aid of the numerous Loyalists who took to the field.

Though no organized Continental force remained in the Carolinas and Georgia, American guerrillas, led by Brigadier Generals Thomas Sumter (1734–1832) and Andrew Pickens (1739–1817) and Lieutenant Colonel Francis Marion (1732–1795), began to harry British posts and lines of communications and to battle the bands of Loyalists. Whigs and Loyalists began to fight each other almost immediately after Clinton's departure, with frequent and bitter skirmishes through the rest of the summer rather than battles between American and British troops. Neighbor fought against neighbor, sometimes taking an opportunity to settle grudges. Neither side took many prisoners. Any prisoners were usually executed soon afterward, especially if they had changed their loyalty to the other side. A bloody, ruthless, and confused civil war ensued, its character determined to a large extent by Tarleton's action at the Waxhaws.

Brattonsville (July 12, 1780)
Williamson's Plantation
Huck's Defeat

Williamson's Plantation (Huck's Defeat): From the intersection of SC 322 and U.S. 321 in McConnells, take SC 322 east 2.5 miles, then turn left on SC 165 for 2.6 miles to the stone monument on the left.

Colonel William Bratton's house, about 200 feet north of Williamson's Plantation, still stands on the edge of some woods. The Daughters of the American Revolution erected a stone monument at the site of Williamson's Plantation to commemorate the engagement which occurred there.

About 500 Patriots attacked Captain Christian Huck (d. 1780), a detested Loyalist officer from Pennsylvania, and his 400 Loyalist and British soldiers at James Williamson's plantation at sunrise on July 12, 1780. Most of the men were sleeping when the surprise attack began. Camped on a lane whose rail fences formed a slaughter pen, the men ran from their tents to fight back, but the attackers blocked the ends of the lane, cutting Huck's men off from their horses.

The defenders made two unsuccessful charges. Huck ran from the Williamson house, jumped on his horse to lead another, and was shot in the throat by a sharpshooter. The Crown forces surrendered soon after the loss of their leader.

The Patriots lost only 1 man killed and liberated 2 men Huck had captured the day before and who were scheduled to be hanged that day. Only about a dozen of Tarleton's Legion and the same number of Huck's mounted infantry managed to escape. The rest of his 115-man command was eliminated: 35 were killed, the rest captured. (See Photo SC-1 showing an example of captured British prisoners.)

This engagement occurred just 2 months after the British captured Charleston on May 12. The victory encouraged about 600 South Carolinians to join Brigadier General Thomas Sumter (1734–1832), who now led the only organized American force in South Carolina.

Great Falls Vicinity (July 30, 1780)
Rocky Mount Engagement

From Great Falls take U.S. 21 south 3.9 miles to SC 45, turn left 2.3 miles to a stone monument on the right of the road.

There are no remaining signs of the Rocky Mount outpost. Only the large rocks that protected the men who threw the torches remain. A stone monument is the only informational device located at this site. (The Fishing Creek Engagement site is also near Great Falls.)

Brigadier General Thomas Sumter (1734–1832) arrived near the British station at Rocky Mount with about 600 men early on July 30, 1780. He camped outside the ditch and abatis surrounding the post just south of where Rocky Creek joins the Catawba River.

Lieutenant Colonel George Turnbull, a Connecticut Loyalist, and about 150 New York Volunteers and some South Carolina militia occupied several log buildings inside the field fortifications.

When Turnbull refused his demand to surrender, Sumter unsuccessfully attacked the post. Lacking artillery, he then decided to burn the enemy out. He sent two men to throw torches at the buildings from behind large boulders. They set fire to one of the buildings which threatened the main structure. However, an unusually heavy rain began to fall and extinguished the flames. Sumter abandoned the attack and withdrew "under as great mortification, as ever any number of men endured."

Heath Springs (August 6, 1780)
Hanging Rock Skirmish

> The site of the Hanging Rock Skirmish is off SC 467, 2 miles south of Heath Springs. Take South Main Street and continue 1.7 miles to SC 467 on the left. Turn onto SC 467 and continue 0.6 mile to a dirt road on the right and take it to the monument at the base of Hanging Rock.
>
> `http://www.royalprovincial.com/history/battles/HangingRock1.shtml`
>
> One may walk the top of Hanging Rock and look across Hanging Rock Creek to where the Loyalist camp was situated. The Daughters of the American Revolution erected a stone monument at the foot of Hanging Rock, the only monument or sign to assist the visitor.

Hanging Rock, so called because of a massive boulder 20 to 30 feet in diameter on the east bank of the Catawba River, was a British post between 1780 and 1781. Brigadier General Thomas Sumter (1734–1832), eager to avenge his loss at the Battle of Rocky Mount in July, 1780, led 600 men against a Loyalist camp of 1,400 shortly after 6:00 AM on August 6, 1780, as the Loyalists finished breakfast and were engaged in morning chores.

Sumter's riflemen fired into the camp catching the Loyalists by surprise. The enemy's left flank broke and fled. The center held and formed a counterattack. They attempted several charges and were involved in savage hand-to-hand fighting. The marksmanship of well-positioned snipers took its toll. At one point, Major John Carden (d. 1783), in command of the Prince of Wales' Regiment with only 9 survivors, resigned his command on the spot in the heat of battle.

A small group of mounted infantry from the British Legion mounted an unsuccessful counterattack on Sumter's right. Sumter repelled the attack and advanced, driving the enemy's center into the right flank of their camp. After 3 hours of fighting and on the verge of a spectacular victory, the Patriot forces began to ransack the camp. This gave the Loyalists time to reorganize. They soon began firing at the looters. Sumter could not re-form his troops and retreated about noon.

The Battle of Hanging Rock was very savage with one of the highest casualty rates for any battle of the War for American Independence. Sumter estimated enemy casualties of 250 and 70 prisoners. He lost 20 dead, 40 wounded, and 10 missing. Sumter himself was one of the wounded, having been shot in the leg.

Great Falls (August 18, 1780)
Fishing Creek Engagement

> The Fishing Creek Engagement site is on Route U.S. 21, 2 miles north of Great Falls at the bottom of Fishing Creek Reservoir.
>
> The battle site itself is now covered by Fishing Creek Reservoir, near the dam. A granite roadside marker on the east side of U.S. 21 tells the story. (See above for the Rocky Mount engagement, also near Great Falls.)

In August, 1780, after his victory at Hanging Rock, Lieutenant Colonel Banastre Tarleton (1744–1833) pursued Brigadier General Thomas Sumter (1734–1832). Sumter, on his way to support Major General Horatio Gates (1728–1806), learned of the American defeat at Camden on August 16, so he chose to retreat. His exhausted troops camped along the west bank of the Wateree River near Rocky Mount on the night of August 17. Tarleton, on the east bank of the river, could see the fires of Sumter's camp and forbade his troops to make fires or noise. He spent the night silently watching his prey.

The next day, Sumter continued his retreat across Fishing Creek where he set up a new camp. Tarleton crossed the Wateree and reached Fishing Creek by noon of the same day, surprising the unprepared American camp. They quickly took a position between most of Sumter's men and their weapons and slaughtered about 150, captured 300, and liberated 100 prisoners, while losing only 16 men. Sumter also lost 2 small artillery pieces, 2 ammunition wagons, 44 other wagons, and over 1,000 weapons.

Sumter leaped onto an unsaddled horse and narrowly escaped into the forest. Within a week, he gathered stragglers from the battle and new recruits and managed to reorganize his unit. Reports of this skirmish made Tarleton a national hero in England.

Camden (August 16, 1780)

> The Battle of Camden site is on Flat Rock Road, SC 58, 5 miles north of Camden. From Camden take U.S. 521 and U.S. 601 north 5.6 miles, bear left, and immediately afterward turn left on County Road 58 for 2 miles to a stone monument on the right. The Battle of Camden site is a national park and the actual site of the battle. The terrain of the battlefield is undeveloped and unmarked, except for the stone memorial erected by the Daughters of the American Revolution in 1909 on the spot where Baron de Kalb was mortally wounded.
>
> The Historic Camden Revolutionary War site is on U.S. 521 south of town. This site is a state park that commemorates the battle. It is a restoration and reconstruction that recreates life in colonial Camden. It includes several of the earthen redoubts constructed by the British and which George Washington explored on a visit on May 25, 1791. It also includes the 1777 powder magazine with 48-inch walls built under the supervision of Joseph Kershaw. General Cornwallis used Kershaw's house (see Photo SC-2), which was burned during the Civil War and reconstructed, as his headquarters. A short stone obelisk in front of Bethesda Presbyterian Church between Lytleton and Broad Streets in Camden marks the grave of Major General Johann Baron de Kalb (1721-1780). Robert Mills (1781-1855), a South Carolinian, designed the monument erected by the Town of Camden in 1825. Marie Jean Paul Joseph du Motier Marquis de Lafayette (1757-1834),

who sailed to America with de Kalb in 1777, laid the cornerstone. The inscription on the monument states de Kalb's "love of liberty induced him to leave the old world to aid the new in their struggle of INDEPENDENCE."

Hobkirk Hill (see below) is another site near Camden.

The British occupied Camden on June 1, 1780, only 19 days after capturing Charleston. They began immediately to develop it as their main interior outpost in South Carolina. On June 22, 2 understrength Continental brigades from General George Washington's (1732–1799) army arrived at Hillsboro, North Carolina, to form the nucleus of a new Southern Army around which militia could rally and which could serve as the nerve center of guerrilla resistance. Major General Baron Johann de Kalb (1721–1780), who commanded this army of about 1,400 men, was the highest ranking Continental officer in the South after Major General Benjamin Lincoln's (1733–1810) surrender at Charleston on May 12, 1780. In July, Congress, without consulting General Washington, provided a commander for this army in the person of Major General Horatio Gates (1728–1806), the hero of Saratoga.

Gates soon lost his northern laurels. Gathering a force of about 2,000 men, mostly militia, he set out to attack the British post at Camden. He arrived in North Carolina on July 25, 1780 and set out 2 days later. Acting against the advice of officers who knew the country, he took the more direct road, 50 miles shorter, through deserted areas where he could not find supplies. The men came down with dysentery from eating green corn and unripened peaches which was the only food they could find. They suffered from exhaustion and debilitation. Gates made rendezvous with 2,000 North Carolina and Virginia militia under Colonel James Caswell on August 3, doubling the size of his army.

After General Henry Clinton's (1730–1795) return to New York, General Charles Cornwallis (1738–1805) left a garrison in Charleston and divided the rest of his army into 3 columns for simultaneous expeditions into the interior in preparation to invade North Carolina. One column would march to Ninety-Six, another would go up the Savannah and Saluda Rivers to Savannah and Augusta, while the third would go to Camden by way of the Santee River.

Cornwallis hurried north from Charleston to reinforce Lord Francis Rawdon (1754–1826) and meet Gates outside Camden which would be the jumping-off point for his campaign. His army of 2,250 British Regulars made contact with Gates by surprise on the night of August 15, 1780 and prepared for battle on August 16. Three prisoners told Cornwallis of Gates's plan to attack on the morning of the 16th, causing him to order his army to be ready to advance at 10:00 PM. Both armies unknowingly approached each other in the night, meeting at Gum Swamp, 8 miles north of Camden, at about 1:00 AM. After an indecisive but sharp 15-minute skirmish, both armies retired and prepared for battle later in the day.

When the soldiers awoke on the morning of August 16, they found themselves in a pine grove with swamps on both sides, giving them no room to maneuver and forcing a head-on collision if they decided to fight. Both armies faced each other across the

Waxhaw Road (now Flatrock Road) which went to the Waxhaw River from Camden and Charlotte. The centers of both lines were located just about at the road.

The Americans had about 3,500 men ready for duty:

Veteran Maryland and Delaware Continentals	900
Charles Armand's Veteran Legion	100
Militia	2,500
Total	3,500

The British had:

Veteran Regular and Loyalist troops	1,500
Banastre Tarleton's Veteran Cavalry	200
Militia and comparable units	550
Total	2,250

Gates deployed the Virginia militia on his left and the North Carolina militia in the center with the Delaware Continentals under Major General Johann de Kalb on the right. Brigadier General Charles Armand's (Charles-Armand Tuffin, Marquis de la Rouerie) (d. 1793) Legion (previously Pulaski's Legion) and the 1st Maryland regiment formed the second line to their rear, with 300 Continentals in reserve. His strength was on his right or west flank, while the militia in the center and on the left were not experienced in battle. The militia were still forming in the hazy dawn when Cornwallis struck, and they fled in panic before the British onslaught, scarcely firing a shot.

Cornwallis, to the south on the same road, posted his best men on his right or east flank, creating an opposite effect to Gates's arrangement. The first line consisted of Loyalist troops on the left and Regulars on the right, aligning British veterans opposite rebel militia. Regulars formed the second line. The Highlanders and Lieutenant Colonel Banastre Tarleton's (1744–1833) cavalry were held in reserve.

The battle began with a cannonade shortly after sunrise. As the British advanced, Gates tried to attack the right before it could deploy, but his militia did not get there fast enough and found the redcoats already in formation, advancing on them. The militia broke and ran, leaving Gates with only one third of his army: the Continentals under de Kalb. Fog, dust, and smoke reduced visibility and contributed to the militia's panic.

After recovering from the confusion caused by the militia's flight, the 1st Marylanders in the second line charged, moving to the left of the 2nd Maryland and Delaware Regiments in the now-ragged first line. The British soon forced it back, eventually sending it racing to the rear.

Cornwallis moved his troops against the 2nd Maryland and Delaware Regiments on his left flank and in front of de Kalb's 900 Continentals. The Continentals held firm for a while, putting up a valiant but hopeless fight against 2,250 men. When de Kalb called for the reserve, those 300 men ran into the fleeing militia which rallied and tried to advance.

Brigadier General William Smallwood (1732–1792) was swept away by the runaways, but his 1st Marylanders formed under General Otho Holland Williams (1749–1794). Williams tried to bring the 1st Marylanders to reinforce the exposed flank of the

2nd Maryland, but Cornwallis prevented them from doing so and soon drove them from the field.

Tarleton's cavalry (see Photo SC-3 of Legion uniform) attacked the Continentals in the rear and captured Baron de Kalb who had 11 wounds and died 3 days later. Tarleton's cavalry pursued the fleeing Americans for 30 miles, killing or making prisoner those who lagged. They also caught up with Brigadier General Thomas Sumter (1734–1832), whom Gates had sent with a detachment to raid a British wagon train, and virtually destroyed his force in a surprise attack at Fishing Creek on August 18. Gates himself fled too fast for Tarleton, riding 60 miles to Charlotte that day and reaching Hillsboro, North Carolina, 180 miles away, in 3½ days.

Gates's army was so badly beaten that there are no accurate reports of his losses. He lost all his stores and baggage, all his 7 brass cannon, and his reputation. He began the battle with almost 4,000 men but only 800 reached Hillsboro. Estimates put the casualties at approximately 800–900 killed and 1,000 captured. Gates reported 700 killed, wounded, and missing. The Continentals suffered 650 casualties, over two-thirds of the total. Hundreds of militia disappeared, probably fleeing to their homes. Tarleton's cavalry killed or captured several hundred more during the days that followed the battle. An official inquiry into Gates's conduct was ordered, but charges were never pressed.

British casualties totaled 324: 2 officers and 66 men killed and 256 wounded, including 18 officers.

The British seemed to have a firm hand on South Carolina. They evacuated Camden, after burning most of it, on May 8, 1781, 15 days after the battle at Hobkirk's Hill because General Nathanael Greene's (1742–1786) campaign to drive the Crown forces out of South Carolina put it in danger.

A Loyalist newspaper printed this notice on September 15 about the British victory:

> REWARD Strayed, Deserted, or Stolen, from . . . [General Horatio Gates], on the 16th of August last, near Camden, in the State of South Carolina, a whole ARMY. . . . Any person or persons, civil or military, who will give information [about it] . . . so that . . . [it] may be recovered and rallied again, shall be entitled to demand from the Treasurer of the United States the sum of THREE MILLION of PAPER DOLLARS. . . .

Cross Anchor (August 18, 1780)
Musgrove Mill Skirmish

The site of the Musgrove Mill Skirmish is on Route SC 56, 3 miles south of Cross Anchor.

The Musgrove Mill State Historic Site (398 State Park Road, Clinton, SC 29325) and its interpretive center are a hub for the Cradle of Democracy project which seeks to further the understanding of South Carolina's pivotal role in the creation of the nation. A memorial stone on the ridge just north of the Enoree River and alongside SC 56 marks Captain Inman's grave and the site of the ambush. The Patriot camp was probably along Cedar Creek about 3 miles from where Captain Inman is buried. Vandals burned the Musgrove house in 1971.

http://www.discoversouthcarolina.com/stateparks/parkdetail.asp?PID=3888

(The Blackstock's Plantation engagement site is also near Cross Anchor.)

After the British returned to South Carolina and occupied Charleston in May, 1780, Loyalist support began to increase, causing fear throughout the region. Two days after the defeat of Major General Horatio Gates (1728–1806) at the Battle of Camden, Colonels James Williams (d. 1780), Elijah Clarke (1733–1799), and Isaac Shelby (1750–1826) led about 200 militia to attack a Loyalist militia unit under Colonels Daniel Clary and Alexander Innes near Edward Musgrove's plantation on the Enoree River in South Carolina on August 18, 1780.

The attackers learned that the enemy had been reinforced during the night and now numbered about 500, so they decided to ambush the Loyalists instead. The Patriot forces hastily assembled a semicircular breastwork of fallen trees and brush 2 miles up river from the Loyalist camp. A volunteer unit of 25 horsemen, led by Captain Shadrack Inman (d. 1780), attacked and fired into the Loyalist camp and raced back toward an ambush position. The lure worked well. The Loyalists ran right into the concealed riflemen who held their fire "till they could distinguish the buttons on their clothes." The Patriots waited for the Loyalists to get within 70 yards before the first shot was fired, followed by a volley. The Loyalists rallied and began gaining on the Patriots' right flank when their leader was wounded. The Patriot right charged, forcing the Loyalists back. The Loyalists retreated, then fled. The rebels, outnumbered more than 2 to 1, killed 63 Loyalists, wounded 90, and captured 70 while only losing 4 dead and 8 wounded, including Inman who was fatally shot in the forehead by a retreating Loyalist.

The Patriot forces left the area before enemy reinforcements arrived. During the retreat, the men ate green peaches and raw corn which, coupled with lack of sleep and exposure to the sun blackened their faces and led to swelling of the eyes. After recuperating, the units separated. Clarke returned to Georgia. Shelby went to the Watauga in North Carolina to recruit additional militia. Williams took the prisoners to Hillsboro, North Carolina, where he later claimed credit for the victory.

The Battle of Musgrove Mill showed that militia could perform just as effectively as professional soldiers in some cases. It also demonstrated that Patriot militia could still maneuver and defeat Loyalist units despite a devastating defeat only days earlier.

York (October 7, 1780)
Kings Mountain

Kings Mountain National Military Park is south of the town of Kings Mountain, North Carolina, off I-85

http://www.nps.gov/kimo/index.htm

Kings Mountain National Military Park, one of the largest military parks in the United States, covers 3,950 acres (see Photo SC-4). It is a spur of the Kings Mountain Range that spreads across York and Cherokee counties in South Carolina. A self-guiding trail winds around the American lines and up to the summit passing all the significant battlefield sites. The park has the United States Monument, Centennial Monument, and other memorial markers. A monument marks the spot where Patrick Ferguson was mortally wounded. (See Photo SC-5.) A traditional Scottish stone cairn covers his grave. The visitor center offers exhibits, a film, and a diorama of the battle.

There is also a Kings Mountain State Park on Route SC 161, 12 miles northwest of the town of York, SC.

Late in 1780, with General Henry Clinton's (1730–1795) reluctant consent, General Charles Cornwallis (1738–1805) set out on the invasion of North Carolina. He sent Major Patrick Ferguson (1744–1780), who had successfully organized the Loyalists in the upcountry of South Carolina, to move north simultaneously with his "American Volunteers," spread the Loyalist gospel in the North Carolina back country, and join the main army at Charlotte, North Carolina with a maximum number of recruits. Ferguson operated independently in the mountains to the west and didn't expect to find any serious opposition, but his advance northward alarmed the "over-mountain men" in western North Carolina, southwest Virginia, and what is now east Tennessee.

After Ferguson warned the frontiersmen to cease attacking the British outposts and threatened to march over the mountains with his Loyalist troops to "lay waste their country with fire and sword," a picked force of mounted militia riflemen gathered at Sycamore Shoals on the Catawba River in western North Carolina and set out to find him on September 26, 1780, the same day Cornwallis arrived at Charlotte. Ferguson learned of their approach from a deserter and retreated east to what he thought was an impregnable position on Kings Mountain, near the border of the two Carolinas, to await the attack. The 900 frontiersmen found him and his 1,100 men early in the morning of October 7.

Kings Mountain is a narrow hogback 60 feet above the surrounding valleys. The plateau is a treeless summit about 600 yards long, 70 feet wide at one end and 120 feet wide at the other. It is surrounded by a hardwood forest and slopes covered with rocks. (See Photo SC-4.) Ferguson believed the summit impregnable, so he built no fortifications. He set the camp at the northeast end, the widest point on the ridge. The Carolinians crept around the flanks of the mountain in groups of one or two hundred, using the trees and rocks as cover. They intended to surround Ferguson and his men.

The battle began about 3:00 PM on October 7 when Ferguson's pickets discovered the mountainmen advancing up the slopes. The opening shots were fired (about where the Visitor's Center is located). As the frontiersmen worked their way up the slopes, fighting from tree to tree, the defenders were unable to get clear shots at their attackers, firing downhill and probably too high.

Ferguson led a bayonet charge to drive the attackers down the hill, but they rallied and moved back up. He led two more bayonet charges to chase the mountainmen down the hill, but each time they returned to kill more Loyalists. The mountainmen pushed the Loyalists back to the summit and into their camp. Ferguson tried in vain to rally them, riding his horse from one end of the ridge to the other, blowing a silver whistle, and waving his sword with his one good arm. (The other had been shattered at Brandywine, Pennsylvania and was practically useless.) Ironically, Ferguson, the inventor of the breech-loading rifle, had to resort to the bayonet to defend himself against men who fired from cover with rifles.

Ferguson, the only person on both sides who was not an American, tried to break through the enemy lines, but 8 or 9 marksmen took aim on him, shooting him off his horse (see Photo SC-5). He died a few minutes later.

Captain Abraham de Peyster (1753–ca. 1799) of New York assumed command and tried to rally the survivors, but he was forced to surrender. When the Loyalists began to lose heart and tried to surrender, few escaped death or capture. Some got the same "quarter" Lieutenant Colonel Banastre Tarleton (1744–1833) had given Colonel Abraham Buford's (1749–1833) men at the Waxhaws. After an hour of fierce fighting, the frontiersmen suffered 90 casualties, including 28 dead and 64 wounded, while they killed 225, wounded 163, and captured 716 Loyalist prisoners, taking with them those who were well enough to walk.

The next morning, the mountain men marched the surviving prisoners away, without food, down the mud-covered road toward Bethabara. Some fell down exhausted and despairing and were abandoned or stepped on and beaten. About 100 others managed to escape. One was shot and wounded trying to escape and was later executed. When they reached Bethabara they endured more brutalities. A drunken captain of the rebel militia kicked a Loyalist officer out of the bed he had at last found. Dr. Johnson, a Loyalist surgeon, was beaten for tending the wounds of an injured prisoner. Lieutenant Anthony Allaire (1755–1838), a friend of this surgeon, escaped with a few friends and found his way to Ninety-Six.

The prisoners were court-martialed a week later, near Gilbert Town. Thirty were condemned to death as traitors, but only 9 were actually hanged. Most of the others eventually escaped, as the mountainmen went back home, leaving them unguarded.

Kings Mountain was as fatal to Cornwallis's plans as Bennington had been to those of Major General John Burgoyne (1722–1792). The North Carolina Loyalists, cowed by the fate of their compatriots, gave him little support. On October 14, 1780, when Lord Cornwallis learned of the defeat at Kings Mountain, he realized that he could not continue his campaign of invading North Carolina. He was unable to raise militia, his supplies at Camden were dwindling, and sickness spread through his army. He decided to withdraw to Winnsboro, South Carolina in the rain with militia harassing his progress. Cornwallis became ill with the fever that also affected many of his men, so he delegated his authority to Lord Francis Rawdon (1754–1826).

Carlisle (November 9, 1780)
Fish Dam

Fish Dam Battleground Monument is on Route SC 72/121, 3 miles east of town, just east of the Broad River bridge on the north side of SC 72/121.

The battle site is undeveloped. Only a sign and stone marker on the east side of the Broad River identify the site. The "fish dam" which is a zigzag chain of rocks built by the Cherokee to trap fish and to cross the river is visible when the water is low during the summer.

Major James Wemyss with 100 mounted troops of the 63rd Foot and 40 dragoons of Tarleton's Legion planned to surprise the camp of Brigadier General Thomas Sumter (1734–1832) at a place called Moore's Mill about 30 miles northwest of Winnsboro. But Sumter had moved his men 5 miles south to the east end of Fish Dam Ford. Wemyss ran into Sumter's pickets about 1:00 AM on November 9, 1780 and drove them back after a quick volley.

Wemyss fell from his saddle with a broken arm and a wounded knee. Tarleton's troopers charged ahead and were badly shot up. The infantry attacked but withdrew after suffering heavy losses. Sumter escaped and returned to his camp about noon the next day to find his men reassembling and a British sergeant left behind to tend to the wounded.

Cross Anchor Vicinity (November 20, 1780)
Blackstock's Plantation

To get to Blackstock's plantation: From the intersection of SC 49 and SC 56 in Cross Anchor, take SC 49 east 2.4 miles, turn left at the sign for Blackstock Battlefield, and follow it 1.2 miles to a road that bears to the right. Follow that road 0.3 mile to a road on the left. The site is 1.3 miles down the road.

None of the plantation buildings remain. A sign and a stone monument on a prominent hill mark the site of this engagement. There are no other informational aids. (See above for the Musgrove Hill skirmish also near Cross Anchor.)

Captain William Blackstock's plantation was situated on high hills on the Tyger River's west bank. It was an advantageous position for Brigadier General Thomas Sumter (1734–1832) when he stopped there about 4:00 PM on November 20, 1780, to strike at Lieutenant Colonel Banastre Tarleton (1744–1833) who was pursuing him. The river protected the plantation's rear and part of its right side. The front of the plantation dropped down to a creek which was bordered by a fence and brushwood. Sumter placed some of his men in the barn and some in small outbuildings on the farm. He put the rest of his 1,000 men near the tops of the hills running roughly northwest of the farm and sent some men forward.

Tarleton, expecting Sumter to cross the Tyger, approached with an advanced corps of about 250 men to try to block him a little after 5:00 PM. However, Tarleton relented and decided to wait for the rest of his force before attacking. Sumter decided to strike before Tarleton's main force arrived. He placed his center on high ground around five log houses and along a rail fence. Colonel Elijah Clarke (1733–1799) led 100 Georgians around Tarleton's right flank to encircle it and to block the advance of his reinforcements. Sumter led the main attack with 400 militia against 80 dismounted Regulars of the 63rd Regiment.

The attack surprised Tarleton, but he rallied quickly. He sent infantry forward, forcing Sumter to retreat back up the hill. The men positioned on the ridgeline blasted Tarleton's troops. Tarleton led a charge but was forced back by the forces on Sumter's right and left. Tarleton attempted a charge on Sumter's left where the hill was less steep. He gained the hilltop after pushing through a stubborn group of Georgia militia, but the Americans in the barn stopped his advance and forced him to retreat.

The battle left 3 Americans dead and 5 wounded, including Sumter who was hit in the chest and right shoulder with buckshot. His wounds incapacitated him for several months. Tarleton's casualties totaled about 50 killed and wounded.

Chesnee (January 17, 1781)
Cowpens

Cowpens National Battlefield is 9 miles northwest of Gaffney and 18 miles northeast of Spartanburg, 0.2 mile east of the junction of State Routes SC11 and SC 110. (See Photo SC-6.)

http://www.nps.gov/cowp/index.htm

Sites of major action are marked by exhibits along a 1.5-mile walking trail and a 3-mile automobile tour road. The visitor center exhibits a lighted map tracing troop movements during the battle as well as oil paintings, woodcarvings, and weapons. It also shows a multi-image laser disc presentation, "Daybreak at the Cowpens." Standing at the monument facing south, the visitor can view the field of battle as Morgan saw it from his command post. The first line of 150 militiamen were lined up at the foot of the slope and stretched across both roads. (Route SC 11 was then called Mill Gap Road.) They were partially concealed in high grass and behind trees. Colonel Andrew Pickens's 300 militia formed the second line across the roads farther up the hill. The third line, Colonel John Eager Howard's Continentals, held the top of the hill. A depression behind the third line concealed the reserve, which included Colonel Washington's mounted troops.

After the Battle of Kings Mountain on October 7, 1780, General Charles Cornwallis (1738–1805) chose to remain in South Carolina. Major General Nathanael Greene (1742–1786), commissioned to reorganize the American forces, sent Colonel Daniel Morgan (1736–1802) to divert Cornwallis's attention from the bulk of the American forces. Morgan threatened Ninety-Six, where there was a British fort, so Cornwallis dispatched Lieutenant Colonel Banastre Tarleton (1744–1833) to stop him.

When Tarleton caught up with Morgan on January 17, 1781, after marching most of the night on bad roads and through deep fords, he was west of Kings Mountain at a place called the "cow pens" because it was used as a spot to round up stray cattle. (See Photo SC-6.) It was an open, sparsely forested area 6 miles from the Broad River. (This was the same location where the frontiersmen would gather to prepare for the Battle of Kings Mountain.) Morgan chose this site to make his stand less by design than necessity, for he had intended to get across the Broad. When he learned that Tarleton was only 10 miles away, he decided to prepare for battle rather than be surprised halfway across the river.

Nevertheless, on ground seemingly better suited to the action of regulars, Morgan achieved a little tactical masterpiece, making the most effective use of his heterogeneous force. Although both sides seemed pretty equal with about 1,100 men, Tarleton had about three times as many trained regulars as Morgan and a cavalry of 300.

Selecting a hill as the center of his position, he placed his Continental infantry from Maryland and Delaware on it, deliberately leaving his flanks open. It seems as if Morgan deliberately picked a place where his men couldn't run or hide and would have to fight. Well out in front of the main line, he posted about 450 militia riflemen from the Carolinas, Georgia, and Virginia in 2 lines, instructing the first line to fire 2 volleys and then fall back on the second, the combined line to fire until the British pressed them, then to fall back to the rear of the Continentals and re-form as a reserve. This specific assignment lessened the possibility that the militia would break and run and lead the Continentals to panic.

Behind the militiamen, on a long ridge of rising ground, Morgan posted his regular troops (about 450 men), the Maryland, Delaware, and Virginia Continentals commanded by Lieutenant Colonel John Eager Howard (1752–1827). Behind the hill, he placed Lieutenant Colonel William Washington's (1752–1810) cavalry, ready to charge the attacking enemy at the critical moment. Every man in the ranks was informed of the plan of battle and the part he was expected to play in it. All the men were rested, well prepared, and ready for the fight.

Tarleton ordered his soldiers to drop all equipment except muskets and ammunition and to attack immediately, expecting to drive the militiamen back into the river. His force slightly outnumbered Morgan's. He put his light infantry on the right, his legion's infantry in the center, the 7th Regiment on the left, and 50 dragoons on each flank. He left 200 of his cavalry in reserve with the 1st Battalion of the 71st Highlanders and advanced about 7:00 AM. When the British infantry got to within about 40 yards, the militiamen, sheltered behind the trees, took careful aim at the officers and sergeants and fired their first volley. They fired a second volley and withdrew. Taking the retreat of the first 2 lines to be the beginning of a rout, Tarleton's Highlanders rushed headlong into the steady fire of the Continentals on the hill.

Colonel Howard ordered a company on his far right to turn to the right 90 degrees to protect his flank against the 71st's fire. Misunderstanding the order, the company retreated, causing the rest of the line to retreat. Morgan galloped up to halt the retreat, reportedly shouting at them "Form! Form! my brave fellows. Give them one more brisk fire and the day is ours! Old Morgan was never beaten yet!" The militia responded by taking a position on the higher ground about 50 paces back of where they had been. They turned about, fired another volley at close range, and followed with a bayonet charge.

Tarleton ordered the 17th Light Dragoons after the retreating militia, but William Washington's fresh cavalry emerged almost immediately from behind the hill to strike Tarleton's right flank. Washington's cavalry now outnumbered Tarleton's dragoons by almost 2 to 1 because Tarleton had divided his force, keeping 200 dragoons in reserve. Washington forced Tarleton's Legion back, giving the militia time to re-form and charge out from behind the hill to hit the British left.

Tarleton and a few other officers with some 40 men of the 17th Light Dragoons made a last desperate charge to save the guns when 200 of his dragoons refused to attack, but they were too late. The American cavalry chased them off the field. Caught in a clever double envelopment, the British surrendered after suffering heavy losses—

about 75% of Tarleton's command: 300 killed and wounded and 525 prisoners of war, 2 3-pounders, 2 regimental flags, 800 muskets, 35 wagons of stores, 100 horses, and 60 slaves. The Americans only lost 12 lives and about 58 wounded. Tarleton managed to escape with only a small force of cavalry he had left in reserve. The battle, which lasted about an hour, was on a small scale, and with certain significant differences, a repetition of the classic double envelopment of the Romans by a Carthaginian army under Hannibal at Cannae in 216 B.C.—an event of which Morgan, no reader of books, probably had no knowledge. The Battle of Cowpens wrecked Tarleton's feared Legion, and ended his reputation of invincibility.

Camden (April 25, 1781)
Hobkirk Hill

Hobkirk Hill Battle Site is on Route U.S. 521 north of Camden. From the center of Camden, follow Broad Street (U.S. 521 and U.S. 601) north 0.2 mile to Greene Street which runs east and west on a ridge.
   `http://www.angelfire.com/folk/scsites/hobkirk's_hill_battle_site.htm`

The location of the battle is along a ridge crossing north Broad Street near the intersection with Kirkwood Lane in Camden. A residential neighborhood covers the site of the battle at Hobkirk Hill. One can only see the ridge above the town where Greene and his men camped.

Camden was also the site of an earlier battle on August 16, 1780 (see above).

Major General Nathanael Greene's (1742–1786) army, in better condition in April, 1781, than 6 months earlier, pushed quickly into South Carolina to reduce the British posts in the interior. He wanted to demonstrate the transience of British control and to teach the British that it is easier to conquer than to occupy. He planned to use partisans to harass the enemy's supply lines; seize their smaller bases, if only temporarily; and interrupt their communications so they could not cooperate effectively. Greene would move against the larger garrisons with his main army which he had to preserve intact. He fought battles against the major British forces but never to the point where he lost so many men that he could not return to fight again.

While he sent Lieutenant Colonel Henry "Light-Horse Harry" Lee (1756–1818) and his Legion to Lieutenant Colonel Francis Marion (1732–1795) to take Fort Watson, Greene marched his army of some 1,200 Continentals and 250 militia plus Lieutenant Colonel William Washington's (1752–1810) 80 cavalry toward Camden against Lord Francis Rawdon (1754–1826). Lord Rawdon commanded 8,000 men in South Carolina and Georgia, but they were mostly Loyalist units scattered throughout the two states in small garrisons. The largest garrison was at Camden, where Rawdon commanded 900 men.

Greene took up a position on Hobkirk Hill, about a mile and a half north of Camden on April 19, 1781. Although he had the larger army, he realized the futility of attacking the strong British position and waited for reinforcements. Rawdon received a description of the rebel position from a deserter and decided to attack Greene's camp on the morning of April 25, 1781.

Lord Rawdon, age 26, armed every man who could carry a weapon and attacked the American outposts at about 10:00 AM. He took his men, mostly American Loyalists, on a long march through the forest to attack Greene's left flank. He used other Loyalists as snipers to pick off as many of their fellow-countrymen as they could as the narrow column pressed the main attack.

Greene's pickets gave him enough time to muster his men and assess the situation. He planned to overlap both flanks of the narrow British column. When Rawdon arrived about 100 yards away at about 10:00 AM, Greene's front line (4th Virginia, 5th Virginia, 1st Maryland, and 5th Maryland Regiments) moved quickly to the right and left, exposing three 6-pounders which immediately opened fire with grapeshot. Rawdon's infantry recoiled under the heavy fire. While Greene's cavalry attacked his rear, 2 battalions of infantry advanced against their center and 2 more against their flanks.

The Continentals tried to outflank Rawdon, who let them advance and pushed his reserves to either side of his front line, outflanking the Americans. He escaped their trap and caught them in his own. Ferocious fighting continued for several minutes. Colonel Washington's cavalrymen surrounded Rawdon, and one of them demanded his sword. Rawdon pretended to comply and seemed to have difficulty in disentangling it. This gave his own infantry time to advance toward him and drive off his prospective captors.

Loyalist sharpshooters brought down several officers of the 1st and 2nd Maryland Regiments. As the 1st Maryland regiment proceeded down the hill, it became momentarily disorganized. Its commander tried to reform the ranks, but the resulting confusion allowed the British to close in on them before they could be reorganized. The 4th Virginia and 5th Maryland regiments also retreated, leaving only the 5th Virginia holding its position. The British almost captured the three 6-pounders in a heated battle that raged around the guns. Greene tugged at the drag ropes himself until Colonel Washington, who had been occupied in taking prisoners, including several surgeons, galloped up to help him get them away. They saved the guns but left 100 men on the field to be taken prisoner. Greene retreated 2 or 3 miles to the old Camden battlefield to reorganize his troops.

American losses were about 19 killed, 115 wounded, and 136 missing; the British lost 28 killed and 228 wounded or missing. Rawdon won an expensive victory like Cornwallis's at Guilford Courthouse. The Battle of Hobkirk Hill marked the beginning of a general British withdrawal from the interior of South Carolina. Rawdon was so weak, despite reinforcements of 500 men of the 64th Regiment who arrived on May 7, he decided to abandon his exposed position at Camden. He was now cut off from his supply base to the east, forcing him to retire to Charleston and leaving Camden to the Americans.

Rawdon began to withdraw to Moncks Corner on the Cooper River 30 miles above Charleston on May 10. He destroyed the fortifications and most of the town before leaving. Greene took over Camden the next day and had Brigadier General Thomas Sumter (1734–1832) destroy the remnants of the British redoubts. The Crown forces lost several forts (Fort Motte, Orangeburg, Fort Granby, Georgetown, and Augusta) in the following months, leaving them with only Charleston and Savannah after a year and a half of campaigning.

Ninety-Six
(November 18–21, 1775; May 22 to June 19, 1781)

Ninety-Six National Historic Site is in Ninety-Six, South Carolina, 2 miles south on State Route SC 248.

http://www.nps.gov/nisi/index.htm

Visitors can explore the earthworks, old road beds, traces of the village, a reconstructed stockade fort, and an early log cabin along a mile-long trail (see Photo SC-7). An observation tower provides an excellent view of the star redoubt and the zigzag trenches used to attack it. Inside the earthworks are the remains of a 25-foot well, dug through the hardpacked clay in a futile attempt to get water for the besieged fort. The Loyalists were forced to rely on slaves slipping past Greene's pickets at night to bring water into the redoubt. The visitor center houses a museum and an auditorium.

Ninety-Six is an interesting site that requires some explanation to understand. It began as a trading post where English traders transacted business with the Cherokees in the 1730s. It received its name because of its location about ninety-six (96) miles from the Cherokee village of Keowee in the Blue Ridge foothills. This trading post was the farthest one from the coast and soon became a settlement. In 1769, it became the center for the court for the Ninety-Six district which covered an area equivalent to 12 of the state's modern counties.

A force of 532 Patriots built a crude fort of fence rails, cowhides, and straw bales on John Savage's plantation. They came under attack by Colonel Joseph Robinson and 1,890 Loyalists on November 18, 1775. The defenders ran low on powder after 3 days of fighting. The aggressors could not capture the fort and its swivel cannon and feared impending reinforcements, so both sides agreed to withdraw and the defenders demolished the fort.

Later, when the British took control of the South, they made their dominant strongholds at Augusta, Georgia, and Ninety-Six. They built a stockade flanked by 2 forts. A covered way connected to both the stockade on the west and to the strong, star-shaped redoubt on the east side of the fort.

After the battle of Hobkirk Hill (April 25, 1781), Lord Francis Rawdon (1754–1826) retired to Charleston. Over the next 5 weeks, other posts fell rapidly: Lieutenant Colonel Francis Marion (1732–1795) and Major General Benjamin Lincoln (1733–1810) took Fort Motte, Brigadier General Thomas Sumter (1734–1832) took Orangeburg, Lieutenant Colonel Henry "Light-Horse Harry" Lee (1756–1818) took Fort Granby (later the site of Columbia), and Marion took Georgetown. Brigadier General Andrew Pickens (1739–1817) and Lee captured Augusta in Georgia on June 5, 1781.

General Nathanael Greene (1742–1786) reassembled his army and marched to Ninety-Six, the last important British outpost on the South Carolina frontier. When he arrived there on May 22, 1781, he examined the position and concluded that, "the fortifications are so strong and the garrison so large and so well furnished that our success is very doubtful."

His army of 1,000 regulars had no heavy artillery, so he decided to lay siege to the garrison defended by Colonel John Harris Cruger (1738–1807) and 550 battle-toughened Loyalists. Greene put Polish engineer Thaddeus Kosciusko (1746–1817) in charge of the siege operation. Kosciusko had the men dig parallel trenches up to the star redoubt and protect them with a zigzag approach pattern (see Photo SC-7). When the third trench line reached 40 yards from the fort, the men built a 30-foot rifle tower. The longest Continental siege of the war was heading into its 28th day in mid-June.

Lord Francis Rawdon brought up a powerful relief column of 2,000 men from Charleston that included 3 fresh regiments from England. Greene had to attack. On June 18, Lieutenant Colonel Henry "Light-Horse Harry" Lee successfully fought through the defenses at the western redoubt, but Greene's initial assessment of the position made a month earlier proved correct. The Continentals could not break into the star redoubt. The 45-minute assault left 40 Patriots dead. Greene ordered a retreat to Charlotte.

The Crown forces soon evacuated Ninety-Six. After a year and a half of campaigning, by August, the British only held Charleston and Savannah, leaving them at the same point they had started. The long summer campaign ruined Lord Rawdon's health and spirit. After chasing Greene in vain after the siege of Ninety-Six, Rawdon turned his command over to Lieutenant Colonel Alexander Stewart (1740–1794) and sailed for England, only to have his ship captured by Admiral François Joseph Paul Comte de Grasse's (1722–1788) fleet.

CHARLESTON AREA

Fort Moultrie is now part of metropolitan Charleston.
    See the map of Southern South Carolina.

Sullivan's Island (June 28–29, 1776; May 6–8, 1780)
Fort Sullivan
Fort Moultrie

Fort Sullivan, called Fort Moultrie after the battle in 1776, is at 1213 West Middle Street, Charleston. It can be reached via U.S. 17B and SC 703.
                    http://www.nps.gov/fomo/index.htm

Fort Sullivan (Fort Moultrie) was neglected after the War for American Independence. Little of it remained by 1791. It was replaced by a new one in 1794, but the sea destroyed it within 10 years. The present fort was built between 1807 and 1811 a little to the rear of the first one. The fort saw no action during the Civil War and remained active until World War II when it was deactivated in 1947. The National Park Service assumed administration of the site as part of Fort Sumter National Monument in January, 1961. (See Photo SC-8.)

After the evacuation of Boston on March 17, 1776, General William Howe (1732–1786) stayed at Halifax, Nova Scotia from March until June, awaiting the arrival of supplies and reinforcements. While he tarried, the British Government ordered another diversion in the South, aimed at encouraging the numerous Loyalists who, according to the deposed royal governors watching from their refuges on board British warships, were waiting for the appearance of a British force to rise and overthrow rebel rule. The British believed large numbers of Loyalists in the South would rise and support the military.

Without an exact plan, they wanted to see which colony offered the best conditions for military operations. General Howe saw this as an opportunity to rid himself of his subordinate, General Henry Clinton (1730–1795), as the two had quarreled over strategy since Howe assumed command from General Thomas Gage (1719–1787) in April, 1776.

Clinton wanted to accede to the wishes of the deposed royal governor, Lord John Murray, 4th Earl of Dunmore (1732–1809), and conduct operations in Virginia. But Admiral Sir Peter Parker's (1721–1811) recent reconnaissance mission to Charleston showed that the rebel fortifications guarding the harbor were not completed, so Clinton agreed to seize the port of Charleston.

Unfortunately, Parker's naval squadron sent from England was delayed and did not arrive in the Charleston area until June 1, 1776. By that time, all hopes of effective cooperation with the Loyalists had been dashed. Loyalist contingents had been completely defeated and dispersed in Virginia, North Carolina, and South Carolina. Parker remained undeterred and determined to attack Charleston, the largest city in the South.

The Second Continental Congress sent Major General Charles Lee (1731–1782) to command 6,500 Continental soldiers and the Southern defenses. Lee and Governor John Rutledge (1730–1800) clashed over the utility of Fort Sullivan. Rutledge wanted to use it against the approaching British fleet. Lee, fearing that the garrison would be easily overwhelmed and defeated, wanted to abandon it.

Fort Sullivan, a fortification located on the western end of Sullivan's Island, was still under construction to guard the entrance to Charleston Harbor. It was made of three walls of palmetto logs. Each one had a forward section of palmetto logs and another section 16 feet behind the first. Sand filled the space between the sections. The combination of the spongy wood of the palmetto logs and the sand acted as a shock-absorber under fire. Moreover, palmetto does not splinter like other woods or shatter like stone. Only the two walls and two bastions facing the sea were completed when the British attacked. (See Photo SC-8.) An existing but old fort, Fort Johnson, guarded the other side of the harbor entrance.

Colonel William Moultrie (1730–1805) commanded a garrison of approximately 750 men at Fort Sullivan, renamed Fort Moultrie after the battle. The defenders consisted of the South Carolina militia and Continentals from North Carolina and Virginia as well as newly raised troops. They manned 25 guns ranging from 9- to 25-pounders.

Admiral Parker decided to attack Fort Sullivan at 11:00 AM on June 28, 1776. The naval attack was an unwise decision, somewhat comparable to that at Bunker Hill.

Fortunately for the defenders, the British had to mount an uncoordinated attack in haste. General Clinton landed his troops on Long Island, now known as the Isle of Palms. After landing 2,500 men on the island, he learned that Breach Inlet, the narrow channel between Long Island and Sullivan's Island, contained very swift currents and deep holes—even at low tide—preventing his troops from wading across. The rebels had also constructed breastworks across Breach Inlet to challenge any attempt to cross from Long Island. The British Army consequently sat idly by while the gunners in Fort Sullivan devastated their warships.

Two 50- and two 28-gun ships moved to within 400 feet of Fort Sullivan. Two 28-gun ships and another with 20-guns positioned themselves behind them. Another 28-gun ship and the *Thunder* with a 10-inch mortar were stationed about a mile and a half southeast of the fort.

The *Thunder*'s mortar exploded when its crew used a larger charge of powder in an attempt to increase its range. About 12:30 PM, the *Sphynx*, *Actaeon*, and *Syren* tried to slip to the western end of the fort and ran aground where Fort Sumter was later built. Some historians speculate that slave pilots who favored the Patriots may have been responsible for grounding the three vessels and for keeping the others at a considerable distance from the fort. The crews managed to extricate the *Sphynx* and *Syren* but could not dislodge the *Actaeon*.

The defenders in the fort were low on gunpowder, so they conserved their cannon fire and concentrated on the two 50-gun vessels. Their limited firing was very effective. The *Bristol*, Parker's flagship, sustained over 70 cannon hits. Her sister ship, the 50-gun *Experiment*, received almost as many hits. Moreover, Sir Peter Parker suffered the ultimate indignity of losing his pants. Some accounts say they were set afire from cannon fire; others say they were destroyed by splinters from a cannon shot.

Meanwhile, the British cannonballs bounced off of Fort Sullivan's walls. The vessels could not get close enough to the fort to allow the marines to snipe at the rebels from the rigging. The British took severe casualties, and many of the ships sustained heavy damage in the engagement. The battle raged until 9:30 PM when the British ships ceased firing. Parker ordered his fleet to withdraw from the harbor entrance about 11:00 PM that night. The crew of the *Actaeon* burned her and sailed with the fleet, but the rebels later salvaged equipment from the ship.

Casualties in this battle vary in different sources. Estimates put the Patriots' losses at 12 men killed and 20 wounded and British casualties at approximately 225, including 64 dead. The *Bristol* alone suffered an estimated 40 battle deaths and 71 wounded. The Continental Congress declared the independence of the 13 American colonies 6 days later.

Clinton's forces remained on Long Island for another 3 weeks and then withdrew from the area by sea. Parker's battered fleet, already behind schedule, sailed northward to join Howe in New York on July 31, 1776. The Continentals used the *Actaeon*'s own guns to fire on the retreating navy. The British left the south unmolested and the many Loyalists there without support for 3 years following the fiasco at Charleston. They returned in 1779 to capture Savannah and then Charleston in 1780. South Carolina added a palmetto tree to its state flag to commemorate the victory at Sullivan's

Island. One grateful Charlestonian sent a hogshead of old Antigua rum to the fort's garrison.

When the British returned to Charleston in early 1780, Fort Moultrie commanded the approach to the harbor and threatened any advance on the city. General Clinton laid siege to the city and sent a landing force of sailors and marines to take the fort on May 6, 1780, prior to capturing Charleston. See below.

Charleston (February 11 to May 12, 1780)

The Old Exchange and Provost Dungeon (122 East Bay Street at Broad Street) was built by the British in 1771 as the Customs House and Exchange for the prosperous city of Charles Towne. The British imprisoned prominent Patriots in the cellars during the American Revolution. (See Photo SC-10) The excavated Half-moon Battery portion of the wall that surrounded Charles Towne in the late 1600s is visible in the dungeon. On December 2, 1774, the *London* landed at Charleston with 257 chests of tea and an assortment of other goods destined for New York. Protesters persuaded merchants not to import the tea. When the 20-day period for payment of the duty expired, customs officers confiscated the tea and put it in storage in the Exchange. One report said that the tea was rotting from dampness. Another account says that it was subsequently sold at auction in July, 1776, to pay for war expenses. George Washington was entertained several times in the Great Hall which also served for the election of delegates to the First Continental Congress, the Declaration of Independence, and the ratification of the U.S. Constitution.
`http://www.oldexchange.com/`

Charleston has many historic buildings and 18th-century sites of interest, but urban development has obliterated any traces of both lines and the parallels the British dug as they moved closer to the Americans. The only remains of the battle is a small section of the defensive hornwork (see Photo SC-9) on the west side (King Street side) of Marion Square.

General Henry Clinton (1730–1795), urged on by the British Government, had determined to push the southern campaign in earnest. Unable to win a decisive victory in the North, he withdrew the British garrison from Newport in October, 1779, pulled in his troops from outposts around New York, and prepared to move south against Charleston with a large part of his force. With Admiral Comte Jean-Baptiste-Charles-Henri-Hector d'Estaing's (1729–1794) withdrawal, the British regained control of the sea along the American coast, giving Clinton a mobility that General George Washington (1732–1799) could not match.

Applying the lessons of his experience in 1776 (see Sullivan's Island above), General Clinton carefully planned a coordinated Army-Navy attack for this attempt to take Charleston. Leaving Lieutenant General Wilhelm von Knyphausen (1716–1800) in command in New York with more than 15,000 men, he set sail on December 26, 1779, with 11 warships and some 8,500 men aboard 90 transports.

Winter storms off the Outer Banks of North Carolina scattered the ships. Two frigates foundered. The transport *George* sank. One transport with Hessian troops even washed ashore on the coast of Cornwall in England. The winds ripped the sails to shreds and blew masts down on the decks. The storm killed many horses, and the troops tossed their carcasses overboard, along with horses they sacrificed to lighten cargoes.

Clinton landed his force on John's Island, about 30 miles south of Charleston, on February 11, 1780, then moved up to the Ashley River invading Charleston from the land side 47 days later. He called for more men from Savannah and from New York who arrived in March and April. This brought his force to about 14,000, including sailors from the fleet. Washington was able to send only piecemeal reinforcements to Major General Benjamin Lincoln (1733–1810) over difficult overland routes.

On April 8, British warships successfully forced the passage past Fort Moultrie (formerly Fort Sullivan), investing Charleston from the sea. The siege then proceeded in traditional 18th-century fashion for almost a month. On April 10, Clinton began cutting the Americans' line of supplies with the north which 3 regiments of cavalry under Brigadier General Isaac Huger (1743–1797) kept open 30 miles upriver at Moncks Corner. Clinton sent Major Patrick Ferguson's (1744–1780) Queen's Rangers and Lieutenant Colonel Banastre Tarleton's (1744–1833) British Legion to destroy the American camp in a surprise attack by night.

General Benjamin Lincoln's 5,150 Continentals and militia were greatly outnumbered, even with the reinforcements Washington sent from Morristown. But they had to try to defend the city for political reasons, even though Lincoln knew that it was more important to preserve his fighting force than to defend the city. He concentrated his forces in a citadel on the neck of land between the Ashley and Cooper Rivers, leaving Fort Moultrie in the harbor lightly manned. Forts Moultrie and Johnson had fallen into disrepair sometime after 1776.

Governor John Rutledge (1730–1800) pressed some 600 slaves into building new fortifications across the neck between the two rivers. The enemy would encounter a water-filled ditch, then two rows of abatis, followed by a trench filled with logs and branches. Large holes in the ground would impede a charge before the enemy reached the redoubts and breastworks. The center of the earthworks consisted of a hornwork made of tabby, a mixture of lime and oyster shells. This hornwork comprised two bastions connected by a curtain or wall and a wall running back from each bastion (see Photo SC-9).

The defenders stood behind these fortifications which the British described ''as a kind of citadel.'' What appeared as a good defense was just an illusion, as the Americans had no escape route if Clinton and the British fleet chose to attack. They also had no hope of getting adequate reinforcements anywhere. Instead of taking advantage of the two rivers as lines of defense, Lincoln left them virtually unguarded.

Clinton landed south of the city, crossed the Stono and the Ashley rivers without opposition, captured Fort Johnson by surprise, and cut the city from the outside world on three sides by April 1. Rather than try to assault the hornworks, he decided to besiege it. He put 1,500 soldiers to work digging entrenchments on the night of April 1. He already had cannon in place within 800 yards of the defenses by April 8. He demanded the city's surrender 2 days later. When Lincoln refused, Clinton's batteries began to bombard the town on April 13.

Clinton's troops moved to the upper side of the Cooper River to seal off one evacuation route on the 14th. His men completed a second set of entrenchments within 250 yards of the American lines 4 days later. Lincoln realized the futility of continued resistance and sent terms to Clinton on April 21. Clinton rejected them and continued bombarding the city.

By May 5, a third parallel opened only 40 yards away from the rebels' earthworks. People could not buy meat, rice, sugar, or coffee. When Clinton learned that a new fleet had set sail from France, he wanted to return to New York as soon as possible. He granted Lincoln a truce to discuss terms which were subsequently refused because he thought the rebels were "not yet sufficiently humbled to accept" British terms. He offered to pardon all rebels who took an oath of loyalty to the royal government and required those who did not actively support the British to be treated as though they were rebels. Instead of clearly differentiating between friends and enemies, these proclamations forced those who had decided to remain neutral to take sides. Loyalists complained that rebels could gain the privilege of British subjects by taking an oath they would break at the first opportunity.

A landing force of sailors and marines took Fort Moultrie on May 6. After the truce expired at 8 PM on May 9, both sides resumed the cannonade which lasted through the night.

General William Moultrie describes the Americans' final desperate act:

> It was a glorious sight, to see them [the shells] like meteors crossing each other, and bursting in the air; it appeared as if the stars were tumbling down. The fire was incessant almost the whole night; cannon-balls whizzing and shells hissing continually amongst us; ammunition chests and temporary magazines blowing up; great guns bursting, and wounded men groaning along the lines: it was a dreadful night! it was our last great effort, but it availed us nothing.

Three days later, at 11:00 A.M on May 12, 1780, with the enemy within 90 feet of the hornwork, the town surrendered after almost ceaseless bombardment. Lincoln accepted the terms that Clinton had offered on April 10; the Union Jack was raised over Charleston at 2:00 PM, causing one Loyalist to gloat that "the thirteen stripes [were leveled] with the dust."

The capture of Charleston, America's fourth largest city, was one of Britain's greatest victories of the war. Although Lincoln had very few casualties—only 240 killed and wounded—he surrendered his entire force of 5,466 men, the greatest disaster to befall the Americans during the war. It ranks as the third largest surrender of Americans in history, after Bataan in World War II and Harpers Ferry in the Civil War. Surprisingly, Clinton's siege took 3 months to accomplish what he might have done in half the time.

Clinton also captured 391 guns and 5,916 muskets, 15 regimental flags, and large quantities of supplies. The British lost 265 men killed and wounded. They lost several more when one of the prisoners threw his loaded musket into a shed that stored gunpowder. The explosion scattered and mutilated bodies so that it was impossible to "make out a single human figure."

Lincoln's army was further humiliated by having to march without music and with flags furled when it surrendered. The British, however, let the officers keep their swords until repeated shouts of "Long Live Congress!" provoked their captors into confiscating them. The British occupied Charleston until they evacuated it on December 14, 1782. (See Photo SC-10 of Charleston's Old Exchange: one of the three most important buildings in the country for democracy—along with Independence Hall in Philadelphia [Photos PA-3 through PA-5] and Faneuil Hall in Boston.)

Southern

See the map of Southern South Carolina.

Port Royal (February 3, 1779)
Beaufort

> Port Royal is in Beaufort County between Charleston and Savannah on U.S. 21.
>
> There are historical markers on U.S. 21 at Grays Hill. A small roadside park with picnic tables and the Beaufort water tower nearby mark the site of the battle. The low, swampy ground in the area may correspond to the swamp area Moultrie mentions in his account of the battle. He wrote that he tried to reach that area before the British, probably to get his men under cover, but the enemy beat him.
>
> The arsenal is now the site of the Beaufort Museum on Craven Street between Scott and Carteret Streets, Beaufort.

British General Augustine Prevost (1723–1786) sent a small force of 200 men north into South Carolina within 1 month of seizing Savannah, Georgia on December 29, 1778. Meanwhile, his main army faced Major General Benjamin Lincoln's (1733–1810) Continentals across the Savannah River.

The British force landed on Port Royal Island, about 30 miles up the South Carolina coast behind the American army, in an attempt to outflank Lincoln. General William Moultrie (1730–1805) assumed command of the 300 local militiamen at Port Royal Ferry (where Highway 21 crosses Whale Branch between Gardens Corner and Beaufort). They gathered at the arsenal (now the Beaufort Museum on Craven Street between Scott and Carteret Streets), on Wednesday, February 3, 1779, and marched north (on what is now Route U.S. 21) to block Prevost's advance from the Broad River.

The two armies met about 4 in the afternoon. Moultrie reported that "he drew up the troops to the right and left of the road, with two field-pieces (6 pounders) in the centre." He was on open ground, while the British enjoyed the protection of bushes and swamp. Moultrie opened fire with his artillery and firing continued very heavy on both sides for almost an hour. Both sides ran out of ammunition and retreated. When Moultrie realized his opponents were retreating toward the ocean, he ordered his men to pursue, but the British managed to reach their boats and return to Savannah.

The engagement at Port Royal Island was successful in blocking the British attempt to outflank Lincoln. It cost the Americans 8 men killed and 22 wounded. We don't know the number of British casualties, but they are assumed to have been very heavy, including every British officer involved in the action wounded.

Moncks Corner (April 14, 1780; October 16, 1781)

> Moncks Corner is about 30 miles northeast of Charleston.

General Henry Clinton (1730–1795) landed his force on John's Island, about 30 miles south of Charleston, on February 11, 1780, then moved up to the Ashley River investing Charleston from the land side. He called for more men from Savannah and from New York who arrived in March and April. This brought his army to about 14,000 including sailors from the fleet.

On April 8, British warships successfully forced the passage past Fort Moultrie, investing Charleston from the sea. On April 10, Clinton began cutting the Americans' line of supplies with the north which 3 regiments of cavalry under Brigadier General Isaac Huger (1742–1797) kept open 30 miles upriver at Moncks Corner. Clinton sent Major Patrick Ferguson's (1744–1780) Queen's Rangers and Lieutenant Colonel Banastre Tarleton's (1744–1833) British Legion to destroy the American camp in a surprise attack by night.

Tarleton struck at 3:30 in the morning of April 14. The attack caught the Americans off guard and dispersed them. General Huger, Lieutenant Colonel William Washington (1752–1810), and other officers fled on foot into the swamps. The British killed those who tried to defend themselves. Tarleton reported: "Four hundred horses belonging to the officers and dragoons with their arms and appointments fell into the hands of the victors. About one hundred, officers, dragoons and hussars, together with fifty wagons loaded with arms, clothing and ammunition, shared the same fate." The British reported only 3 casualties.

The successful attack closed the American supply route to Charleston which would surrender on May 12. It was also very brutal. Tarleton's British Legion were so ferocious that they outraged Major Ferguson who threatened to have some of the worst offenders shot—which he would have done if he had not been restrained. Tarleton then became known as "the Butcher."

A second engagement occurred at Moncks Corner on October 16, 1781 when an American raiding party attacked a British encampment and captured 80 men.

Moncks Corner Vicinity (July 17, 1781)
Biggin Church

> To get to the Biggin Church site, at the intersection of US 17 and SC 6 in Moncks Corner go 0.8 mile east on SC 6 to SC 52. Turn left and go north 2.8 miles, then turn right on SC 402 for 0.6 mile.
>
> The Biggin Church ruins and cemetery are on the right on SC 402. The church was rebuilt and destroyed again by a forest fire in 1886. A historical marker explains the site.
> ```
> http://www.rootsweb.com/~scbchs/Biggin.html
> ```

Lieutenant Colonel John Coates withdrew the 19th Regiment from Moncks Corner when he learned that Brigadier General Thomas Sumter (1734–1832) was approaching in July, 1781. He crossed to the east side of the Cooper River to St. John's about a mile and a half away on Biggin Creek. He stored his weapons and supplies in the church. When he left the area to move closer to Charleston, about 29 miles to the south, on the evening of July 16, he ordered his men to burn the church and all the supplies he could not take with him.

The fire broke through the church's roof about 3:00 AM, long after Coates had departed. The fire burned itself out after destroying the church. Only the church's 3-foot brick walls remained. It was reconstructed after the war, destroyed again by a forest fire in 1886, and never rebuilt. All that remains are parts of the west and south walls.

Rhems (September 14, 1780)
Black Mingo Creek

> Black Mingo Creek is about 20 miles north-northwest of Georgetown near Rhems, South Carolina, at the junction of SC 41 and SC 51.
>
> The site of the battle is undeveloped. Visitors can view the battle area, but there are few interpretive markers.

A bridge crosses Black Mingo Creek about 2 miles from the Waxhaws. Lieutenant Colonel Francis Marion (1732–1795) attacked a band of about 46 Loyalists under Colonel John Corning Ball here on Thursday, September 14, 1780. Shepherd's Ferry (about where SC 41 and SC 51 cross the Black Mingo) served the crossing at that time; the nearby Dollard's Tavern accommodated the ferry passengers. Marion, at one of his camps north of the creek on the Peedee River, learned that Colonel Ball and his men were stationed here as an outpost for the British in Georgetown, so he decided to attack. A sentry heard them around midnight as they crossed a bridge at Willtown, a mile upstream, and alerted Ball. Marion swung around the ferry and attacked from the south (along what is now Route SC 41).

Ball's men were deployed in a field and hit Marion's center column by surprise, inflicting heavy casualties. Marion rallied his men, turned Ball's right flank and ended the battle in 15 minutes. The Loyalists fled into the swamp. There were only about 50 men engaged on each side. Marion lost 2 dead and 8 wounded. The Loyalists lost 3 dead and 13 wounded and captured.

Santee (February 28 and April 16–25, 1781)
Fort Watson

> Fort Watson was near Santee, 8 miles south of Summerton South Carolina, off SC 301 and SC 15. Near the sign for the site, turn right on the road next to it and follow it to the site.

No trace of the fortifications remain. Water now covers most of the ground to the east of Fort Watson, probably including the site of the well and the trench the defenders dug. Granite memorials mark the common grave of the American dead. One of the stones replaces the original marker which is no longer legible.

Steps lead to the top of the 30 to 50 foot high Native American mound. The mound probably dates from around 1200 to 1500 A.D. and probably served as either a burial or temple structure.

When the British took control of South Carolina, they established a series of outposts to support the line of communication between Charleston and Camden. When General Nathanael Greene (1742–1786) assumed command of the American army in the south, he embarked on a campaign to destroy these interior posts. He made Fort Watson his first objective. The fort was constructed atop an ancient 30-foot Native American mound overlooking the Santee River.

First Battle

Brigadier General Thomas Sumter (1734–1832) launched a frontal assault against Fort Watson on February 28, 1781 which was repulsed with heavy casualties. After three quick defeats in 1 month, Sumter's men suffered from poor morale that led to many desertions, so he withdrew from the area. He later had to explain his conduct during the campaign in a long discourse to his disgruntled men.

Second Battle

Greene then sent Lieutenant Colonel Henry "Light-Horse Harry" Lee (1756–1818) and his Legion to Lieutenant Colonel Francis Marion (1732–1795), the "Swamp Fox," to take Fort Watson. They converged at the fort on April 16, 1781. Marion's men immediately took control of the nearby lake which lay outside the Native American mound and served as the fort's water supply. The 80 defenders had sufficient ammunition and food to withstand a siege until relieved, but without water, they could not endure very long. When demanded to surrender, British lieutenant James McKay politely declined and ordered his men to dig a well at the base of the Native American mound. They struck water on April 18.

Lee realized the great difficulty of forcing the defenders to surrender after they had acquired a source of water. He knew that he could not successfully assault the fort without any cannon, so he asked General Greene for a fieldpiece to destroy the walls of the fort. Greene sent a small cannon, but the soldiers bringing it got lost trying to find Fort Watson and turned back. About this time, smallpox broke out among Marion's men. This caused many militia members to return home.

The Americans had no cannon and would not risk storming the fort. Lieutenant Colonel Hezekiah Maham found a solution. He proposed building a tower of logs outside the walls, higher than the stockade. Marion's men constructed a 60-foot tower of notched logs over the next 5 days. It had an oblong base and a platform on top that was protected on the fort side by a palisade, allowing the riflemen to shoot everything that moved inside the fort. Two units assaulted the stockade at dawn on April 23 while the riflemen shot at the defenders. McKay soon surrendered. The tower eventually came to bear Maham's name (see Photo SC-11).

The capture of Fort Watson is significant in that it was the first of the interior forts to fall to the Patriot cause after the return of General Greene to South Carolina in April, 1781. The Americans would capture several more outposts over the next month; the British would withdraw from Camden on May 10. The siege of Fort Watson was also the first use of the Maham Tower, which would become a standard fixture of American sieges in South Carolina and Georgia.

Fort Motte (May 12, 1781)

> Fort Motte stood on the Congaree River near its junction with the Wateree to form the Santee River.
>
> Patriotic ladies erected a granite monument in 1909 on the site of Rebecca Motte's home which became the fort/supply depot, but it is about 0.5 mile from the nearest road.

When the British occupied South Carolina, they selected the mansion of widow Rebecca Brewton Motte as their principal supply depot between Charleston and Camden. The mansion fortified with a stockade, ditch, and abatis, was garrisoned by 150 infantry and a few dragoons on May 8, 1781 when Lieutenant Colonel Francis Marion (1732–1795) and Lieutenant Colonel Henry "Light-Horse Harry" Lee (1756–1818) arrived after their victory at Fort Watson.

They intended to lay a formal siege to the fortress and had already begun digging trenches when they learned that Lord Francis Rawdon (1754–1826) was abandoning Camden and might rescue Fort Motte on his way to Charleston. Lee devised a plan to capture the fort by using fire arrows to ignite the shingle roof of the house which was dry after a period of sunny weather. Mrs. Motte, who was living in a nearby farmhouse which Lee and Marion made their headquarters, not only granted her permission but also produced a fine East Indian bow and a bundle of arrows.

When one of the siege trenches got within range of the house about noon, one of Marion's men shot two arrows onto the roof. His artillery prevented anybody from knocking the burning shingles to the ground, forcing the defenders to surrender about 1:00 PM. After the fire was extinguished, Mrs. Motte served a sumptuous dinner to the officers on both sides. The only casualties of the action were 2 of Marion's men. The prisoners were paroled.

Cayce (May 15, 1781)
Fort Granby
The Congarees

> Fort Granby is on the Congaree River south of Columbia.
>
> A graveyard and historical marker just south of Cayce in Lexington County identify the site of Fort Granby.

Granby, once known as The Congarees, was built in 1718 as a trading post with the Native Americans. It had grown into an important river depot by 1754. The British fortified the Cayce House, a strong two-story frame house built in 1765, with a parapet with bastions and guns, a ditch, and the usual abatis from 1780 until May 15, 1781 when Lee's Legion captured it. It was garrisoned by 352 men, including 60 German mercenaries under the command of Major Andrew Maxwell, a Maryland Loyalist.

The day after the capture of Fort Motte, Lieutenant Colonel Henry "Light-Horse Harry" Lee (1756–1818) left for Fort Granby and placed a 6-pounder within 600 yards of the fort during the night of May 14. When the fog cleared the following morning, Lee fired the cannon while his infantry advanced to fire on Maxwell's pickets.

When Lee demanded Maxwell's surrender, he agreed to do so on condition that he and his men be allowed to keep their plunder and be kept at Charleston as prisoners of war until exchanged. Lee expected Lord Francis Rawdon (1754–1826) to arrive to save the fort, so he agreed and added the condition that all horses fit for service be surrendered. Maxwell's mercenaries, who were mounted, objected; and negotiations were suspended until Lee learned that Lord Rawdon was approaching Fort Motte and agreed to Maxwell's terms. Maxwell surrendered before noon on May 15 and departed with 2 wagons of plunder.

Neither side suffered any casualties, and the Americans captured an important post along with a large supply of ammunition, the garrison's weapons, 2 cannon, a number of horses, and some salt and liquor.

Huger (July 17, 1781)
Quinby Bridge

> Quinby Bridge is on SC 98 just west of Huger. Coming up SC 41, turn left before the junction of SC 41 and SC 402 in Huger and follow the road 0.25 mile to Quinby Bridge. A state historical marker on the right immediately before the bridge (west of it) marks the battle site.
>
> A modern house sits on the site of the Quinby Plantation. The site is not marked.

Lieutenant Colonel Henry "Light-Horse Harry" Lee (1756–1818) and his Legion, arrived at Quinby Bridge about noon on July 17, 1781, ahead of Brigadier General Thomas Sumter's (1734–1832) infantry. They were in pursuit of Lieutenant Colonel John Coates, who had withdrawn from Biggin Creek after the battle at Moncks Corner.

Having made a rapid march of 18 miles that day, the British held a strong defensive position on the other side of Quinby Bridge. They loosened the planks on the bridge over the wide and deep creek, intending to remove the flooring when the rear guard got across.

Some of the Legionnaires spotted the enemy across the creek. They captured Coates's rear guard, and 2 sections of cavalry galloped over the bridge, catching the enemy by surprise. Crossing the bridge, they knocked many planks into the water, making it impossible for the main force to repair the bridge in time to join the action on the other side. All but a few redcoats fled, leaving Coates alone with only a few men. They rallied, and the dragoons escaped to cross a ford further upstream where they were met by Lee with his main body and Marion's men.

Meanwhile, Coates used the rail fences and outbuildings of Captain Thomas Shubrick's plantation (now Quinby Plantation) to form a hollow square. He placed a single howitzer to cover his front, but Sumter left all of his artillery behind. Lee and Marion decided that the position was too strong to attack without artillery. When Sumter arrived with the rest of the infantry about 5:00 PM, he overruled Lee's and Marion's decision and ordered an attack without waiting for a 6-pounder to arrive.

Colonel Thomas Taylor's infantry began the attack by charging across an open field and forming a line along a fence. Coates counterattacked and retook the position. Marion's infantry re-captured the fence line but were driven back with heavy losses while Sumter's men fired from behind the buildings.

The Americans retreated across the repaired bridge. Sumter ended the attack after Colonel Taylor, whose unit lost many men, declared, "I will never more serve under you!" Lee and Marion, also angry over the loss of their men, marched away with their troops the next morning. With reinforcements coming to join Coates, Sumter withdrew his remaining men. He retired from the army shortly afterward.

Eutawville (September 8, 1781)
Eutaw Springs

Eutaw Springs Battlefield is on Route SC 6, 3 miles east of Eutawville.
            http://sciway3.net/outdoors/park-eutawsprings.html

The site of the battlefield is now under Lake Marion created by damming the Santee River. A small park with interpretive signs marks the site of the British camp. There are two informational exhibits that describe the engagement and a stone erected by the Daughters of the American Revolution to commemorate it. Major Marjoribanks was originally buried at a spot now submerged beneath the lake; his remains were moved to the park in 1941.

After the siege of Ninety-Six, General Nathanael Greene (1742–1786) rested his army for 6 weeks on the banks of the Wateree south of Camden. The long summer campaign ruined Lord Francis Rawdon's (1754–1826) health and spirit. After chasing Greene in vain after the siege of Ninety-Six, Rawdon turned his command over to Lieutenant Colonel Alexander Stewart (1740–1794) and sailed for England, only to have his ship captured by Admiral François Joseph Paul Comte de Grasse's (1722–1788) fleet.

On August 22, 1781, Greene moved his army of 2,300, about half of them Continentals, north to Camden and turned south toward Lieutenant Colonel Alexander Stewart's (1740–1794) camp at Eutaw Springs about 50 miles northwest of Charleston.

Stewart left the initiative to the rebels on the morning of September 8, 1781. His army numbered about 2,000, including Colonel John Harris Cruger's (1738–1807) men evacuated from Ninety-Six. Stewart learned of Greene's approach about 8:00 AM when some of his men sent to harvest yams for the army's rations encountered the advancing front line. They fled to tell Stewart who deployed his men about 100 yards to the west of his camp.

He placed most of his men in a line crossing the road that led to Charleston. He reinforced his exposed left flank with some infantry and his cavalry. Major John Marjoribanks (d. 1781) took his position with 300 men by the waters of Eutaw Springs. He placed the Guards and Grenadiers on his right flank, near a tangle of blackjack oak. The cavalry were on the left and his 3 guns on the road in the middle of the front line.

Greene had the advantage of knowing the enemy's location. Declining Loyalist support for the British allowed his army to get 4 miles from Stewart's camp without friendly citizens informing him. About a mile from the enemy, Greene arranged his troops into battle order. He put the South and North Carolina militia in the first line, the Continentals in the second, and the light infantry and cavalry in the third.

Shortly after 9:00 AM, Brigadier General Andrew Pickens (1739–1817) and Brigadier General Francis Marion (1732–1795) led the South and North Carolina militia against Marjoribanks. They encountered very heavy cannon and musket fire as artillery on both sides fired grapeshot at each other. One of Stewart's guns and two of Greene's were put out of action. The militia did not falter, astounding the Regulars on both sides. They fired about 17 rounds before the 64th Regiment and some Loyalist troops charged with the bayonet and drove them back.

The British right and center held for a while, but Greene sent 3 brigades of North Carolina Continentals under Major General Jethro Sumner (1735–1785) to reestablish the line. He followed with a charge by the relatively fresh Maryland and Virginia Continentals as the Americans on the right poured heavy fire into the British left, collapsing that flank and then Stewart's front. The redcoats soon retreated with heavy losses. Only Marjoribanks continued to fight on the right.

Greene sent Lieutenant Colonel William Washington's (1752–1810) cavalry forward, but Marjoribanks routed them as they attempted to reach his rear. Washington's horse was hit by a musket ball and he was captured.

When the American infantry pushed the British into their camp (see Photo SC-12), the Americans ran into the tents and plundered the camp. They opened casks and bottles and drank so heavily that they were soon uncontrollable. This gave Major Marjoribanks time to organize his troops, rush forward to capture the American guns, and drive off the looters, shooting many of them as they drank. Sharpshooters also killed several officers. Although mortally wounded, Marjoribanks ordered an attack that forced the Americans back. Greene's units, completely disorganized, stopped fighting and withdrew instead of risking the destruction of his army.

Greene's cavalry covered the retreat, while Stewart's cavalry tried to stop them. After collecting his exhausted men, Greene left Stewart in possession of the battlefield. The Americans suffered about 25% casualties: 139 killed, 375 wounded, and 8 missing. The number of missing is undoubtedly higher because a large part of the army was involved in plundering British tents and drinking. Stewart reported British casualties as 85 killed, 351 wounded, and 257 missing—35% of his army, the highest percentage of losses sustained by any force during the war. Stewart returned to Charleston, and the

British did not leave their strongholds in Charleston and Savannah for the rest of the war.

The 4-hour Battle of Eutaw Springs was one of the most violent of the war. It essentially ended the campaign in the south, forcing the enemy back to Charleston, where they remained cooped up until they evacuated it in December, 1782, and leaving Greene master in South Carolina. Greene had lost battles but won a campaign. In so doing, he paved the way for the greater victory to follow at Yorktown. The Whigs regained control of South Carolina and Georgia.

16

GEORGIA

Georgia sent 2,679 men to the Continental Army.

The British evacuated Philadelphia, Pennsylvania in June, 1778, partly because they needed to supply troops for operations in the Caribbean and Florida. General Henry Clinton (1730–1795) sent 5,000 troops to St. Lucia in the West Indies in November, 1778, and another 3,000 under Lieutenant Colonel Archibald Campbell (1739–1791) to join Major General Augustine Prevost (1723–1786) in St. Augustine, Florida.

By moving south, the British were closer to the West Indies where the fleet could protect their interests and guard against the French. The Loyalists were also more numerous in the South, especially in the Carolinas and Georgia. The king's ministers hoped to bring the southern states into the fold one by one and, from bases there, to strangle the recalcitrant North. A small British force operating from Florida quickly overran thinly populated Georgia in the winter of 1778-1779.

The Allied defeat at Savannah confirmed the British as masters of Georgia and paved the way for the offensive that would capture Charleston and most of South Carolina the following year. When the Patriots captured Augusta, they won the support of the Georgia backcountry for their cause.

See the Georgia map.

Midway (November 25, 1778) and Sunbury (January 6–9, 1779)
Battle of Fort Morris

The Battle of Fort Morris is also known as the Battle of Midway. Fort Morris State Historic Site is at 2559 Fort Morris Road, 7.9 miles northeast of Midway, Georgia. At the intersection of Interstate I-95 and U.S. 84, travel east for 4.6 miles following signs. Turn left after 2.5 miles, then bear right on a dirt road for 0.6 mile to the fort.

`http://www.cr.nps.gov/goldcres/sites/morris.htm`

Visitors can still see remains of the breastworks, embrasures, and the moat, take a walking tour, or use the picnic facilities. A museum interprets the history of the site.

The Continentals withdrew to Midway Church as the Crown forces under Lieutenant Colonel James Mark Prevost advanced on the town of Midway. The church's cemetery is the burial place of a number of Patriots, including Brigadier General James Screven (1744–1778).

`http://roadsidegeorgia.com/site/midwaycemetery.html`

Sunbury no longer exists. It was protected by Fort Morris about a 0.25 mile to the north.

The Continental Congress commissioned Fort Morris in 1776. Slaves built the large earthworks on a bluff overlooking the Midway River. It was Georgia's largest fortification, measuring 275 feet in length along the east (river side), 191 feet on the northern side, 240 feet on the west and 140 feet on the south. Besides the marshes on three sides, the fort was surrounded by a moat 10 feet deep and 10 feet wide at the bottom and 20 feet wide at the top. It had 7 embrasures, each about 5 feet wide to accommodate 25 guns of various sizes, ranging from 4- to 24-pounders, mounted on platforms. American Patriots garrisoned the post to protect the port of Sunbury against British forces in both the War for American Independence and the War of 1812.

Sunbury was a town south of Savannah and a little more than a quarter of a mile south of the fort. With a population of more than 1,000 people during the War for American Independence, it was the second largest port in Georgia, but it had completely disappeared by the Civil War.

Sunbury was the key for any American force planning to attack St. Augustine, Florida, or for any British unit with aims at occupying Savannah. It served as the advance camp for the Patriot forces under Colonel William Moultrie (1730–1805) who planned to attack the Loyalists in East Florida in 1776. However, the heat and malaria began decimating the troops at the rate of 15 a day, causing Moultrie to return to Charleston, South Carolina.

Lieutenant Colonel James Mark Prevost, younger brother of Major General Augustine Prevost (1723–1786) led a small army of 400 Regulars, Loyalists, and Native Americans north from Florida in the fall of 1778. He traveled by land as a second force of 500 men led by Colonel L. V. Fuser was headed to the port town of Sunbury by sea. The two forces were supposed to rendezvous at Sunbury and then proceed to Savannah to join with Lieutenant Colonel Archibald Campbell's (1739–1791) force of 2,000 men sailing from New York. The Battle of Midway prevented the two forces from joining.

As Prevost approached the town of Midway, Colonel John White and a group of 100 Continental Army regulars with 2 pieces of light artillery and 20 mounted militiamen under the command of Brigadier General James Screven (1744–1778) formed to block him. The Crown forces attacked, wounding and capturing Screven who died in captivity shortly afterward.

The Continentals withdrew to Midway Church and formed a new defense line in the town. White wrote a letter which looked like an order to retreat so as to draw the Crown forces in pursuit. It also mentioned a large body of cavalry coming to attack Prevost from behind. White made sure Prevost received the letter. As Fuser had not arrived, Prevost withdrew and returned to Florida after burning a few buildings, including the Congregationalist meeting house which was used to store arms and ammunition.

Colonel Fuser, delayed by head winds, arrived at Sunbury on November 25, 1778, after Colonel Prevost had already left for Florida. He immediately besieged Fort Morris. Expecting the arrival of Colonel Prevost, Fuser demanded the surrender of the fort. Lieutenant Colonel John McIntosh (1755–1826) abruptly refused, telling him: "Come and take it." When Fuser learned that Prevost had withdrawn, he sailed down the coast to Fort Frederica on St. Simons Island. The Georgia Assembly later voted to present McIntosh with a sword with the engraving "Come and take it!"

A few weeks later, in December, 1778, Major General Robert Howe (1732–1786) and 950 men who had marched to Sunbury departed to counter the Crown forces near Savannah. They left about 200 Continentals at Sunbury. After the fall of Savannah, General Augustine Prevost returned on January 6, 1779, with a more formidable force of 2,000 men and laid siege to Sunbury and Fort Morris. The defenders held out for 3 days until a brief bombardment caused the 159 Continentals and 45 militia to surrender on January 9. The Americans lost 1 captain and 3 privates killed, 7 wounded, 24 guns and a quantity of supplies while the Crown forces had 1 man killed and 3 wounded. This ended any fighting in eastern Georgia.

Savannah
(December 29, 1778; September 23 to October 18, 1779)

Railroad tracks cover most of the Savannah battlefield. The Savannah History Museum occupies the site of the Spring Hill Redoubt. Nothing remains of the breastworks and ditch. The swamps and wooded marshes through which the militia units got entangled have been filled and converted to industrial use. The causeway over which the attackers advanced no longer exists. Railroad embankments and tracks cover the spot where d'Estaing was wounded trying to rally his men and where Pulaski was shot from his horse. Markers and memorials between Louisville Road and French Jones Street identify where the fortifications were and where the important actions took place. The only remaining site of the battlefield is the old Jewish burial ground where the French gathered for the final attack.

Raids

Savannah, the largest town and port in Georgia, was the key to controlling the colony. Patriot forces seized the powder supplies there on May 11, 1775. The deposed Royal Governor, Sir James Wright (1714–1785), launched a raid with British naval forces against the town on March 7, 1776. They captured 11 merchant ships carrying rice and posed a direct threat to the city. The Patriots counterattacked and defeated the British at the Battle of Hutchinson's Island.

Battle

The British evacuated Philadelphia in June, 1778, partly because they needed to supply troops for operations in the Caribbean and Florida. General Henry Clinton (1730–1795) sent 5,000 troops to St. Lucia in the West Indies in November, 1778, and another 3,000 under Lieutenant Colonel Archibald Campbell (1739–1791) sailed from New York on November 27 to join Major General Augustine Prevost (1723–1786) in St. Augustine, Florida.

By moving south, the British were closer to the West Indies where the fleet could protect their interests and guard against the French. The Loyalists were also more numerous in the South, especially in the Carolinas and Georgia. The king's ministers hoped to bring the southern colonies into the fold one by one, and from bases there to strangle the recalcitrant North. A small British force operating from Florida quickly overran thinly populated Georgia in the winter of 1778–1779.

Instead of going to St. Augustine, Campbell sailed directly to Savannah where he disembarked on Tynbee Island at the mouth of the Savannah River on December 29, 1778. He commanded 2 battalions of Brigadier General Simon Fraser's (1737–1777) Highlanders, 2 of Germans, and 4 of American volunteers, including deserters of Irish descent from General George Washington's (1732–1799) army. There were so many deserters who switched sides that Lieutenant Colonel Lord Francis Rawdon (1754–1826) formed an entire battalion of them in Philadelphia and called them the Volunteers of Ireland.

General Prevost planned to march north from Florida to meet Campbell, but he was delayed. Campbell learned that the American officer in command, Major General Robert Howe (1732–1786) of North Carolina, had just returned from a predatory expedition into East Florida. He decided to strike immediately before Howe's expected reinforcements arrived.

The same day as Campbell's army of 3,500 landed at the mouth of the Savannah River, Howe marched to oppose him with a force of only 700 Continentals and 150 militia. Campbell re-embarked his men and sailed upriver to a landing place less than 2 miles below Savannah. He crossed a causeway between rice swamps and proceeded to Howe's camp on Girardeau's Plantation about half a mile east of Savannah. Howe positioned his flanks on the edge of the swamps and waited for the British to attack. Colonel Campbell induced an African-American named Quamino Dolly "to conduct the Troops, by a private Path through the Swamp, upon the Right of the Americans" for a small reward.

Campbell struck the American right flank as the main army assaulted the center. The Americans panicked and fled into the swamps where many drowned. Campbell then occupied Savannah, looting and burning the homes of Patriots. The Americans lost 83 men dead (battle casualties and drownings) and 453 captured, 48 cannon, 23 mortars, and a large supply of powder. The Crown forces had only 3 battle deaths and 10 wounded.

The British thought that the easy capture of Savannah would let them expand their occupation into a center of loyalism. After Prevost arrived from Florida with another 1,000 men, Campbell went up the Savannah River to recruit Loyalist volunteers. About 1,400 Loyalists joined Campbell at Augusta, but, on February 14, at the Battle of Kettle Creek, the American militia ambushed another 700 on their way to enlist. News that Major-General Benjamin Lincoln (1733–1810) was coming with an army of more than 1,500 men convinced the Crown forces to withdraw to Savannah.

Siege
Admiral Comte Jean-Baptiste-Charles-Henri-Hector d'Estaing (1729–1794) sailed north from the Caribbean and arrived off the coast of Georgia with a strong French fleet of 33 ships and 6,000 troops on September 11, 1779. The *Paris Gazette* reported that the troops landed there consisted of 2,979 "Europeans" and 545 "Colored: Volunteer Chasseurs, Mulattoes, and Negroes, newly raised at St. Domingo." The Volunteer Chasseurs, called the Fontages Legion after its French commander, included young men who would become famous in the Haitian revolution, such as André Rigaud,

Louis Jacques Beauvais, Martial Besse, Jean-Baptiste Mars Belley, and Henri Christophe, future king of Haiti. Christophe was 12 years old at Savannah. He volunteered as a freeborn infantryman and served as orderly to a French naval officer.

Major General Benjamin Lincoln hurried south with 1,350 Americans to join d'Estaing on September 15 in a siege of the main British base at Savannah. The following day, d'Estaing demanded that General Augustine Prevost surrender the city, but he gave Prevost 24 hours to consider the terms. This gave Prevost enough time to strengthen his defenses and receive reinforcements of 800 Regulars from the garrison at Beaufort, South Carolina. D'Estaing got upset as the redcoats dug their trenches. He sent Prevost a letter saying, "I am informed that you continue intrenching yourself. It is a Matter of very little Importance to me, however for Form's sake, I must desire that you will desist." With his total manpower raised to 3,250, Prevost declined to surrender.

Unfortunately, the Franco-American force had to hurry its attack because d'Estaing was unwilling to risk his fleet in a position dangerously exposed to hurricanes, remembering Rhode Island where he was caught in one. On October 9, the French and Americans abandoned their plan to make a systematic approach by regular parallels and mounted a direct assault on the Crown forces who were aided by hundreds of "armed blacks" gathered from the countryside to build redoubts, mount cannon, and serve as guides and spies. Their "incessant and cheerful labours, in rearing those numerous defenses which were completed with so much expedition as to astonish the besiegers, ought not to be forgotten in a history of this memorable siege."

Prevost chose the Spring Hill Redoubt, off the town's southwest corner, as the strongest point of his defense. The French and Americans began digging siege trenches on September 23 and installed cannon by October 3. Early the next morning, allied gunners fired the first shots of a bombardment hoping to weaken enemy resistance. Some drunken French gunners hit their own lines. After being reprimanded, they resumed firing "with more vivacity than precision." The cannonade failed to produce the desired result.

When d'Estaing learned, on October 8, that the assault trenches would not be completed until 10 days later, he demanded an immediate attack. Lincoln, in charge of some 5,000 troops agreed somewhat grudgingly. He ordered the main attack against the Spring Hill Redoubt to begin at 4:00 AM on October 9.

The French under General Dillon would emerge from a swamp while Brigadier General Isaac Huger (1743–1797) would lead a secondary assault. However, Dillon's men got lost and the British forced Huger to retreat under heavy fire. The French and American allies fought a long and bloody battle in the ditch outside the Spring Hill Redoubt, trying to get to the top. As soon as they placed French and American colors on it, they were immediately knocked down.

The Crown forces, in strongly entrenched positions, repelled the attack in what was essentially a Bunker Hill in reverse. The French and Americans suffered staggering losses. British grenadiers and marines charged, throwing their foe into confusion and finally into flight. After the repulsion of other thrusts, Lincoln gave up. The Fontages Legion, stationed as a reserve in the rear guard, prevented the annihilation of the allied force. Brigadier General Count Casimir Pulaski (1747–1779) led his Legion in a cavalry assault that resulted in his death. Martial Besse and Henri Christophe were slightly wounded and returned to Saint Domingue (now Haiti). Count d'Estaing was also wounded trying to reorganize the French forces.

The Americans suffered approximately 150 casualties while the French sustained approximately 650 officers and men wounded. We don't know the British losses in the battle, but they range from approximately 55 to 155 men.

The French army departed the area and boarded their ships on October 20, 1779. D'Estaing then sailed away to the West Indies. General Lincoln marched his army back to Charleston, which would fall the next year. The second attempt at Franco-American cooperation ended in much the same atmosphere of bitterness and disillusion as the first. As in Rhode Island, this affair displayed poor coordination between the Americans and the French. Each allied commander disliked his opposite and departed Savannah with a mutual distrust. American and French coordination and cooperation would improve at the Battle of Yorktown in 1781.

The Allied defeat at Savannah confirmed the British as masters of Georgia and paved the way for the offensive that would capture Charleston and most of South Carolina the following year. The British would later evacuate Savannah on July 11, 1782.

Washington (February 14, 1779)
Kettle Creek

> The Kettle Creek Battlefield is on Warhill Road off Route GA 44 west of town. From Washington, take GA 44 west for 6.8 miles, turn right at the state historical marker for Kettle Creek Battleground after 1.2 miles, then turn left for 1.2 miles and take a final left on a dirt road for 1.6 miles to a stone obelisk.
>
> `http://www.kudcom.com/www/att05.html`
>
> The road leading to the battleground ends at the hill marked with a 20-foot-high stone obelisk. The monument, erected in 1930, commemorates the battle. Two memorial stones honor John Shank and John Lindsey, two soldiers of the War for American Independence. Pickens and his men camped near here the night before they attacked Boyd's men, but the exact site of the camp is unknown. There are no markers explaining the action or describing the battlefield.

In the battle of Kettle Creek on February 14, 1779, Colonel Andrew Pickens (1739–1817) and about 300 South Carolina and Georgia militiamen ambushed a group of 700 North Carolina Loyalists, who were plundering their way through South Carolina on their way to enlist in the British army at Augusta. The new recruits would have increased Loyalist opposition in the area.

The Loyalists commanded by Colonel John Boyd crossed the Savannah River near Cherokee Ford and overwhelmed Pickens's sentries. As they continued on toward Augusta, the Loyalists were unaware that Pickens and his men were near them. Boyd camped on the north side of Kettle Creek near where it joins the Savannah River. On the morning of February 14, as the horses were grazing and the Loyalists were having breakfast, Pickens attacked.

A first surprise assault took the hilltop. Boyd rallied about 100 of his men behind a fence but was forced to retreat when his left was outflanked. The bitter fight went on for about an hour when Boyd fell with two mortal wounds. The Patriots responded with coordinated flank attacks that enabled them to cross the creek and attack the Loyalists from the rear. The inexperienced troops failed to complete the maneuver, and Pickens had to bear the brunt of the enemy fire. The Patriots forced the Loyalists to retreat across the creek. The battle lasted another half hour before the Loyalists surrendered.

The Patriots suffered 9 dead and 23 wounded but killed about 40 men and wounded or captured another 75. They brought charges of treason against 70 Loyalists and hanged 5 of the leaders. Southern militiamen were not inclined to have mercy on those who sided with the Crown forces because the British encouraged African-American slaves to run away from their masters and employed them on fatigue duties in British camps.

Fewer than 300 North Carolinians proceeded to Augusta to join the Crown forces. The victory at Kettle Creek checked the string of British victories to regain control of Georgia, strengthened the desire for independence in the colony, and lowered the morale of the Loyalists in the interior of Georgia and South Carolina. It also encouraged Patriot militia to join the forces assembled under Major General Benjamin Lincoln (1733–1810).

Lincoln decided to recover Georgia, but attempts to do so in February and March, 1779, failed. A stronger effort in April caused Major General Augustine Prevost (1723–1786) to move to Charleston, South Carolina in May, and Lincoln withdrew from Georgia. Neither side gained much ground in these engagements, and the Patriots suffered much heavier losses.

Sylvania (March 3, 1779)
Briar Creek

> Briar Creek Battleground: Briar Creek Bridge, East Ogeechee Street, 11 miles east of Sylvania. Turn left to cross the bridge over Briar Creek
>
> A large historical marker has a map showing the movements of the two forces and a lengthy description of the battle. There is no other development at the site except for a causeway running through it. The east bank of the creek is used for camping.

Major General Augustine Prevost's (1723–1786) army faced Major General Benjamin Lincoln's (1733–1810) American army across the Savannah River in early 1779. After the fall of Savannah, the Americans were trying to retake the colony while the Crown forces were consolidating their hold on it. Although the Crown forces had taken Augusta with little effort, American pressure across the river forced them to abandon it during the night of February 13, 1779.

American Brigadier General John Ashe (1720–1781) crossed the Savannah River with 1,400 men and some 100 Georgia Continentals in pursuit of the Crown forces withdrawing down to Savannah. The redcoats destroyed a bridge across Briar Creek and continued marching until they reached Hudson's Ferry, a fortified post about 15 miles below the creek. The Patriots camped at Briar Creek while they rebuilt the bridge, but they failed to take adequate defensive precautions. They also awaited reinforcements which they received with the arrival of 207 South Carolinians.

General Prevost saw this as an opportunity to strike. He ordered a small diversionary force out from Savannah to march toward the Americans while his younger brother, Lieutenant Colonel James Mark Prevost led a second force of 900 professional soldiers to circle around the American force and come down from the north. The flanking maneuver caught General Ashe completely by surprise, cornering him against the swamp and the unrepaired bridge around 4:00 PM on March 3, 1779. The militia fled immediately. The small number of Continentals remaining exchanged volleys briefly before fleeing into the swamp where many drowned in a desperate attempt to swim across the Savannah River.

Nearly 200 Americans were killed or drowned and 11 wounded. They lost another 200 prisoners, 7 guns and many small arms, their baggage, and colors. Ashe was court-martialed for being unprepared to meet the enemy. This terminated his military career. The Battle of Briar Creek destroyed Ashe's force and allowed the Crown forces to reoccupy Augusta, confirming their position in the South and ending General Lincoln's hope of retaking Georgia. The Patriots would not be able to retake Georgia until after the Crown forces left 2 years later.

Augusta (January 29, 1779; September 14–18, 1780; May 22 to June 5, 1781)
Fort Cornwallis (Fort Augusta)

The site of Fort Cornwallis is at 6th and Reynolds Streets, Augusta, Georgia. The fort was built by James Oglethorpe in 1735 as protection for traders on the Savannah River. Named Fort Augusta, after the Princess of Wales, it was renamed Fort Cornwallis in the Patriot attack on Augusta in September, 1780. Fort Cornwallis was torn down in 1786. St. Paul's Church marks the site of Fort Cornwallis. It is the fourth one to do so.. When this church was first built in 1750, it stood "under the curtain of the fort." A Celtic cross behind the church marks the site of Fort Augusta; one of James Oglethorpe's cannons stands at the foot of the cross. There are no apparent remains of Fort Cornwallis.

There is a marker for the site of the Maham tower a few feet off Reynolds on 8th Street. The site is presently occupied by a cotton exchange building which houses a business school and a motel.

Fort Grierson: The approximate location of the temporary British stronghold commanded by Colonel James Grierson (d. 1781) is 11th and Reynolds Streets, 1 mile west of Fort Cornwallis.

Capture
Lieutenant Colonel Archibald Campbell (1739–1791) captured Augusta on January 29, 1779 with virtually no opposition. The Crown forces held the fort until February, 1780, when American pressure across the river forced them to abandon it.

First Battle

Colonel Elijah Clarke (1733–1799) and more than 400 militia men attacked and quickly captured Forts Grierson and Cornwallis in September, 1780. They then advanced on the town itself where the Crown forces fortified the McKay House and waited for reinforcements. A relief column arrived from Ninety-Six, South Carolina, on September 18, 1780, forcing the Patriots to withdraw after a 2-day siege. The Patriots suffered approximately 60 total casualties. There is no record of Crown forces casualties which are believed to have been mostly Native American allies.

Second Battle

During Major General Nathanael Greene's (1742–1786) 1781 campaign to recapture South Carolina from the Crown forces, Lieutenant Colonel Henry "Light-Horse Harry" Lee's (1756–1818) Legion joined the forces of Brigadier General Andrew Pickens (1739–1817) and Brigadier General Elijah Clarke (1733–1799) in an attack upon Augusta, Georgia. They focused on Fort Grierson, the smaller of 2 forts guarding the town with a garrison of only 80 men. They attacked from three sides on Wednesday, May 23, 1781. The defenders tried to withdraw to the larger Fort Cornwallis a half mile away. Clarke's men offered stiff resistance, killing 30 and capturing the rest. Colonel James Grierson (d. 1781), the commander, was taken prisoner and shot by an unknown Georgian according to the Richmond County Historical Society. Benson Lossing identifies him as Captain Samuel Alexander of the Georgia militia.

Unable to take Fort Cornwallis by storm, the militia began a siege and started digging siege trenches. The Crown forces mounted 2 sorties, and the Patriots decided to build a Maham tower (at what is now the corner of 8th and Reynolds Streets). The tower, made of logs and filled with earth, had an embrasure at the top that accommodated a 6-pounder, allowing the Patriots to deliver deadly cannon and musket fire from it into the fort. The height of the Maham tower constructed at Augusta is unknown, but it was tall enough to dominate the interior of Fort Cornwallis which was just 2 modern blocks away. (See Photo SC-11.) The 300 defenders tried unsuccessfully to destroy it and were forced to surrender on June 6, 1781. Patriot casualties totaled 40 men; Crown forces lost about 52 officers and men killed and 334 were made prisoners. The capture of Augusta won the support of the Georgia backcountry for the American cause.

17

(Re)Living History

Visiting a museum or a historic site with friends or family is a very different experience than doing so alone. The sharing of thoughts, impressions, and reactions enriches the experience and adds to the enjoyment. Having a guide or guidebook provides context and interpretation. Going to a living history event or a re-enactment whether as an observer or a participant adds a totally different dimension.

Re-enactors, sometimes called living historians, try to re-create history by portraying the look and actions of a person from a particular time period. Interacting with the public, explaining their equipment, lifestyle, and activities are an important part of what they do. The aphorism that teachers learn from their students also applies to re-enactors. Nobody can be an expert on everything, so an important part of re-enacting is learning from fellow re-enactors.

Re-enactors get a particular thrill when an event is held on the original site because they realize they are on hallowed ground where their forefathers camped, fought, and died. They also realize that they are re-creating important events in our history. Usually events are held on the weekend closest to an anniversary. Sometimes an event occurs on the same date or at the same time as the original.

Many of the sites of the War for American Independence are national parks. Because National Parks Service regulations prohibit opposed firing very few re-enactments occur there. They do allow "commemorations" at which re-enactors can fire muskets at an imaginary enemy.

Because so many sites are national parks or are obliterated by urban development, finding an appropriate site that has similar terrain to the original site and can accommodate the numbers of participants and spectators can be difficult. Often, these sites are on privately owned farms or in city or state parks.

State historic parks are ideal locations. Not only are they the site of the original action, but they usually try to re-create the same environmental conditions. For example, if a battle was originally fought in a cornfield, re-enactors may have a cornfield to re-create the event (see Photo RLH-1).

Re-enactors experience some of the difficulties and hardships of their forefathers—not only in living conditions but also in experiences. Many of them sleep in tents, lean-tos, or under the stars. (See Photo RLH-2, Native American lean-to.) They eat foods of the period, prepared over camp fires. However they don't have to suffer the shortages their ancestors endured. They do not have the limited rations or periods of starvation. They don't have to endure the illnesses of smallpox, the "itch," and camp fever.

A visitor to a battlefield can try to visualize the tactics and imagine the thoughts and emotions the soldiers may have felt. Re-enactors relive part of the experience. For example, charging up a hill on a hot summer day, a re-enactor not only suffers the heat and fatigue of the assault, he can also be awed and frightened facing cannons and hundreds of muskets. Even knowing that the "enemy" are only firing powder and will not fire directly at them, re-enactors can appreciate the courage of their ancestors. A tourist can hike up the same hill to re-create the experience, but it's not the same as doing it carrying a musket in the face of enemy fire.

Who Are Re-enactors?

As previously stated, re-enactors re-create history by portraying the look and actions of a person from a particular time period. The organizations involved in re-creating the era of the War for American Independence are dedicated to re-creating the life and times of the common soldiers. They also demonstrate the life and activities of an 18th-century military camp. This is not to say that only "soldiers" are admitted to membership. The war affected entire families and even displaced many of them, forcing them to accompany the army. Consequently, the camps also portray a spectrum of civilian life, particularly as it was affected and influenced by the war.

Re-enactors come from all walks of life as did the men who served in George Washington's army. They include teachers, doctors and nurses, dentists, lawyers, librarians, policemen and firefighters, plumbers, mechanics, museum curators, printers, musicians, engineers, photographers, authors, craftspeople—even postal workers. The list is almost endless. They all have one thing in common: a strong interest in history.

Some people join because it caters to the inner child—playing soldier with "real" toys. Others join because their children become interested after attending an event. Re-enacting allows families to share common experiences and to deepen their relationships. Re-enacting is a personal experience, and there are as many reasons for joining the hobby as there are participants.

Many people stay involved because they enjoy educating the public about history. Others enjoy being with friends, demonstrating a particular talent or craft, or simply escaping the complexities of modern life for a weekend. Going back to "the good old days" develops a deeper appreciation for the lifestyles of our ancestors and the difficulties they endured. It also fosters a deeper appreciation of our own lives.

Some people portray specific characters, but most depict a representative of a particular class of people. While the largest number of participants are soldiers, there are officers' wives, camp followers, laundresses (see Photo RLH-5), tinkers, surgeons, craftspeople (such as blacksmiths, tinsmiths, leather workers, potters, spinners), refugees, etc. Sutlers or merchants follow the camps to sell their wares to the soldiers. They are also a great source for interesting and unusual souvenirs.

Children can participate in re-enacting at any age (see Photo RLH-3), but they have to be at least 12 years old to go on the battlefield and at least 16 to bear arms. Children under the age of 16 are encouraged to join the music, learning to play the fife or drum. This is consonant with the practice in the Continental Army where children as young as 11 are known to have served as musicians. Music plays an important role in the army. Band music raises morale, provides a cadence for marching, and increases the pomp of ceremonies, whether joyful or solemn. The musicians' most important function, however, is to convey orders and signals. Drums and fifes furnish most of the signals for the infantry and artillery because they can be heard in battle much more clearly than the human voice. Dragoons (cavalry) rely on a trumpet or bugle horn because these instruments can be played with one hand while holding reins with the other.

How to Become a Re-enactor

The three national and international organizations re-creating the period of the War for American Independence include the Brigade of the American Revolution, the Continental Line, and the British Brigade. These are "umbrella" organizations made up of many units. While one can join these organizations as an individual, normal membership is through a member unit. The organizations can refer individuals to appropriate member units in a particular area or a particular "politic" or impression (Patriot, Loyalist, British, French, Hessian, Native American). Local historic sites are another source of information.

Attending a re-enactment is a good way to see and experience the variety of units one can join. Each army also offers opportunities to portray infantry, artillery, cavalry, musicians, artificers, engineers, riflemen, militia, naval forces, marines, and other military and civilian personnel. Attending a re-enactment provides the opportunity for spectators and prospective re-enactors to ask a lot of questions about the various people, their clothing, equipment, lifestyle, activities, etc. When one decides to join a unit, he or she only needs to express that interest to the leader or a member.

> **Re-enactor Organizations: War for American Independence**
> Brigade of the American Revolution
>   `http://www.brigade.org/`
> The Continental Line
>   `http://www.continentalline.org/`
> The British Brigade
>   `http://www.britishbrigade.org/`

Outfit and Equipment

Re-enacting can be an expensive hobby for the beginner. The musket alone costs several hundred dollars. Then, there's the clothing: shirt, pants, socks, shoes, waistcoat, haversack, uniform coat, hat, canteen, and cartridge box which can total $1,000 or more. That's not counting some cooking utensils, bedding, backpack, tent, etc. Re-enactors refer to their clothing and equipment as their *kit* and the persona they portray as their *impression.*

Joining a unit first can save a lot of money. Many units have extra clothing and equipment for people to borrow. People who leave the hobby sometimes sell or give away their equipment. Units may have such extra equipment to loan to new recruits until they are ready to make or purchase their own. Some unit members also have extra clothing that they can share. So, new recruits can usually participate even if they don't have a full kit. Some units may have craftsmen or members with particular skills to help members make or repair parts of their kit, thereby saving money.

Recruits need not acquire a complete kit all at once. They can obtain pieces as they have funds available. Some items make good gift ideas for birthdays, Father's Day, Christmas, etc. Equipment and hardware are more likely to be interchangeable with various units while clothing tends to be less so.

Merchants, called sutlers, attend the various re-enactments and may be a good source for clothing and accoutrements. People interested in joining the hobby should avoid rushing to purchase kit items before joining a unit. Just because someone is selling something at an event doesn't mean that it's authentic or appropriate. It often takes time and experience to determine whether or not something is "period." Also, something may be authentic for the period but not for a particular unit. For example, buckskin and leggings which are authentic for frontiersmen, riflemen, rangers, and scouts (see Photo RLH-4) are not appropriate for an urban militia or a coastal unit.

Most units have had various types of uniforms at various stages of the war. They generally choose a primary impression to depict the unit at a particular period. They may prefer certain sutlers over others. Some may use private tailors to maintain some consistency or a particular level of authenticity. This may result in garments costing less than if bought "off the rack." As one matures in the hobby, one may opt to acquire extra items to have a secondary impression.

Many photographs in this book show re-enactments and re-enactors, and give a sense of the details associated with some of the uniforms and equipment. Photos RLH-1 through RLH-6 are intended to portray the "life" in a re-enactors' event.

Safety

Safety is a primary concern for re-enactors as the battlefield can be a dangerous place with musket and artillery fire and various types of edged weapons. The Brigade of the American Revolution, established in 1962, led the way in developing guidelines for the safe use and handling of black powder. Each organization also has its own safety rules which unit commanders are required to implement and monitor. When the organizations join together for re-enactments, the safety rules are agreed upon prior to the event and publicized so participants know which rules apply. Safety officers monitor each event and may interrupt it until a safety violation is corrected. Safety regulations cover the kitchen and animals in addition to the weapons.

Modern safety concerns have required modifications to weapons and practices. Very few authentic muskets have flash guards attached to the lock. The re-enacting organizations require that the modern reproductions have "positive stop" flash guards to prevent or minimize a fellow re-enactor getting powder burns. The positive stop prevents the flash guard from slipping if the frizzen screw becomes loose.

The drill manual has also been modified to eliminate steps that could possibly result in injury. Ramrods used to pack the powder and ball in the musket barrel are not used in re-enactments because soldiers can forget to secure them in the heat of battle. A ramrod forgotten in the barrel can become a projectile. Ramrods are withdrawn at safety inspections before and after an event to ensure that nothing remains in the barrel. Also, re-enactors don't put the paper from the cartridges down the barrel. The paper does not always burn completely upon discharge and can become a projectile. Edged weapons are usually not withdrawn on the battlefield to prevent injuries.

Background Reading

The average American's view of the War for American Independence is often a series of disjointed scenes or vignettes: Paul Revere's ride, the Battle of Bunker Hill, the Battle of Saratoga, the surrender at Yorktown. A new re-enactor can find it difficult to transcend these initial images in an attempt to understand the nature and scope of the war. There have been several books published in recent years that focus on what life was like for ordinary citizens in the colonial and revolutionary periods. Other books focus on the politics of the period or the roles of particular groups or classes of people, such as women, Quakers, or sailors.

The Brigade of the American Revolution, the Continental Line, and the British Brigade all have newsletters and publications available for their members. Some of these materials may also be available from their web sites.

Diaries and memoirs offer a re-enactor a rich source of understanding. Joseph Plumb Martin's narrative *Private Yankee Doodle: Being a Narrative of Some of the Adventures, Dangers, and Sufferings of a Revolutionary soldier* is one of the most entertaining and captivating narratives of a soldier's life during the War for American Independence. First published in 1830, it is sometimes criticized for being written long after the end of the war. Nonetheless, it is an entertaining firsthand account of a Connecticut soldier who served from the Battle of Bunker Hill to the surrender at Yorktown. It has been republished many times and is available in inexpensive paperback editions.

There are many diaries and memoirs authored by participants in all the armies involved in the war. Locating one written by a member of the unit one wants to re-create is particularly valuable. There are also many histories of the war in general or of specific battles or campaigns. Most of the standard sources were written from the Patriot point of view. Recent histories are re-examining events from other points of view. Christopher Hibbert's *Redcoats and Rebels: The American Revolution through British Eyes*, for example, looks at the events from the British perspective. Nancy Wolock's *Women and the American Experience* examines the experiences and contributions of women. Other books treat the experiences of people like the Quakers, African Americans, Loyalists, etc.

Philip R. N. Katcher's book *Rebels & Loyalists: The Revolutionary Soldier in Philadelphia* is a short (79 pages) and simple book about a soldier's life. It was written during the Bicentennial to explain the everyday experiences of soldiers in and from Philadelphia. David Freeman Hawke's *Everyday Life in Early America* is broader in scope, discussing civilian life in the period.

Harold Leslie Peterson's *The Book of the Continental Soldier; Being a Compleat Account of the Uniforms, Weapons, and Equipment with Which He Lived and Fought* is a standard work on the clothing, equipment, and branches of the Continental Army. *A*

Respectable Army: The Military Origins of the Republic, 1763–1789 by James Kirby Martin and Mark Edward Lender is a general history of the war and its aftermath that synthesizes the work of several military historians who attempted to put the battles, leaders, and armies of the war in a broader political and social context.

Charles Royster's book, *A Revolutionary People at War: The Continental Army and American Character, 1775–1783*, makes us think about why men joined and stayed with the Continental Army despite terrible hardships.

A People's Army: Massachusetts Soldiers and Society in the Seven Years' War by Fred Anderson provides important information on diet, attitudes toward service, and the social structure of camp life. It focuses on the service of the Massachusetts militia during the Seven Years War (1754–1763), but there are obvious comparisons to be drawn with the Continental Army.

Every re-enactor needs to be familiar with the drills and manual of exercise adopted by his unit. Colonel Timothy Pickering (1745–1829) authored a manual which several American troops follow, but the most commonly used one, particularly after the winter at Valley Forge, was Friedrich Wilhelm Ludolf Gerhard Augustin Baron von Steuben's drill manual (*Baron von Steuben's Revolutionary War Drill Manual: A Facsimile Reprint of the 1794 Edition*). Von Steuben's drills proved so effective that at the Battle of Monmouth, the first battle after the winter at Valley Forge, American troops fought on equal footing with British Regulars, particularly with the bayonet. The Crown forces have other drill manuals, depending on whether they portray British, Hessian, or Loyalist forces.

A re-enactor should also have some knowledge of the history of the unit he helps portray. Robert K. Wright, Jr.'s *The Continental Army* provides a highly detailed organizational history of the army and includes a good bibliography of regimental histories that can identify other titles which may prove interesting. The "History and Historiography" chapter of Martin and Lender's *A Respectable Army* will also be useful.

APPENDIX 1

ALPHABETICAL LIST
OF BATTLES, ACTIONS, AND SKIRMISHES

This appendix lists the battles and actions of the war. Colonies are listed in the geographical order found elsewhere in this book. Within each colony, locations are arranged *alphabetically* with chronological data. It was compiled from several sources with Francis B. Heitman's *Historical Register of Officers of the Continental Army* (Washington, DC: The Rare Book Shop Publishing Company, Inc., 1914) serving as the primary source. Some battles, such as the First Battle of Saratoga (also known as the Battle of Freeman's Farm) or Bunker Hill (also known as Breed's Hill) have several names and appear under more than one designation to facilitate retrieval. There are more battles listed in the appendix than are covered in the text. This volume covers the major actions and some minor ones. The author is working on another volume that will cover the remaining engagements. The text covers places like Philadelphia, Valley Forge, Morristown, and Wethersfield that are important for the outcome of the War for American Independence but are not listed in this appendix.

Canada
Cedars, The, 19 May 1776
Fort Cumberland, Nova Scotia, 20 Nov. 1776
Fort St. John, 14 May 1775
Isle aux Noix, 24 June 1778
Montreal, 25 Sept. and 12 Nov. 1775
Plains of Abraham, 6 May 1776
Quebec, siege of, 8–31 Dec. 1775
Sorel, 19 Nov. 1775
Sorrel River, 24 July 1776
St. John's, 18 Sept. and 3 Nov. 1775
Three Rivers, 8 June 1776
Vandreuil, 26 May 1776

Maine
Falmouth, Massachusetts (Portland, Maine),
     18 Oct. 1775
Machias (naval), 12 June 1775
Penobscot Bay, 25 July 1779
Pownalborough, 1775, 1779

Vermont
Bennington, 16 Aug. 1777
Hubbardton, 7 July 1777

New York
Bedford, 2 July 1779
Bemis Heights, 19 Sept. 1777
Bronx, 22 Oct. 1776
Brookland, Long Island, 28 Aug. 1776
Brooklyn, 27 Aug. 1776
Bushwick, Long Island, 27 Aug. 1776
Cambridge, 13 Aug. 1777
Canajoharie, 2 Aug. 1780
Canandaigua, Sept. 1779
Catherine's Town, 31 Aug. 1779
Caughnawaga, 22 May 1780
Cayuga Lake raid, Sept. 1779
Chatterton's Hill (White Plains), 28 Oct. 1776
Chemung, 29 Aug. 1779; see Elmira
Cherry Valley, 11 Nov. 1778
Cobleskill, 1 June 1778
Coram, Long Island, 21 Nov. 1780
Croton River, 14 May 1781
Crown Point, 12 May 1775; 14 Oct. 1776; 16
     June 1777
Currytown, 9 July 1781
Diamond Island, 23 Sept. 1777
East Chester, 18 Jan. 1780

Elmira, 29 Aug. 1779
Esopus, 13 Oct. 1777
Flatbush, 22–23 Aug. 1780
Fort Anne, 8 July 1777
Fort Clinton, 6 Oct. 1777
Fort Cock-hill, 16 Nov. 1776
Fort Edward, 27 July 1777
Fort Dayton, Herkimer, 6 Aug. 1781
Fort George, 18 Nov. 1776; 11 Oct. 1780
Fort George, Long Island, 21 Nov. 1780
Fort Keyser, 19 Oct. 1780; see Stone Arabia
Fort Lafayette (Verplanck's Point), 1 June 1779
Fort Montgomery, 6 Oct. 1777
Fort Plain, 2 Aug. 1780; 7 Sept. 1781
Fort Schuyler (Fort Stanwix), 4–22 Aug. 1777
Fort Stanwix, 4–22 Aug. 1777
Fort St. George, Long Island, 23 Nov. 1780
Fort Ticonderoga, 10 May 1775; 6 July 1777
Fort Tryon, 16 Nov. 1776
Fort Washington, 16 Nov. 1776
Four Corners, 3 Feb. 1780
Fox's Mills, see Klock's Field
Freeman's Farm, 19 Sept. 1777
Geneseo, 14 Sept. 1779
German Flats, 29 Oct. 1780
Harlem Cove, 16 Nov. 1776
Harlem Heights, 16 Sept. 1776
Harlem Plains, 16 Sept. 1776
Harpersfield, 2 April 1780
Highlands, 24 March 1777
Indian Field and Bridge, 31 Aug. 1778
Jamaica, Long Island, 28 Aug. 1776
Jefferd's Neck, 7 Nov. 1779
Jerseyfield, 30 Oct. 1781
Johnson Hall, 24 Oct. 1781
Johnstown, 22 May 1780; 24 Oct. 1781
Kanassoraga, 23 Oct. 1780
King's Bridge, 17 Jan. 1777; 3 July 1781
Kingston (Esopus), 13 Oct. 1777
Kip's Bay, 15 Sept. 1776
Klock's Field (Fox's Mills), 21 Oct. 1780
Lake Champlain, 11–13 Oct. 1776
Lake George, 18 Sept. 1777
Lloyd's Neck, 5 Sept. 1779
Long Island, 27 Aug. 1776; 10 Dec. 1777
Mamaroneck, 21 Oct. 1778
Manhattanville, 18 Nov. 1776
Middleburg, 15 Oct. 1780
Minisink, 19–22 July 1779
Mohawk Valley, 2 Aug. 1780
Montressor's Island, 24 Sept. 1776
Morrisania, 5 Aug. 1779; 22 Jan. 1781;
    4 March 1782

Moses Kill, 2 Aug. 1777
Mount Washington (Washington Heights),
    8 Nov. 1776
New Rochelle, 18 Oct. 1776
Newtown, 29 Aug. 1779
New York City, attack on, 29 Aug. 1775;
    occupied by British Troops, 15 Sept. 1776 to
    25 Nov. 1783
North Hoosick, see Bennington, Vermont
Onondagas, 20 April 1779
Oriskany, 6 Aug. 1777
Peekskill, 22 March 1777
Pelham Manor, 18 Oct. 1776
Pell's Point, 18 Oct. 1776
Phillips Heights, 16 Sept. 1778
Poundridge, 2 July 1779
Sagg Harbor, 23 May 1777
Saratoga, 7–17 Oct. 1777; see also Freeman's
    Farm and Bemis Heights
Schoharie, 17 Oct. 1780
Sharon Spring Swamp, 6 Aug. 1781
Skenesborough, 7 July 1777
Smith's Point, 23 Nov. 1780
Staten Island, 21 and 22 Aug. 1777
Stillwater, 19 Sept. and 7 Oct. 1777
Stone Arabia, 19 Oct. 1780
Stony Point, 1 June and 16 July 1779
Tappan, 28 Sept. 1778
Tarrytown, 30 Aug. 1779; 15 July 1781
Threadwell's Neck (Treadwell's), 10 Oct. 1781
Throg's Neck, 12 Oct. 1776
Valcour Island, 11 Oct. 1776
Valley Grove, Long Island, 26 Aug. 1776
Verplanck's Point (Fort Lafayette), 1 June 1779
Ward's House, 16 March 1777
Warwarsing, 22 Aug. 1781
Washington Heights, see Mount Washington
West Canada Creek, 30 Oct. 1781
West Chester, 16 Sept. 1778
West Chester County, 16 March 1777
West Farms, 25 Jan. 1777
White Plains, 28 Oct. 1776
Young's House, 25 Dec. 1778; 3 Feb. 1780

Massachusetts
Boston, siege of, 17 June 1775 to 17 March
    1776
Breeds Hill (Bunker Hill), 17 June 1775
Bunker Hill (Breeds Hill), 17 June. 1775
Charlestown, 8 Jan. 1776
Concord, 19 April 1775
Dorchester Heights, 4–17 March 1776
Falmouth (Portland, Maine), 18 Oct. 1775

Gloucester, 13 Aug. 1775
Grape Island, 21 May 1775
Great Brewster Island (Light House Island),
    31 July 1779
Hog Island, 28 May 1775
Lechmere Point, 9 Nov. 1775
Lexington, 19 April 1775
Martha's Vineyard, 5 May 1775
Nantasket Point raid, 21 July 1775
Noddles Island, 27 May 1775
Nooks Hill, 8 March 1776
Phipp's Farm, 9 Nov. 1775
Plowed Hill, 8 Aug. 1780
Roxbury, 8 July 1775
Salem raid, 26 Feb. 1775

Rhode Island
Block Island, 6 April 1776
Bristol, 7 Oct. 1775; 24 May 1778
Butts Hill, 29 Aug. 1778
Dutch Island, 2 Aug. 1777
Fogland Ferry, 10 Jan. 1777
Narragansett Bay raids, late 1775–1776
Newport (naval), 10 Aug. 1778
North Ferry, 5 Aug. 1777
Prudence Island, 12–14 Jan. 1776; 4 Sept. 1777
Quaker Hill, 29 Aug. 1778
Rhode Island, 29 Aug. 1778
Sakonnet Passage (naval battle of Rhode Island),
    5 Aug. 1778
Tiverton, 31 May 1778
Warren raid, 24 May 1778; late April 1781

Connecticut
Compo Hill, 28 April 1777
Danbury Raid, 25–27 April 1777
Fairfield, 8 July 1779
Fort Griswold, 6 Sept. 1781
Green's Farms, 9 July 1779
Greenwich, 19 June 1779
Groton Hill, 6 Sept. 1781; see Fort Griswold
Horseneck, 26 Feb. 1779; 9 Dec. 1780
New Haven, 5 July 1779
New London, 6 Sept. 1781
Norwalk, 12 July 1779
Ridgefield (Danbury), 27 April 1777
Stonington, 30 Sept. 1775.
West Greenwich, 26 March 1779
West Haven, 1 Sept. 1781

New Jersey
Amboy, 8 March 1777
Ash Swamp, 26 June 1777; see Short Hills

Assunpink Bridge, 2 Jan. 1777
Bergen, 19 July 1780
Block House, 21 July 1780; see Bull's Ferry
Bordentown, 8 May 1778
Bound Brook, 13 April 1777
Brunswick, 1 Dec. 1776; 26 Oct. 1779
Bull's Ferry, 21 July 1780
Chestnut Creek, 6 Oct. 1778
Connecticut Farms, 7–23 June 1780
Egg Harbor, 15 Oct. 1778
Elizabethtown, 25 Jan. and 6 June 1780
Fort Lee, 18 Nov. 1776
Fort Mercer, 22 Oct. 1777
Hackensack raid, 14 Dec. 1776
Hancock's Bridge, 21 March 1778
Herringtown, 28 Sept. 1778
Jersey City, 18 July 1779; see Paulus (Powles)
    Hook
Middletown, 27 April 1779; 12 June 1780
Millstone (Somerset Courthouse), 22 January
    and 17 June 1777
Mincock Island, 15 Oct. 1778
Monmouth, 28 June 1778
Mount Holly, 21 Dec. 1776; March 1781
New Bridge, 15 April 1780
New Brunswick, 19 June 1777
Newark, 25 Jan. 1780
Paramus (now Ridgewood), 22 March and
    16 April 1780
Paulus Hook (Powles Hook), 19 Aug. 1779
Princeton, 3 Jan. 1777
Quinton's Bridge, 18 March 1778
Rahway Meadow, 26 June 1781
Red Bank, 22 Oct. 1777
Short Hills (Ash Swamp), 26 June 1777
Somerset Court-House, 20 Jan. 1777
South River Bridge, Hillsborough, 25 Oct.
    1779
Springfield, 17 Dec. 1776; 23 June 1780
Tinton Falls raid, 26 April 1779
Tom's River, 19 July 1780
Trenton, 26 Dec. 1776; 2 Jan. 1777
Weehawken, 19 Aug. 1779
Woodbridge, 19 April 1777

Pennsylvania
Barren Hill, 20 May 1778
Black Horse Tavern (Bryn Mawr, Harrington
    House, or Rebel Hill), 11 Dec. 1777
Brandywine, 11 Sept. 1777
Bryn Mawr, see Black Horse Tavern
Bristol, 17 April 1778
Chadd's Ford (Brandywine), 11 Sept. 1777

Chestnut Hill, 6 Dec. 1777
Crooked Billet (now Hatboro), 1 May 1778
Edge Hill, 7 Dec. 1777
Fort Mifflin, 23 Oct. and 10–15 Nov. 1777
Germantown, 4 Oct. 1777
Gulphs Mill, 11 Dec. 1777
Harrington House, see Black Horse Tavern
Paoli, 20 Sept. 1777
Philadelphia, occupied by the British, 26 Sept.
    1777 to 18 June 1778
Rebel Hill, see Black Horse Tavern
Washington's Crossing, 28 Dec. 1776
White Horse Tavern or Warren Tavern, 16 Sept.
    1777
Whitemarsh, 5–8 Dec. 1777
Wyoming, 1–4 July 1778

Illinois

Fort Kaskaskia, Ellis Grove, 4 July 1778
Fort Massac, Metropolis, summer, 1778

Indiana

Vincennes, 17 Dec. 1778; 25 Feb. 1779

Kentucky

Blue Licks, 19 Aug. 1782

Delaware

Cooch's Bridge, 3 Sept. 1777
Iron Hill, see Cooch's Bridge

Maryland

Saint George's Island raid, 16 July 1776

Virginia

Charles City Court-House, 8 Jan. 1781
Charlottesville, Raid on, 4 June 1781
Chesapeake Bay, 8–10 July 1776
Chesapeake Bay, Virginia Capes (Yorktown
    Campaign, naval battle), 5 Sept. 1781
Fort Nelson, 9 May 1779
Gosport, Portsmouth (Hampton Roads),
    16 May 1779
Great Bridge, 9 Dec. 1775
Green Spring, 6 July 1781
Gwyn's (or Gwynn's) Island, Chesapeake Bay,
    8–10 July 1776
Hampton, 2 Sept. 1775; 24 Oct. 1775
Jamestown Ford, see Green Spring
Kemp's Landing, 14 Nov. 1775
Norfolk, 1 Jan. 1776; 9 May 1779
Osborne's, 27 April 1781
Petersburg, 25 April 1781

Point of Fork (Fork Union), 1 June 1781
Richmond, 5 Jan. 1781
Spencer's Ordinary (Tavern), 28 June 1781
Westham raid, 5 Jan. 1781
Wheeling, Virginia (now West Virginia), 1 Sept.
    1777; 26–28 Sept. 1778
Yorktown, 28 September to 19 Oct. 1781

North Carolina

Bruce's Cross.Roads, 12 Feb. 1781
Cane Creek, 12 Sept. 1780; 13 Sept. 1781
Clapp's Mill, 2 March 1781
Cowan's Ford, 1 Feb. 1781
Earle's Ford, 15 July 1780
Guilford, 15 March 1781
Hart's Mill, Jan. 1781
Haw River, see Pyles' Defeat
Hillsborough, 25 April 1781
King's Mountain, 7 Oct. 1780
Lindley's Mill, 13 Sept. 1781; see Cane Creek
Moore's Creek Bridge, 27 Feb. 1776
Pacolett River, 14 July 1780
Pyles' Defeat, 25 Feb. 1781
Ramsour's Mill, 20 June 1780
Shallow Ford, 6 Feb. 1781
Tarrant's (Torrence's) Tavern, 1 Feb. 1781
Tearcoat Swamp, 25 Oct. 1780
Watagua, July 1776
Wetsell's (Wetzell's or Whitsall's) Mills, 6 March
    1781
Wilmington, 1 Feb. 1781

South Carolina

Barton's Post, Colleton City, 8 April 1781
Beach (or Beech) Island, Aiken City, 15 May
    1781
Beaufort, 10 Aug. 1776; 3 Feb. 1779; see Port
    Royal
Beattie's Mill, 21 March 1781
Beckhamville, near Great Falls, Chester County,
    6 June 1780
Bee's Plantation, 23 March 1780
Bellevue Plantation, 22 Feb. 1781
Biggin Church, 17 July 1781
Biggin's Bridge, Moncks Corner, Berkeley
    County, 14 April 1780
Black Mingo, 14 April 1780
Black Mingo Creek, 14 Sept. 1780
Black River, 25 Oct. 1780
Black Stoks (Blackstock), near Cross Keys,
    Union County, 20 Nov. 1780
Blue Savannah, Little Pee Dee River, 4 Sept.
    1780

Bowling Green, Marion County, 3 June 1782.

Brandon's Camp, Union County, 12 July 1780

Brattonville, 12 July 1780

Brierly's Ferry or Ford, 18 Nov. 1780

Broad River, 12 Nov. 1780

Bryan's Station, South Carolina (now Kentucky), 15 Aug. 1782

Buford Massacre (Waxhaws), near Lancaster, Lancaster County, 29 May 1780

Camden, Kershaw County, 16 Aug. 1780; 25 April and 10 May 1781

Cane Brake, 22 Dec. 1775

Capers' Scout, Berkeley County, 9 April 1780

Catawba Ford, 18 Aug. 1780

Cedar Springs, 13 July and 8 Aug. 1780

Charleston, siege of, 11–13 May 1779 and 29 March to 12 May 1780; sortie from 24 April 1780; occupied by the British, 12 May 1780 to 14 Dec. 1782

Charleston Neck, 11 May 1779

Charlestown Road, Berkeley County, 31 Aug. 1781

Cheraw, Great Pee Dee River, Chesterfield County, 20 Dec. 1780 to 28 Jan. 1781

Cherokee Ford, Savannah River, 14 Feb. 1779

Cherokee Indian Town, 13 July 1780

Clouds Creek, 7 Nov. 1781

Combahee Ferry, 27 Aug. 1782

Coosawhatchie, Coosawhatchie, Jasper County, 11–13 May 1779

Cowpens, Cherokee County, 17 Jan. 1781

Cunningham's Raid, Laurens County, 1 Aug. 1781

Dean Swamp, near Salley, Aiken County, 24 May 1782

De Peyster's (or De Peister's) Capture, 19 Jan. 1781

Dorchester, 1 and 29 Dec. 1781; 24 April 1782

Dutchman's Creek, Fairfield County, March 1781

Eggleston's Capture, Lexington County, 8 July 1781

Esseneca Town, Seneca Old Town, Pickens County, 1 Aug. 1778; see Seneca

Eutaw Springs, Eutawville, Orangeburg County, 8 Sept. 1781

Fair Lawn, Moncks Corner, Berkeley County, 27 Nov. 1781

Fish Dam Ford, near Carlisle, Chester County, 9 Nov. 1780

Fishing Creek, 18 Aug. 1780

Flat Rock, 20 July 1780

Fork of Edisto, Orangeburg County, Aug. 1781

Fort Balfour, 12 April 1781

Fort Carey (Camden), 15 Aug. 1780

Fort Charlotte, 12 July 1775

Fort Dorchester, near Summerville, Dorchester County, 1 Dec. 1781

Fort Dreadnought, see Fort Galphin

Fort Galphin, near Jackson, Aiken County, 21 May 1781

Fort Granby (now Columbia), 15 May 1781

Fort Johnson, 14 Sept. 1775

Fort Motte, near Fort Motte, Calhoun County, 12 May 1781

Fort Moultrie, 28 June 1776; 7 May 1780

Fort Prince/McDowell's Camp, near Wellford, Spartanburg County, 15 July 1780

Fort Sullivan, 28 and 29 June 1776

Fort Thickety, 30 July 1780

Fort Watson, near Summerton, Clarendon County, 15–23 April 1781

Four Holes, 7 and 15 April 1781

Friday's (or Fridig's) Ferry, Richland County, 1 May 1782

Georgetown, 24 Jan. 1781

Gibson's Meeting House, see Mobley's Meeting House

Gowen's Old Fort, near Gowensville, Spartanburg County, 13 July 1780; 1 May 1781

Gowen's Fort (Prince's Fort), Greenville County, Nov. 1781.

Great Cane Brake, near Simpsonville, Greenville County, 22 Dec. 1775

Great Savannah, 20 Aug. 1780; see Nelson's Ferry

Green Spring, 1 Aug. 1780

Gum Swamp, 16 Aug. 1780

Haddrell's Point, 1780

Halfway Swamp, near Rimini, Clarendon County, 12 Dec. 1780; see Singleton's Mill

Hammond's Mill, Edgefield County, April 1781

Hammond's Store, Abbeville County, 28 Dec. 1780

Hanging Rock, near Heath Springs, Lancaster County, 1–6 Aug. 1780

Hayes' Station, near Joanna, Laurens County, 9 Nov. 1781

Hobkirk Hill, near Camden, Kershaw County, 25 April 1781

Horner's Creek or Corner, April 1781

Hunts Bluff, near Blenheim, Marlboro County, 1 Aug. 1780

Indian Villages, Oconee County, March 1782

James Island, July 1782

John's Island, 4 Nov. 1782

Winnsboro, 29 May 1780

Witherspoon's Ferry, Georgetown County, March 1781

Wofford's Iron Works, 8 Aug. 1780

Wright's Bluff (Fort Watson), 27 Feb. 1781

Georgia

Augusta, 29 Jan. 1779; 14–18 Sept. 1780; 22 May to 5 June 1781.

Brewton Hill, 29 Dec. 1778, see Savannah

Briar Creek, 3 March 1779

Bulltown Swamp, Savannah, 19 Nov. 1778

Cherokee Ford, 10 Feb. 1778

Ebenezer, 23 June 1782

Fort Anderson (Fort Thickety), 23 July 1780

Fort Cars (Carrs, Kerrs), 10 Feb. 1779

Fort Cornwallis, 14 Sept. 1780; 5 June 1781

Fort Darien, late 1778 to early 1779

Fort Dreadnought (Fort Galphin), 21 May 1781

Fort Galphin, 21 May 1781

Fort Grierson, 14 Sept. 1780; 24 May 1781

Fort McIntosh, 2–4 Feb. 1777

Fort Morris, 9 Jan. 1779

Fort Thickety, 23 July 1780

Frederika (Rebecca & Hinchinbrook), 19 April 1778

Hickory Hill, 28 June 1779

Hutchinson's Island (Battle of the Rice Boats), 7 March 1778

Kettle Creek, 14 Feb. 1779

Medway Church (Midway), 24 Nov. 1778

Ogeechee Road, 21 May 1782

Savannah, occupied by British troops, 29 Dec. 1778 to 11 July 1782; siege of, 23 Sept. to 18 Oct. 1779

Sharon, Georgia (near), 24 May 1782

Spencer's Hill, 19 Nov. 1778

Spring Hill Redoubt, Savannah, 1779

Sunbury, 6–9 Jan. 1779

White House, 15 Sept. 1780

Wiggins Hill, April 1781

Yamacrow Bluff (Savannah), 4 March 1776

Florida

Alligator Bridge, 30 June 1778

Amelia Island, 18 May 1777

Pensacola, 9 May 1781

Thomas Creek, 17 May 1777

Miscellaneous

Cherokee Campaign of 1776, 1 July to 19 Sept. 1776

Cherokee Campaign of 1782

Fort Saint Joseph, Detroit, Michigan, 12 Feb. 1781

Mobile, Alabama, 9 Feb. 1780

Nassau raids, Bahamas, 3–4 March 1776

Piqua, Ohio, 8 Aug. 1780

Saint Louis, Missouri, 26 May 1780

Sandusky (Upper Sandusky), Ohio, 4 June 1782

Upper Sandusky, Ohio, 4 June 1782

Whitehaven naval raid, England, 27–28 Sept. 1778

APPENDIX 2

CHRONOLOGICAL LIST
OF BATTLES, ACTIONS, AND SKIRMISHES

This appendix reorganizes the alphabetical list of Appendix 1 in chronological order. There are more battles listed in the appendix than are covered in the text. This volume covers the major actions and some minor ones. The author is working on another volume that will cover the remaining engagements.

1775
1775, Pownalborough, Maine
Feb.   26, Salem (raid), Massachusetts
April   19, Concord, Massachusetts
         19, Lexington, Massachusetts
May   5, Martha's Vineyard, Massachusetts
         6, Plains of Abraham, Canada
         10, Fort Ticonderoga, New York
         12, Crown Point, New York
         14, Fort St. John, Canada
         21, Grape Island, Massachusetts
         27, Noddles Island, Massachusetts
         28, Hog Island, Massachusetts
June   12, Machias (naval), Maine
         17, Bunker Hill (Breed's Hill), Massachusetts
         17 to March 17, 1776, Boston (siege),
            Massachusetts
July   2, Fort Charlotte, South Carolina
         8, Roxbury, Massachusetts
         21, Nantasket Point (raid), Massachusetts
         24, Sorrel River, Canada
Aug.   13, Gloucester, Massachusetts
         29, New York City (attack), New York
Sept.   2, Hampton, Virginia
         14, Fort Johnson, South Carolina
         18, St. John's, Canada
         25, Montreal, Canada
         30, Stonington, Connecticut
Oct.   7, Bristol, Rhode Island
         18, Falmouth, Massachusetts (Portland,
            Maine)
         24, Hampton, Virginia
Nov.   3, St. John's, Canada
         9, Lechmere Point (Phipp's Farm),
            Massachusetts
         12, Montreal, Canada

         14, Kemp's Landing, Virginia
         19, Sorel, Canada
         19–26, Ninety-Six, Greenwood County,
            South Carolina
Dec.   8–31, Quebec (siege), Canada
         9, Great Bridge, Virginia
         22, Cane Brake, near Simpsonville,
            Greenville County, South Carolina
late 1775–1776, Narragansett Bay (raids),
            Rhode Island

1776
Jan.   1, Norfolk, Virginia
         8, Charlestown, Massachusetts
         12–14, Prudence Island, Rhode Island
Feb.   27, Moore's Creek Bridge, North
            Carolina
March   3–4, Nassau (raids), Bahamas
         4, Yamacrow Bluff, Georgia
         4–17, Dorchester Heights, Massachusetts
         8, Nook's Hill, Massachusetts
April   6, Block Island, Rhode Island
May   19, Cedars, Canada
         26, Vandreuil, Canada
June   7, Watagua, North Carolina
         8, Three Rivers, Canada
         28, Fort Moultrie, South Carolina
         28–29, Fort Sullivan, South Carolina
July   1 to Sept. 19, 1776, Cherokee Campaign
            of 1776
         8–10, Chesapeake Bay, Virginia
         8–10, Gwyn's Island, Virginia
         15, Rayborn Creek, South Carolina, see
            Lyndley's Fort, South Carolina
         15, Lyndley's Fort, near Laurens,
            Laurens County, South Carolina

16, Saint George's Island (raid), Maryland

Aug. 1, Oconore, South Carolina

1, Seneca, South Carolina

10, Beaufort, South Carolina (Port Royal, South Carolina)

11, Ring Fight, near Tamassee, Oconee County, South Carolina

11, Tomassy, South Carolina

26, Valley Grove, New York

27, Brooklyn, New York

27, Bushwick, New York

27, Long Island, New York

28, Brookland, New York

28, Chatterton's Hill, New York

28, Jamaica, New York

Sept. 15, Kip's Bay, New York

15 to Nov. 25, 1783, New York City (occupation), New York

16, Harlem Heights (and Plains), New York

24, Montressor's Island, New York

Oct. 11, Valcour Island, New York

11–13, Lake Champlain, New York

12, Throg's Neck, New York

14, Crown Point, New York

16, Harlem Heights, New York

18, Pelham Manor, New York

18, Pell's Point, New York

22, Bronx, New York

28, White Plains, New York

Nov. 8, Mount Washington (Washington Heights), New York

16, Fort Cock-hill, New York

16, Fort Tryon, New York

16, Fort Washington, New York

16, Harlem Cove, New York

18, Fort George, New York

18, Fort Lee, New Jersey

18, Manhattanville, New York

20, Fort Cumberland, Canada

Dec. 1, Brunswick, New Jersey

14, Hackensack (raid), New Jersey

17, Springfield, New Jersey

21, Mount Holly, New Jersey

26, Trenton, New Jersey (Washington's Crossing, Pennsylvania)

1777

Jan. 2, Assunpink Bridge, New Jersey

2, Trenton, New Jersey

3, Princeton, New Jersey

10, Fogland Ferry, Rhode Island

17, King's Bridge, New York

20, Somerset Courthouse, New Jersey

22, Millstone (Somerset Courthouse), New Jersey

25, West Farms, New York

Feb. 2–4, Fort McIntosh, Georgia

March 8, Amboy, New Jersey

16, Ward's House, New York

16, West Chester County, New York

22, Peekskill, New York

24, Highlands, New York

April 13, Bound Brook, New Jersey

19, Woodbridge, New Jersey

25–27, Danbury (raid), Connecticut

27, Ridgefield (Danbury), Connecticut

28, Compo Hill, Connecticut

May 17, Thomas Creek, Florida

18, Amelia Island, Florida

23, Sagg Harbor, New York

June 16, Crown Point, New York

17, Millstone (Somerset Courthouse), New Jersey

19, New Brunswick, New Jersey

26, Ash Swamp, New Jersey

26, Short Hills (Ash Swamp), New Jersey

July 6, Fort Ticonderoga, New York

7, Hubbardton, Vermont

7, Skenesborough, New York

8, Fort Anne, New York

27, Fort Edward, New York

Aug. 2, Dutch Island, Rhode Island

2, Moses Kill, New York

4–22, Fort Schuyler (Fort Stanwix), New York

4–22, Fort Stanwix, New York

5, North Ferry, Rhode Island

6, Oriskany, New York

13, Cambridge, New York

16, Bennington, Vermont

21–22, Staten Island, New York

Sept. 1, Brandywine, Pennsylvania

1, Wheeling, Virginia (now West Virginia)

3, Cooch's Bridge (Iron Hill), Delaware

4, Prudence Island, Rhode Island

11, Chadd's Ford (Brandywine), Pennsylvania

16, White Horse Tavern or Warren Tavern (Battle in the Clouds), Pennsylvania

18, Lake George, New York

19, Bemis Heights, New York

19, Freeman's Farm, New York
19, Stillwater, New York
20, Paoli, Pennsylvania
23, Diamond Island, New York
26 to June 18, 1778, Philadelphia (occupation), Pennsylvania
Oct.   4, Germantown, Pennsylvania
6, Fort Clinton, New York
6, Fort Montgomery, New York
7, Stillwater, New York
7–17, Saratoga, New York
13, Esopus, New York
13, Kingston, New York
22, Fort Mercer, New Jersey
22, Red Bank, New Jersey
23, Fort Mifflin, Pennsylvania
Dec.   5–8, Whitemarsh, Pennsylvania
6, Chestnut Hill, Pennsylvania
7, Edge Hill, Pennsylvania
10, Long Island, New York
11, Black Horse Tavern (Bryn Mawr, Harrington House, or Rebel Hill), Pennsylvania
11, Gulphs Mill, Pennsylvania

1778

Feb.   10, Cherokee Ford, Georgia
March 7, Hutchinson's Island (Battle of the Rice Boats), Georgia
18, Quinton's Bridge, New Jersey
21, Hancock's Bridge, New Jersey
April 1–4, Wyoming, Pennsylvania
17, Bristol, Pennsylvania
19, Frederika, Georgia (Rebecca & Hinchinbrook)
May   1, Crooked Billet, Pennsylvania
8, Bordentown, New Jersey
20, Barren Hill, Pennsylvania
24, Bristol, Rhode Island
24, Warren raid, Rhode Island
31, Tiverton, Rhode Island
June   1, Cobleskill, New York
24, Isle aux Noix, Canada
28, Monmouth, New Jersey
30, Alligator Bridge, Florida
July   4, Fort Kaskaskia, Illinois
Aug.   1, Essenecca Town, Seneca Old Town, Pickens County, South Carolina
10, Newport (naval), Rhode Island
29, Butts Hill, Rhode Island (Battle of Rhode Island)
29, Quaker Hill, Rhode Island (Battle of Rhode Island)

29, Sakonnet Passage (naval battle of Rhode Island), Rhode Island
31, Indian Field and Bridge, New York
summer, Fort Massac, Illinois
Sept. 16, Phillip's Heights, New York
16, West Chester, New York
18, Herringtown, New Jersey
26–28, Wheeling, Virginia (now West Virginia)
27–28, Whitehaven (naval raid), England
28, Tappan, New York
Oct.   6, Chestnut Creek, New Jersey
15, Egg Harbor, New Jersey
15, Mincock Island, New Jersey
21, Mamaroneck, New York
Nov.   11, Cherry Valley, New York
19, Bulltown Swamp, Georgia
19, Spencer's Hill, Georgia
24, Medway (Midway) Church, Georgia
Dec.   17, Vincennes, Indiana
25, Young's House, New York
29, Brewton Hill, Georgia
29 to July 11, 1782, Savannah (occupation), Georgia
late 1778 to early 1779, Fort Darien, Georgia

1779

1779, Pownalborough, Maine
Jan.   6–9, Sunbury, Georgia
9, Fort Morris, Georgia
29, Augusta, Georgia
Feb.   3, Beaufort, South Carolina (Port Royal Island) South Carolina
10, Fort Cars (Carrs, Kerrs), Georgia
14, Cherokee Ford, Savannah River, South Carolina
14, Kettle Creek, Georgia
25, Vincennes, Indiana
26, Horseneck, Connecticut
March 3, Briar Creek, Georgia
26, West Greenwich, Connecticut
April 20, Onandagas, New York
26, Tinton Falls (raid), New Jersey
27, Middletown, New Jersey
May   9, Fort Nelson, Virginia
9, Norfolk, Virginia
11, Charleston Neck, South Carolina
11–13, Charleston (siege), South Carolina
11–13, Coosawhatchie, Coosawhatchie, Jasper County, South Carolina
16, Gosport (Hampton Roads), Portsmouth, Virginia

June   1, Fort Lafayette (Verplanck's Point),
          New York
       1, Stony Point, New York
       19, Greenwich, Connecticut
       20, Stono Ferry, near Rantowles,
          Charleston County, South Carolina
July   2, Bedford, New York
       2, Poundridge, New York
       5, New Haven, Connecticut
       8, Fairfield, Connecticut
       9, Green's Farms, Connecticut
       16, Stony Point, New York
       18, Jersey City, New Jersey
       19–22, Minisink, New York
       25, Penobscot Bay, Maine
       31, Great Brewster Island (Light House
          Island), Massachusetts
Aug.   5, Morrisania, New York
       19, Paulus Hook (Powles Hook), New
          Jersey
       19, Weehawken, New Jersey
       29, Chemung, New York
       29, Elmira, New York
       29, Newtown, New York
       30, Tarrytown, New York
       31, Catherine's Town, New York
Sept. Canandaigua, New York
       Cayuga Lake, Raid, New York
       5, Lloyd's Neck, New York
       14, Geneseo, New York
       23 to Oct. 18, 1779, Savannah (siege),
          Georgia
Oct.   9, Spring Hill Redoubt, Georgia
       25, South River Bridge, New Jersey
       26, Brunswick, New Jersey
Nov.   7, Jefferd's Neck, New York

1780
1780, Haddrell's Point, South Carolina
Jan.   18, East Chester, New York
       25, Elizabethtown, New Jersey
       25, Newark, New Jersey
Feb.   3, Four Corners, New York
       3, Young's House, New York
       9, Mobile, Alabama
March 8, Salkahatchie, South Carolina
       22, Paramus, New Jersey
       23, Bee's Plantation, South Carolina
       23, Pon Pon, South Carolina
       27, Rentowle, South Carolina
       29 to May 12, 1780, Charleston (siege),
          South Carolina
April 2, Harpersfield, New York

       9, Capers' Scout, Berkeley County,
          South Carolina
       9, Port's Ferry, Richland County, South
          Carolina
       14, Biggin's Bridge, Moncks Corner,
          Berkeley County, South Carolina
       14, Black Mingo, South Carolina
       14, Monck's Corner, South Carolina
       15, New Bridge, New Jersey
       16, Paramus, New Jersey
       24, Charleston (sortie), South Carolina
May   6, Lenud's (Le Nud's or Lanneau's)
          Ferry, Jamestown, Berkeley County,
          South Carolina
       8, Sullivan's Island, South Carolina
       12 to Dec. 14, 1782, Charleston
          (occupation), South Carolina
       18, Le Nud's Ferry, South Carolina
       22, Caughnawaga, New York
       22, Johnstown, New York
       26, Saint Louis, Missouri
       29, Buford's Massacre (Waxhaws), near
          Lancaster, Lancaster County, South
          Carolina
       29, Waxhaws, near Lancaster, Lancaster
          County, South Carolina
       29, Winnsboro, South Carolina
June   Mobley's (or Gibson's) Meetinghouse,
          South Carolina
       6, Beckhamville, near Great Falls,
          Chester County, South Carolina
       6, Elizabethtown, New Jersey
       7–23, Connecticut Farms, New Jersey
       12, Middletown, New Jersey
       20, Ramsour's Mill, North Carolina
       23, Springfield, New Jersey
July   12, Brandon's Camp, South Carolina
       12, Brattonville, South Carolina
       12, Stallions, South Carolina
       12, Williamson's Plantation, Brattons-
          ville, York County, South Carolina
       13, Cedar Springs, South Carolina
       13, Cherokee Indian Town, South
          Carolina
       13, Gowen's Old Fort, near Gowensville,
          Spartanburg County, South Carolina
       14, Pacolett River, North Carolina
       15, Earle's Ford, North Carolina
       15–16, Fort Prince/McDowell's or
          McDonnell's Camp, near Wellford,
          Spartanburg County, South Carolina
       19, Bergen, New Jersey
       19, Tom's River, New Jersey

20, Flat Rock, South Carolina

21, Block House (Bull's Ferry), New
    Jersey

23, Fort Anderson (Fort Thickety),
    Georgia

23, Fort Thickety, Georgia

30, Fort Thickety, South Carolina

30, Rocky Mount, near Great Falls,
    Fairfield County, South Carolina

Aug.   1, Green Spring, South Carolina

1, Hunt's Bluff, near Blenheim,
    Marlboro County, South Carolina

1–6, Hanging Rock, near Heath
    Springs, Lancaster County, South
    Carolina

2, Canajoharie, New York

2, Fort Plain, New York

2, Mohawk Valley, New York

2, Murray's Ferry, South Carolina

8, Cedar Springs, South Carolina

8, Old Iron Works (2nd Cedar Springs),
    South Carolina

8, Piqua, Ohio

8, Plowed Hill, Massachusetts

8, Wofford's Iron Works, South Carolina

15, Fort Carey (Camden), South
    Carolina

15, Wateree, Ford of the, South
    Carolina

16, Camden, Kershaw County, South
    Carolina

16, Gum Swamp, South Carolina

18, Catawba Ford, South Carolina

18, Fishing Creek, South Carolina

19, Musgrove's Mills, near Cross
    Anchor, Spartanburg County, South
    Carolina

20, Great Savannah, South Carolina

20, Nelson's Ferry, South Carolina

22–23, Flatbush, New York

27, Kingstree, South Carolina

Sept.   4, Blue Savannah, Little Pee Dee River,
    South Carolina

4, Tarcote, South Carolina

12, Cane Creek, North Carolina

14, Black Mingo Creek, South Carolina

14, Fort Cornwallis, Georgia

14, Fort Grierson, Georgia

14–18, Augusta, Georgia

15, White House, Georgia

21, Wahab's Plantation, South Carolina

Oct.   7, King's Mountain, near Blacksburg,
    York County, North Carolina

11, Fort George, New York

15, Middleburg, New York

17, Schoharie, New York

19, Stone Arabia (Fort Keyser), New
    York

21, Klocks Field (Fox's Mills), New York

23, Kanassoraga, New York

25, Black River, South Carolina

25, Tarcote (or Tearcoat) Swamp, North
    Carolina

29, German Flats, New York

Nov.   9, Fish Dam Ford, near Carlisle, Chester
    County, South Carolina

12, Broad River, South Carolina

15, White's Bridge, South Carolina

18, Brierly's Ferry or Ford, South
    Carolina

20, Black Stoks (Blackstock), Cross
    Keys, Union County, South Carolina

20, Tiger River, South Carolina

21, Coram, New York

21, Fort George, New York

23, Fort St. George, New York

23, Smith's Point, New York

Dec.   4, Rugeley's Mills, Clermont, South
    Carolina

9, Horseneck, Connecticut

11, Long Cane, near Troy, McCormick
    County, South Carolina

12, Halfway Swamp, near Rimini,
    Clarendon County, South Carolina

20 to 28 Jan., 1781, Cheraw, Great Pee
    Dee River, Chesterfield County,
    South Carolina

28, Hammond's Store, South Carolina

31, Williamson's Plantation, Brattons-
    ville, York County, South Carolina

1781

Jan.   Hart's Mill, North Carolina

Sampit Road, South Carolina

5, Richmond, Virginia

5, Westham (raid), Virginia

8, Charles City Courthouse, Virginia

14, Waccamaw Neck, South Carolina

17, Cowpens, Cherokee County, South
    Carolina

19, De Peyster's Capture, South
    Carolina

22, Morrisania, New York

24, Georgetown, South Carolina

24, Singleton's Mill—Halfway Swamp,
    South Carolina

24, Wadboo (Wiboo, Wyboo, Watboo), South Carolina

Feb. 1, Cowan's Ford, North Carolina

1, Tarrant's Tavern, North Carolina

1, Torrence's Tavern, North Carolina

1, Wilmington, North Carolina

6, Shallow Ford, North Carolina

12, Bruce's Cross Roads, North Carolina

12, Fort Saint Joseph, Michigan

22, Bellevue Plantation, South Carolina

23, Thompson's Plantation, South Carolina

25, Pyle's Defeat, (Haw River) North Carolina

27, Wright's Bluff (Fort Watson), South Carolina

March Dutchman's Creek, South Carolina

Lower Bridge, Black River, Williamsburg County, South Carolina

Mount Holly, New Jersey

Sampit Bridge, South Carolina

Witherspoon's Ferry, South Carolina

2, Clapp's Mill, North Carolina

2, Mud Lick, South Carolina

6, Lynch's Creek, South Carolina

6, Wetsel's (Wetzell's or Whitsall's) Mills, North Carolina

6, Wiboo Swamp, South Carolina

9, Mount Hope Swamp, near Greeleyville, Williamsburg County, South Carolina

15, Guilford, North Carolina

21, Beattie's Mill, South Carolina

late March, Snow Island, Johnsonville, Marion (Florence) County, South Carolina

April Four Holes, South Carolina

Hammond's Mill, South Carolina

Horner's Creek or Corner, South Carolina

Mathew's Bluff, South Carolina

Wiggins Hill, South Carolina

7–15, Four Holes, South Carolina

8, Barton's Post, South Carolina

8, Pocotaligo Road, South Carolina

9, Waxhaws Church, near Lancaster, Lancaster County, South Carolina

12, Fort Balfour, South Carolina

15–23, Fort Watson, near Summerton, Clarendon County, South Carolina

25, Camden, Kershaw County, South Carolina

25, Hillsoborough, North Carolina

25, Hobkirk's Hill, near Camden, Kershaw County, South Carolina

25, Petersburg, Virginia

27, Osborne's, Virginia

late April, Warren (raid), Rhode Island

May 1, Gowan's (or Gowen's) Old Fort, South Carolina

7, Fort Moultrie, near Gowensville, Spartanburg County, South Carolina

9, Pensacola, Florida

10, Camden, Kershaw County, South Carolina

11, Orangeburg, South Carolina

12, Fort Motte, near Fort Motte, Calhoun County, South Carolina

14, Croton River, New York

14, Nelson's Ferry, South Carolina

15, Beach Island, South Carolina

15, Fort Granby, South Carolina

21, Fort Dreadnought (Fort Galphin), Georgia

21, Fort Galphin, near Jackson, Aiken County, South Carolina

21, Silver Bluff, South Carolina

22 to June 5, 1781, Augusta, Georgia

22 to June 19, 1781, Ninety-Six, Greenwood County, South Carolina

24, Fort Grierson, Georgia

June Mydleton's (Middleton's) Ambuscade, South Carolina

1, Point of Fork (Fork Union), Virginia

4, Charlottesville (raid), Virginia

5, Fort Cornwallis, Georgia

18, Juniper Spring , South Carolina

20, Stono Ferry, South Carolina

26, Rahway Meadow, New Jersey

28, Hickory Hill, Georgia

28, Spencer's Ordinary (Tavern), Virginia

July Washington's Raid, South Carolina

3, King's Bridge, New York

6, Green Spring, (Jamestown Ford) Virginia

7, Fort Plain, New York

8, Eggleston's Capture, South Carolina

9, Currytown, New York

12, Norwalk, Connecticut

15, Quarter House, South Carolina

15, Tarrytown, New York

16, Wadboo (Wiboo, Wyboo, Watboo), South Carolina

17, Biggin Church, South Carolina

17, Quinby's Bridge, near Huger, Berkeley County, South Carolina

Aug.   1, Cunningham's Raid, South Carolina

6, Fort Dayton, New York

6, Sharon Spring Swamp, New York

22, Fork of Edisto, South Carolina

22, Warwarsing, New York

24, Johnson Hall, New York

30, Jerseyfield, New York

31, Charleston Road, South Carolina

31, Parker's Ferry, South Carolina

Sept.   1, West Haven, Connecticut

5, Virginia Capes (naval), Virginia

6, Fort Griswold, Connecticut

6, Groton Hill, Connecticut

6, New London, Connecticut

6, Turkey Creek, South Carolina

8, Eutaw Springs, Eutawville, Orangeburg County, South Carolina

13, Cane Creek, North Carolina

13, Lindley's Mill (Cane Creek), North Carolina

28 to Oct. 19, 1781, Yorktown, Virginia

Oct.   5, Stevens Creek, South Carolina

10, Threadwell's Neck (Treadwell's), New York

16, Monck's Corner, South Carolina

24, Johnstown, New York

30, West Canada Creek, New York

Nov.   Gowen's Fort (Prince's Fort), South Carolina

Moore's Surprise, North Carolina

Richard Hampton's Surprise, South Carolina

7, Clouds Creek, South Carolina

9, Hayes' Station, near Joanna, Laurens County, South Carolina

27, Fair Lawn, Moncks Corner, Berkeley County, South Carolina

Dec.   1, Fort Dorchester, near Summerville, Dorchester County, South Carolina

29, Fort Dorchester, near Summerville, Dorchester County, South Carolina

1782

Cherokee Campaign of 1782

Jan.   3, Videau's Bridge, between Huger and Cainhoy, Berkeley County, South Carolina

Feb.   14, Wambaw Creek, near McClellanville, Charleston County, South Carolina

24, Savannah River, South Carolina

25, Tidyman's Plantation, South Carolina

March   Indian Villages, South Carolina

Oconee River, South Carolina

4, Morrisania, New York

13, Port Royal, South Carolina

April   24, Dorchester, South Carolina

May   Lorick's Ferry, Edgefield County, South Carolina

1, Friday's (or Fridig's) Ferry, Richland County, South Carolina

21, Ogeechee Road, Georgia

24, Dean Swamp, near Salley, Aiken County, South Carolina

24, Sharon (vicinity), Georgia

June   3, Bowling Green, Marion County, South Carolina

4, Sandusky (Upper Sandusky), Ohio

23, Ebenezer, Georgia

July   James Island, South Carolina

Aug.   15, Bryan's Station, South Carolina (now Kentucky)

19, Blue Licks, Kentucky

27, Combahee Ferry, South Carolina

Nov.   4, John's Island, South Carolina

19–21, Ninety-Six, South Carolina

BATTLE SITES GROUPED AND KEYED TO MAJOR CITIES/LOCATIONS

This appendix is intended as an aid for planning visits to sites in or near one city or in a geographical area, or side trips centered on a major city. It may be helpful for visitors and tourists unfamiliar with an area, who may have the names of larger cities in mind but are not familiar with smaller cities or battle sites. Consult the maps and the text given each town/battle site for more information and directions. The list below follows the general schema of north to south, east to west. States are listed in the geographical order found elsewhere in this book.

How much the visitor can see depends on time and driving constraints. Some states, like Rhode Island, are small; other states are larger, with distances of 50 or more miles between sites. Generally the sites within a geographical area would be day or weekend trips, depending on how much one wants to cover.

Sites indicated with **boldface** type indicate the tourist may want to allow extra time, as these sites have been developed with exhibits, museums, monuments, etc. and/or are in historically significant cities. Keep in mind that many sites feature special seasonal or commemorative events such as re-enactments or thematic ranger presentations—the visitor may want to check in advance for these and plan accordingly.

Maine
Coast, midstate: Castine/Fort George. The nearest major cities are Bar Harbor and Bangor.

Vermont
Rutland area: East Hubbardton site.

Bennington: The Battle of Bennington was fought mostly in Hoosick Falls, New York, although there is a monument in Vermont. Other sites in this general area are the Battle of Saratoga and Fort Edward (New York).

New York
Upper Hudson River Valley: Valcour Island (Plattsburgh), **Fort Ticonderoga**, Crown Point, Hubbardton (Vermont).

Saratoga/Glens Falls area: Fort Edward, sites related to **Battle of Saratoga (Stillwater, Schuylerville)**, also Hoosick Falls, for Battle of Bennington, Bennington (Vermont).

Albany/Amsterdam: Johnstown, Cherry Valley, Schoharie.

Rome: Fort Stanwix, Oriskany.

Elmira: Newtown Battlefield.

Port Jervis: Minisink Battlefield Memorial.

Lower Hudson River Valley: **West Point (and Fort Putnam)**, Fort Montgomery, Fort Clinton, Stony Point, White Plains.

New York City: Fort Washington (Fort Lee is across the Hudson River in New Jersey), Harlem Heights, Kip's Bay, Brooklyn Heights.

Massachusetts
Lexington, Concord, Arlington: These cities all have monuments, battle sites, and historically important buildings in the Minute Man National Historic Park.

Boston: **Boston, Bunker Hill (Charlestown)**, Dorchester Heights.

Rhode Island coastal area
Portsmouth, Newport, Rhode Island Sound.

Connecticut

New London: Fort Griswold.
Hartford: Wethersfield.
New Haven.
Danbury: Danbury and Ridgefield.

New Jersey

Northern New Jersey/Hudson River: Fort Lee. There's a retreat route (with route markers) from Fort Lee to New Bridge Landing, New Jersey. Also Fort Washington (New York).

Newark/Jersey City: Paulus Hook, Springfield. Morristown.

Trenton/Delaware River: Trenton, **Princeton**, **Washington Crossing State Park** (also Washington Crossing, Pennsylvania), Monmouth Battleground (Freehold; between Trenton and the coast).

Central/Delaware River: Red Bank Battlefield/ Fort Mercer (National Park). The Philadelphia metropolitan area is across the river.

Pennsylvania

Wilkes-Barre area/Bloomsburg: Wyoming Massacre site.

Delaware River Valley: Washington Crossing State Park (also Washington Crossing, New Jersey). Valley Forge.

Paoli/Malvern area: Paoli Massacre (Malvern), Battle of the Clouds (Frazer).

Philadelphia: Independence National Historical Park has many sites of historical significance, including Independence Hall, Carpenters' Hall, and Washington Park (for more, see the text under Philadelphia or consult the Park's website).

Philadelphia metropolitan area: Germantown (northeast), Fort Mifflin (southeast). Except for Wyoming Valley, most of the sites in Pennsylvania are within driving distance of Philadelphia, although it is doubtful that one would want to cover them all in the same day.

Southwest of Philadelphia: Chadd's Ford/ Brandywine Battlefield Park.

Indiana

Vincennes.

Illinois

Chester/Ellis Grove/Mississippi River: Fort Kaskaskia State Historic Site.
Metropolis: Fort Massac.

Delaware

Newark: Cooch's Bridge Battlefield.

Virginia

Williamsburg: Green Spring Battlefield is part of the Colonial National Historial Park and is near **Colonial Williamsburg.**

Yorktown: **Yorktown** battle sites and battle-related buildings are mostly in the Colonial National Historical Park, Yorktown.

Hampton: Newport News is a nearby city.

Portsmouth, Norfolk: Engagements in these cities and Great Bridge, which is near Portsmouth.

Kentucky

Mount Olivet: The Blue Licks Battlefield State Park is nearby.

North Carolina

Burlington: Alamance and Pyle's Defeat battle sites are both south of Burlington.

Greensboro: **Guilford Courthouse** National Military Park is north of Greensboro.

Charlotte: Cornelius/Battle at Cowan's Ford. Charlotte is also within 40 or 50 miles of the Kings Mountain National Military Park (see under South Carolina: York, Kings Mountain).

Wilmington/Cape Fear: Moore's Creek National Battlefield is in Currie, about 20 miles from Wilmington.

South Carolina

York: This is the closest large city to the **Kings Mountain** National Military Park and the Kings Mountain State Park. Williamson's Plantation/ Huck's Defeat (Brattonsville) is south of York. The Cowpens battle site is about 30 miles driving distance from the King's Mountain site.

Spartanburg/Gaffney: Cowpens National Battlefield (Chesnee).

Lancaster /Kershaw area: Battle of the Waxhaws (Lancaster), Hanging Rock (Heath Springs), Fishing Creek (Great Falls), Rocky Mount (Great Falls).

Union/Laurel/Clinton area south of Spartanburg: Sites in this area are Musgrove Hill and Blackstocks Plantation (near Cross Anchor) and the Fish Dam Engagement (Carlisle).

Camden: The city is the site of both the Battles of Camden and Hobkirk Hill.

Abbeville/Saluda: The closest medium-size cities to **Ninety-Six** National Historic Site, in western South Carolina.

Columbia: Fort Granby is nearby.

Congaree River from Columbia: A series of forts were built along the Congaree River, downstream and southeast from Columbia: Fort

Granby, Fort Motte, Fort Watson (Santee). Continuing southeast: Eutaw Springs, Moncks Corner/Biggin Church, Quinby Bridge (Huger)

Georgetown/Rhems: Black Mingo Creek engagement.

Charleston : **Charleston** and Fort Moultrie. (Moncks Corner and the Quinby Bridge site are within about 30 miles of Charleston.)

Beaufort (southeastern coast):Port Royal.

Georgia

Augusta is the site of Fort Cornwallis and Fort Grierson. The Kettle Creek Battlefield (Washington) is about 40-50 miles farther west in the same general area of the state.

Sylvania: Briar Creek Battleground.

Savannah: Some historical sites related to the battle are in Savannah. Fort Morris (Midway) is south of the city along the coast.

GLOSSARY

ABATIS: Sharpened branches pointing out from a fortification at an angle toward the enemy to slow or disrupt an assault.

ACCOUTREMENT: Piece of military equipment carried by soldiers in addition to their standard uniform and weapons.

BARRACKS: Building used to lodge soldiers.

BASTION: Fortification with a projecting part of a wall to protect the main walls of the fortification.

BATTALION: The basic organizational unit of a military force. Most regiments consisted of a single battalion which was composed of ten companies.

BATTEAU: A light flat-bottomed riverboat with sharply tapering stern and bow.

BATTERY: Two or more similar artillery pieces that function as a single tactical unit; a prepared position for artillery; an army artillery unit corresponding to a company in an infantry regiment.

BAYONET: A long, slender blade that can be attached to the end of a musket and used for stabbing. Most 18th-century bayonets were triangular.

BLUNDERBUSS: Short musket with a wide muzzle used to fire shot with a scattering effect at close range.

BOMBPROOF: Structure built strong enough to protect the inhabitants from exploding bombs and shells.

BRIG: Small two-masted sailing vessel with square-rigged sails on both masts.

BRIGADE: Military unit consisting of about 800 men.

CHEVAUX-DE-FRISE: Obstacles consisting of horizontal poles with projecting spikes to block a passageway. They were used on land and modified to block rivers to enemy ships.

COMPANY: The smallest military unit of the army consisting of about 100 men.

CROWN FORCES: The allied forces supporting King George III. They consisted primarily of the British army, Hessian mercenaries, Loyalists, and Native Americans.

CUTTER: (1) Single-masted sailing vessel similar to a sloop but having its mast positioned further aft; (2) a ship's boat, usually equipped with both sails and oars. In the 18th century, the terms sloop and cutter seem to have been used almost interchangeably.

DEMILUNE: Fortification similar to a bastion but shaped as a crescent or half-moon rather than as an arrow.

DRAGOON: A soldier who rode on horseback like cavalry. Dragoons generally fought dismounted in the 17th and 18th centuries.

EARTHWORKS: Fortification made of earth.

EMBRASURE: Slanted opening in the wall or parapet of a fortification designed for the defender to fire through it on attackers.

ENVELOPMENT: The act of completely surrounding an enemy.

FASCINE: Long bundle of sticks tied together, used in building earthworks and in strengthening ramparts.

FORAGE: To go from place to place looking for food and supplies; to plunder.

FORLORN HOPE: A group of soldiers sent on a very dangerous if not hopeless mission.

FRAISE: Sharpened stakes built into the exterior wall of a fortification to deter attackers.

GABION: Cylindrical basket made of wicker and filled with earth for use in building fortifications.

GALLEY: Long boat propelled by oars. These boats had a shallow draft and were particularly useful in rivers, lakes, and other shallow bodies of water.

GENERAL ENGAGEMENT: An encounter, conflict, or battle in which the majority of a force is involved.

GRAPESHOT: A number of small iron balls tied together to resemble a cluster of grapes. When fired simultaneously from a cannon, the balls separate into multiple projectiles.

GRENADIER: Soldier armed with grenades; a specially selected foot soldier in an elite unit selected on the basis of exceptional height and ability.

GUN: Cannon. Guns were referred to by the size of the shot they fired. A 3-pounder fired a 3-pound ball, a 6-pounder fired a 6-pound ball.

GUNDALOW: Flat-bottomed vessel equipped with both sails and oars, designed to carry heavy loads, usually armed with one gun at the bow and two mid-ship.

HESSIAN: German mercenary soldier who fought with the British army. Most of the German soldiers came from the kingdom of Hesse-Cassel, hence the name. Other German states that sent soldiers include Brunswick, Hesse-Hanau, Waldeck, Anspach-Bayreuth, and Anhalt-Zerbst.

HORNWORKS: Earthworks.

HOWITZER: Cannon with a short barrel and a bore diameter greater than 30 mm and a maximum elevation of 60 degrees, used for firing shells at a high angle of elevation to reach a target behind cover or in a trench.

JAEGER: A hunter and gamekeeper who fought with the Hessians for the British army. They wore green uniforms, carried rifles, and were expert marksmen.

LIGHT INFANTRY: Foot soldiers who carried lightweight weapons and minimal field equipment.

LOYALIST: An American who supported the British during the American Revolution; also called Tory.

MAGAZINE: Structure to store weapons, ammunition, explosives, and other military equipment or supplies.

MAHAM TOWER: Gun tower to give attacking forces an advantage in height over defenders in a siege. It gets its name from Hezekiah Maham who designed the first one used during the Battle of Fort Watson. They were also built for the Siege of Ninety-Six and the Second Battle of Augusta.

MAN-OF-WAR: Warship.

MATROSS: A private in an artillery unit who needed no specialized skills. Matrosses usually hauled cannon and positioned them.

MILITIA: Civilians who are part-time soldiers who take military training and can serve full-time for short periods during emergencies.

MINER: A soldier who digs tunnels for a siege or who lays, detects, and disarms mines.

MINUTEMAN: Member of a special militia unit, called a Minute Company. A minuteman pledged to be ready to fight at a minute's notice.

MISCHIANZA: A lavish party organized by Major John André and Oliver de Lancey to honor General William Howe on May 18, 1778, prior to his return to England.

MORTAR: Cannon with a relatively short and wide barrel, used for firing shells in a high arc over a short distance, particularly behind enemy defenses. They were not mounted on wheeled carriages.

MUSKET: Firearm with a long barrel, large caliber, and smooth bore. It was used between the 16th and 18th centuries, before rifling was invented.

OPEN ORDER: Troop formation in which the distance between the individuals is greater than in close order (which is shoulder to shoulder). Also called extended order.

PARLEY: A talk or negotiation, under a truce, between opposing military forces.

PAROLE: Promise given by a prisoner of war, either not to escape, or not to take up arms again as a condition of release. Individuals on parole can remain at home and conduct their normal occupations. Breaking parole makes one subject to immediate arrest and often execution. From the French *parole* which means one's word of honor.

PORTAGE: Overland route used to transport a boat or its cargo from one waterway to another; the act of carrying a boat or its cargo from one waterway to another.

RAMPART: Earthen fortification made of an embankment and often topped by a low protective wall.

RAVELIN: Small outwork fortification shaped like an arrowhead or a V that points outward in front of a larger defense work.

REDOUBT: Temporary fortification built to defend a prominent position such as a hilltop.

REGIMENT: Permanent military unit usually consisting of two or three battalions.

REGULAR: Belonging to or constituting a full-time professional military or police force as opposed to, for example, the reserves.

SAPPER: Soldier who specializes in making entrenchments and tunnels for siege operations.

SCHOONER: Fast-sailing ship with at least two masts and with fore and aft sails on all lower masts.

SCOW: Flat-bottomed sailboat with a rectangular hull.

SHELL: Explosive projectile fired from a large-bore gun such as a howitzer or mortar.

SHIP OF THE LINE: Large warship with sufficient armament to enter combat with similar vessels in the line of battle. A ship of the line carried 60 to 100 guns.

SLOOP: Small single-masted sailing vessel with sails rigged fore-and-aft and guns on only one deck. In the 18th century, the terms sloop and cutter seem to have been used almost interchangeably.

SLOOP OF WAR: Three-masted, square-rigged naval vessel with all her guns mounted on a single uncovered main deck.

SONS OF LIBERTY: Patriots who belonged to secret organizations to oppose British attempts at taxation after 1765. They often resorted to violence and coercion to achieve their purposes.

SPIKE [a gun]: To destroy a cannon by hammering a long spike into the touchhole or vent, thereby rendering it useless.

TARLETON'S QUARTER: The refusal to let the enemy surrender and massacring the survivors. Derived from the Battle of Waxhaws when Lieutenant Colonel Banastre Tarleton attacked retreating Continental soldiers, killing more than 100 of them.

WHIG: Somebody who supported independence from Great Britain during the American Revolution. The name comes from the British liberal political party that favored reforms and opposed many of the policies of the king and Parliament related to the War for American Independence.

BIBLIOGRAPHY

Adams, James Truslow, et al., eds. *Dictionary of American History.* 8 vols. Concise edition. New York: Charles Scribner's Sons, 1983.

Adams, Leslie, et al., eds. *Visiting Our Past: A Supplemental Guide to Selected Sites.* Washington, DC: National Geographic Society, 1986.

Anderson, Fred. *A People's Army: Massachusetts Soldiers and Society in the Seven Years' War.* Chapel Hill: University of North Carolina Press, 1984.

Bailyn, Bernard. *The Ideological Origins of the American Revolution.* Cambridge, MA: Harvard University Press, Belknap Press, 1967.

Bancroft, George. *The History of the United States of America from the Discovery of the Continent.* Abridged and edited by Russel B. Nye. Chicago: University of Chicago Press, 1966.

Barbour, R. L. *South Carolina's Revolutionary War Battlefields: A Tour Guide.* Gretna, LA: Pelican Publishing Co., 2002.

Beard, Charles A., and Mary R. Beard. *New Basic History of the United States.* Rev. ed. New York: Doubleday, 1968.

Boatner, Mark Mayo. *Encyclopedia of the American Revolution.* 3rd ed. New York: McKay, 1980.

—. *Landmarks of the American Revolution: A Guide to Locating and Knowing What Happened at the Sites of Independence.* Harrisburg, PA: Stackpole Books, 1973.

Bradford, Samuel Sydney. *Liberty's Road: A Guide To Revolutionary War Sites.* New York: McGraw-Hill, 1976.

Bridenbaugh, Carl. *Early Americans.* New York: Oxford University Press, 1981.

Brogan, Hugh. *The Longman History of the United States of America.* New York: William Morrow and Co., 1985.

Chambers, S. Allen. *National Landmarks, America's Treasures: The National Park Foundation's Complete Guide To National Historic Landmarks.* New York: J. Wiley and Sons, 2000.

Commager, Henry Steele, and Milton Cantor. *Documents of American History.* 10th ed. New York: Prentice Hall, 1988.

Cordes, Kathleen A. *America's National Historic Trails.* Norman: University of Oklahoma Press, 1999.

Davis, David Brion. *The Problem of Slavery in the Age of Revolution, 1770–1823.* Ithaca, NY: Cornell University Press, 1975.

Fischer, David Hackett. *Washington's Crossing.* Oxford, New York: Oxford University Press, 2004.

Foner, Eric, and John A. Garraty, eds. *The Reader's Companion to American History.* Boston: Houghton Mifflin Co., 1991.

Freidel, Frank, ed. *Harvard Guide to American History.* 2nd ed. Cambridge, MA: Harvard University Press, 1974.

Gelbert, Doug. *American Revolutionary War Sites, Memorials, Museums, and Library Collections: A State-by-State Guidebook to Places Open to the Public.* Jefferson, NC: McFarland, 1998.

Hawke, David Freeman. *Everyday Life in Early America.* New York: Harper and Row, 1988.

Heitman, Francis B. *Historical Register of Officers of the Continental Army.* Washington, DC: The Rare Book Shop Publishing Company, 1914.

Hibbert, Christopher. *Redcoats and Rebels: The American Revolution through British Eyes.* New York: Avon Books, 1991.

Higginbotham, Don. *Atlas of the American Revolution.* Chicago: Rand McNally and Co., 1974.

Hofstadter, Richard. *America at 1750: A Social Portrait.* New York: Random House, 1973.

Johnson, Thomas H. *The Oxford Companion to American History.* New York: Oxford University Press, 1966.

Katcher, Philip R. N. *Rebels and Loyalists: The Revolutionary Soldier in Philadelphia.* Philadelphia: Atwater Kent Museum, 1976.

Ketchum, Richard M., and L. Edward Purcell, eds. *American Heritage Book of the Revolution.* New York: American Heritage Publishing Co., 1958.

Lingeman, Richard. *Small Town America: A Narrative History 1620–the Present.* New York: Putnam, 1980.

Lossing, Benson J.. *Pictorial Field Book of the Revolution.* 2 vols. New York: Harper and Brothers,

1850/1859. Available online at http://freepages.history.rootsweb.com/~wcarr1/Lossing1/Contents.html

Martin, James Kirby, and Mark Edward Lender. *A Respectable Army: The Military Origins of the Republic, 1763–1789.* Arlington Heights, IL: H. Davidson, 1982.

Martin, Joseph Plumb. *Private Yankee Doodle: Being a Narrative of Some of the Adventures, Dangers, and Sufferings of a Revolutionary Soldier.* Edited by George F. Scheer. Boston: Little, Brown, 1962. Also published as *A Narrative of Some of the Adventures, Dangers and Sufferings of a Revolutionary Soldier.* New York Times, 1968.

Mays, Terry M. *Historical Dictionary of the American Revolution.* Lanham, MD: Scarecrow Press, 1999.

Meinig, D.W. *The Shaping of America.* Vol. 1, *Atlantic America, 1492–1800.* New Haven, CT: Yale University Press, 1986.

Morison, Samuel Eliot. *A Concise History of the American Republic.* 2nd ed. New York: Oxford University Press:, 1983.

—. *The Growth of the American Republic.* 2 vols. 7th ed. New York: Oxford University Press, 1980.

Peterson, Harold Leslie. *The Book of the Continental Soldier, Being a Compleat Account of the Uniforms, Weapons, and Equipment with Which He Lived and Fought.* Harrisburg, PA: Stackpole, 1968.

Purvis, Thomas L. *Revolutionary America 1763 to 1800.* New York: Facts on File, 1985.

Royster, Charles. *A Revolutionary People at War: The Continental Army and American Character,* *1775–1783,* Chapel Hill: University of North Carolina Press, published for the Institute of Early American History and Culture, Williamsburg, VA, 1979.

Smith, Page. *A New Age Begins: A People's History of the American Revolution.* New York: McGraw-Hill, 1976.

Stember, Sol. *The Bicentennial Guide to the American Revolution.* New York: Saturday Review Press, 1974; distributed by Dutton.

Steuben, Friedrich Wilhelm Ludolf Gerhard Augustin Baron von. *Baron von Steuben's Revolutionary War Drill Manual: A Facsimile Reprint of the 1794 edition.* New York: Dover Publications, 1985.

Turner, Frederick Jackson. *The Frontier in American History.* Arizona: Kreiger Publishing Co., 1985.

U.S. News and World Report. *200 Years: A Bicentennial Illustrated History of the United States.* Washington, DC: U.S. News & World Report, 1973.

Wolock, Nancy. *Women and the American Experience.* New York: Alfred A. Knopf, 1984.

Wood, Gordon S. *The Radicalism of the American Revolution.* New York: Alfred A. Knopf, 1992.

Wright, Louis B. *The American Heritage History of the Thirteen Colonies.* New York: American Heritage, 1981.

Wright, Robert K., Jr. *The Continental Army.* Washington, DC: Center of Military History, U.S. Army, 1983.

Zinn, Howard. *A People's History of the United States.* New York: Harper and Row, 1981.

INDEX